Taming Ethnic Hatred

Syracuse Studies on Peace and Conflict Resolution
Louis Kriesberg, *Series Editor*

OTHER TITLES IN SYRACUSE STUDIES ON PEACE AND CONFLICT RESOLUTION

Cooperative Security: Reducing Third World Wars
I. WILLIAM ZARTMAN and VICTOR A. KREMENYUK, eds.

Cultures of Peace: The Hidden Side of History
ELISE BOULDING

From Cold War to Democratic Peace: Third Parties,
Peaceful Change, and the OSCE
JANIE LEATHERMAN

Global Liberalism, Local Populism: Peace and Conflict
in Israel/Palestine and Northern Ireland
GUY BEN-PORAT

Making Peace Prevail: Preventing Violent Conflict in Macedonia
ALICE ACKERMANN

Preparing for Peace: Conflict Transformation Across Cultures
JOHN PAUL LEDERACH

Radical Pacifism: The War Resisters League
and Gandhian Nonviolence in America, 1915–1963
SCOTT H. BENNETT

Scare Tactics: The Politics of International Rivalry
MICHAEL P. COLARESI

Thinking Peaceful Change: Baltic Security Policies
and Security Community Building
FRANK MÖLLER

Transnational Social Movements and Global Politics:
Solidarity Beyond the State
JACKIE SMITH, CHARLES CHATFIELD,
AND RON PAGNUCCO, eds.

Taming Ethnic Hatred

Ethnic Cooperation and Transnational
Networks in Eastern Europe

Patrice C. McMahon

With a Foreword by Max van der Stoel

Syracuse University Press

Data for figures 1–6 are drawn from the Minorities at Risk (MAR) data set; see Minorities
at Risk Project (2005), Center for International Development and Conflict Management,
College Park, Md. Retrieved from http://www.cidcm.umd.edu/inscr/mar/ on September 2003.
MAR tracks 285 politically active ethnic groups throughout the world from 1945 to 2003. MAR focuses
on ethnopolitical groups and nonstate communal groups whose contemporary political significance derives
from their world status and political actions. In profiling strategies of "unconventional politics" used by
ethnopolitical communal groups or states, MAR created three categories of collective action: conflict, rebellion,
and protest. Ethnopolitical conflict could be targeted at or initiated by an ethnopolitical group.

The paper used in this publication meets the minimum requirements
of American National Standard of Information Sciences—Permanence
of Paper of Printed Library Materials, ANSI Z39.48–1984∞™

For a listing of books published and distributed by Syracuse University Press,
visit our Web site at SyracuseUniversityPress.syr.edu.
ISBN-13: 978-0-8156-3137-8
ISBN-10: 0-8156-3137-5

Library of Congress Cataloging-in-Publication Data
McMahon, Patrice C.
Taming ethnic hatred : ethnic cooperation and transnational networks
in Eastern Europe / Patrice C. McMahon ; with a foreword by Max van der Stoel.—1st ed.
p. cm.—(Syracuse studies on peace and conflict resolution)
Includes bibliographical references and index.
ISBN-13: 978–0–8156–3137–8 (cloth : alk. paper)
ISBN-10: 0–8156–3137–5 (cloth : alk. paper)
1. Europe, Eastern—Ethnic relations. 2. Conflict management—Europe,
Eastern. 3. Pluralism (Social sciences)—Europe, Eastern. I. Title.
DJK26.M39 2007
305.800947—dc22
2007002135

To Jeff, Hana, and Julia

PATRICE C. McMAHON is associate professor in the Department of Political Science at the University of Nebraska, Lincoln.

Contents

Figures

Foreword

MAX VAN DER STOEL

Armed conflict is associated by many with war between states. In reality, increasingly most of these conflicts take place within states, often in the form of interethnic violence. It was especially the bloody conflict within Yugoslavia, which began without any significant international effort to prevent it even though there were many indications that the danger of civil war was constantly growing, that led to an international discussion on how to find effective ways to prevent such conflicts in the future.

The steps taken by the international community in Europe since then have been described in this fascinating study by Dr. Patrice McMahon. It is a book rich in content, even more so because it looks back to the international approach to minority problems since the First World War, for instance, by describing the efforts of the League of Nations in this field.

The author has done an impressive amount of research on her subject, not only through a wide-ranging study of international literature in this field but also by conducting a great number of interviews. Especially striking is her balanced approach. She never mentions one side of an argument without paying attention to different views. Although her main subject is taming ethnic hatred in post-cold war Europe, she also points out that there are examples of minorities and majorities managing to live together in peace and without major tensions.

McMahon especially emphasizes that the defusing of potentially dangerous interethnic problems in Eastern Europe since 1989 was due, apart from the influence of moderate forces within the countries themselves, to the interplay of various international actors. She concludes that since 1990, if not before, the CSCE/OSCE has distinguished itself as the most forward-looking and proactive organization regarding conflict prevention, but she also demonstrates that various other actors, such as the Council of Europe, the European Union, and NATO have made their contributions, as well as some major nongovernmental organizations.

Mutual trust and willingness to cooperate instead of to compete gradually led to the development of what Dr. McMahon calls "transnational networks" aiming at overcoming interethnic controversies.

As high commissioner on national minorities for the Organization for Security and Cooperation in Europe (OSCE) from 1993 to 2001, I was myself an actor in many of the events described by Dr. McMahon. I can testify that she has succeeded brilliantly in describing the main aspects of the involvement of the various actors regarding interethnic tensions in Romania and Latvia, the two countries she selected for special case studies.

Interethnic questions will undoubtedly have a high place at the international agenda in the years to come. We have to learn from the lessons of the past. Also, against this background, I express the hope that the well-documented and balanced study of Dr. McMahon will be read by many.

Preface

Without realizing it, my grandmother made me distinctly aware of ethnicity and of difference. As an adult living in Eastern Europe and then working in Washington, D.C., I often wondered if ethnic differences would be disregarded as these countries revived their national traditions. With every trip to Central Europe in the 1990s, I realized that while ethnic violence had tragically destroyed the multiethnic ideal in Yugoslavia, Central Europeans were confronting ethnic differences and their past in a variety of ways. This book allowed me to explore the changes in ethnic relations in Eastern Europe and, in the process, better understand my own ethnic identity.

Grants from the National Research Council, the National Council for East European and Eurasian Research, and the University of Nebraska-Lincoln provided significant support for this research and for necessary interviews throughout Europe and the U.S. Thanks also to the Nebraska National Guard and to Major General Lemke in particular for supporting one of my trips to Bosnia in 2003. These trips provided more than data to support an argument about the effects of transnationalism. They also conveyed a reality that is emerging around the world but is easy to overlook. It is a new architecture of governance and resides in the changing role of the state in international politics and the growing interdependence of states and nonstate actors.

What I realized long ago was that despite the ease and low cost of travel, a surprising amount of research on ethnic conflict and cooperation takes place without travel, without interaction with people, and without firsthand experiences. I am grateful that this research provided me with the opportunity to witness and experience firsthand how international politics has changed and how governmental and nongovernmental actors have responded to ethnic conflict in an increasingly interconnected world.

I am deeply grateful for the training and support I received as a graduate student at Columbia University. This training pushed me to understand and embrace complexity rather than assume it away. I benefitted tremendously from the research project supported by the Carnegie Corporation of New York on international nongovernmental organizations (NGOs). The project and its participants not only reminded me of the growing relevance of international nonstate actors but helped me examine these issues systematically.

My research benefitted tremendously from colleagues and students in the U.S. and Europe who commented and helped along the way, including, among others, Fiona Adamson, Shiela Croucher, Zsusza Csergo, Stephen Deets, Svekis Elmars, John Glenn, Michael Johns, Walter Kemp, Alexander Motyl, Stephen Saideman, Jack Snyder, Rajan Menon, Andrew Wedeman, and Jon Western. A special thanks to David Forsythe, who has read more drafts of this book than he would like to remember, but whom I will not soon forget.

I enjoy conducting interviews, particularly when I admire the people I have the opportunity to meet. My research benefitted significantly from the cooperation of representatives from the Organization for Security and Cooperation in Europe (OSCE) and the office of its high commissioner on national minorities, the European Union Commission, and the U.S. Agency for International Development. I am grateful for the OSCE staff in Prague and to Martina Steiner and Maartje Breakman Monika for their translations and research assistance. Alice Nemcova's connections within the OSCE and beyond strengthened my interviews tremendously. Meeting with representatives from various governmental and nongovernmental organizations who have tirelessly (and usually without much financial support) worked for peace, like Max van der Stoel, was an unexpected gift.

On a more personal note, I am grateful to my supportive friends and especially the many teachers and childcare helpers. Thank you, Kris, for keeping me sane and my family safe. Without Hana and Julia, however, I never would have worked so hard to finish this if they hadn't taught me the difference between work and play. As much as I enjoyed writing this book, I always longed for more time with them. There is no way I could have undertaken this project without my husband, Jeff Cole, who has always provided me with an endless supply of support, faith, editing advice, but most of all, a sense of humor and perspective.

Taming Ethnic Hatred

ONE

Ethnic Cooperation in Eastern Europe

Clash of civilizations, age-old ethnic hatreds, warring tribalism; these are, unfortunately, the terms associated with ethnic identity. Vivid images from Europe, Africa, and Asia seem to provide us with unforgettable mental pictures of what happens when groups mix. At first glance, ethnic mixing appears to be a bloody, chaotic affair. Yet, is it true—as some contend—that ethnic conflicts have become the source of political violence in the world, and that these hostilities show no sign of abating?[1] The simple but conclusive answer is no. Various quantitative studies conclude that there has been a shift away from violence to more peaceful resolutions of ethnic difference.[2] Research on the former Soviet bloc in particular highlights these positive trends, as new democracies choose minority-friendly legislation and adopt international norms.[3] It is thus fair to say that ethnic and religious groups are not, at this juncture, lying in wait for one another, nourishing age-old hatreds.

As a 2005 United Nations Human Security Report confirms, what has been largely ignored by scholars and policymakers alike is that the 1990s was a unique and peaceful decade.[4] Not only did the number of inter- and intrastate conflicts drop, but some one hundred-odd conflicts ended quietly or were contained. From Romania, to Indonesia, to Nigeria, the story that increasingly needs to be told is one of different groups living side by side in peace, as they have done for centuries. Thus, while conflict might be typical of politics in ethnically heterogeneous societies, we cannot forget that outcomes are varied, and even the most severely divided societies rarely pursue violence.[5] The continued need to study violence and war will not go away, but more research clearly needs to focus on peace and the transformations of conflict.

In Eastern Europe and the former Soviet Union, where the potential for bloodshed in the early 1990s appeared almost endless, violence has been, in the words of one scholar, "recent, repulsive, but rare."[6] Post-Soviet Russia, predicted by many to be a major threat to regional security, did not adopt an aggressive foreign policy, nor did it seek to redeem its ethnic kin abroad.[7] Any similarities that once existed between post-Soviet Russia and Weimar Germany have been overshadowed as the former superpower works through and with the international community to deal with

1

its concerns for ethnic Russians living outside its borders.[8] Ethnic Hungarians living in Romania, Slovakia, and Ukraine have helped build, rather than dismantle, the states in the region, and Hungary, once predisposed to aggressive nationalist policies, has become a model for countries in the East and West to emulate.[9] Even Bosnia, home to the worst violence seen in Europe since World War II, has been pacified, and despite ongoing challenges within the state, close observers are optimistic about the prospects for peace.[10]

This book describes the evolution of ethnic politics in Eastern Europe in the 1990s, and it analyzes a chief reason behind this outbreak of peace. I contend that the postcommunist experience is better characterized as one of ethnic cooperation rather than ethnic conflict because of the efforts of a transnational network of public and private organizations that labored in complementary, reinforcing ways to manage ethnicity. Spearheaded by the Conference on Security and Cooperation in Europe (CSCE) in 1990, this network evolved throughout the decade as governments, intergovernmental organizations, and nongovernmental organizations (NGOs) each responded to the resurgence of ethnic tensions.[11] By 1995, this decentralized arrangement included several intergovernmental organizations such as the Council of Europe (CoE) and the European Union (EU) and involved national governments as well as private, nongovernmental actors.[12] Although each actor had its own reason for participation, they all modified their behavior and organizational cultures to work collaboratively to tame ethnic conflict.[13] By explaining the historical development of this network and describing the overlapping policies its members adopted, the research shows how the interaction and coordination of public and private actors created a decentralized form of governance that ultimately helped transform ethnic conflict in this region.

In exploring these interactions and the network effects, this book focuses on two central concerns: *how* the actors comprising the "international community" behaved toward each other in the first decade after the cold war's collapse; and *how* they worked to contain rising ethnic tensions. In response to both, this research asserts that after the fall of the Soviet Union, international influences (particularly in Europe) cannot be conceptualized solely in terms of states or governmental policies. Intergovernmental organizations and NGOs work side by side with governments, and it is increasingly difficult to untangle the governmental-nongovernmental knot. Similarly, thinking of international influences on ethnic politics in terms of bilateral treaties, governmental assistance, or conditionality misses the numerous bottom-up initiatives and grassroots interactions that fundamentally shape domestic structures, policies, and societies.

As Robert Keohane and Joseph Nye predicted decades ago, international influences associated with preventing ethnic conflict in the 1990s evolved into a web of interlocking institutions; no single actor dominated in all respects, but several actors—international and domestic, both governmental and nongovernmental—simultaneously pushed for the same outcome.[14] The new architecture of public-private governance that this book describes to explain ethnic cooperation has been observed in a variety of other areas and in both domestic and international contexts. In areas as diverse as human rights law, terrorism, and peace building, scholars in international relations and comparative politics use networks to explain how international and domestic actors mesh to respond to shared problems and accomplish common objectives.[15] In each network, actors have their own objectives, mandates, and capabilities, but their decisions are contingent on the behavior of others, information is shared, financial interdependence common, and a division of labor evident. The book's main contention is that rising ethnic tensions in Eastern Europe in the early 1990s pushed the international community to act; its response was historically unique and multileveled. The common objectives, shared values, and high level of trust among public and private actors, alongside their inability to solve these complex problems alone, resulted in a new way of interacting with each other and innovative strategies for managing ethnic conflict.

It would be too simplistic and empirically incorrect to assert that international factors alone explain the trend toward peace in postcommunist countries, and this is not the argument that I make. Despite a temptation to exaggerate the influence of international-level variables and transnational networks, domestic factors remain critical to the timing of specific accommodating policies and to the effectiveness of transnational networks. Yet, I maintain that international factors are central to understanding domestic politics in Eastern Europe, elite motivations, and definitions of self-interest. Transnational involvement also sheds light on the form and content accommodating legislation assumed, as well as overt changes in civil society to push cooperation from the bottom up. Put differently, this transnational network bent on containing ethnic tensions provided the *message*, the *motivation*, and the *means* for Eastern European states and their leaders to eschew ethnic violence and move toward cooperation.

Why This Matters

For good reason, policymakers care deeply about ethnic politics and want to know when and how international actors can make a difference in mediating ethnic conflict. Such concerns are not totally new, and as this book explains in chapter 2, the international community has always been attentive to ethnic and religious minorities, specifically their destabilizing potential. In recent history, however, it was Yugoslavia's implosion in 1991 that put ethnic conflict back on the international community's agenda. With over two hundred thousand casualties, over two million people on the move seeking refuge, and stories of rape and concentration camps, the Bosnian tragedy, more than anything else, pushed the West to think seriously about ethnicity.[16] Given that there were several other places throughout the former Soviet bloc where ethnic minorities were isolated from their home country and could destabilize politics in their host country (Albania, Latvia, Macedonia, Montenegro, and Romania, to name a few) or in the region, the West realized the importance of stemming the tide of ethnic violence.[17] As the director of the U.S. Army Strategic Institute warned, "Ethnic conflict has reemerged with a vengeance in Europe, and policymakers need to be prepared to respond."[18]

The revival of ethnic tensions was not limited to Europe; nonetheless, the West devoted substantial resources to preventing further bloodshed on the continent. Throughout the 1990s, a wide range of governments, intergovernmental organizations, and NGOs flooded the former Communist bloc with the aim of promoting peaceful, democratic, and market-oriented change. The bulk of international assistance came from the European Union, but the U.S. government and Japan responded as well, and by the end of the decade the United States alone provided a total of $14 billion of assistance to countries in Eastern Europe and the former Soviet Union.[19] In Bosnia, where ethnic bloodshed resulted in military intervention and extensive political engineering, a decade of international involvement topped more than $9 billion. Yet, in all cases, governments did not work alone. Private foundations and international NGOs arrived in the East in untold numbers, and they too were bent on promoting peaceful change. Given the extraordinary investment in peace and stability in Eastern Europe, policymakers and members of the NGO community are no doubt interested in understanding why and when their efforts pay off.

The dramatic increase in scholarship on ethnic conflict in the 1990s makes plain the interest among academics in this topic. The volume of literature denotes a certain amount of development in this field of study, but its focus is exceedingly narrow. That is to say, writings on ethnic politics tend to be concentrated on explaining violent ethnic conflict, and research on *ethnic cooperation* or *ethnic peace* is scarce, especially when compared with the publications centered on conflict and war. Similar trends and discrepancies exist in relation to journals and newspaper articles, as well as other scholarship in English and other languages (see Appendix).[20]

A focus on violent conflict may be understandable, given assumptions about ethnic identity and nationalism and the tendency, especially among international relations scholars, to focus on violence and war. As the historian Geoffrey Blainey once put it, for every thousand pages on the causes of war, there is less than one page on the causes of peace.[21] While perhaps an exaggeration, even when authors do not explain the conditions that are likely to lead to ethnic conflict, they take vilence for granted.[22] As the late Senator Daniel Patrick Moynihan once observed, violence follows ethnic tensions just as night follows day, and while nation states no longer seem inclined to go to war with one another, ethnic groups fight all the time.[23] Such beliefs clearly inform the bulk of writings on ethnic politics in Eastern Europe.[24] Without addressing the topic extensively, George Schopflin notes that academic research on Eastern Europe tends to overlook the success stories of ethnonational conflict regulation and concentrates solely on the pathologies.[25]

In the last decade of the twentieth century, a substantial amount of literature on the causes of ethnic conflict developed, mostly by scholars' intent on explaining the newest threat to international security. Despite the variety of explanations offered, research centers on three broad approaches:[26] Ethnic conflicts are caused by so-called ancient hatreds, are due to an array of structural conditions, or are the result of manipulative elites who pursue ethnic claims for their parochial interests.[27] A unified theory to explain ethnic conflict never developed, but a combination of factors convinced many that it was on the steady rise and overdetermined in the post-communist context.[28]

The need to study the causes of ethnic conflict was obvious, at least if one looked superficially at events in Eastern Europe and broader international trends. As figures 1 and 2 show, the collapse of Communism coincided with a rise in the number and strength of ethnopolitical conflicts in the 1990s. Yet, because of tragic and horrible events in places such as Bosnia and Rwanda, scholars and policymakers overlooked less dramatic—but equally important—trends. Research conducted under the auspices of the Minorities at Risk Project tracks more than 280 politically active ethnic and religious groups for over half a century, and while ethnopolitical conflict, protest, and rebellion *did* increase substantially with the cold war's end, this increase was in fact a culmination of a much-longer trend that began after World War II, as figure 3 shows.

With the myth of global ethnic conflict in full swing, other events and trends were also obscured; that is to say, despite the spike in violence in the early 1990s, eth-

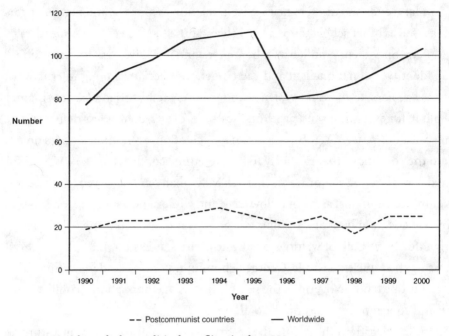

Figure 1. Number of ethnopolitical conflicts in the 1990s.

nic conflict declined precipitously within a couple of years.[29] Further evidence of the peaceful trend in the 1990s is demonstrated by the change in the balance between escalating and de-escalating conflicts, and the number of new ethnic conflicts that began after 1995.[30] In Eastern Europe, these trends are even more pronounced; since the mid-1990s there has been a decline in the strength of ethnopolitical conflicts, rebellion, and protest, as figures 4, 5, and 6 demonstrate. Finally, it is true but generally glossed over that the *actual* cases of ethnic violence in the former Soviet Union were vastly fewer than the cases of *potential* violence. As James Fearon and David Laitin put it, "Even in the extremely unsettled post-Soviet world, while some ethnic violence has been horrible, it is far from ubiquitous."[31]

This is not to say that academics totally ignored the burst of interest among governments, intergovernmental organizations, and NGOs in conflict prevention and management in the post-cold war era, but much of this literature tends to be normative, pointing out what intergovernmental organizations and governments *ought* to do to prevent ethnic violence.[32] For instance, before Western engagement in Eastern Europe began, scholars proposed ways the international community might forestall violent ethnic conflict in the post-Soviet bloc. Surprisingly, little research examined the response or the effects of this involvement by the international com-

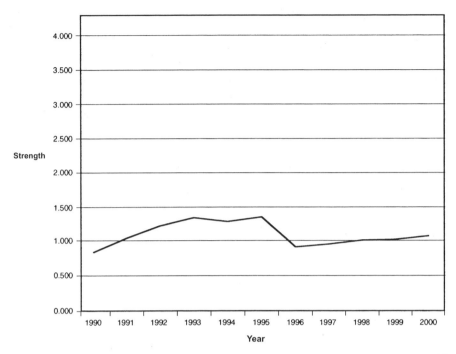

Figure 2. Strength of ethnopolitical conflicts in the 1990s. A coding of a 1 to a 1.5 would include individual acts of harassment against property and persons with no fatalities, political agitation, and campaigns urging authorities to impose restrictions on a group.

munity.[33] Ethnic wars in the 1990s fueled research on the role of international intervention in ethnic conflicts, establishing the conditions and possible mechanisms available for intervention.[34] Yet, this literature dealt almost exclusively with military intervention to end violent conflicts or the international community's peacekeeping or peace-building efforts. Only rarely did scholarship focus on how external actors can *transform* internal ethnic conflicts that have not yet erupted into violence.[35] These gaps should not come as much of a surprise, since efforts by outsiders to mediate intrastate ethnic tensions during the cold war were few and far between.[36]

Students of comparative politics, international law, and experts on European integration certainly realize that ethnic pluralism does not always culminate in violence. However, scholars writing from these perspectives tend to address the effects of the international community's actions on minority politics. To a large extent, the dependent variable is specific minority-friendly policies and the independent variable the European Union, though at least some admit that separating the effects of different international actors on such policies is difficult because international ac-

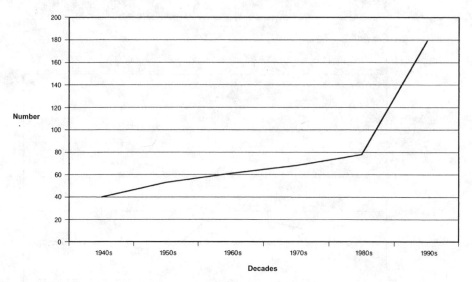

Figure 3. Trends in ethnopolitical conflicts since World War II. These numbers are the totals for conflicts in each decade and thus are different from the number of ethnopolitical conflicts given in figure 1.

tors' goals and behavior became so intertwined in the 1990s.[37] Nonetheless, this reframing of the issue—from a focus on ethnic conflict to minority issues—is important. The lens used by those who study European integration brings into clearer focus the relative importance of intergovernmental actors to domestic changes in Eastern Europe, but it ignores the transformative aspect of ethnic politics throughout the region. This helps explain why those who study ethnic politics in Eastern Europe in terms of EU integration tend to downplay the role played by the United States, NATO, and other regional organizations, or NGOs, and more significantly fail to highlight the seismic shift that occurred in international relations in the 1990s.

In total, this means that existing literature either ignores ethnic cooperation altogether, or it seeks to specify the relationship between a particular organization and certain policies to exact a single cause to explain what is a much broader outcome: ethnic cooperation. This book engages several distinct literatures, mostly within political science, to fill this gap and explain the international community's impact on the transformation of ethnic conflict to ethnic cooperation. Using insights from literature on transnationalism, network analysis, conflict management, and European integration, it explores why and how a transnational network formed in the 1990s to tame ethnicity in Eastern Europe.

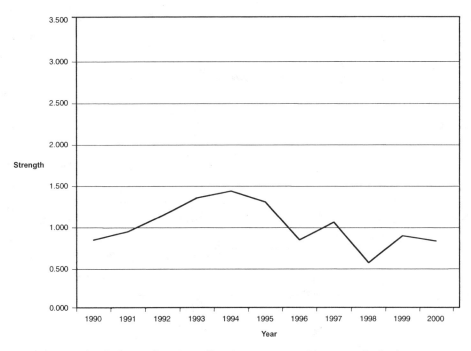

Figure 4. Strength of ethnopolitical conflicts in postcommunist countries in the 1990s.

The Argument

In the chapters that follow, I argue that ethnic conflicts in Eastern Europe were positively shaped by the unique responses of governments and nongovernmental actors. These responses are conceptualized in terms of a transnational network. *Networks* should be understood as sets of relatively stable relationships among public and private actors that are nonhierarchical and interdependent; actors have common interests and share information, acknowledging that cooperation is the best way to achieve their goals.[38] This transnational network not only dampened the escalation of ethnic disputes in Eastern Europe, but it also encouraged cooperation between and within states. To be clear, I do not argue that this transnational network alone is the sole reason for ethnic cooperation in Eastern Europe. Instead, I contend that without the development of this network, the story of postcommunism would have been quite different and possibly more violent.

Further, I contend that the CSCE/OSCE, rather than any national government or nongovernmental organization, helped establish the framework within which

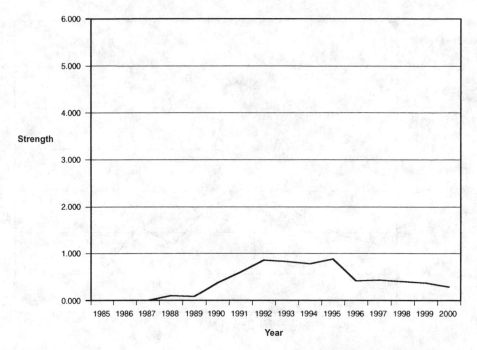

Figure 5. Strength of ethnopolitical rebellions in postcommunist countries in the 1990s.

this transnational network could flourish, providing the general and specific princi-ples associated with ethnic conflict prevention and minority rights. It encouraged information exchange and collaboration among governments, intergovernmental organizations, and nongovernmental organizations. The CSCE/OSCE's multifac-eted approach to conflict prevention also meant that ethnic conflict management did not rely on a single strategy but, instead, addressed these issues multilaterally and strategized on multiple levels. Interviews with representatives of government agencies, intergovernmental organizations, as well as politicians, NGO officials, and academics in Europe and the United States helped reveal this complex reality. What emerges from these interviews, alongside primary and secondary research, is a pic-ture of numerous governmental and nongovernmental organizations working col-laboratively, adapting their missions to fit with the objectives and normative framework of other actors.

In Eastern Europe, these overlapping initiatives are rarely distinguished as sep-arate or isolated events. When, for example, I asked Latvian government officials which international actor was most important in influencing ethnic relations in Latvia, I received a variety of responses. One former Latvian adviser to the presi-

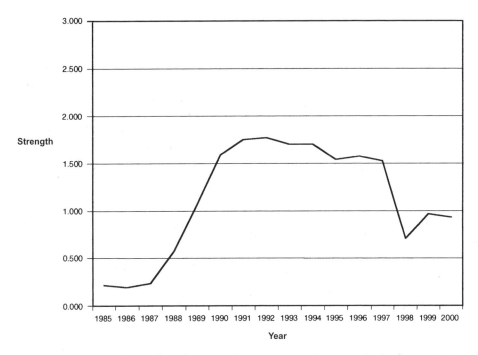

Figure 6. Strength of ethnopolitical protests in postcommunist countries in the 1990s.

dent, when pushed to be specific about *the* international actor that had been the most influential in affecting Latvia's relationship to its Russian minority in the 1990s, put it this way:

> At the time, when I was working in the president's office, I did not distinguish among all the international actors. Like most Latvians, I put international representatives and officials into one group. I labeled them "the West." Basically, Latvians knew that the West, whether it was voiced by the HCNM [High Commissioner on National Minorities], an official from the EU or the Council of Europe, or a foreign ambassador, wanted Latvia to change its policies toward its Russian population. Who said what and when was not really that important.[39]

The point is that while academics strive to identify a two-pronged relationship between one organization and ethnic politics in Eastern Europe, this simple causal chain masks a far more complex, dynamic, and historically unique relationship.

The Origins of Transnational Networks

This argument is based on the now extensive literature on transnationalism, developed and popularized in the early 1970s.[40] The transnational "revolution" marked a turning point in theory development in the subfield of international relations because it challenged the traditional realist paradigm and the centrality of states. However, the debate ended somewhat prematurely, largely because the initial focus was on transnational interactions and included such a broad array of actors and activities that it was impossible to assess their effects systematically. As Samuel Huntington put it, transnationalism achieved popularity at the price of precision, and the first wave of this literature was criticized for its creation of a partial, even idealized view of its effects.[41] Without intending to, some of this early literature left the impression that transnational activity occurred at the expense of nation states, and it clearly did not.[42]

A second wave of transnational research emerged in the early 1990s in response to the Soviet Union's collapse and the explosion of NGOs. These studies, according to Thomas Risse-Kappen, tried "to overcome the conceptual and empirical hurdles that plagued earlier research."[43] Using insights from comparative foreign economic policy, this research emphasized a state's domestic structure to explain the success of transnational actors in specific sectors. Others, influenced by the normative turn in international relations and the development of constructivist ideas, emphasized the role transnational actors play in promoting change. Perhaps the best-known concept to emerge from the marriage of transnationalism and the social movement's literature is Margaret Keck and Kathryn Sikkink's concept of "transnational advocacy networks,"[44] which are defined as the array of governmental and nongovernmental organizations that are united by similar principles and work simultaneously to promote policy change.

Borrowing the term *network* from sociology allowed these scholars to capture the numerous interactions among actors that operate in both domestic and international politics.[45] Sidney Tarrow explains the crucial difference between transnational social movements, which are the bases for contentious politics *within* domestic societies and have sustained domestic roots, and transnational advocacy networks, which originate *outside* a state, provide a mechanism for the diffusion of collective action frames, and help domestic groups construct their own social movements.[46] Among the reasons for the popularity of this concept is that it helped to bridge the largely artificial divide between international relations and comparative politics, and students of both subfields found it useful for understanding how domestic and international forces work together to affect change.[47] Advocacy networks also allow the traditionally state-centered literature in international relations to incorporate the role of nongovernmental organizations, as most of the existing literature on NGOs comes from development studies and not political science.[48]

While numerous kinds of transnational advocacy networks exist and scores of different campaigns have been launched to promote change of one kind or another, human rights networks have been investigated the most and are considered by scholars to be both the strongest and most institutionalized advocacy networks.[49] However, these human rights networks had little to say when it came to ethnic conflict management or minority rights.[50] As Communism crumbled and ethnic disputes escalated, it was clear that existing international organizations and transnational advocacy networks were either unable or unwilling to respond to the complex, volatile issues associated with ethnic conflict. Moreover, although NGOs became involved in ethnic politics in Eastern Europe, they were not central players in all cases. Instead, it was the CSCE/OSCE that put ethnic conflict management and minority rights on the international radar screen in 1990, producing specific statements that acknowledged "that questions relating to national minorities can only be satisfactorily resolved in a democratic political framework."[51]

Due to the attention and coordinating efforts of the CSCE/OSCE in this issue area, overlapping relationships developed throughout the decade, emphasizing coordination, transparency, information sharing, as well as a pooling of resources to prevent ethnic-based conflict. Thus, although existing transnational literature provides important insights into the story of ethnic peace in Eastern Europe, it cannot explain the evolution of ethnic politics for at least three reasons. First, its emphasis on NGOs fails to anticipate a central role for intergovernmental organizations that may in fact behave like a NGO, leading a transnational campaign while still relying on and often deferring to other actors. Second, existing literature does not anticipate the definitive shift that occurred in the post–cold war era between governments, international organizations, and NGOs. In this new configuration, states were not pushed aside, but a more diverse army of actors worked together to achieve common goals. Finally, while the term network is used by scholars, there is little theoretical discussion of this concept and its usage. Does network merely mean lots of actors? Or does it say something about the relationships between the actors?

This book contends that the network response in the 1990s was not simply uncoordinated behavior by several actors, but it reflected a clear desire among governments and NGOs to bring their resources and authority to bear on the shared problem of ethnic conflict.

How Networks Operate

Although transnational efforts to prevent ethnic conflict started in 1990, it was not until the mid-1990s that an actual network was in place, whereby actors with similar interests collaborated with like-minded individuals from other organizations to achieve common goals.[52] This corresponded directly to U.S.-led NATO intervention in Bosnia, and the network congealed as Western governments and leaders of intergovernmental organizations negotiated their roles and promised to support stability, democracy, and ethnic cooperation in Eastern Europe.[53] The goal of this network was simple: to exploit a range of strategies and tools to prevent ethnic-based violence in other postcommunist countries. In addition to military force, transnational actors crafted a combination of material and ideational strategies to encourage states and societies in the East to opt for peaceful ways of managing ethnic pluralism.

The theoretical framework for this research was inspired by fieldwork conducted in Bosnia, first in 2000 and then in 2001 and 2002, where international and local officials regularly commented that Yugoslavia's unraveling had contributed to important changes in the ways governments and nongovernmental organizations behaved.[54] This is because the Dayton Peace Accords, signed in December 1995, reflected the clear need for multiparty and multilevel involvement to rebuild Bosnia after ethnic conflict ravaged the country. Ultimately, at least seven international organizations, six national governments, numerous ad hoc committees, and an untold number of international NGOs committed themselves to re-creating a multiethnic Bosnian state.[55]

In Bosnia, I identified several strategies transnational actors used to prevent future violence and encourage ethnic cooperation. In addition to military measures, they used an array of strategies, including special political institutions, economic development programs, as well as large doses of financial assistance to promote democracy and strengthen civil society.[56] The behavior in Bosnia reflected the close, interdependent relationships that had evolved among interested actors, including NATO, the EU, the CSCE/OSCE, and the Council of Europe, which were supported by governments and reinforced by dozens of international NGOs. The international community's response to the conflict in Bosnia by 1995 seemed to signify a unique, if not unprecedented model of international cooperation and decentralized governance. The question was: did these same strategies and nonhierarchical, collaborative relationships exist elsewhere to counter ethnic tensions? And if so, what were the effects?

Like others concerned with conflict prevention, this research analytically separates transnational influences into top-down and bottom-up strategies.[57] The top-down strategies include: conditionality, mediation, and normative pressure, but transnational actors did not stop there. They also aimed to positively influence ethnic politics from below by promoting democracy, NGO development, and regional initiatives. Put differently, this decentralized arrangement of public and private actors relied on a complex array of modalities to influence outcomes from above and below. The following causal diagram (figure 7) represents *how* transnational strategies influenced ethnic politics in Eastern Europe as well as the characteristics of ethnic cooperation.

In some places and at certain points, transnational influence included all of these strategies, while elsewhere it involved a single strategy or a smaller combination of strategies. To clarify what I conceived as the "the Bosnia effect," I conducted interviews in the summer of 2003 with former and current officials from the U.S. Agency for International Development (USAID) and from private foundations that had worked in Eastern Europe during the 1990s, testing the plausibility of my ideas about transnationalism and networks. In the spring and summer of 2004, I interviewed similar officials from the EU and the CSCE/OSCE.[58] The point of these interviews was to confirm what secondary sources suggested about the nature of the "Western mission" in postcommunist Eastern Europe and the burgeoning security framework in Europe. During the summer of 2004, I had unlimited access to CSCE/OSCE reports, restricted documents, mission correspondence, and correspondence with regional organizations and national governments. I also interviewed current and former CSCE/OSCE officials in Brussels, Vienna, and The Hague. Importantly, these interviews included a one-on-one interview with the first high commissioner on national minorities, Max van der Stoel (1993–2001), considered to be "the face of Europe" when it came to ethnic issues in postcommunist countries.[59] In total, more than sixty interviews with officials from intergovernmental organizations, governments, and NGOs provide crucial evidence of the intentions and strategies employed by members of this transnational network and their effects, which supplement my secondary sources.

Two aspects of this transnational behavior are highlighted: how strategies overlapped, and the high level of interdependence among international actors. Network analysis provides a powerful tool for addressing these concerns, specifically for conceptualizing the complex, nonhierarchical relationships among international actors interested in ethnic conflict management. A representative of the CSCE/OSCE describes the relationships in the 1990s in this way: "Transnational actors were united

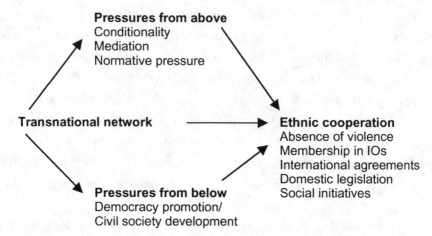

Figure 7. Transnational networks and ethnic cooperation.

by the same goals and guided by similar principles, and together they created a vector of activities that all flowed in the same direction."[60]

Although my research indicates that this network was spearheaded by the CSCE/OSCE, I must emphasize that there was never an explicit leader or hierarchy among the parties focused on ethnic conflict. Conflict management instead emerged organically from a division of labor by governmental and nongovernmental organizations. In the early 1990s, the CSCE/OSCE and the CoE crafted the international community's message related to ethnic problems, identifying the obstacles to cooperation and suggesting how international actors and targeted states should respond. This message was often used by moderate politicians in Eastern Europe to further their own agendas. Working closely with governments and NGOs, these transnational messengers provided Eastern European states with possible legal and political solutions to mediate escalating tensions.

In the second half of the 1990s, with the message defined, the EU and NATO became crucial network members, furnishing states in the East with the motivation to transform ethnic conflict because of their ability to sanction and reward states. Supported by powerful governments such as that of the United States, these intergovernmental organizations possessed the necessary "teeth" to push difficult domestic changes in the East. Nongovernmental organizations were also instrumental, supplying the means for ethnic cooperation by providing significant financial and in-kind assistance to initiate dialogues, establishing local NGOs, and fostering an environment conducive to ethnic cooperation. What was most striking about this transnational network was how intertwined the relationships and activities were among governmental, regional, and nongovernmental actors.[61] Oftentimes, it was difficult to discern when governmental work ended and NGO activities began.

Given the characteristics of networks, which are explained in greater detail in chapter 3, this research posits that members of transnational network will: (1) share common principles and goals; (2) make interdependent decisions; and (3) exchange information and expertise. Although relationships will be close, no formal hierarchy among actors will develop, and thus no one actor will dominate this arrangement. This research also posits that when a network forms (such as the one on ethnic conflict management formed by 1995), its members will be more successful in affecting desired outcomes through the network than when they work alone.

Alternative explanations

The most common argument made to explain the current trajectory of ethnic politics in Eastern Europe singles out the European Union and focuses on its strategy of conditionality to change the behavior of Eastern European states.[62] In short, the European Union's Copenhagen criteria, adopted in June 1993, provided transitioning states with a set of political and economic requirements that had to be met before EU membership would be considered. Under this not-so-veiled threat, the EU mandated that if Eastern European states did not resolve interethnic conflicts peacefully and undertake initiatives to protect and preserve minority rights, it would deny them financial assistance and bar them from entering the union. This argument certainly offers insight into specific legislation, especially in the second half of the 1990s, as Eastern European states realized that EU enlargement was not only inevitable but their inclusion plausible.

Yet by the time EU enlargement became a genuine possibility, ethnic crises in Eastern Europe were largely contained and violence considered quite unlikely.[63] The argument fails to explain the containment of ethnic conflict for at least three additional reasons. First, although respect for and the protection of minority rights was indeed a criterion identified to assess accession states' progress, specific laws or mechanisms aimed at ensuring the protection of minority rights never materialized. The EU's official foray into conflict resolution did not emerge until its sponsorship of the Stability Pact (which was not adopted until 1999). Second, despite the adoption of the Copenhagen criteria in 1993, the EU did not monitor these issues closely or independently until about 1997 (and even after this point, the EU continued to rely on other governmental and nongovernmental actors). Finally, research that looks at the relationship between conditionality and accommodating ethnic policies suggests that there is not even a strong correlation between EU monitoring reports and minority-rights protection legislation in Eastern European states.[64]

A second set of explanations credits the conflict prevention activities of the CSCE/OSCE for the East's peaceful turn. This research concludes that the work of the CSCE/OSCE, specifically in the area of democratization and human rights, had a significant effect on the containment of ethnic conflict in many postcommunist countries.[65] Without discounting other regional organizations entirely, scholars like P. Terrence Hopmann assert that the "OSCE deserves a place of at least equal status with other regional organizations when evaluating the role of multilateral institutions in ethnic conflict prevention."[66] This is because it was the CSCE/OSCE (and not the EU or NATO) that was the primary player pushing for a focus on ethnic conflict and the development of a minority rights regime. A few studies discuss the CSCE/OSCE's democracy promotion activities, its standard-setting behavior, or its in-country missions, but most research centers on the activities of the Office of the High Commissioner on National Minorities and Max van der Stoel's behavior as a "normative entrepreneur."[67]

Claims about the CSCE/OSCE's importance do not go unchallenged. Among others, Judith Kelley argues that many of the recommendations made by the HCNM fell on deaf ears, and it was only the EU's support of the CSCE/OSCE and of the HCNM's recommendations that ultimately influenced Eastern European leaders' behavior.[68] That is to say, conditionality and material costs and benefits were far more important than the standards promoted by the CSCE/OSCE. Other criticisms explicitly or implicitly dismiss the activities of the CSCE/OSCE since the organization lacks both the teeth and the resources necessary to affect leaders' decisions.

A third body of research points to the role played by the international community in promoting democracy in the postcommunist region. While the mechanisms are often underspecified, the argument made is that the management of ethnic conflicts in Eastern Europe is a byproduct of successful democracy-promotion activities.[69] Democracy promotion no doubt affected ethnic policies in the East, but there are at least three problems with this argument. First, it is difficult to obtain reliable data on the huge array of actors that were involved in democracy-promotion activities and to discern which of these governmental or nongovernmental organizations were interested specifically in ethnic conflict management. This is especially true of NGOs; interviews with officers from U.S.-based foundations involved in democracy promotion activities, including The German Marshall Fund and The Open Society Institute, reinforce this point.[70] That is, although NGOs may not have had an explicit program defined in terms of ethnic conflict or minority rights, they were clearly interested in preventing violence and promoting stability. Thus, although NGOs assumed that engagement in other areas of civil society would indirectly encourage ethnic cooperation, this was not a top priority.

Second, if gathering data on democracy-related initiatives is difficult, evaluations of these projects and their cumulative impact on interethnic relations is nearly impossible. As an EU evaluation of its democracy promotion programs points out, "Outcomes are influenced by a multitude of factors which cannot be separated from each other."[71] Finally, research on the connections between democratization and violence conflict may in fact undermine claims that link democracy promotion and ethnic peace. Democratization, at least in the short run, may increase rather than decrease ethnic conflicts.[72] Thus, concentrating on democracy promotion alone is unlikely to explain the peaceful trajectory of ethnic politics in Eastern European.

Each of these explanations describes a slice of reality and helps explain why certain minority-friendly policies were adopted. However, they not only ignore other potential international influences, but they miss the broader shifts in international politics, the new ways governments and nongovernmental organizations behaved, and the synergistic effects of public-private relationships. That is to say, existing explanations for the peaceful trajectory overlook the transnational network that developed in the second half of the 1990s to tame ethnic hatreds in Eastern Europe.

Defining the Terms

Problems of definition, or a failure to clearly define one's terms, may be at the heart of misperception that links ethnic diversity so closely with violence and bloodshed. What distinguishes ethnic conflicts from other types of intranational or internal disputes? Michael Brown asserts that the term *ethnic conflict* is often used haphazardly to describe a range of intrastate conflicts that are not, in fact, ethnic at all.[73] Another scholar claims that *ethnic conflict* has merely become a euphemism for substate conflicts that we can neither explain nor comprehend.[74] Others suggest that terms such as *ethnic conflict* are applied strategically by governments and international organizations to justify a retreat from the world, suggesting that certain conflicts, by their very nature, are insolvable.[75] In response to genocide in Rwanda and ethnic cleansing in Bosnia, policymakers latched on to certain labels while consciously avoiding others because of legal implications and an obligation to respond. Thought of in this light, ethnic conflicts are not only internal disputes with a long historical tradition, but are violent conflicts that cannot be affected by external involvement. This book defines ethnic conflict as substate disputes between groups of people who believe that they are members of different identity groups; it is *discord* among groups whose ethnicity has political consequences—including violence.[76] Thought of in this way, ethnic conflict is more about the *form* the conflict takes rather than its actual cause.

Ethnic cooperation

Ethnic cooperation or ethnic accommodation, the outcome this research explores is defined as any actions or policies developed for the purpose of managing or resolving ethnic disputes without resorting to violence or secession.[77] Unlike ethnic violence, which has a fairly clear beginning and end, capturing what is meant by ethnic cooperation is more difficult; the absence of violence is a necessary, though not sufficient, indicator of cooperation. As Robert Keohane suggests, cooperation requires that the actions of separate individuals or groups be brought into conformity with one another and that each party changes his or her behavior contingent on changes in the other's behavior.[78] To demonstrate cooperation or a country's move toward ethnic peace, I look at an array of indicators, including a state's foreign and domestic policies connected to ethnic politics.

Ethnic cooperation is evidenced, at least to a minimal extent, by a state's participation in international and regional bodies and agreements that govern ethnic relations. More consequential, however, is a state's or group's willingness to accept international mediation or to implement international standards associated with conflict management and minority rights. Domestic changes are crucial to sustaining interethnic cooperation; new laws, monitoring bodies, and institutions that hold the state accountable all demonstrate that, in the words of Thomas Risse and Kathryn Sikkink, behavior is gaining "prescriptive status."[79] Therefore, domestic legislation and the existence of institutions meant to prevent and manage ethnic conflicts, including governmental and nongovernmental organizations, are crucial evidence of institutionalized change and, thus, ethnic cooperation.

Transnational actors

Just as words dealing with ethnicity have multiple meanings, the explanation I offer suffers from definitional and conceptual ambiguity. External actors or the international community are central to my argument. Who or what constitutes the "international community," however, is far from clear. Like others who study the numerous organizations and processes comprising the subfield of international relations, I think of the external sources of ethnic cooperation in Eastern Europe in terms of transnationalism. Simply, *transnational influences* describe the movement of tangible or intangible items across state boundaries when at least one actor is not an agent of a government.[80] *Transnational,* rather than *external* or *international,* is used for a variety of reasons. *International* is limiting because it is often used to contrast activities or groups found in domestic politics, and it suggests a global dimension that is not entirely accurate in Eastern Europe. Similarly, the word *external* does not capture the fluidity of actors and relationships that transgress borders. *Transnational* refers to the nature of the involvement, which is not regulated, rather than just an identification of the actors involved. Transnational influences in Eastern Europe thus include the efforts of Western governments, regional and multilateral organizations, and NGOs that operate across borders.[81]

No single book could examine all the transnational influences in Eastern Europe in the 1990s. I primarily consider the activities of regional actors such as the CSCE/OSCE, the EU, the CoE, and NATO.[82] I also address the initiatives of the United States and the work of international nongovernmental organizations, such as the Helsinki Committee and the Open Society Institute. When talking about transnational behavior, I use the word *strategy* to define mechanisms of influence or explain how transnational actors attempt to contain ethnic conflicts.

Eastern Europe

Defining a region is always contested, and Eastern Europe is hardly an exception.[83] The states in this region have been described in many, often confusing ways, including Central Europe, East Central Europe, or South Central Europe. Yet, it is not clear what criteria are used when including certain countries or defining one region as distinct from another, and thus there is little consistency when speaking of the countries that should be included or excluded.[84] Is it religion, culture, or political history that unites what might otherwise be considered diverse countries into a seemingly cohesive region?

The imposition of Communism after World War II by the Soviet Union changed the political, social, and cultural landscape of numerous countries, which previously had few historical or cultural ties. The countries that came under the sway of Soviet domination were suddenly and definitively grouped together, and the term *Eastern Europe* was firmly established. Despite the understandable disdain of this term by many inhabitants of the region, I use it because of its clarity and my interest in the postcommunist experience.[85] Therefore, in this context, Eastern Europe will refer to all former Communist countries in Europe, including portions of eastern Germany, the former Yugoslavia, and post-Soviet states.

The Plan of the Book

Although this is not a history book, chapter 2 provides a historical summary of the international community's response to ethnic conflict, explaining why the West was so ill-prepared for Yugoslavia's demise in 1991. It also accounts for the unique perceptions of ethnic politics in Eastern Europe that helped lay the foundation for a network organizational arrangement in the mid-1990s. Chapter 3 initially takes a theoretical turn, discussing and defining transnational networks, their characteristics, and their behavior. It then analyzes the development of the transnational network focused on ethnic conflict, explaining the specific top-down and bottom-up strategies (which were often used simultaneously)to contain ethnic conflict in Eastern Europe.

In chapters 4 and 5, I apply these arguments to two similar cases in Eastern Europe: Romania and Latvia. Although Romania and Latvia are different in many respects, and ethnic politics in these countries in the 1990s differed significantly from those in Bosnia, they share commonalities but also differences that make them suitable for comparative research. Both are postcommunist countries considered to be new democracies; not only do they share Communist legacies, but their access to the West, as well as the density of civil society in 1990 was, while not identical, arguably quite similar. Each country is home to what has been described as a "divided nation"; that is, the county has at least one ethnic minority group that has ethnic kin living in a neighboring country. (Bosnia has two divided nations: Serbs and Croats.) Rogers Brubaker, among others, has looked at these situations because of the historical and destructive role played by divided nations, and the so-called "triadic nexus of relations" created by nationalizing states, ethnic minorities, and external national homelands.[86] Finally, both Romania and Latvia were identified as hotspots in the early 1990s because of the intractability of ethnic conflicts that many feared could turn violent.[87] Thus, it is not surprising that in both countries the move toward ethnic cooperation was neither immediate nor continuous.

While Romania and Latvia share a common recent history, important political, economic, and social differences remain. One obvious difference was their regime type during the early 1990s and their attitudes toward the West. Upon regaining its independence, Latvia immediately declared its desire to become a liberal democracy and rejoin the West, while in Romania, a democratic, solidly pro-Western government was not firmly in place until late 1996. Nonetheless, Latvia's move toward ethnic cooperation did not begin immediately. In fact, despite its Western orientation and small population, it successfully resisted international recommendations on these matters for quite some time.

In both cases, however, transnational actors followed a similar path, relying on the same strategies at roughly the same time. Outcomes were not identical, but ethnic politics improved at about the same juncture in both Romania and Latvia. Despite the intensity of ethnic relations at different points in the 1990s, both countries joined international organizations, adopted legislation, and behaved in remarkably similar ways to manage majority-minority relations. Thus, these chapters look at the evolution and transformation of ethnic politics in Romania and Latvia. They address similar questions and concerns in these disputes: What transnational actors became involved? What strategies did they employ? How effective were they? And how can we tell that transnational involvement made a difference?

Evaluating the effects of this transnational network on the management of ethnic conflict in these case studies is not an easy task. For one, it has become almost commonplace to state that the results of conflict prevention are impossible to measure, as no one really knows whether violence would have broken out if this or that policy had not been implemented.[88] In short, it is always more difficult to explain precisely and definitely why something did *not* happen rather than why it did. To make matters even more complex, transnational networks attempt to promote change in a variety of places, and effects are difficult to trace. Previous research on human rights and democratization provides a useful framework for evaluating the influence of this transnational network.[89] As Risse and Sikkink have shown, transnational-network influence can be conceptualized in terms of stages.[90] Although desired changes in foreign and domestic policies does suggest some influence, we know that states often make decisions for instrumental reasons. Thus, other evidence is crucial, such as the creation of domestic bodies that allow different actors access to the decision-making process or to monitor government behavior. A key objective of the transnational network I describe is the empowerment of local governmental and nongovernmental actors, including NGOs that will advocate for minority rights, increase awareness of the problems faced by minorities, or promote government transparency. Ultimately, transnational networks promote change by working from both the top down and the bottom up.

Employing the technique of process tracing or historical analysis, I explore the chain of events from transnational involvement to policy decisions and social changes. Ideally, the evidence would include a close sequencing of events that would demonstrate clearly that transnational involvement was followed by or contributed directly to accommodating ethnic behavior. This is not always possible, but I do try to demonstrate, through primary and secondary sources, the transnational inspiration of many foreign policies and domestic changes. I also highlight the importance of the synergy among transnational actors to the trajectory of ethnic conflict in these countries.

Chapter 6 concludes with a summary of the findings and the lessons of ethnic conflict management in Eastern Europe, including a discussion of the negative and unintended consequences of this transnational network.

A Summary of the Main Findings

At least three theoretical and policy-relevant findings emerge from this research. First, while it is understandable that violent ethnic conflict attracts a great deal of attention from academics and policymakers, ethnic pluralism—common throughout the world—does not necessarily lead to violence. Like violent ethnic conflict, ethnic cooperation also requires an explanation. Even research that allegedly focuses on managing ethnic conflict does not spend much time on the avoidance of conflict or how deescalation takes place.[91] This means that more research needs to focus on the ethnic conflicts that do not result in violence and on the transformation of ethnic conflicts.

Second, the "international community" however defined has never been able to solve the problems associated with majority-minority relations, and it likely never will. However, transnational actors, using a broad array of instruments and engaging in networklike behavior, can perform crucial functions for ethnic peace. As in Eastern Europe in the 1990s, international actors can identify common issues that intensify majority-minority relations and propose legal and political solutions. They can induce change through appropriately crafted incentives and constraints. Finally, they can assist states and societies financially by helping establish domestic instruments and innovative social programs. Put differently, the international community can provide the *message*, the *motivation*, and the *means* to push tense majority-minority relations away from violence and toward ethnic cooperation.

Finally, by tracking the enormous changes that took place in the last decade of the twentieth century in this one area, this book highlights a new, nascent architecture of global governance. In the transnational network it describes, governments and intergovernmental organizations are the main players, but realizing the need for responsiveness, flexibility, but most of all burden-sharing, network members adopt novel ways of dealing with the threat of ethnic conflict. While not always successful, this transnational network had an obvious and positive impact on the legislation, policies, and societies in Eastern Europe. As in domestic politics, governing by network is a growing reality in international politics. This research draws attention to the possibilities of this arrangement—where states work closely with regional organizations and NGOs—to manage shared problems.

T W O

Historical Responses to Ethnic Conflict

The democratic transitions of 1989–91 made it abundantly clear that the post-World War II international order was disappearing. Initially, the elation associated with Communism's collapse was palpable. As President H. W. Bush put in 1989, "We live in a peaceful, prosperous time . . . for a new breeze is blowing, and a world refreshed by freedom seems reborn."[1] Later that year, European heads of state proclaimed that "each day in Central and Eastern Europe change is asserting itself more strongly. Everywhere a powerful aspiration toward freedom, democracy, human rights . . . and peace is being expressed."[2] Unfortunately, the winds changed course quickly, and just four years later, President Bill Clinton described a different world indeed. "Today, a generation raised in the shadows of the Cold War assumes new responsibilities in a world warmed by the sunshine of freedom but threatened still by ancient hatreds and new plagues."[3] By this point, European leaders had already recognized the need to accelerate economic and political integration to ensure stability and peace on the continent.[4]

Such actions characterize well the contradictory interpretations of the post-cold war world, and they help clarify the international community's initial, rather clumsy response to the reemergence of ethnic tensions. This chapter explains the historical roots of the international community's response, shedding light on the peculiar political and ideological conditions in the early 1990s that ultimately gave rise to a network of governmental and nongovernmental actors working together to calm ethnic tensions. Most discussions of the international community's involvement in ethnic conflict management in Eastern Europe are normative; this chapter is not.[5] In trying to discern the unique aspects of transnational involvement in the 1990s, it provides a historical backdrop to the international community's efforts in this area.

To do so, it makes three related arguments. First, international involvement in ethnic conflict management is not a new practice but is instead based on a long, albeit interrupted history. Second, the West's initial, uneven response to ethnic conflict in the early 1990s was influenced by two different, if not opposing intellectual traditions: the paradigm of liberal democracy and the concept of eastern nationalism. The former contributed to the initial optimism as Communism collapsed, while the latter caused scholars and policymakers to misinterpret and exaggerate emerging ethnopolitical disputes.[6] These diverging tendencies unfortunately meant that in the course of a few years, the policy pendulum swung from overlooking ethnicity completely to seeing violent ethnic conflict in every potential situation.[7] Consequently, as violent ethnic conflict broke out in the 1990s, international actors were both ill-prepared and unwilling to manage these conflicts alone. Unique international circumstances, alongside a culture of consensus, gave way to new strategies and relationships, providing the necessary foundation for a network to form.

Historical Precedents

Often ethnic conflict management is considered in context of the changes associated with the cold war's end, or it is believed to be proof of how the institution of sovereignty has evolved.[8] International involvement and the promotion of minority rights, while seemingly sudden and novel, is not a new phenomenon.[9] This section will demonstrate that the post-cold war era *re*awakened, rather than awakened, concerns over ethnicity and the role of minorities in international politics.

World War I and the Minority Problem

A detailed account of the history of international attempts to manage ethnic tensions and protect minorities would require a great deal more space, and it is readily available elsewhere.[10] However, it is important to point out that every major peace treaty since the Treaty of Westphalia in 1648 contained provisions for the protection of minorities, particularly religious minorities.[11] Regardless of whether international involvement concerned religious, ethnic, or linguistic minorities, its goal was the same: to promote stability and keep the peace. During the Congress of Vienna in 1815, the first international guarantees related to the protection of *ethnic*, rather than religious, groups were established. These guarantees were regarded by ruling elites as neither some kind of novelty nor as something that would in any way restrict the sovereignty of new states.[12] Vienna recognized the partitions of the Polish state while it simultaneously recognized the need for the Great Powers to guarantee a special position for the Polish nation to inhibit rebellion and promote regional stability.

On the surface, the stipulations identified by Vienna did not help the Polish nation much, at least not in the short term. Vienna did not lead to the creation of more ethnically inclusive institutions in countries where Poles were a minority, nor, as the

Great Powers had hoped, did interethnic harmony result. These agreements did, however, succeed in their important security function: They helped prevent a general European war. With the exception of the Crimean War, no conflict seriously jeopardized the balance of power in Europe for almost a hundred years. At the same time, although Vienna sanctified the division of the Polish state, its recognition of the rights of Polish minorities helped to unify and sustain the nation. Ironically, this aspect of international involvement contributed to the reemergence of the Polish state after World War I.[13]

World War I had significant implications for Eastern Europe as a region but also for the development of international mechanisms governing ethnic politics, as an "international regime" governing minority rights took shape.[14] Nationalist movements seeking independence from multiethnic empires had looked to the Allied powers to support their causes. Assistance was not easy to come by because the Allies had initially planned to merely readjust the balance of power in Europe, favoring the preservation of the Austro-Hungarian monarchy in order to counterbalance the ambitions of the Prussian and Russian empires. Historical legacies aside, President Woodrow Wilson was initially dismissive if not openly hostile to Eastern European nationalist movements because he viewed the establishment of small nation states in this region as politically irrational. Support for the Austro-Hungarian monarchy became increasingly untenable as the empire succumbed to nationalist movements. Thus, only out of necessity were ethnic differences mediated by the international community.

Adapting to the new situation, President Wilson became the driving force behind the commitment to national self-determination.[15] Although Wilson exalted this principle, he did so without realizing that in practice this would contribute to instability in Europe.[16] Thus, while Wilson can be credited for putting national self-determination on the international agenda, this did not mean that he ever aimed or planned to resolve majority-minority problems. The famous but generally misrepresented Point Ten (of his Fourteen Points) did not in fact mention national independence at all; instead, it read that nations should be accorded the freest opportunity for autonomous development.[17] Moreover, his declarations about nations and nationalism were pointed; he was thinking primarily about the Polish nation, not about the numerous other small ethnic groups that were intermingled throughout the region. Even at this point, Wilson saw the continued existence of the Austro-Hungarian empire as a political necessity for stability in Europe.[18]

Interwar mechanisms to prevent ethnic conflict were addressed through a carpet of treaties, declarations, and policies, many of which, unfortunately, lacked the clarity or the supervision to be effective. From these, four basic strategies can be discerned: (1) border changes and population transfers; (2) local plebiscites; (3) legal promises reflected in peace agreements, bilateral treaties, and unilateral national declarations; and (4) the creation of a monitoring body within the League of Nations. To encourage more homogenized nation states in the lands between Germany and the Soviet Union, but also to reward certain nations and punish others, borders were drawn largely along ethnic boundaries, and minority populations were transferred to their ethnic homeland. For example, the delineation of German-Polish and German-Czechoslovak border resulted in over 3.5 million ethnic Germans being resettled in the German state.[19] In markedly contentious areas where ethnic sorting proved impossible, plebiscites were held to allow citizens to decide on their citizenship. Although the United States did not support the German proposal to hold plebiscites, Great Britain's Lloyd George insisted upon it, even if the outcomes were not decisive, because he believed this strategy would promote long-term ethnic stability.[20] To a large extent, ethnic cooperation would emerge as groups were forced to live in homogenous states.

Sorting and separating was not always possible, and the Great Powers pushed weaker states to promise that they would protect the rights of ethnic minorities. In May 1919, the Commission on New States and Minorities was established to develop minority-protection clauses in peace agreements and initiate guarantees for minority rights within the framework of basic human freedoms.[21] Globally, more than a dozen countries would eventually agree to these clauses and freedoms.[22] Minority rights were also embedded in national laws, specifically in basic constitutional guarantees, which could not be altered without the approval of the League of Nations. The task of monitoring and enforcing minority rights was also put in the hands of the League of Nations.

No obligations relating to minority protection were included in the league's covenant but several articles (including Article 23) provided the basis for putting the issue under the aegis of its authority.[23] Given its imprecise authority, the League of Nations set up a specialized mechanism, the Council, to address the concerns of minority groups. The Council did have some success in ameliorating difficult ethnic relations, such as in Upper Silesia where the shared Germany-Polish ownership of this industrial region lasted for about fifteen prosperous years.[24] In numerous other cases, the Council established ad hoc committees to investigate complaints and, in the majority of these cases, the committees were able to work out some type of compromise, rather than recommend legal proceedings.[25] Yet, the league's Council faced numerous problems, most of which reflected the broader weaknesses of international efforts to deal with the problems of peace.

Instead of averting ethnic conflict and strengthening minority rights, these international initiatives at times exacerbated ethnic tensions because of the unwillingness of larger, more powerful states (such as Germany) to abide by their dictates. Thus, although the interwar period was a significant step forward, and it represented the first time in modern history that states tried to provide systematic international legal protections for minorities and prevent ethnic-based conflicts, ethnic problems were not in fact internationalized.[26] The difficulties of the 1930s (including the growth of fascism and the burgeoning social and economic problems throughout the world) make it difficult to evaluate objectively the achievements of this embryonic international regime because Nazi Germany and other irredentist states did all that they could to exploit ethnic tensions and manipulate international instruments.

World War II and Individual Rights

When the states of Europe were resurrected after World War II, the basic outlines of the Versailles map remained intact. Although unresolved minority issues played an important role in causing these conflicts, the war yielded a different attitude toward ethnic conflict and minority rights for several reasons. First, migration and the forced resettlement of peoples during the interwar years had created more ethnically homogenous states, providing a weaker justification for international involvement in these matters. Precise figures on each country are not available, but the number of minorities in Eastern Europe was reduced to between eight and ten million, or less than 10 percent of the population.[27] Second, many believed that the League of Nations had not only failed to prevent ethnic conflicts but may have even assisted aggressive nationalist states in regaining lost territory and people. Thus, international involvement was not viewed as a particularly positive force.

At the same time, notions about liberal democracy, which pervaded Western thinking, were optimistic about the inevitable demise of nationalism, mainly because the power of the market would serve as a check on unprofitable ethnic instincts.[28] Moreover, liberal democracy claimed that ethnic conflict was not a problem with national minorities per se but was a problem of individuals struggling to have their rights recognized and respected in undemocratic environments.[29] A final, decisive reason for the shift away from ethnic concerns was the influence of the United States, which implicitly believed that since it had no problems with ethnic minorities, it was opposed to any broad international effort to revive the interwar minority rights regime or to recognize the rights of groups.[30] In a rare moment of international consensus, the victors of the war elbowed aside minority rights in favor of individual, human rights. While similar in many ways, the league's successor, the United Nations, had a more limited scope, and its involvement in a state's domestic politics was constrained by Article 2 (7) of the United Nations charter, which protected states from external interference in their internal affairs. Consequently, despite its name, the United Nations worked on behalf of states (not nations); its influence on ethnic issues was shaped, first and foremost, by the overriding importance attached to state sovereignty.

In December 1947, the UN Human Rights Commission sought the opinion of the Economic and Social Council on whether minority protection treaties signed after World War I should be considered valid and binding. It was decided then that the situation regarding national minorities had changed to such an extent that the problem ceased to exist.[31] Put differently, ethnic minorities were no longer a leading threat to peace and thus should be ignored. In drafting the Universal Declaration of Human Rights, UN members explicitly rejected a proposal to include the rights of minorities.[32] The emphasis on individual rights was mostly the result of American preferences, based on the belief that ethnic differences could ultimately be resolved through the integration or assimilation of such populations. As Eleanor Roosevelt, the first U.S. representative to the UN Human Rights Commission, argued, since the best solution to the problem of minorities was to encourage respect for individual rights, the UN should not cater to group identities.[33]

Although no specific references to protect minorities were included in the UN charter, the organization did not absolve itself completely from the management of ethnic disputes. The phrase *national self-determination* was even included, but its meaning is conspicuously vague, especially as to how this principle might relate to ethnic minorities. Instead, the post–World War II international order emphasized only the "internal dimension" of the self-determination principle: that states have exclusive control over the internal affairs in their country and are free from foreign intervention.[34] The "external dimension" of this principle, which would specify the particular groups that could take advantage of the right to national independence, was noticeably less clear. In theory, most countries supported the rights of dependent territories or former colonies to national self-determination, independence, and self-government, but the application of these rights was still controversial. While both Eastern European and Asian countries supported a broad interpretation of this right, Western countries were more reluctant, being concerned about interfering in the domestic affairs of another country.[35] When it came to the rights of national minorities within an already existing state, UN members were united and uniformly unsympathetic.

Involvement by the UN in minority issues came in other ways, however, starting in 1948 with the Convention on the Prevention and Punishment of the Crime of Genocide and the Sub-committee on the Prevention of Discrimination and Protection of Minorities.[36] In the decades that followed, it was increasingly, albeit reluctantly, drawn into internal ethnic disputes, even while it maintained a strict observance of the principle of noninterference to prevent interstate war. By 1960, the UN General Assembly was forced to revisit its commitment to noninterference, and it officially approved of national self-determination in the colonial context. In 1966, two international human rights agreements—the International Covenant of Civil and Political Rights (ICCPR) and the International Covenant on Economic, Social, and Cultural Rights (ICESCR)—were drafted that embraced support for all peoples to the right of self-determination. The ICCPR in particular suggested that the principle of self-determination was not clear and that general rules in the field of human rights were sometimes insufficient for ensuring minorities' rights. As Article 27 puts it: "In those States in which ethnic, religious, or linguistic minorities exist, persons belonging to such minorities shall not be denied the right, in community with other members of their group, to enjoy their own culture and practice their own religion or use their own language."[37]

While the ICCPR does not endow minority groups with special rights, the skillfully worded compromise opened the door to the *exercise* of collective rights, demonstrating how international guarantees related to individual rights can be applied to minority individuals.[38] Although military intervention was rare and tended to occur in cases of colonial wars or when a government totally collapsed, the growing influence of less-developed countries in the UN made it difficult for this organization to continue discounting ethnic conflicts.[39] In specific situations, the UN made exceptions to the inviolability of sovereignty, becoming closely involved in ethnic disputes in various settings.[40] In 1970, its commitment to national self-determination was further muddled by the General Assembly's unanimous approval of Resolution 2625 and the Declaration on the Principle of International Law concerning Friendly Relations and Cooperation among States. This resolution, while still emphasizing the preservation of a state's territorial integrity, established a category of "peoples" who possessed the right to national self-determination out-side the colonial context.[41]

During the cold war, superpower support or opposition to an ethnic group's de-sire for self-determination was not the result of some coherent policy toward the rights of minorities or the principle itself. Instead, it was the consequence of a spe-cific situation and how a particular ethnic dispute played into the larger ideological battle between the East and the West. Tremendous pressure was put on all states to maintain the territorial status quo and resist border changes of any kind, regardless of a country's internal problems. A clear sign of this sentiment is that throughout the cold war era, the international community only endorsed one full-fledged seces-sion effort (in Bangladesh).

To supplement UN principles and better manage inter- and intrastate ethnic disputes in the West, states embraced democratic liberalism, institutionalizing the rights of individuals, and nondiscrimination in domestic laws and regional organi-zations as a way to protect minority rights, prevent ethnic conflict, and promote sta-bility. Architects of European integration consciously aimed to create institutions that would transcend the identities of European nations, thereby making a future war in Europe impossible.[42] At the same time and similar to the sentiment expressed in UN documents, Western leaders assumed that ethnic identity was fleeting and that liberal democratic governments would eventually galvanize civic cultures, causing ethnic divisions to disappear.[43] Universalism and individualism, rather than specific policies, would manage ethnic disputes. In total, these beliefs provided the foundation for the West's general tenor toward ethnic conflict and minority rights: assimilate and ignore while holding out the promise of individual rights. Embodied in multilateral development projects such as the Marshall Plan, and institutional-ized in regional organizations such as the European Coal and Steel Community (ECSC) and the Council of Europe, the management of ethnic pluralism was a nearly incidental concern when compared to containing Communism.

By the early 1960s in Western Europe, such policies were proving unsatisfying and ineffectual as ethnic tensions resurfaced in several countries. The most violent situation was in Northern Ireland, but ethnic groups desiring independence or more autonomy were also problematic in Spain, France, Italy, and Belgium. As dis-putes continued into the 1970s, Western European leaders reluctantly acknowl-edged the limits of liberal democracy, human rights policies, and the forces of modernization as adequate correctives, and many countries developed unique na-tional structures and instruments to accommodate ethnopolitical demands.

On a regional level, Western European politicians occasionally called for, but never really acted on, a more systematic response to ethnic conflict. For example, the Council of Europe, which was established in 1949 as an intergovernmental body to protect and promote human rights, recognized in its first year the importance of the protection of national minorities—even while it maintained a concentration on individuals and human rights and did little to put these pronouncements into practice.[44] Precursors to the European Union proposed a "Europe of Regions," with less-centralized national states, claiming that the development of regions would play an important role in mediating ethnic problems by encouraging regional identities; this regionalism would purportedly strengthen democracy and peace from the bottom up.[45] Yet, it was only with Communism's collapse that the West developed a comprehensive compendium of strategies for the explicit purpose of managing ethnic conflict, thereby restoring the issue as an international concern.[46]

The Return of Eastern Nationalism?

Although the level of international involvement in majority-minority relations varied, its geographical inspiration hardly wavered. The problem of minorities in Eastern Europe, evident for more than a century, brought about more than just treaties and international offices; it also contributed to a certain mindset about the region and its penchant for nationalism and ethnic violence. That is to say, the concept of Eastern nationalism also informed the international community's responses at the cold war's end. Overlaid on post-World War II attitudes, these conflicting influences—one that predicted the demise of ethnicity and the other that highlighted the unique and virulent strain of nationalism in the East—pushed leaders of the West to think differently about ethnic conflict management when it came to countries in Eastern Europe. When Communism's implosion in the 1990s again raised the specter of ethnic violence in the region, governments and intergovernmental organizations recognized the value of working together to achieve what no one actor could accomplish alone.

The Origins of Eastern Nationalism

Nationalism, as many have argued, emerges from a variety of contexts, and the political principle manifests itself differently from country to country.[47] Yet, for the countries in Eastern Europe, conventional wisdom held that the history of these countries was so similar that the entire region should be seen through the lens of ethnicity and the region's struggle for national self-determination.[48] Put differently, nationalism in the East does not vary from country to country, and it is different from nationalism in the West. John Plamentz may have been the first to define and distinguish nationalism in the West with its deep links to the Enlightenment and liberal ideas, from nationalism in the East with its ties to romanticism and a focus on group identity.[49] In short, Western nationalism was relatively benign and nice, asserts Plamentz, while the Eastern kind was doomed to nastiness by the conditions that gave rise to it.[50]

Plamentz's arguments are tied to several factors, including regional history and the role of the state, but most decisively to the region's culture. Unlike the West, Eastern nationalism did not operate on behalf of an already-existing, well-defined, and codified high culture; instead it was an aspirant or "in-the-making culture," which affected both its content and vigor. Plamentz focused largely on culture, while others developed a whole range of arguments to justify what they believed to be the fundamental differences between the East and the West and the implications of these differences on nationalism. Obvious empirical shortcomings aside, the contention arose that nationalism in the East was predestined to bloodshed while in the West it was peaceful and polite. Through these interpretations of Eastern culture and conflict, however invalid, the myth of Eastern nationalism and the inevitability of ethnic conflict in the region took root.

Other scholars put forth different reasons for the uniqueness of Eastern Europe and its nationalism. One argument often used by political economists focuses on the region's geographic location, vis-à-vis the great empires of Europe and Asia.[51] Eastern Europe's distance from the heart of economic development, combined with lower population density and different agricultural traditions, meant that while it was part of the Prussian, Russian, Habsburg, and Ottoman empires, it was always on the periphery of what was happening at the center. To borrow Immanuel Wallerstein's terminology, Eastern Europe's peripheral location profoundly shaped its political and social development.[52] Its geographical position, scholars like Daniel Chirot argued, contributed to its economic backwardness as early as the Middle Ages.[53]

Backwardness and dependence on Western Europe intensified the political subordination of Eastern Europeans, shaping the institutions and ideas that took hold in these countries. Consequently, in the nineteenth century, Eastern European elites formed intense nationalist ambitions and sought to build strong states to overcome their inconsequential position in the past, becoming "amusing imitators of the West" but also the "object of mockery."[54]

For some, romanticism's sway in the East contributed to the unique form of nationalism that emerged in this region. In reaction to the Enlightenment's emphasis on the universality of human reason, of scientific law, and the significance of the individual, romanticism stressed the diversity of nature and the spirit unique to each nation.[55] Given the subordinated positions of Eastern European nations, it is not surprising that these ideas resonated so loudly, contributing to the Springtime of the Nations revolts in 1848. Romanticism's emphasis on struggle offered a means for solving the problem of oppression and discrimination using culture and a shared history, which some believe influenced how Eastern nations came to understand the function of states. Romantic philosophy not only influenced the nation's relationship to the state, but it also produced a strong group tradition in the East.[56]

The Effects of Eastern Nationalism

Right or wrong, the collision of culture, geography, economics, and history provided the multiform foundation for what many referred to as Eastern nationalism. Its effects were purportedly reflected in the behavior of both elites and the masses. Years of persecution and political domination not only fomented a feeling of isolation among the masses but also cultivated an intense, nearly obsessive identification with one's nation. In Poland, the "Christ of nations," intellectuals and political leaders alike emphasized the uniqueness of the noble Polish nation and the need for nationalism to evolve and mature if it was ever to regain its statehood.[57] In place of religious tolerance, humanitarianism, and equality among groups, assaults against Jews, the Roma population, and minority groups were not uncommon in Eastern Europe.[58] Born of struggle, desperation, and internal oppression, Eastern nationalism foretells the politics Eastern European states experienced in the twentieth century.[59]

After World War I, historical states reemerged, and the states of Albania, Bulgaria, Estonia, Hungary, Latvia, Lithuania, Poland, and Romania all became independent. Political agreements and compromise also allowed totally new states, such as Yugoslavia and Czechoslovakia, to be established.[60] Like their predecessors, however, all these new Eastern European states—the newly independent historical states and the totally new ones—were multinational; that is, each comprised several ethnic groups. In 1914, half of the inhabitants of Eastern Europe were members of a minority group within their country. Although this proportion did decline in the postwar period, it remained substantial: after the war nearly one-third of the region's inhabitants still lived as minorities or subjugated peoples.[61] Each of the four largest states, Poland, Romania, Czechoslovakia, and Yugoslavia, were home to significant minority populations, and all struggled with the challenges posed by ethnic diversity.[62] Within a few years, border disputes, discrimination against minorities, and zones of violent conflict broke out on the Polish-German border, the Russo-Polish border, and in Transylvania between the Hungarians and the Romanians. The mismatch between political and ethnic borders gave rise to numerous irredentist conflicts throughout the interwar period.[63] While Germany's expansionist ambitions would start tearing the continent apart in the second half of the 1930s, Hungary and Bulgaria maintained similar claims, seeking to retrieve territory and people each considered to be part of their nation.[64]

Irredentist nationalism was the strongest spur to violence, but other situations also caused ethnic conflicts; in fact, there was not a country in the entire region that was free of ethnic dispute.[65] In most Eastern European countries, problems during this period were the result of an exclusivist conception of the state; that is, the state was the embodiment of one nation rather than ethnically diverse peoples unified by certain principles.[66] Alternatively invoking ethnic or historical claims to specific territories, leaders in Eastern Europe demonstrated that they had difficulty moderating their political behavior. As a representative of the Romanian delegation explained, Romania had fought for the right to impose her will on the Hungarian minority in Transylvania.[67] Thus, the breakup of semiauthoritarian, multiethnic empires resulting from World War I intensified, rather than diminished, ethnic conflicts throughout much of the region.

Even countries that varied historically and culturally in many ways, such as Yugoslavia, Czechoslovakia, Romania, and Poland, responded in remarkably similar ways to their minority populations. Each of these states resisted minority demands for autonomy, pursued policies of linguistic assimilation, and adopted land-reform packages that discriminated against ethnic minorities.[68] Despite the rash of other problems the region faced during this period, ethnic conflicts, according to Joseph Rothschild, constituted Eastern Europe's most vivid and distinctive political knot, which proved to be both debilitating and impossible to untangle.[69] By the 1940s, as German power on the continent spread to Eastern Europe, so too did fascist and radical nationalist movements. Ethnic bloodshed became common. In Yugoslavia, for instance, violent encounters perpetrated by the Croat Ustase regime resulted in the death of at least six hundred thousand Serbs, and thereby helped to sow the seeds for future violence.[70]

Communism as the Solution

Communist thinkers were hardly united on the relevance of ethnicity to political development, let alone in agreement on how states should handle ethnic diversity. Karl Marx and Friedrich Engels, for instance, claimed that ethnic differences would inevitably disappear because class consciousness would transcend all. Therefore, Communism did not need to address ethnic pluralism. Vladimir Lenin clearly saw things differently, and in the context of a turbulent and multiethnic Russia, he relied on national movements to become allies of the Bolshevik cause. In a 1914 tract, Lenin championed the rights of oppressed minorities, arguing that minority nations in multinational empires had the right to secession and to the formation of independent national states.[71]

It was not Lenin but Joseph Stalin who developed the Soviet Union's framework for managing ethnic pluralism. In *Marxism and the National Question,* Stalin not only acknowledged the staying power of ethnicity, but he articulated in a systematic way the need for states to develop institutional mechanisms to channel national demands. His ideas were eventually embodied in the Soviet Union's 1936 constitution, which subsequently became the model for managing ethnic diversity in all Communist states. In theory, Communism took an assertive stand against nationalism: It was the duty of the proletariat of the majority nation to adhere to class identity and insist upon the equal rights of all nationalities.[72] In reality, the fathers of Communist theory were also the progenitors of its impotence, addressing nationalism capriciously, using and misusing it as either a tool to advance the Socialist revolution or as a mechanism for consolidating their own power.[73] Under Russian leadership, the Soviet Union imposed Communist ideology (as well as the Russian nation) on the other nations, in part "to suppress all the overt and latent conflicts in the region, between states, nationalities, ethnic groups, and religions."[74]

To guarantee equality for all nationalities, Stalin called upon Communist states to resocialize the population under the banner of class rather than ethnicity or nation. In practice, this meant a developmental straitjacket for how ethnic relations were handled in Communist countries. Ethnic conflict management rested on the proclaimed goals of socialist friendship, and it submerged minority grievances. Anyone who deviated from officially determined objectives and rhetoric was regarded as a threat or a conspirator against the system. Communist practices for managing ethnic diversity differed slightly from country to country, but all shared the goal of harnessing and subjugating expressions of nationality. According to Rogers Brubaker, Communist systems accomplished this by draining nationality of its content even while it legitimated its existence.[75] Put differently, the Soviet Union's solution meant that nations could be seen but not heard.[76] As the Soviet Union "liberated" Eastern Europe, it retained the concept of national self-determination or the "will of the people." However, the application of this principle was closely tied to Soviet interests and the theoretical will of the working class rather than to support minority rights or national autonomy.[77] Communism was no panacea, but certain economic, political, and social achievements were evident in the region and, paradoxically, the system brought a measure of stability and security to an area long troubled by aggrandizing states and ethnic turmoil.

To be sure, Communism was effective at containing obvious manifestations of ethnic conflict, and there were few overt conflicts, protests, or rebellions in Communist states after World War II. This contributed to the tendency of Sovietologists to downplay the importance of national minorities, and only a handful bothered to focus on majority-minority relations in Communist countries.[78] In a way, Western scholars believed the proclamations of Communist leaders; that is, that while different ethnic groups existed in these countries, ethnic identity played an insignificant role in politics. Soviet leaders from Lenin to Gorbachev had undoubtedly pushed these ideas, consciously downplaying interethnic politics.[79] In 1981, for example, Brezhnev claimed that while all of the problems between national groups were not resolved, the Soviet people were more united than ever.[80] This oversight did not mean that ethnic disputes or violence disappeared altogether in Eastern Europe, especially when directed toward German minorities.[81]

In some cases, Communist parties kept ethnic identities alive temporarily to maintain administrative unity and social cohesion, but these states did not attempt to create genuinely multiethnic societies. Depending on the country, intolerance for divergence from official Communist doctrine and class solidarity led to various forms of repression against ethnic and religious minorities. Minorities in the Soviet Union suffered the most at the hands of Stalin, but throughout Eastern Europe Stalin's minions followed suit, repressing ethnic and religious minorities in their alleged attempts to create a Socialist identity. These countries lacked democratic procedures; thus, minority groups had few opportunities to engage in independent social or cultural activities. Communism's desire to destroy all forms of social interaction meant that there were few ways for ethnic groups to either articulate their interests or contest existing power arrangements. Combined with the ideological antagonism to political diversity, this meant that while Communism did not put all ethnic conflicts in a deep freeze, as some suggest, it did prevent the potential for the evolution of cross-cutting, multilayered identities. Ironically, as George Schopflin observes, Communism's attempt to squash ethnic nationalism meant that individuals tended to see themselves "largely as members of an ethnic group and not much else."[82]

To ensure their own power, Communist leaders needed to maintain the appearance of fellowship. Thus, ethnic disputes were often carried out behind the scenes by means of ideological or historical discussions. In some places, however, accommodating practices were established. Yugoslavia modeled itself on the Soviet Union, creating an ethnoterritorial federal state with six national republics, the autonomous region of Voivodina and the autonomous province of Kosovo, but it had a different attitude to ethnicity. In contrast to the Soviet government, the Yugoslav leadership rejected the idea of national assimilation, realizing that it was impossible to create a single nation.[83] Although Tito emphasized the need to foster brotherhood and unity while acknowledging different nations, ethnic crises punctuated the country's history into the 1970s. The 1974 constitution and the 1978 proposal for collective leadership did bring about a certain amount of ethnic accommodation and stability. Yugoslavia's "golden age," which emerged subsequently, allowed regime ideologues to imagine a new Socialist society, one rid of all forms of exploitation and ethnic difference.[84] Stability and optimism did not last long after Tito's death, and by the late 1980s, chauvinistic nationalism threatened the federation's existence.

Czechoslovakia had its share of interethnic problems. In short, Slovaks felt dominated and mistreated by their Czech brethren. The Communist purge of Slovak "bourgeois nationalists" in 1948 quieted Slovak nationalism for a while, but the sentiment reemerged during the spring of 1968 in Prague. While Czechs saw this period of political liberalization as a revolt against Soviet-style Communism, Slovaks saw it as the culmination of national urgings meant to ensure equality.[85] After 1968, the state became a federation and gave more power to the Slovaks, but ethnic friction remained. The country's 1989 "Velvet Revolution" was followed just two years later by its "Velvet Divorce," which solved the country's long-standing ethnic problems by creating the Czech Republic and Slovakia.

Of all Communist countries, Romania was often viewed as the most generous toward its minority. Despite the creation of an Autonomous Magyar Region in 1952, allegedly to accommodate its large Hungarian population, this act should not be misconstrued.[86] Although a concession to ethnic Hungarians, the region was set up in eastern Romania. Even though heavily populated by Hungarians, the Autonomous Magyar Region was established as far as possible from Hungary's border. Moreover, this solution to the country's ethnic conflict was not Romania's idea but was "encouraged" by the Soviet Union. This incident demonstrates both the complex "political trading" that went on between the Soviet Union and its satellite states and the continued relevance of ethnic identity in Communist Eastern Europe.[87] Romania's commitment to the rights of Hungarians waxed and waned during the Communist period. By the end of the Ceausescu regime, either the government had shouldered out most of the Hungarian nationalists or, like their Romanian brethren, Hungarians lived in fear of Romania's dictator.

In spite of these tensions, the dynamic of East-West relations during the cold war largely overlooked internal ethnic issues. For policymakers in the West, avoiding violent confrontation with the Soviet Union while nurturing democracy and individual rights overshadowed any desire to address ethnic conflicts directly. Perhaps some believed that although Communism had not solved the problem of eastern nationalism, any recognition of ethnic disputes would threaten the status quo and undermine East-West stability. With the emergence of the CSCE in the 1970s, ethnic politics and minority rights resurfaced on the international agenda. In 1975, thirty-five heads of state signed the Helsinki Final Act, which accepted post-World War II political realities, solidified existing borders, and established respect for human rights and other fundamental freedoms. Addressing the rights of individuals and minority groups, Section VII of the Helsinki Final Act notes: "Participating States on whose territory national minorities exist will respect the right of persons belonging to such minorities to equality before the law, will afford them the full opportunity for the actual enjoyment of human rights and fundamental freedoms and will, in this manner, protect their legitimate interests." [88]

At the time, the Final Act was condemned by many in the West as a supreme concession to Soviet totalitarianism; recent analyses of this document and process have been more positive. Daniel Thomas, for example, claims that the Final Act not only revised and codified human-rights norms in Europe, but it set in motion transnational changes that rippled through Eastern Europe.[89] Though marginal to the 1975 agreement, it also laid the foundation for the CSCE's future role in ethnic conflict management. At Follow-Up Meetings in the 1980s, CSCE countries vowed to sustain efforts to implement human rights with respect to persons of national minorities.[90]

The relationship between nationalism and Communism was complicated and contested, but judgments on its effect were not: As long as Communist governments remained powerful, the virulence of eastern nationalism was held in check. With Communism's sudden demise, catching "Western social scientists off guard like no other political transformation," a dramatic change in the study of the region and ethnic politics occurred.[91] As expressions of national identity asserted themselves, observers concentrated on the differences and the historical problems of the region. As J. F. Brown put it, in contrast to the West, Eastern Europe and the former Soviet Empire seems to be "one vast open wound" and thus, "after years of oppression and humiliation, there is liable to occur a violent counter reaction."[92]

With the nearly simultaneous breakup of the Soviet Union, Yugoslavia, and Czechoslovakia, a rapid, massive, and concentrated reconfiguration of political space arose like the sleeping giant. The creation of almost two dozen new political entities from the rubble of multiethnic empires led scholars to imperceptibly revert to the notion of Eastern nationalism and the region's history to inform their predictions of Eastern Europe's likely future.[93] Some maintained that the similarities between the recent reconfiguration of states and the interwar period were superficial and the differences between 1918 and 1989 likely to be consequential.[94] Among the reasons for the difference was the benign international environment at the end of the twentieth century. That is to say, the Great Powers were generally satisfied with the status quo, and they were openly supportive of conflict management. At the same time, several intergovernmental and nongovernmental organizations blossomed, possessing the will and finding the way to firmly shape and contain ethnic conflict.

Ethnic Conflict after Communism

Once ethnicity started to reassert itself forcibly in Yugoslavia in 1991, policymakers and scholars shed their rosy assumptions about democracy and ethnicity's demise and began to think the worst. A grim though distorted portrait of postcommunism emerged, as optimism morphed into apocalyptic predictions about "ancient hatreds" and a return to the "Balkanization of Europe."[95]

Intergovernmental Responses

The United Nations: The cold war's end and the growth of internal conflict necessitated a fundamental rethinking of security challenges and a retooling of available mechanisms. In January 1992, the UN Security Council held a meeting to examine the future responsibilities of the organization, especially with regard to conflict resolution.[96] In an exceptional demonstration of international consensus, members of the Security Council asked Boutros Boutros-Ghali, the newly elected UN secretary general, to evaluate the UN's role in the post-cold war era. The secretary general's response came in June 1992 in his report *An Agenda for Peace,* which identified preventive diplomacy as the most desirable and efficient option for managing the growing number of internal disputes and linking human rights and peace to democratic forms of governance.

Drawing upon ideas from member states, regional, and nongovernmental organizations, Boutros Boutros-Ghali acknowledged changes in the concept of sovereignty and the need for international responses to change as well. Tellingly, the need for such a shift was closely tied to ethnicity's revival in the East. As the UN's *Agenda for Peace* explains, in this new environment, "fierce new assertions of nationalism and sovereignty spring up, and the cohesion of States is threatened by brutal ethnic, religious, social, cultural or linguistic strife." [97] In the same report, the secretary general acknowledged the work of the League of Nations in this area, and that the one requirement for a solution to ethnopolitical problems lies in a commitment to human rights—with a special sensitivity to those of minorities. The cold war's abiding focus on individuals and human rights, however, meant that international law had little to offer as a solution to threatening assertions of ethnic identity.

The UN tried to address this oversight with the October 1992 Declaration on the Rights of Persons Belonging to National or Ethnic, Religious and Linguistic Minorities. [98] In a significant departure from previous policies, it proclaims that states shall protect the existence and the national or ethnic, cultural, religious, and language identity of minorities within their respective territory and shall encourage conditions for the promotion of that identity. Included in this declaration are provisions related to opportunities for minorities to learn in their own language and gain knowledge of their societies. Article 2 (5), moreover, acknowledged the existence of cross-border or divided nations and the need for members of a national group to maintain contacts with their ethnic kin in other countries. As such, nations have the right to establish linkages across boundaries with the aim of fostering a coherent national identity.

This global acknowledgment of the challenges posed by ethnic conflict came only after regional organizations in Europe, namely the CSCE and the CoE, had issued similar proclamations. [99] Interestingly, it was the CSCE's activities that provided the UN with the necessary impetus and example for how it should proceed; it did so by drafting documents related to ethnic minorities and initiating investigations into ways to prevent violent intrastate conflict. [100] In 1993, at the World Conference on Human Rights, the UN developed the concept of "civil states" and "ethnic states," emphasizing the need to codify strong obligations with respect to the treatment of minorities that all UN member states would accept. To allay third world fears that the Great Powers were using human rights as a modern excuse to impose their will on smaller states, and to avoid a repeat of the problems encountered by the League of Nations, powerful UN states committed themselves to abiding by these principles.

Despite the originality of these documents, they were not legally binding. No monitoring mechanisms were created, and the UN's ability to address internal ethnic disputes was limited.[101] This did not mean that the UN played no role in mediating ethnic conflicts in Eastern Europe or in reducing the potential for violence elsewhere. In the 1990s, the UN became directly involved in Bosnia, Croatia, and Macedonia, and UN offices including the UN Development Program (UNDP) were active in several Eastern European countries throughout the 1990s. What it did mean was that the UN did not try to assume all of the responsibilities for conflict management but, instead, consciously positioned itself to share these responsibilities with other governmental and nongovernmental organizations. As the secretary general conceded in early 1995, "If United Nations' efforts are to succeed, the role of the various players needs to be carefully coordinated into an integrated approach to human security."[102] In other words, although its weaknesses kept the UN from attempting to assume total responsibility for ethnic conflict management, it did not prevent it from adapting to the situation and seeking out other organizations for assistance.

North Atlantic Treaty Organization (NATO): The return of ethnic nationalism to Eastern Europe left Europe's most important regional security arrangement similarly ill-equipped to counter ethnic conflicts that originated outside its borders. In this situation, NATO could either maintain the status quo and, in the process, risk becoming a relic of the previous era (as its Eastern counterpart, the Warsaw Pact, had), or it could adapt to the changing international environment.[103] Like the UN, NATO adapted to the changing times and the threat of ethnic conflict without trying to assume a leading position. Created in 1949 with an official mandate to deter military aggression and protect its members from external threats, the North Atlantic treaty, the basis of the organization, was carefully worded to ensure that members' obligations stopped at NATO's boundary.[104]

Consistent with realist arguments about alliances, several scholars predicted that Communism's demise and the loss of an identifiable enemy would lead to NATO's disintegration. In short, NATO had achieved its goals and outlived its usefulness when the Soviet Union collapsed.[105] Yet, NATO survived the cold war, and there are several reasons why this crucial period led to its revival rather than its ruin.[106] A major reason was its willingness to take on "new security issues," specifically the threat of ethnic conflict. In November 1991, NATO revised its strategic concept in direct response to ethnic conflict in Yugoslavia. As its revised charter now states, members believe that threats to their security are less likely to come from "calculated aggression" from other states than from "the adverse consequences of instabilities that may arise from serious economic, social, and political difficulties, including ethnic rivalries and territorial disputes."[107] In effect, to maintain NATO members' security, it needed to do something to help manage crises that originated outside its designated area of involvement, and to remain relevant, it needed to care about ethnopolitical conflict.

Changing NATO's mandate, or the security goods it would provide, coincided with pressures from some NATO members, specifically the recently reunified Germany, to enlarge the security organization, which constituted a second reason for NATO's continued relevance.[108] Its post-cold war character would not only include a redefinition of security, but its mandate would embrace a larger moral imperative that involved helping spread stability and democratic norms throughout Europe. NATO agreed to play a role in managing what many believed would be an epidemic of conflict, driven by border disputes and concessions over minority rights, by linking bilateral security agreements and assistance to key domestic reforms, with the goal of socializing Eastern European states into new patterns of behavior.[109]

Initially, NATO's message about ethnic conflict and minorities was tentative. In 1991, for example, the North Atlantic Cooperation Council was created to develop an institutional link between NATO and former Warsaw Pact countries. The council's specific message for these states was: Liberal democracy is conducive, though not a requirement, for closer relations. At this point, although NATO recognized the new security issues that were emerging and the importance of promoting stability in non-NATO countries, its members remained generally unprepared and unwilling to shoulder any missions outside its members' territory.[110] By 1992, as violence escalated in Yugoslavia, NATO leaders were confronted with a profound dilemma: Exactly how would this political-military entity, with its exclusive membership, affect security in non-NATO states in the throes of internal ethnic disputes?[111] Its answer, like the UN's, was that it would undertake steps to contain ethnic conflict, but it would do so only in the context of broader, global efforts. NATO's response was clear: It would help contain ethnic conflict in the East, but it would not attempt to do this alone.

The Conference on Security and Cooperation in Europe/Organization on Security and Cooperation (CSCE/OSCE): NATO was not the only regional organization forced to consider its role in a post-cold war world. Even earlier, as hostilities between the East and West diminished, representatives of the CSCE were working to give meaning and structure to the largest (and most unfamiliar) security organization in the world. The CSCE not only matured with post-cold war opportunities, but it was the only intergovernmental organization to "seize the moment," establishing specific offices for ethnic conflict management and prevention. Given its cold war history and its attention to ethnic minorities stretching backing to 1975, the CSCE was uniquely situated to focus on ethnic conflict management and minority rights in post-Soviet Eastern Europe.[112]

In 1990, the CSCE established itself as a leader in the field of human rights, producing what many refer to as a remarkable human rights document, with annexes concerning the rule of law and individual rights as well as the rights of national minorities.[113] The Copenhagen document, followed by the Charter of Paris for a New Europe six months later, proved crucial to putting ethnic conflict management on the international radar screen. The Copenhagen Document provided a detailed list of the protections for minorities. Articles 31–38, in particular, concentrate on the right to express one's ethnic, cultural, linguistic, or religious identity, the right to speak in one's mother tongue in public, to have special institutions of higher learning, and the right to maintain contact with members of one's own group residing in other states.[114]

The Charter of Paris contained what would become the normative framework for the emerging transnational network: a commitment to the peaceful resolution of conflicts through pluralist democracy and minority rights. The link that the CSCE made between the protection of ethnic minorities, democracy, and peace in Europe was clear. As the charter states,

> We are determined to foster the rich contribution of national minorities to the life of our societies. We reaffirm our deep conviction that friendly relations among our peoples, as well as peace, justice, stability and democracy require that the ethnic, cultural, linguistic and religious identity of national minorities be protected and conditions for the promotion of that identity be created. We declare that questions related to national minorities can only be satisfactorily resolved in a democratic political framework.[115]

While somewhat open-ended in terms of how these principles would be put into practice or how they might be monitored, these ideas influenced not only the trajectory of the CSCE's development, but they also informed the proclamations and behavior of other governmental and nongovernmental organizations. Seeking the same outcomes in Eastern Europe, it is notable that throughout the 1990s transnational actors increasingly referred to and often explicitly quoted CSCE principles verbatim when launching their own policies or standards. In essence, these declarations helped transform the CSCE from a forum for pressure into an organization with specific tools for ethnic conflict management.[116]

In July 1991, the CSCE convened a meeting of international experts to develop a protocol for dealing with ethnic diversity and conflict, which included decentralizing governments, the inclusion of minorities in advisory and decision-making bodies, and transfrontier cooperation.[117] Three months later, the CSCE established the Moscow Mechanism that allowed the CSCE to send an expert mission of investigators to any CSCE country to monitor human rights, explicitly internationalizing internal ethnic conflicts. However, it was not until the Helsinki Summit in July 1992 that the "muddy stench of fear" prompted fundamental changes in the organization's structure.[118] At that meeting, CSCE members realized that since no government or intergovernmental organization was stepping up to the challenge, it needed to develop more tools to prevent ethnic conflict.[119] With the establishment of short-term fact-finding missions, long-term in-country missions, and the appointment of personal representatives with mandates to focus on ethnopolitical conflicts, the ad hoc CSCE was transformed into a comprehensive organization devoted to security in Europe.

In the course of 1992, the CSCE developed a clear operational capacity to respond quickly and noncoercively to emerging ethnopolitical conflicts. Importantly, the Office of the High Commissioner on National Minorities (HCNM) was established to help avert ethnic-based violence, particularly where the problems of minorities could interact with and escalate the so-called problem of divided nations separated by political borders.[120] With Dutch diplomat Max van der Stoel appointed as the first high commissioner, the office's official mandate was clear: to provide early warning and (if necessary) early action to prevent violent ethnic conflict in CSCE states.[121] Although this organization lacked the coercive and financial power of other regional organizations, it did possess various instruments that allowed it to focus squarely on ethnic conflict management.

The European Community/European Union (EC/EU): As the most influential organization in Europe, the European Community could not stand idly by as ethnic tensions surfaced in Eastern Europe. As an economic organization first and foremost, however, it did not have the capacity in 1989 to think about ethnic issues or conflict prevention, and in this area its efforts trailed that of other intergovernmental organizations. At the same time, given its own difficulty restructuring and expanding in the three decades prior, this economic body could ill afford to allow the potential negative consequences of Communism's collapse to threaten over thirty years of economic and political achievement. After a decade or so of stagnation and Euro-skepticism, events in the East forced the EC to jumpstart the integration process whether member states wanted to or not. Put differently by Elizabeth Pond, the question in 1989 for Western Europeans was no longer, should economic and political integration continue? but, how could European integration be used effectively to leverage behavior and ensure stability throughout Europe?[122]

In some respects, the EC reacted swiftly and unambiguously to the transitions in Eastern Europe through trade liberalization, promises of aid, and negotiations aimed at economic cooperation. In July 1989, it established the Poland and Hungary: Assistance for Restructuring Their Economies (Phare) Programme and the European Bank for Reconstruction and Development (EBRD) to facilitate broad-based economic reform in the East. By the end of the 1990s, the EC and its member states would become the largest contributor to Eastern Europe's transition.[123] The EC economic focus remained steadfast for the first few years of the new era. The Phare program, for example, stipulated *only* economic and trade issues; no political areas or human rights considerations were identified.[124] Various documents from 1989 until early in 1992 related to the Phare program, Association Agreements, and the aims of the EBRD all point to the EC's singular focus on economic assistance and market reform; rarely do documents mention political changes, let alone ethnic conflict or minority rights.[125]

In June 1991, the EC did turn its attention to the instability in the Balkans; it did so, however, by declaring its support for the unity of the Yugoslavia state as Slovenia and Croatia proclaimed their desire for independence. By the beginning of 1992, the EC's position on Yugoslavia changed noticeably with its endorsement of the *uti possidetis* principle, providing "that states emerging from decolonization shall presumptively inherit the colonial administrative borders that are held at the time of independence."[126] In simple terms, the EC changed its position and sanctioned Slovenia and Croatia's bid for independence. As if to counterbalance this decision in an attempt to manage ethnic conflicts, two months later the EC identified the conditions necessary for its recognition of new states. The Declaration on the Guidelines on the Recognition of New States in Eastern Europe and the Soviet Union made recognition conditional upon the state guaranteeing the rights of ethnic and national groups within the framework identified by the CSCE.[127] Putting conditions on the recognition of states was not unprecedented; what was striking was the incorporation of minority protections as a specific strategy to manage this ethnic dispute.

The EC did not pin all of its hopes for forestalling ethnic violence on mere legislation; starting in late 1991, European diplomats "plunged into tireless diplomacy."[128] Yet, like all of the other efforts prior to the Dayton Peace Accords, European-inspired peace initiatives failed to stop the bloodletting. Balkan instability had a significant impact on the EC's own development and move toward a more political orientation to stem the tide of instability in the East. The Maastricht treaty, signed in February 1992, illustrates the clear link that emerged between events in the East, the need for additional tools to promote stability, and the need for the advancement of the European Community into the European Union. As the treaty states:

> RECALLING the historic importance of the ending of the division of the European continent and the need to create firm bases for the construction of the future Europe,
>
> CONFIRMING their attachment to the principles of liberty, democracy and respect for human rights and fundamental freedoms and of the rule of law,
>
> RESOLVED to implement a common foreign and security policy . . . reinforcing the European identity and its independence in order to promote peace and security and progress in Europe and in the world.[129]

By the year's end, the European Council recognized that current intergovernmental arrangements did not adequately meet the needs for a more coherent security structure.[130] It was at the December 1992 meeting that EU leaders decided that it was time to change and upgrade their strategies, developing specific criteria to prepare Eastern European countries for future membership. In the process, the EU would use its economic resources and political clout to help manage ethnic conflicts, leveraging the political and foreign-policy behavior of these states. Given its traditional economic focus, the EU acknowledged that it could not respond to these problems alone. Thus, although the EU's mandate broadened by late 1992, it still looked elsewhere for guidance and direction when it came to ethnic issues.[131]

The Council of Europe (CoE): As the leading actor in the European human rights regime, and with a long history of promoting international reconciliation, mutual understanding, and increased cooperation among Western European states, it is perhaps not surprising that the CoE was the first regional organization to respond programmatically to political changes in Eastern Europe. Yet, concern with political change and even promoting democracy did not necessarily translate into recognition of the problems posed by ethnic conflict. Like other European organizations, the council's cautious policies in the first few years after Communism's fall betrayed its futile hope that treaties, international law, and an emphasis on liberal democracy alone would contain ethnic violence.

In June 1989, the council established a special guest status for the transitioning states of Eastern Europe, on condition that they incorporate the principles of the CSCE's Helsinki Final Act and the UN Covenant on Human Rights into their domestic practices. After granting guest status immediately to Hungary, Poland, the USSR, and Yugoslavia, and upon realizing its diminishing ability to influence outcomes as a result, the council constructed a formal process for transitioning states in the region that wanted to become CoE members. Although the council had examined the situation of minorities on several occasions since its creation in 1949, ethnic conflicts in the 1990s revealed not only the limitations of the council's mission and its focus on individual rights, but also its inadequate framework for affecting political change. Starting in 1990, with Recommendation 1134, the Parliamentary Assembly of the Council recommended a number of political and legal measures to the Committee of Ministers that it considered necessary for the protection of national minorities.[132]

The mutation of this organization into one capable of influencing inter- or intrastate behavior associated with ethnicity was nearly impossible, given that its primary mission was to ensure that European states became and remained liberal democracies.[133] Hungary's recent membership in the CoE was important for pushing this organization toward more progressive thinking in this area. As the first postcommunist country to become a full member of the council, Hungary lobbied its members for fundamental changes in the way it addressed ethnic minorities. It encouraged them to embrace a new, post-cold war identity, which included helping formerly Communist countries transition into liberal democracies and promoting stability. In early 1991, the council developed small programs to help accession countries complete the democratic transition and encourage peaceful change.

In part, the CoE's dilemma was a function of its reluctance to shift its fundamental focus away from human rights and individuals to minority rights and groups, leaving it bound by the 1950 European Convention for the Protection of Human Rights and Fundamental Freedoms. Thus, like the UN, the CoE maintained an emphasis on all people as individuals, giving little attention to the protection and promotion of minority groups. The Council of Europe's impotence in the face of the Yugoslavia tragedy and rising ethnic tensions was as plain as the inadequacies of the other intergovernmental organizations struggling with the realities of a post-cold war world and ethnic instability. However, by the end of 1991, in the context of developments in Yugoslavia, the steering committee for human rights was given the task of considering the conditions under which the council could undertake an activity related to the protection of national minorities, in light of the ongoing efforts of the CSCE and the UN.

With the passage of the Maastricht treaty, which made a single European currency a reality and introduced the Common Foreign and Security Policy pillar, council leaders shifted their organization's focus both to ethnic conflict and to national minorities, initiating specific legal standards related to their protection.[134] Its most important and practical contribution (although it was not opened for signature until 5 November 1992) was the adoption of the European Charter on Regional and Minority Languages. Although not specifically an instrument to protect minorities, it was a sign of things to come for an organization that just a year earlier had barely recognized the ethnic tensions brewing in Yugoslavia, suspending its special-guest status because of the so-called political impasse within the country.

The U.S. Response

As the world's only remaining superpower, the United States heartily supported the transformation of the Communist bloc, even if its actions fell short of Eastern Europe's expectations.[135] However, the time between the fall of the Berlin Wall and the beginning of ethnic violence in Yugoslavia was too short, and the United States did not develop an early or keen interest in the conflict. Part of the problem was simply lack of knowledge and foresight among U.S. policy makers; as David Callahan notes, during the cold war, briefings concerning ethnic conflict simply never reached top decision makers.[136] At the same time, the first post-cold war years were hardly blissful for the United States, and an array of international concerns pushed the superpower's foreign policy into disarray. Consequently, as the threat of ethnic conflict reemerged, the United States was ill-equipped and too distracted to deal systematically or comprehensively with conflicts radiating from the former Eastern bloc.

During the cold war, two principles had dictated U.S. policy in this region: geographically containing and avoiding war with the Soviet Union. The botched war in Vietnam further contributed to the resistance within the U.S. military to become involved in internal disputes of any kind. Instead of developing a specific policy to prevent ethnic conflicts, the U.S. government relied on economic assistance, encouraged equality between ethnic groups, and concentrated its efforts on economic-development projects. Even with the main rationale for overlooking ethnic-based conflicts gone and with potentially explosive situations developing in Yugoslavia, Czechoslovakia, and the Soviet Union, the United States only inched toward a focus on ethnic conflict, maintaining the fiction that economic assistance alone was all that was needed to reduce tensions. In November 1989, with the Support of East European Democracy (SEED) legislation, the government identified over fifty specific initiatives it would either take or refrain from taking in order to support democratic and economic change in the transitioning countries of Eastern Europe.[137] It was clear from these and related policies and statements that ethnic conflict prevention was not yet a priority for the United States. The country's interest in the region was tied to vestiges of cold-war thinking and reflected an almost singular reliance on economics and the magic of the market to ensure peaceful, democratic change.

Yugoslavia's disintegration did put a wrench in this thinking, and the government reluctantly acknowledged the need to address ethnopolitical issues directly. In May 1991, for example, the then Acting Secretary of State Lawrence Eagleburger acknowledged that despite the achievements and progress in Eastern Europe, the resurgence of both ethnic strife and nationalist tensions were significant obstacles to the future of democracy.[138] Roughly four months later, paralleling a strategy used by the EC, the Bush administration articulated a new foreign policy toward the recognition of new states, noting its support for existing international borders, respect for rule of law and democratic processes, human rights (including minority rights), and the responsibility of states to abide by international laws and obligations.[139] The U.S. government also established some new instruments and a few programs to manage ethnic conflict without changing its fundamental assumption that economic development policies—if better designed and implemented—would reduce, mitigate, and prevent ethnic violence. It was evident from the focus of State Department briefings during these years that despite U.S. proclamations and its genuine desire for political and economic change in the Eastern bloc, other international issues clearly took priority.[140]

In September 1992, as the International Conference on the Former Yugoslavia was set up to confer on the country's future, the EC and the UN were main players while the United States preferred to take a "more back-seat role."[141] In the minds of many Americans, particularly those who were reluctant to become embroiled in another European war, this was "Europe's hour to shine"—not the time for the United States to overextend itself.[142] After decades at the front of European security, Americans did not mind sharing the burden of security provision—as long as it did not jeopardize America's leadership in the Western alliance or NATO. In fact, as the

United States contended with challenges in the Middle East and Africa, many were beginning to believe that it was time for Europeans to step up to the plate and show they could act as a unified power.[143]

The NGO Invasion

Reactions to Communism's collapse and the rebirth of ethnic tensions were not limited to intergovernmental organizations and national governments. The extensive involvement of nongovernmental organizations in fact became a hallmark of Eastern Europe's development in the 1990s. Responding to the changes and challenges in the East with unprecedented vigor, these organizations involved themselves with many aspects of political, economic, and social change.[144] This unwieldy group of nonstate actors included public and private foundations, international humanitarian organizations, and specialized sets of organizations, such as human rights and women's groups.[145] Many of these groups were financed in part or in whole by governments or regional organizations, although they remained autonomous from the structure and machinery of states and governmental bodies.

At least three factors explain why NGOs became significant players in the transition of Eastern Europe and in the embryonic transnational network focused on ethnic conflict management. First, the end of ideological conflict between the East and the West, coupled with growing transnational problems, made states in the East and West less suspicious of nonstate actors and provided alternative ways of solving problems. During the cold war, both sides relied on nonstate actors, but they were often forced to do the superpowers' bidding. With ideological differences put aside, security was beginning to be defined in broader ways and included political, economic, environmental, and societal security.[146] As a consequence, "additional pressure for NGO involvement grew around such issues as economic development and ethnonationalism."[147] In Eastern Europe, opportunities and needs fueled the onslaught of NGOs to the region.

International trends were accompanied by new domestic circumstances—namely, affluence, increased leisure time, and rising levels of education—which allowed and encouraged individuals to engage in more autonomous civic activities, both in domestic and international politics.[148] Some refer to these changes when talking about the creation of a global civil society because they provided more venues for voluntary, associational activities. These factors, combined with technological changes that diminished the importance of distance and borders, contributed to the growing importance of NGOs in ethnic conflict management and to the army of NGOs that descended on Eastern Europe in the early 1990s.[149]

Nongovernmental actors would not have been as prolific if not for the significant support and resources that they were able to attract in the 1990s from national governments and the UN, which increasingly came to rely on NGOs to supplement or implement their policies.[150] Support also came from public and private foundations, many of which established their own conflict management or human rights initiatives. Thus, public and private actors alike had come to see NGOs as an important answer to, but also a mechanism for, managing the problems facing Eastern Europe.

Some foundations, such as Germany's Friedrich Ebert and Konrad Adenauer foundations, had been involved in Eastern Europe for a long time, providing as much, if not more, development aid than the U.S. government did on the region during the Communist period.[151] This sector changed precipitously in 1989–90, as public and private foundations from other parts of Western Europe and the United States flocked to former Communist countries. Governmental actors spent most of their resources on economic reform while foundation assistance, particularly in democracy-related activities, often equaled if not surpassed government support.[152] The ability of NGOs to react quickly and strategically meant that they often made a bigger impact on change than numbers alone would suggest.

Private U.S.-based foundations had significant resources at their disposal to divert to the former Communist bloc. In 1991, for example, there were more than a million such tax-exempt organizations in the US, with annual revenues of over $33 billion; this made the total assets of the foundation sector slightly larger than the U.S. defense budget or about five percent of the country's GNP.[153] Moreover, a few American foundations, such as the Ford Foundation and the Carnegie Corporation, had long and impressive histories of strengthening democracy at home and abroad, particularly when it came to the development of mechanisms designed to extend public debate. Before 1989, American private foundations had a small presence in Communist Eastern Europe, but as "children of private enterprise" and unique products of affluent industrialists, they gravitated to Eastern Europe in Communism's wake. In a way, Communism's failure validated their liberal philosophy and their belief in the superiority of democratic market systems.[154] It also opened the door wide to NGO involvement in ethnic conflict management.

In the early period of transition, from roughly 1989–92, public and private foundations together supplied more than $450 million to certain transitioning countries in the East; as a point of comparison, USAID provided less then $350 million during roughly the same period.[155] By the decade's end, even though government funding far surpassed private donations, foundations emphasized democracy promotion and civil society development, and relied on different strategies to accomplish their goals. Thus, the influence of nonstate actors in Eastern Europe's transition cannot be ignored. As Kevin F. F. Quigley explains, "In some regards, foundations' programs may be important not only because of what they invest in, but because of whom they invest in and how they invest."[156] As the backbone of civil society in Western countries, creating, funding, and nurturing organizations that either mediated between citizens and the state or provided alternative services to those offered by the state, foundations were ideally situated to become central players in transnational efforts to manage ethnic conflicts.[157] The different comportment of foundations in this regard ensured that their involvement played a critical, albeit moderate role in guiding change in Eastern Europe. Appreciating their resources and experience, Eastern Europeans readily approached foundations and international NGOs, requesting financial and in-kind assistance to rebuild their countries' civil societies and lay the cornerstones for democracy.

It is extremely difficult to know how many nongovernmental actors were truly active in the region in the first few years after Communism's fall, how much money was spent, and for what purposes, primarily because there were always multiple donors who dispensed a mix of grants and loans for a wide variety of often overlapping purposes.[158] It is known that by the mid-1990s, more than sixty European and North American foundations were involved in democracy assistance activities in Eastern Europe.[159] The main problem with exacting NGO involvement in ethnic conflict management was that international groups realized quickly that their efforts were better received and positive outcomes more likely if they avoided any references to ethnicity or conflict management. At one point in post-Dayton Bosnia, for example, there were about 250 international NGOs, many of which were working to promote ethnic cooperation but failed to specify their activities as such.[160] In other countries, such as Latvia, only a handful of Western foundations and international NGOs were working on ethnic conflict prevention, yet they tended to define their work in terms of democracy, national integration, or civil society development.[161]

Without a doubt, the most important nongovernmental actor involved in the region's transition was the Soros foundations network, which was established by Hungarian émigré financier George Soros. Soros's money and foundations proliferated quickly, establishing a sustained presence in over two dozen countries throughout the former Communist bloc. While it is easier to identify the numerous projects funded or implemented by these foundations, the effects of this investment are still difficult to track because of the sheer number of organizations it sponsored, its regular collaboration with other public and private actors, and its conscious goal to create numerous spin-off organizations and foundations. Despite this, the Soros response to the problems facing Eastern Europe is straightforward: encourage open societies through bottom-up, grassroots changes, thereby transforming attitudes and creating an environment conducive to democracy, stability, and peace. As explained by an official of the East-West Institute, a U.S.-based NGO involved in ethnic conflict management in Eastern Europe, this bottom-up approach used by most NGOs is not surprising. Even those nongovernmental actors with a lot of money lack the experience and clout to rival or punish states; thus, they focus on bringing people together, providing information, and encouraging compromise through attitudinal changes.[162]

In Eastern Europe, numerous NGOs, representing various narrow interests, were active in ethnic conflict prevention, minority rights, and human rights, including, among many others: the Catholic Relief Services, the Center for Preventive Action, the East-West Institute, the International Crisis Group, the International Red Cross, the Helsinki Committee, the Project on Ethnic Relations, and the Search for Common Ground. Usually, these NGOs identified the broader goals of reconstruction, education, or civil society development, seeing achievement in these areas as an indirect way of managing ethnic conflict and promoting stability.[163] A representative of the German Marshall Fund of the United States reinforced this point, noting that even when American foundations did not focus explicitly on ethnic conflict management in Eastern Europe, the desire for peaceful change and the promotion and protection of minority issues always influenced their activities.[164]

Conclusion

This chapter provided some background on the international community's responses to ethnic conflict, highlighting what some perceived as unique ethnic problems in Eastern Europe. It argued that the network response in the 1990s must be seen in the context of a long history of international involvement in the protection of minorities as a way of promoting regional stability. Although interrupted by the cold war and superpower rivalries, several different international mechanisms were used to mediate ethnic disputes both between and within states. In part because of the international community's efforts to contain violence in the East, the perception of Eastern nationalism resurfaced in the cold war's wake, and events in the region were seen through the constrictive prism of the region's mythic nationalist past. Almost overnight, ethnic relations in Eastern Europe were deemed both unique and menacing.

The post-1989 world order was ideal for the establishment of a comprehensive international organization to manage ethnicity, but there was no one actor willing or able to focus on ethnic conflict management or minority issues. However, by 1992, with fear in the West escalating, governmental and nongovernmental agencies alike rushed to respond, employing a variety of instruments based on different theoretical assumptions about conflict management.[165] This chapter explained the circumstances that gave rise to the international community's inability to respond adequately to ethnic conflict in Yugoslavia, while the next illustrates how ad hoc efforts to tame ethnicity from 1993 onward transformed into a transnational network. Put differently, while this chapter reviewed how the orders of Versailles and Yalta dealt with ethnic conflict, the next explains how the post-cold war international order responded to the revival of ethnopolitical tensions.

THREE

The Network Response in the 1990s

The term *network* has become a fashionable catchword in several disciplines, providing, as one scholar puts it, a new paradigm for the architecture of complexity.[1] Like other clichéd concepts, *network* is used in confusing ways, both as a verb and a noun, and in a variety of contexts. In international relations, scholars tend to use it as a metaphor to mean a large number of actors, and not as it is used here, as an analytical tool to characterize relationships and understand governance in a specific issue area. In this work, networks are "identifiable systems of formal and informal organizations characterized by horizontal power relations, interdependence, and close, open lines of communication."[2] *Transnational networks* are unique arrangements comprised of domestic and international actors; members operate as relative equals, relying on close association and a dense exchange of information to achieve specific, shared goals. Although complex, transnational networks are not unrestricted and amorphous; they are identifiable arrangements governed by specific characteristics and behavior.

In the previous chapter, it becomes painfully obvious that as ethnic tensions resurfaced, Western governments and intergovernmental organizations each had their own reasons for overlooking mounting ethnic friction. The turning point was 1992. Throughout the year, as fear of instability mounted, the international community acknowledged the shifting challenges associated with political change and the dire need for comprehensive international attention. Self-interest can explain *why* members of the international community started to respond to ethnic conflict, but self-interest alone cannot explain *how* these organizations pursued their objectives or the nature of the interorganizational relationships that burgeoned.

Since others have explained in detail how transnational influences relate to broader debates in political science, this research is not reiterated here.[3] Instead, this chapter provides a theoretical discussion of networks, with expectations for how transnational networks should behave in international politics. It then probes the shift in organizational behavior and the multilateral, multilevel strategies designed to respond to the growing menace of ethnic conflict.

Transnational Networks in International Relations

Although networks are most often discussed in economics and business, these arrangements are not new to political science. Traditionally what are known as *policy networks* have been the preserve of public policy analysts, who use network analysis in three different ways: to describe government policymaking; as a method for analyzing policymaking; or as a prescription for reform.[4] Using insights from economics, organizational management, and sociology, this section highlights the characteristics and behavior of networks.

Networks characteristics

Because of the pioneering work of economists such as Ronald Coase, social scientists agree that institutions, or the rules of the game in a society, structure both political and economic behavior.[5] For a long time, it was the belief that individual behavior was influenced either by self-interest and spontaneity, the so-called "invisible hand of the market," or was shaped by organizations with clear lines of authority and decision-making procedures, what might be called the "visible hand of management."[6] In the 1980s, scholars began to draw attention to other organizational forms; organization-management theorists, for example, made a distinction between markets and hierarchies on the one hand and networks on the other. In his seminal piece, Robert Powell explained that networks capture the "diversity of organizational designs that are neither fish nor fowl, nor some mongrel hybrid, but a distinctly different form."[7]

Network arrangements are based on a different logic than markets. While markets are the result of spontaneous coordination, limited personal involvement, and little trust, networks develop from repeated interactions of individualistic actors and decisions based on the behavior of others. Furthermore, networks encourage indebtedness among its members. In direct contrast to markets, hierarchies represent the other end of the organizational spectrum, where one actor controls the actions of others and the lines of authority are clear. Although networks are more coordinated than markets, they are "lighter on their feet" than hierarchies or organizations; networks hover in the middle, expressing neither the criteria of the market nor the familiar paternalism of hierarchy; they represent a unique institutional arrangement.[8] Scholars in sociology embrace and emphasize the social dimension of networks; that is, since organizations are made up of individuals who form relationships with parallel individuals in other organizations, these relationships—both organizational and individual—reflect on political outcomes and the possibilities for cooperation.[9]

Without rejecting the importance of individuals, the focus here is on organizations and how networks develop from autonomous but close-knit organizations that work together to accomplish shared goals. Five characteristics inform my expectations for how transnational networks should behave in international relations. First, actors' preferences and policy choices are interdependent; that is, organizations regularly consider the actions and expectations of others. The interdependence of actors is not necessarily reflected in a centralized plan or the creation of a new organization but is expressed through shared principles, common objectives, and regular collaboration.[10] For example, throughout the 1990s, the EU and the Council of Europe increasingly adopted similar (if not identical) standards and principles on democracy, human rights, and minority rights to reinforce each other's policies and send a common message to transitioning countries in the East on appropriate behavior.

Interdependence can mean a pooling of resources to achieve common goals, or a situation where one member is financially dependent on another. A unique form of interdependence exists between Western governments and NGOs. In 1991, for example, about a quarter of development assistance from governments flowed through NGOs, and almost all bilateral and multilateral donor agencies established permanent units to act as liaisons with NGOs.[11] The public-private partnerships that emerge from governmental agencies contracting out to NGOs is more common as more private actors crop up, seeking the same outcomes as governments.

A second, related feature of networks is the relative equality among network members. This means that even where there is interdependence between actors or financial support by one for another, such relationships do not translate into control of one organization by another nor entail an established hierarchy between them. In short, the relationships within networks are loose and relatively flat, and members' positions and relative influence are derived from their competencies and the specific situation. Again using the example of a national government and an NGO, it would be fair to say that although governments possess political and economic clout, NGOs have their own skills and resources, including an ability to act quickly and to be seen as neutral. Therefore, although NGOs may receive significant government funding, governments do not dictate their programs or determine their strategies.[12] In fact, some scholars maintain that in certain circumstances NGOs even shape donor states' policies and behavior.[13] Because of their independent status, NGOs are not construed as government minions or even implementers of government policy; instead, most governments tend to view them as junior partners, and sometimes even challengers to their authority.

Third, the value of the goods to be exchanged or the outcomes achieved in networks is as important as the relationship itself; that is, while networks emerge in response to specific situations and seek certain outcomes, they simultaneously reinforce preexisting alliances and strengthen trust, thereby serving other "intangible" functions. The point is that while network members do not agree on everything, and while networks may constrain its members in the short-term, these arrangements are built upon relationships that serve broader, multifaceted goals. As Wolfgang Reincke and Francis Deng put it, networks are "protean things," both resilient and mutable, serving different purposes.[14] What unites all networks is that they are pragmatic and are built to utilize the resources that each participant brings to the fore. The bridges created by networks allow for the pooling of know-how and the exchange of experience, thereby serving both specific and diffuse purposes.

For example, the U.S. government provided a small amount of financial support to the Princeton-based Project on Ethnic Relations (PER) to carry out ethnic-conflict prevention programs in Eastern Europe as a part of its effort to help stabilize the region. Even though the government has often ignored the warnings and advice of PER officials, the partnership was not severed; instead, personal relationships and trust continued to inform this public-private collaboration and the respective policies of its partners. As a former U.S. State Department official stationed in Romania remarked, even though the U.S. government did not always heed the advice of PER officials, it valued their experience.[15] Officials of the Stability Pact for South Eastern Europe explained the nature of government-NGO relationships somewhat differently, noting that a purpose of this EU-inspired institution was to bring governmental and nongovernmental organizations together on somewhat equal terms to encourage stability in the Balkans. International and local NGOs are thus able to meet directly and regularly with donor governments and regional organizations.[16]

A fourth characteristic of all networks is the emphasis placed on transparency, communication, and the sharing of information and knowledge.[17] The dense exchange of information among network members cultivates the open-ended, relational feature of networks and deters explicit quid pro quo behavior. "What do members of networks do?" Anne Marie Slaughter asks and answers, "They talk a lot . . . and they exchange ideas and information."[18] Among numerous CSCE/OSCE reports, one published in 2000 describes the importance of information exchange to security in Europe, facilitating what it refers to as the "web of interlocking institutions" in Europe. Crucial to weblike relationships is an exchange of information that helps foster coordinated approaches, avoids duplication, and ensures the efficient use of resources.[19]

A final, pivotal characteristic of networks are the informal interactions among individuals working within these organizations.[20] As sociologists underscore, individuals form the human bridges that link organizations, and these interactions "congeal alongside formal structures."[21] Such informal linkages are neither new nor rare; government officials often move in and out of the nonprofit sector, but in networks, information exchange and interaction is more intense, regular, and focused. In terms of ethnic conflict management in the 1990s, for instance, the pool of people with the necessary expertise was not large, and with no time to spare, everyone involved in these issues sought to acquaint themselves with one another.

Walter Kemp, a senior adviser to the CSCE/OSCE, explained that after 1993, when the EU started to think about ethnic conflict management, EU officials would regularly call the Office of the High Commissioner on National Minorities for information, contacts, and recommendations.[22] Knowing the right people in other organizations committed to conflict management was crucial to making decisions and implementing policies. Max van der Stoel concurs: "The relationships between the organizations depended on the personalities of individuals within them rather than on formalized, institutional relationships; and since it takes time for such relationships to evolve, they were neither easily broken nor taken for granted."[23]

NGO officials and government representatives working on conflict management similarly stressed the importance of human contacts and individual relationships.[24] Given the complex nature of promoting interethnic stability—with its political, economic, and social components—the contacts between individuals are crucial to the realization of projects and broader objectives. As the director of Latvia's Center for Human Rights, Ilze Brands Kehris, explains, everyone in Latvia who works on ethnic issues or minority rights knows each other, and generally when an international actor organized a meeting, the same people and organizations were represented; working for a number of similar organizations is often just a matter of time.[25] Case in point, Latvia's current minister for national integration was the former director of the Center for Human Rights (which was established with funding from the Soros Foundation-Latvia), and before that he worked on national minority issues at the Soros Foundation-Latvia in Riga.

When Networks Form

There is no consensus on why networks spring up in some areas and not in others; in economic terms, self-interest and a desire to "minimize transaction costs" are undeniably important. Alone, these motivations could easily lead to the creation of other, more recognizable organizational forms. Powell suggests that *know-how, speed,* and *trust* are important conditions for the inception of networklike behavior among actors.[26] Networks are thus more likely to arise in situations that rely on knowledge-intensive activities or exchanges that are based on the unique abilities of individuals rather than specific resources. Consequently, networks emerge when the alternatives for cooperation are difficult to come by.

Networks arrive when speed is important, since they are based on complex channels that allow a rapid and nearly effortless stream of information. In the economic realm, they become the most efficient type of organization when competition is less dependent on price but instead requires innovation and the ability to quickly translate ideas into practical outcomes. In politics, this would mean that networks are more likely to form when unique solutions and specific expertise are needed, rather than a standard formula and general knowledge. Context, however, appears to be *the* crucial precondition for the development of networks; where relations have been lasting and continuous, and members are relatively homogenous, networks are more likely to form.

Influenced by a multitude of changes associated with globalization and the collapse of Communism, scholars have arrived at an important conclusion: Overlapping, nonhierarchical relationships among international actors, working on both the international and domestic front, are increasingly common in international politics.[27] Initially, the main concern of what could be called "the network approach" was to challenge realist understandings of how international relations function.[28] As Slaughter puts it, the main conclusion was this: The unitary state is a useful fiction but a fiction nonetheless. Transnational networks help scholars understand how governmental and nongovernmental actors exchange information and coordinate their efforts to achieve common outcomes.[29] Words such as *transnational network, transnational advocacy network,* or *global public policy network* are thus regularly used in international relations and comparative politics to explain everything from changes in human rights practices to democracy promotion to agricultural policy. Even though the characteristics of these networks are rarely defined, they all suggest joint action by public and private actors.[30]

In the 1990s, as governments groped for a response to the resurgence of ethnic conflict, the necessary conditions were in place for a transnational network to form: Ethnic conflict management required unique know-how that no single actor possessed at the time, and responses to the complex social, political, and economic problems associated with ethnic conflict needed to be fast and effective. At the same time, Western governments had a long history of cooperation as well as a newfound confidence in the ability of private actors to help manage problems in the East. Without fundamentally changing their organizational structures, governments looked to other actors, both public and private, for assistance in ethnic conflict management, adopting overlapping, complementary strategies. With time, they adopted similar principles, made interdependent decisions, and readily shared information and expertise. The unique competencies and authority of these different agents allowed each actor to play a different but reinforcing role, and no one actor dominated this arrangement.

The Postcommunist Context

By the beginning of the 1990s, a virtual army of internationals had descended on Eastern Europe. Whether they were interested in economic reform, democratic change, or human rights, this coalition of governmental and nongovernmental representatives assumed that the success of their efforts depended upon stability in the region. Idealistically believing that money, advice, and good intentions could magically fill the breach opened by the retrenching Communist state, transnational actors—largely from Western Europe and North America—pledged large sums of money to facilitate change. In addition to money, governments and foundations supported a number of projects, internships, and training programs under the banner of "democracy promotion." The success of this mission depended on significant resources from the West, but it also entailed a shift in thinking about international politics, and the need for actors to work together to promote peaceful change.

The West approached the East with a missionary zeal, but it would be incorrect to assume that their practices were either consistent or even well-coordinated, at least initially, though this changed by the mid-1990s. It is however safe to say that from the very beginning, transnational actors employed noncompetitive, multilateral strategies, implicitly agreeing on the goals, instruments, and principles that should guide behavior in this region.[31] The sense of common purpose and the need for collaboration to manage ethnic conflict was particularly evident by 1992, as the missed opportunities in Yugoslavia grew more glaring and ethnic problems elsewhere grew more urgent. In April of the following year, for instance, the European Commission acknowledged forthrightly its historical friendship and ties with the United States, the possibility of pooling its resources with its North American ally, and the need for Europe and the United States to find common answers to emerging political crises.[32] There was, moreover, remarkable congruence among Western governments in their support for existing international organizations and what they hoped these organizations would be able to accomplish in postcommunist Eastern Europe.[33] More than anything else, trust and a compatibility of core values characterized the West's general tenor toward the transitioning countries in Eastern Europe, their desire for peaceful change and the embrace of democracy and the market.

Although numerous actors became involved in efforts to usher in peace and stability to the region, what was most apparent was how similarly these governmental and nongovernmental actors approached change. West Germany had the most contact with Eastern Europe during the cold war, providing more assistance to the region than any other Western country.[34] Although it kept its leading position in the first few years, providing nearly a third of all the aid coming from the West, it was eager to "multilateralize" assistance to the region, partly to assure countries in the East that it had no ill intent and did not want to revive historic ethnic tensions.[35] Meanwhile, despite its superpower status, the United States had barely a noticeable presence in the Eastern bloc. In the late 1980s, the U.S. government provided about $3.5 million of aid to the region while U.S.-based private foundations spent between $5 million and $8 million annually to support projects in the Communist bloc.[36] As other Western countries, including the United States, stepped up their efforts in Eastern Europe, they consistently coordinated their assistance, pooling their resources to avoid duplication, thereby marking an important behavioral departure from traditional power politics.[37]

In July 1989, the European Community set up the Poland and Hungary: Assistance for Restructuring Their Economies (Phare) Programme and made plans to establish the European Bank for Reconstruction and Development (EBRD). In the same year, the Group of Seven (G-7) countries convened meetings to create the Group of Twenty-Four (G-24), which included G-7 countries plus most of the countries in Western Europe.[38] Created for the specific purpose of coordinating economic assistance to transitioning countries in the East, the G-24 was chaired by the Commission of the European Communities in Brussels and the EU was given an unprecedented role in dispersing assistance to postcommunist countries.[39] All of these efforts were meant to coordinate resources and facilitate regular interaction, with the aim of cultivating a community of likeminded individuals in the West that was committed to democratic market reform in Eastern Europe. It also helped lay the necessary foundation for the network response to ethnic conflict.

Throughout the decade, the European Union's Phare program became the largest assistance program to the postcommunist bloc; from 1990 through 1998, Phare pledged almost $11 billion to fourteen Eastern European countries, and by the end of 1998, it had provided almost $7 billion in payments.[40] Assistance from the United States to the region also increased dramatically during this same period; within one year, from 1989 to 1990, USAID funding for Eastern Europe and the former Soviet Union combined jumped from less than $4 million to over $90 million. Because of events in Bosnia and fear of ethnic instability elsewhere, funding peaked in 1994. By the end of the 1990s, the United States had provided a total of $14 billion of assistance to countries in Eastern Europe and the former Soviet Union (see figure 8).[41] Yet, even with this increase in funding, the United States never became the economic hegemon in Eastern Europe, largely because much of its funding went to Russia to help it create a market economy.

The combined support of the European Commission and EU member states, together with bilateral assistance from other non-EU European countries, meant that Europe provided some 85 percent of all official aid to Eastern Europe, while the United States contributed only 12 percent. In other words, it was Europe—rather than the United States—at the financial center of transnational efforts to promote political and economic change in Eastern Europe (see figure 9). However, the economic importance of European states did not negate U.S. influence, especially in military and security areas. Instead, the economic power of Europe was combined with the unparalleled military might of the United States (as well as its substantial economic power), creating several poles of power that diffused authority and influence, depending on the issue area.

Although the lion's share of Western assistance programs focused on creating markets and spurring economic reform, they did contain vaguely worded political objectives that identified the domestic political conditions necessary for these transitioning states to receive aid. EBRD, for example, was created to assemble support for the region so that it could promote private and entrepreneurial activities in "countries committed to applying the principles of multiparty democracy, pluralism, and market economics."[42] Thus, although the Western mission remained concentrated on economic rather than political change, multilateral assistance

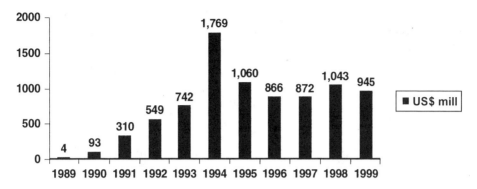

Figure 8. U.S. funding to Eastern Europe and the former Soviet Union. *Source:* USAID financial information system in *A Decade of Change: Profiles of USAID Assistance to Europe and Eurasia* (2000). For the purposes of this table, the funding graphed here went to 27 countries: 12 from the former Soviet Union (Russia, Belorussia, Ukraine, Moldova, Georgia, Armenia, Azerbaijan, Kazakhstan, Kyrgyzstan, Uzbekistan, Turkmenistan, Tajikistan,); 8 from the northern tier of Europe (Estonia, Latvia, Lithuania, Poland, the Czech Republic, Slovakia, Hungary, and Slovenia) and 7 from the Southern tier of Europe (Albania, Bosnia, Bulgaria, Croatia, Macedonia, Romania, and the former Republic of Yugoslavia).

programs steadily highlighted the need to define common political criteria for how transitioning countries should be treated, nourishing both a broader political agenda and interdependent decision making for Western involvement. As the U.S. State Department confirms, not only were the emerging objectives of Western assistance the same for the G-24 countries, but so too were the political and economic criteria for this assistance—the most important of which was the requirement that aid recipients be democratic, pluralistic societies and that states be committed to human rights.[43]

The conversion of Eastern Europe entailed more than just a different configuration of traditional assistance mechanisms and a strengthening of relationships between governments. The need to respond to events in Eastern Europe quickly as well as a confluence of other factors pushed Western states to restructure their traditional relationships with NGOs to accelerate the process of change.[44] For example, the political significance of Communism's collapse led Western governments to set up special mechanisms to streamline financial assistance to the region. In the United States, the Support for Eastern European Democracies (SEED) Act called upon the expertise of more than thirty government agencies to help allocate the funds that Congress had appropriated for this region.[45] About two-thirds of this money even-

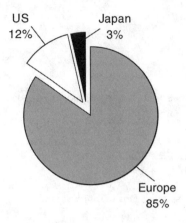

US
12%

Japan
3%

Europe
85%

Figure 9. Sources of aid to Eastern Europe, 1990–1998. *Source:* Adapted from Janine R. Wedel's OECD table, "Total Official Aid to Central and Eastern Europe from bilateral and multilateral sources 1990–98." *Collision and Collusion. The Strange Case of Western Aid to Eastern Europe* (New York: Palgrave, 2001), 210. The aid graphed consists of the actual disbursements of assistance rather than commitments or obligations. For the purposes of this table, the countries included are Albania, Bulgaria, Czech Republic, Hungary, Poland, Romania, and Slovak Republic. The former Yugoslavia and the Baltic States are excluded.

tually flowed through organizations that previously had been uninvolved in traditional aid programs, such as enterprise funds, EBRD, and parallel financing with the World Bank, the EC Commission, and NGOs.[46]

A similar process was evident in other Western democracies, as they looked to regional organizations and contracted out to NGOs to help distribute government assistance. Consequently, as many scholars detail, the Eastern European transitions were guided by Western governments, but assistance was implemented by an array of actors, including public and private foundations and NGOs.[47] Put simply, the Western mission in the East was a multiparty enterprise, consisting of a hodgepodge of functionally different governmental and nongovernmental organizations, working side by side to encourage rapid but peaceful change in the region.

The delicate thread holding the Western mission together was neither a single organization nor a comprehensive plan for how governments and NGOs would function in Eastern Europe. Instead, these transnational efforts coalesced around vague but unmistakable notions of stability, democracy, and market reform. In this context and as ethnic conflicts arose, transnational actors admonished themselves for overlooking ethnic relations and failing to prevent the bloody dissolution of Yugoslavia. Yet, as inept and disappointing as the elusive "international community" was in Bosnia, the West did not reject the fundamental premise that responses to the potential reprisal of Eastern nationalism should remain multilateral. Instead, it collectively embraced multilateralism and adopted unique, reinforcing ways of countering ethnicity's resurgence. Moreover, with no time to spare, the response to rising ethnic tensions could not rely on a single strategy; instead, governmental actors and

NGOs relied on a variety of policy instruments to affect different levels of government.[48]

The CSCE/OSCE as a Linking-Pin Organization

In the past, the precariousness caused by ethnic conflict had either inspired the inception of new institutions or, as after World War II, resulted in the international community seeking circuitous ways of averting ethnic conflict. Because of the unique international environment at the cold war's end and the close-knit relations among the actors involved in promoting change in the East, the reemergence of ethnic conflict prompted a totally different response, which reflected not only the binding trust between Western governments but also the "power shift" that had occurred between states, intergovernmental organizations, and NGOs.[49] As explained in chapter 2, the CSCE/OSCE can be credited with spearheading a transnational campaign to manage such conflicts in the 1990s. Yet, this organization never labored alone, nor did its leaders imagine that European security could be guaranteed by one institution. Instead, it became the linking-pin organization in this transnational network, not because it possessed the greatest resources or had coercive power but because the CSCE/OSCE came to occupy a central, strategic position connecting constituent organizations devoted to ethnic conflict management.

As the CSCE/OSCE transformed from an ad hoc institution into an organization with several discrete offices charged with conflict management, it steadfastly referred to the future of European security as reliant on "interlocking" institutions, structures, and processes that would provide the foundation for transatlantic stability.[50] Other security organizations, such as NATO, envisioned a similar framework, using precisely the same words to describe the future security architecture in Europe and recognizing the unique role of the CSCE/OSCE. As early as May 1990, the secretary general of NATO described a projected intertwined security structure for Europe "embodying a range of intergovernmental actors."[51] Instead of provoking rivalry, NATO, the EC, and the CSCE would each rely on its unique competencies to develop complementary strategies in collaboration with countries from the former Warsaw Pact. Given NATO's own identity crisis in the initial post-cold war years, it recognized the distinctive contribution of the CSCE to conflict prevention and post-cold war security while it acknowledged its own need to adapt its principles to those of the UN Charter and the CSCE. NATO's 1991 Rome Declaration on Peace and Cooperation, for instance, underscores the organization's intent to adapt to the new situation, establishing a new security system to counter regional discord but in the context of a unique framework of interlocking and mutually reinforcing organizations.[52]

Initially, some Council of Europe representatives were concerned that the CSCE might be duplicating some of its functions, but this intergovernmental organization quickly arrived at a similar conclusion: Promoting peace and thwarting ethnic conflict in Eastern Europe required multiple actors and extensive interorganizational cooperation. In an address to the Council of Europe in May 1992, François Mitterrand discussed the principles underpinning his vision of "Greater Europe," which would be developed according to the "specific areas of competence" of various institutions that would share work. Moreover, there would not be a single organization charged with ensuring stability. As Mitterrand explains, in this Greater Europe there should be no hierarchy of organizations; flexibility and adaptability must be the rule.[53]

Despite European calls for U.S. support with Yugoslavia's unfolding crisis, its leaders generally hoped that Europe, and not the United States, would take the lead in managing this conflict and restoring stability to the continent. In June 1991, for example, as fighting broke out in Slovenia, Luxembourg's foreign minister famously declared, "It is the hour of Europe," and "If anybody can achieve things, it is the European Community."[54] Yet, even as Europe failed to stop the violence, the emphasis nonetheless remained on more, rather than fewer, actors to guarantee stability in Europe.

In the United States, a similarly collaborative, if not deferential attitude toward European states was evident when it came to Yugoslavia. Even as crisis turned to violence there, the United States was satisfied to be just one of several actors pushing for peaceful change in the East. This is because although the United States was unwilling to disengage from Europe completely, it was eager for Western European countries to take more of the lead in conflict prevention and the political transitions in the East. Not only was the United States less vulnerable to the effects of instability in the East, but it needed its allies to start shouldering greater financial burden for European security in order to concentrate on neglected domestic needs and other international concerns.[55] Consumed by developments in the Middle East, the Clinton administration made "tenacious diplomacy" a guiding principle of its foreign policy, which included supporting multilateral institutions rather than relying on its own military power.[56] The quandary Washington faced with regard to the tragedy of Yugoslavia was significant; although Americans would find the death of American soldiers in Yugoslavia unconscionable, NATO's legitimacy—and perhaps its survival—might be at stake if the United States simply sat by. Thus, administration officials reasoned that the best response to ethnic violence in Europe, at least in some contexts, was to forfeit leadership and engage other governments, intergovernmental organizations, and NGOs on somewhat equal terms.[57]

Although no single country or any one organization wished to be responsible for managing these conflicts, a certain consensus had arisen on the leading role of the CSCE/OSCE in Europe. Since 1990, it had distinguished itself as the most forward-thinking and proactive organization regarding conflict prevention, human rights, and ethnic politics.[58] Throughout the decade, the CSCE/OSCE consciously sought to act as the node through which this transnational network would be loosely joined, involving itself both directly and indirectly in ethnopolitical disputes throughout Eastern Europe.[59] As Patrick Thornberry puts it, the CSCE/OSCE was "the first in line" to meet the challenges posed by ethnic conflict.[60] The importance of the 1990 Copenhagen document was obvious since it contained a codification of minority rights that was, in qualitative terms, the most far-reaching international instrument up until that point. Together, the Copenhagen document and the Treaty of Paris prompted other regional organizations, including the EU, the CoE, and NATO, to acknowledge minority rights and the problem of ethnic conflict, and all took turns adopting CSCE/OSCE principles as their own. Wolfgang Zellner points to the organization's unabashed support for democratic pluralism and its embrace of human and minority rights, not merely as worthy humanitarian goals but as effective instruments of conflict prevention; this unique normative groundwork is the foundation for all of the CSCE/OSCE activities.[61]

The attention the CSCE/OSCE gave to ethnic conflict and minority rights after the cold war was equal in significance to its own historical development during that period. Its origins and inclusive membership allowed this organization to become what other intergovernmental organizations only aspired to be: the sturdy bridge between the West and the East. When the Warsaw Pact dissolved, its former members looked hopefully to the only regional organization that had granted them membership. Shortly thereafter, in July 1990, NATO countries turned to the CSCE as their only link with former enemies. NATO affirmed a desire for a role in securing Europe but simultaneously underscored support for the CSCE, which "should become more prominent in Europe's future, bringing together the countries of Europe and North America."[62] Moreover, NATO documents confirm this organization's belief that the CSCE/OSCE had a central role to play in expanding "the network of cooperative relationships" developing across Europe.[63]

As NATO contemplated its future relations with Eastern Europe, it looked to the CSCE/OSCE for guidance, partly because its members realized that this inclusive organization was unlikely to be construed as a threat to either the Soviet Union or the United States. President George H. W. Bush was in favor of strengthening the CSCE/OSCE but wanted do so without weakening NATO; he believed a weaker NATO would mean less U.S. influence in Europe.[64] These factors, along with the CSCE/OSCE's substantive work in the area of human rights, made it the most logical and most suitable organization to handle sensitive internal issues associated with ethnic identities. NATO's reliance on the CSCE/OSCE in certain areas demonstrated what the NATO secretary general referred to in 2000 as a "unique division of labor" that reflected the principles on which institutional relationships should be built: cooperation instead of competition, synergy rather than hierarchy.[65]

Another reason this emergent transnational network fused around the CSCE/OSCE were the principles that had buttressed the oft—mentioned "CSCE process," which started in the 1970s. In the post-cold war era, terms like *complex security, cooperative engagement, preventive diplomacy,* and *human security* were alternately used to characterize the forthcoming security environment. Despite important differences between them, what these terms shared were notions of *common, cooperative,* and *collective*—in other words, the notion that state and nonstate actors needed to work together to accomplish shared goals and offer security by modifying their own behavior. These were the principles upon which the CSCE/OSCE based its notion of *comprehensive security* since the 1970s; that is, security between states is rooted in cooperation, and it is indivisible and unbreakable. Galvanized through cooperation, it is both possible and necessary to enhance the security of others while providing one's own.[66]

During the cold war, the CSCE/OSCE's approach to security translated into greater transparency in interstate affairs, an emphasis on mutual consent, comprehensive security, and state accountability.[67] In the post-cold war period, the CSCE/OSCE recognized forthrightly that states' security would be enhanced not by preparations for war, but by creating the conditions for peace.[68] Its ideational approach to security was so influential that in 1994, as NATO developed its Partnership for Peace (PfP) program with Eastern European states, it reaffirmed its specific commitment to the CSCE/OSCE and its newly adopted *comprehensive approach* to security, highlighting its own internal and external changes in light of the need for a new cooperative security architecture in Europe.[69]

There was one additional reason for the CSCE/OSCE's status as the knot binding this emerging transnational network: the development of a unique competency in ethnic conflict prevention. By 1993, several newly created agencies within the organization were primarily concerned with ethnic conflict and national minorities. In particular, the Office of High Commissioner on National Minorities, which became operational in January 1993, quickly became the hub of information about activities directed toward ethnic conflicts in the former Eastern bloc. Within the first few months of 1993, the HCNM visited Estonia, Latvia, and Lithuania to address allegations of discrimination against the Russian-speaking minorities there. It then directed its attentions to Slovakia, Romania, and Hungary to concentrate on the difficulties associated with the divided Hungarian nation.[70] By the year's end, the HCNM had visited the former Yugoslav Republic of Macedonia and Albania to deliberate on the Albanian minority dispersed in the region.

Uniquely and narrowly focused on the dangerous potential of majority-minority relations in the East, the CSCE/OSCE established the transnational network's message on this shared problem. It identified the common issues that exacerbated interethnic relations and then considered their relevance in light of international norms and practices. To fulfill its mandate of providing early warning, the HCNM was given significant autonomy from the complicated structure of the CSCE/OSCE, thereby enabling representatives of his office to travel easily to the region and work behind the scenes, engaging in "quiet diplomacy." Its relative autonomy allowed the HCNM office to obtain crucial regional and field expertise in the former Soviet bloc, establishing a first-hand, functional knowledge of ethnic conflict prevention and national minorities.[71] EU officials substantiate the claims of van der Stoel and other HCNM officials; throughout the mid-1990s, the HCNM office was *the* source of information on ethnic disputes and national minorities in Eastern Europe.[72] Government officials and NGO representatives in Romania and Latvia put the HCNM's role somewhat differently, explaining that because of van der Stoel's frequent visits to the region, he was often the only person from the West identified with these issues. For better or for worse, van der Stoel was alternately referred to as "the face of Europe" or the "father of minorities."

The HCNM office was not the only instrument within the CSCE/OSCE structure to address ethnic conflict. Other CSCE/OSCE institutions were directly and indirectly engaged in halting and handling ethnic disputes, including most notably missions. In 1992, the CSCE established long-term in-country missions; considered more intrusive than the approach of the HCNM office, these missions operated for least six months, and their scope was more general than the focused activities of the HCNM. Like the high commissioner's office, the first function of missions is to provide up-to-date information to member states and to the Conflict Prevention Center (CPC) in Vienna on ongoing or emergent crises. Because of their higher profile, missions vary operationally from the "quiet diplomacy" of the HCNM. Although active throughout the country, they are often quite visible in a country's capital. While designed to meet the individual needs of the situation on the ground, they are often charged with the broader tasks of working closely with local actors, facilitating discussions, and encouraging conditions for conflict resolution.[73] Mission representatives make frequent, regular reports to the chairman in office (CIO), who passes this information on to the CPC. The CPC then circulates relevant information to the member states, other regional organizations, and relevant NGOs.[74]

As intent as the CSCE/OSCE was to avert violent ethnic conflict in Eastern Europe, its approach to conflict prevention was diffuse and comprehensive. Statements made after 1990 emphasized the organization's general attitude to ethnic violence: instability would be countered by eliminating the root causes of tension, through respect for human rights (including those of national minorities), through building democratic institutions, and by fostering economic and social progress.[75] By design as well as by default, the CSCE/OSCE's institutional development cultivated its spearheading efforts, assuring that it would guide the efforts of governments, intergovernmental organizations, and NGOs.[76]

From the beginning, CSCE/OSCE officials made information and its exchange an organizational priority, aware that more and better information was crucial to improving transparency between states and thus indispensable for establishing stability and peace. For example, the 1975 Helsinki Final Act devotes almost five pages to the importance of information and information exchange: "*Conscious* of the need for an ever wider knowledge and understanding of various aspects of life in other participating States; *Acknowledging* the contribution of this process to the growth of confidence between peoples."[77]

The CSCE/OSCE's organizational emphasis on early warning and early action in situations involving inter- or intrastate ethnic disputes encouraged it to reach out directly to other organizations involved in the former Eastern bloc. At the beginning of 1992, the CSCE invited the CoE, the EC, NATO, the Organization for Economic Cooperation and Development (OECD), and the EBRD, as well as other European and transatlantic organizations, to provide its secretariat with information relevant to CSCE activities.[78] Although these initial efforts were not that successful in creating a sustained arrangement for information exchange under CSCE auspices, the emphasis placed on information and transparency was the "first concrete step towards increased contacts and cooperation" among these organizations.[79]

This exchange of information was crucial to closer collaboration among international organizations bent on harmonizing their activities to achieve common goals. At the same time, this emerging interlocking framework would only be successful if the institutions involved concentrated their strengths on this purpose and maintained objectives that they were best suited to pursue.[80] In other words, this new security framework would work only if some efficient division of labor was constructed. As early as 1992 and with no other organization taking the lead in addressing ethnic conflict, the CSCE recognized that its role in consolidating security in the East depended upon its ability to gain the support of powerful governments and other intergovernmental organizations, drawing upon their particular competencies.[81] Consequently, it made "pragmatic cooperation" with other intergovernmental organizations and member states a priority for exerting its influence, not just as a goal in and of itself but as a way to achieve comprehensive security in Europe.[82]

Throughout the 1990s, at the headquarters and the field levels, the CSCE/OSCE unwaveringly joined with other regional organizations and national governments to exchange information, design joint needs-assessments, and establish common projects.[83] Its closest partners in ethnic conflict prevention were the CoE, the UN, the EU, and NATO. In many cases, these latter organizations provided funding for projects that grew out of CSCE/OSCE recommendations, or they put their projects under CSCE/OSCE management, such as the EU-sponsored Stability Pact for South Eastern Europe, concluded in June 1999.

Acknowledging the CSCE/OSCE's groundbreaking involvement in ethnic issues, CoE representatives were initially somewhat concerned that the upstart organization would duplicate some of its functions. These problems proved ephemeral; through necessity and interaction in the field, council-CSCE/OSCE relations improved substantially during 1992–93, with both affirming that future cooperation would be aimed at creating structures that avoided wasteful overlap and duplication. More importantly, these two groups achieved the "synergy effects" that can result from innovative forms of coordination.[84]

During the same period, the CSCE and the UN engaged in similar discussions, intending to improve collaboration, information exchange, and the coordination of policies.[85] By 1993, the CoE, UN, and CSCE were conducting regular high-level meetings, and each sent representatives to conferences held by the other two. In recognition of the importance accorded ethnic conflict management, this body expanded in 1996 to include the HCNM, the UN's High Commissioner on Refugees (UNHCR), and representatives of a few international NGOs.[86] At several points in the 1990s, the CSCE/OSCE articulated its evolving security model for Europe, which was based on deepening its relations with other regional and nongovernmental organizations, including the EU, NATO, and several international NGOs.

The CSCE/OSCE's collaborative framework was echoed by leaders of other Euro-Atlantic organizations and national governments, all faced with the immense and unwanted task of ethnic conflict prevention. In the eyes of the Council of Europe's leadership, the new order of Europe was well established and consisted of a complex range of institutions and organizations, some solely European and others part of the Euro-Atlantic community, yet all complemented one another to promote security, peace, and democracy. The president of the European Community noted that by cooperating, each organization could do what it did best. The secretary general of NATO was more specific: "I said earlier that no single organization could guarantee security. . . . We need interlocking institutions working together so as to create a network of relationships."[87]

In sum, Europe possessed a plenitude of governments, regional organizations, and NGOs that were interested in ethnic conflict management. Among the array of actors, only the CSCE/OSCE had the mandate, membership, and motivation to be at the forefront of transnational efforts to mange ethnic tensions. It was not until the middle of the decade that problems linked to interethnic friction spurred the formation of a transnational network of public and private actors that orbited around the CSCE/OSCE with the conjoined purpose of forestalling and regulating ethnic conflicts in Eastern Europe. It must be restated that since the CSCE/OSCE had few resources to directly influence governments or prevent ethnic violence, it never attempted to act in isolation. Given the unique competencies of actors with strikingly similar objectives, as well as the need to respond quickly and uniquely to crises, the network response was—by design—multilateral and multilevel. Yet, even as governmental organizations adapted to this new environment, and public and private relationships evolved throughout the decade, the CSCE/OSCE retained a unique place in Europe's evolving security architecture when it came to ethnic conflict management. As the NATO secretary general stated in 2000, "The OSCE remains the sole organization capable of setting standards of security behavior, preventive diplomacy, democracy building, and for addressing the myriad of minority issues in Europe."[88]

Top-Down Strategies

The majority of the literature on the international community's involvement in ethnic conflict in Eastern Europe emphasizes its shortcomings, especially its blatant failures in the former Yugoslavia.[89] The international community eventually did intervene to stop the violence in Bosnia-Herzegovina, however belatedly, and by the spring of 1994, NATO was using its airpower against the Serb-controlled Yugoslav army. After a successful air campaign that ended in September 1995, the international community effectively coerced Bosnia's neighbors to sign the Dayton Peace Accords that December. Yet, the West had no intention of making Bosnia a precedent for future international involvement in ethnic conflict. The twofold lesson that emerged from Bosnia's wreckage was clear: A new preemptive strategy toward ethnic conflict was necessary, and this strategy should rest on other less intrusive and less costly initiatives originating from various sources.

By July 1996, the International Commission on the Balkans confirmed the need for what it called top-down and bottom-up initiatives and "a network of regional commissions to work on specific problems including ethnic and minority relations."[90] Apparently unbeknownst to the commission authors, such an arrangement was already in the works and directed at other potentially explosive situations. Although states were undeniably important in this emerging configuration, the impetus and leadership came from regional organizations, and the implementation of many programs was carried out largely by NGOs. Thus, as Phillipe Schmitter remarks about the origins of democratic change in Eastern Europe, there is good reason to believe that the world both above and beneath the nation state played an important role in affecting the trajectory of ethnic conflicts in Eastern Europe.[91]

As complex as the configuration of actors and range of strategies was, the goal of all these strategies was straightforward: to prevent ethnic violence in Eastern Europe. Although transnational actors employed a mixture of strategies and tools (often simultaneously), it is worthwhile to consider the top-down strategies of *conditionality, mediation,* and *normative pressure* individually, while emphasizing their complementary nature.[92]

Conditionality

Although there is no consensus on the use of positive incentives to alter states' behavior, explicit or implicit forms of political *conditionality* were used by several transnational organizations interested in preventing ethnic violence and promoting stability in Eastern Europe. *Explicit conditionality* identifies specific qualifications that are often part of legislation, while *implicit conditionality* derives largely from the types and timing of the foreign assistance provided to countries.[93] The EU, NATO, the CoE, most Western governments, and international financial institutions all used forms of this strategy throughout the 1990s, with some offering membership in their organizations while others used financial assistance as both an incentive and a reward for compliant behavior outlined by the international community.

The EU's incremental use of leveraging aspiring members' behavior by providing limited rewards to states that abided by certain conditions while holding off membership made it, according to one scholar, "a master of political conditionality."[94] Largely because of its use of membership conditionality, the EU is recognized by some as the quintessential actor that influenced ethnic relations the most in the region.[95] With this said, this strategy was not fine-tuned until 1997 at the earliest, though the origins of the EU strategy started much earlier. The EU's initial instrument was contained in its Common Foreign and Security Policy (CFSP), which was developed with the Maastricht treaty in 1992. As a part of this initiative, in early 1993, the EU proposed the Pact on Stability in Europe to foster good neighborliness through, among other means, signing bilateral treaties that confirmed current borders and established minority rights within them. Adopted formally by fifty-two member states in March 1995 and concerned with states in Central and Eastern Europe and the Baltic region, the pact contained several provisions dealing with minority rights and urged close cooperation among intergovernmental organizations. However, scholars contend that, more than anything else, this pact illuminated the incoherence between planning and execution within the EU system and the powerlessness of the EU at this time to sway nationalist politicians.[96]

Perhaps the most tangible effect of the EU's 1993 initiative was its explicit recognition that resolving historical grievances, the consolidation of borders, and the assurance of minority rights were crucial to regional stability, and these issues would be a priority in relations with states seeking membership.[97] Yet, at this juncture all East European states needed to do was to promise to implement certain initiatives to comply with international standards. In 1999, with the failures of this pact in mind, the EU sponsored another stability pact focused on South Eastern Europe. In an interview, a current political adviser to the Stability Pact for South Eastern Europe explained the impact of the earlier initiative this way: "The Pact on Stability in Europe launched in 1993 was a very good idea; it was based on the notion that the EU needed to encourage good neighborly relations in Eastern Europe as a first step to closer relations with the EU. Getting the EU, the CSCE/OSCE, the Council of Europe, and NGOs to coordinate and work together was a part of this goal; the problem was that nothing really happened."[98]

At approximately the same point in 1993, the EU developed another mechanism to quell ethnic conflict. At the European Council meeting in Copenhagen, the

EU embedded the goal of conflict prevention into the criteria it outlined for future EU member states. Borrowing from CSCE best practices, the Copenhagen criteria defined the political and economic standards for all new EU members, including the stability of institutions, democracy, rule of law, human rights, and respect for and protection of minorities. At the heart of these conditions was the importance of democracy and human rights, including those of minorities. Looking to the principles and practices of the CSCE, the Copenhagen European Council stated: "Considerable progress has been made along the road to democracy, peace, and the unity of Europe. The Helsinki Final Act, the Charter of Paris, the Copenhagen document, the Helsinki 1992 document, as well as bilateral agreements on good neighborly relations are milestones in this process. But we must go further and make these achievements irreversible."[99]

With specific criteria defined and the decision made to enlarge the union, an explicit policy of political conditionality based on CSCE and CoE criterion emerged, and what are called "European standards" related to ethnic conflict prevention arrived. The attention paid to minority rights was undoubtedly part of a broader transnational campaign to waylay ethnic conflict in the East since the most recent EU members from Southern Europe had not been required to meet any criteria related to national minorities.[100] Yet, the EU's strategy depended crucially on the input of other regional organizations and local NGOs to evaluate and monitor states' behavior, indicating that the EU never intended to manage ethnic conflicts alone but merely meant to use its power and resources to empower and reinforce the ongoing efforts of other actors.

After the development of political criteria for membership, a handful of "pre-accession steps" were added to provide an effective mixture of incentives and constraints to guide ethnic relations in transitioning countries. The Europe Agreements, for example, provided the framework for relations between the EU and transitioning countries in Eastern Europe that fulfilled the Copenhagen criteria and entailed both short—and long-term support to help these countries meet and implement European standards. Important to note, however, was that minority rights per se were not developed further in EU law. Instead, the EU referenced the principles established by the CSCE in its Copenhagen document and the Treaty of Paris, as well as standards and laws found in the Council of Europe's Framework Convention and the European Charter of Regional and Minority Languages.[101]

The EU's adoption of preexisting criteria elaborated by the CSCE and the CoE indeed signaled the importance of minority issues as a pan-European question informed by two general principles: the principle of universality and the growing irrelevance of the doctrine of nonintervention in internal affairs.[102] The EU's formalization of this process, along with its references to CSCE and CoE documents, not only solidified the common principles upon which different intergovernmental actors agreed, but they reflected a clear layering of authority and governance that was later reinforced through the multilateral management and monitoring of ethnic conflicts and minority-majority relations.

Yet, despite the slow incorporation of ethnic issues into the EU's purview, it did not adopt its own monitoring process until 1997. Until this point, the EU regularly relied on proxies for information related to ethnic politics and national minorities, and it mainly solicited information from the HCNM office and Council of Europe, which indirectly allowed these actors to shape EU policies and its relationships with Eastern European states. According to one scholar, the EU essentially delegated to the CSCE/OSCE's Office of the High Commissioner on National Minorities the task of judging whether Central and Eastern European countries had "done enough" in terms of minority rights.[103] Falk Lange, a longtime adviser to the HCNM office, commented that he was initially somewhat surprised by the lack of knowledge of other actors when it came to ethnic conflicts in the East, but later he appreciated that this was understandable given for example that the EU was an economic organization, had no direct experience in this area, and could not spare people for fieldwork in this area until the late 1990s.[104] It simply cannot be forgotten that during the early 1990s, the EU's main concerns centered on economic issues.

EU officials concur that from the beginning of its involvement in Eastern Europe until 2004, relations among the EU, the CSCE/OSCE, NATO, the CoE, and NGOs are largely complementary rather than competitive. The EU's success in various areas depended on its willingness to defer to other more experienced organizations for information and advice. As the decade progressed, the relationships between the interested parties became closer and more mutually reinforcing as responsibilities were delegated according to each organization's capabilities.[105] Franz Cermak, an official of the EU Enlargement Directorate General, explained the connections between the organizations in this way: "The EU had the money, but the CSCE/OSCE had the knowledge," and regular meetings with them took place on ethnic and human rights issues.[106] The CSCE/OSCE provided the EU with important information and expertise that the EU simply did not have. The CSCE/OSCE, specifically the high commissioner, traveled regularly and understood the unique problems of each country, thereby raising consciousness within the EU about issues needing immediate attention. While this still did not mean that the EU always followed van der Stoel's recommendations, it did value his insights. The EU did not have people on the ground with the kinds of connections that the CSCE/OSCE had; plus, "van der Stoel was the expert and everyone trusted him."[107]

Starting in 1993, the EU also relied on a different tactic, adopting landmark antidiscrimination legislation to ensure that states that eventually became EU members adopted such laws. This legislative move seemed to be the best, if not the only way, that the EU could shift ethnic politics at that time. Instead of trying to resolve ethnic disputes or impose solutions, the EU put the burden for peacemaking on the states themselves, urging them to nurture their own competencies as soon as possible. In 1997, at the Amsterdam European Council meeting, the Copenhagen criteria were strengthened by Article 6 of the European Union treaty, which asserts that since the union is founded on the principles of liberty, democracy, and respect for human rights and fundamental freedoms, it should follow that these principles should serve as conditions for all members. Article 49 of the EU treaty thereby confirmed that any European states respecting these principles may apply to become a member. Since 1997, the EU has produced regular reports on accession members, monitoring compliance by measuring the countries' adoption of laws as well as their practical implementation.[108] The EU Commission claims that it is not content with the mere recognition of minority rights in national and bilateral treaties; instead, its assessment is also based on its perception of the implementation of these laws with input from other regional actors and local NGOs.

In 1999, with the crisis in Kosovo over, the EU added even more tools to grow its repertoire of conflict prevention strategies centered on conditionality by revitalizing its Common Foreign and Security Policy (CFSP) in a few key ways. The position of the high representative of the CFSP, responsible for representing the EU externally, was created, as was a Policy Planning and Early Warning Unit (PPEWU). The EU also developed closer links with the Western European Union, mandating it to deal with tasks related to humanitarian and rescue missions, peacekeeping, and crisis management. Although the EU's tools for dealing with conflict prevention increased substantially throughout the 1990s, officials from the External Relations Department of the European Commission admit that even in 2004, the EU still relied on and deferred to the expertise of other governmental and nongovernmental organizations to monitor situations on the ground and to provide information.[109] As others have noted, rather than viewing the EU's strategy of conditionality in isolation, it is more appropriate to conceptualize it in a more diffuse, multilateral light, and thus the process of enlargement as consisting of an "accession constellation" of organizations that influence domestic politics in transitioning countries through the coordination of their efforts.[110]

The EU's final major conflict prevention initiative of the decade, the Stability Pact for South Eastern Europe, was a reflection of many of the lessons learned in the early 1990s, particularly the importance of governmental collaboration and outreach to NGOs. Unlike previous EU initiatives, this stability pact embraces a network form of governance in all respects, identifying roles for some forty countries, plus intergovernmental and nongovernmental organizations, with the ultimate goal of promoting regional security. Under OSCE authority, this pact is based on CSCE/OSCE principles and the conviction that democracy and human rights, as well as economic development, were crucial to stability and to drawing the countries of South Eastern Europe closer to Euro-Atlantic institutions and processes. Although the European Union plays a leading role, it collaborates closely with the OSCE, other intergovernmental organizations, including the Council of Europe, the UN, and NATO, as well as NGOs. The uniqueness of the pact lay in both its cooperative public-private composition and its appreciation of the need for multidimensional strategies to promote peace.[111] A Stability Pact officer further claims that pact representatives foresee an essential role for NGOs because of their on-the-ground experience and their ability to recreate ethnically divided societies.[112]

North Atlantic Treaty Organization (NATO): While sometimes overlooked, the EU was hardly the only actor to use membership conditionality as a strategy to influence ethnic conflicts. The wars in Yugoslavia, which ultimately resulted in NATO intervention, triggered ongoing debates within NATO over how this organization would or should adapt to the post-cold war environment, using its power and prestige to foster regional security.[113] In 1993, NATO began to consider enlarging its membership and, like the EU, made membership contingent on fulfilling certain requirements. Its expansionist agenda aimed to coax states "into the fold" not by providing security guarantees *a priori* but by fostering a web of military and political institutions modeled on the most successful components of the NATO alliance.[114] At the same time, this agenda marked another significant turning point because NATO simultaneously admitted that its goals would be furthered only by expanding and intensifying ties with other organizations that shared similar objectives in Eastern Europe, such as the CSCE/OSCE, the Western European Union (WEU), and the UN.[115]

The United States ambassador to NATO between 1993 and 1998 explains NATO's evolution by underscoring that in the United States, "strategic calculation, ethnic politics, and the vision of an inclusive Europe were major factors for decision makers," adding approval for the enlargement of the organization but also U.S. support for other multilateral organizations.[116] NATO's sudden willingness to share—

and even hand over—activities to other intergovernmental organizations was un-derstandable in light of the range of post-cold war activities that were starting to mount for NATO, without a corresponding increase in personnel or resources.[117] Consequently, NATO leaders also used conditionality as a way of mediating ethnic conflicts and promoting regional security. In fact, the coalition within NATO in favor of a more comprehensive response to events in the East (including Germany's foreign and defense ministers, NATO's secretary general, and key U.S. senators) be-lieved that including former Communist countries in the NATO structure could be a highly effective way of cultivating political stability both between and within states.[118] According to this view, extending the security umbrella to Eastern Europe was a precondition for the establishment of proper socioeconomic foundations, which were seen as necessary for democracy to take root.[119]

Membership in NATO thus would serve both as a reward for good behavior and an incentive to make the transitions irreversible. As a report to the U.S. Congress put it, the purpose of NATO enlargement is "to integrate more countries into the exist-ing community of values and institutions, thereby enhancing stability and security for all countries in the Euro-Atlantic area."[120] As advocates for NATO enlargement such as Jeanne Kirkpatrick maintained, the values and institutions embodied in NATO "would be the only reliable guarantees against aggression and preserving and strengthening democracy in Central and Eastern Europe."[121] In January 1994, NATO acted on these urgings, initiating its Partnership for Peace program (PfP), a military and political process designed for the specific purpose of responding to the instability, tension, and conflict that accompanied the climate of cooperation.[122] Al-though the program was really a substitute for admitting new members into NATO, it did signal NATO's willingness to work with other intergovernmental organiza-tions on issues related to ethnic conflict management. According to a NATO press release, the partnership program acknowledges "NATO's new role in preventive diplomacy," as the program is based on forging new relationships with non-NATO states, largely from the former Warsaw Pact in an effort to "expand and intensify po-litical and military cooperation throughout Europe, increase stability, and diminish threats to peace."[123]

The program provided a framework for NATO's evaluation of states' candidacy for alliance membership; within a year, its success was evidenced by the fact that twenty-six states had indicated a desire to join, nineteen of which had already pro-vided documents to NATO, and twelve of which had signed Individual Partner Pro-grams with NATO.[124] Despite the importance of NATO membership, there is reason to believe that Eastern European leaders saw NATO as only a single component of an evolving security structure based on common principles and standards and general organizations.[125]

By late 1995, with NATO's successful air campaign completed in Bosnia but with its troops intimately involved in postconflict reconstruction and peace building, NATO realized the extent to which its goals and room for maneuver were dependent upon other intergovernmental organizations.[126] According to NATO's assistant secretary general for political affairs, Bosnia demonstrated that interlocking institutions created a system of synergy rather than of hierarchy among transnational organizations.[127] Thus, while NATO was important to the overall formula for preventing ethnic violence, other organizations provided unique and crucial functions that were necessary to cultivating long-term peace in the region. Most clearly, post-Dayton Bosnia demonstrated that without NATO-led military security, the OSCE could not have organized democratic elections; without elections and some political stability, economic and social reconstruction, led by the EU, the UN, and the USAID, and implemented by scores of NGOs, could not have moved forward. The difficult task of rebuilding Bosnia spelled out the importance, if not the urgency, of collaboration among public and private organizations hoping to tame ethnic conflict.

By July 1997, the Czech Republic, Hungary, and Poland were invited to become NATO members. The invitations were extended to these countries for a variety of reasons, but mostly because they had shown a readiness and ability to commit to "the military and political obligations of membership, including domestic political and economic reforms and ending any lingering claims against their neighbors."[128] In the United States, supporters of NATO's expansion emphasized the organization's ability to project stability into a region that had long suffered from a security vacuum. Responding to the voices of criticism against expansion, due in part to the potential for U.S. casualties in places that were not vital to U.S. security interests, Secretary of Defense William Cohen responded that U.S. interests in fact would be served by NATO's enlargement—because it would dampen nationalism and ethnic tension by bringing new member states into the security framework.[129]

As a consensus-building organization with elaborate and highly institutionalized norms and procedures for decision making, NATO greatly valued its integrated command and multinational force structure, which was an indirect way of managing interstate ethnic tensions. That is to say, NATO would deal with ethnic conflicts in the East as it had dealt with them with in the West—by using multinational commands and integrating NATO forces. To be clear, its emphasis on multinationalism is not for efficiency's sake but, instead, serves as a way of promoting trust among its members and preventing the renationalization of defense policies.[130] Essentially, NATO's plans to enlarge signaled that this military defense organization was trying to build upon its historical success, homogenizing and reproducing standard expectations that had helped stabilize international order during the cold war.[131] Without ever addressing ethnic conflicts in a comprehensive way, NATO did weigh in on certain situations, hoping that it would contribute to European security by assisting the internal management of crises among aspiring members such as Hungary and Romania.[132] Like the EU, NATO emphasized that future members must be willing to undertake the military and political obligations of membership.

By the second half of the 1990s, NATO developed a clear message for Eastern European states: Cooperation with other intergovernmental organizations and states in the region was crucial to Europe's security and to future membership in NATO. As leaders confirmed in 1996, because current challenges to security are more diverse and diffuse, they necessitate complex responses that rely on a multiinstitutional approach to security.[133] According to the assistant security general of NATO, it was Bosnia that convinced NATO leadership that the model for future cooperation and future European safety was based upon comprehensive security or principles that underpinned the CSCE/OSCE process.[134] Ethnic conflict prevention and the management of tensions required that organizations with different specific missions work together in practical ways.[135]

Some observers are rightfully skeptical of NATO's independent ability to promote democracy or to minimize ethnic disputes; as one author notes, its goal of "promoting stability" in the former Warsaw Pact is clearly specious because the countries that were admitted in 1999 were in fact already quite stable.[136] Moreover, while fears of an epidemic of ethnic conflict in Eastern Europe (driven by border disputes and concessions for minority rights) did not come to pass, there is evidence that links peaceful outcomes in the East with NATO's involvement, at least indirectly. Rather than NATO preventing ethnic violence, it is far more likely that it, as Dan Reiter puts it, was part of "a web of institutions that helped lessen disputes and promote democracy and stability in this region."[137]

Mediation

The strategy of conditionality may have been effective because it was not used alone; instead, it worked alongside mediation efforts, undertaken primarily by the CSCE/OSCE. Starting in 1993, the CSCE/OSCE's Office of the High Commissioner on National Minorities became involved in more than a dozen ethnic conflicts in the region; representatives of this office also made visits to Georgia, Uzbekistan, Montenegro, and Kosovo, and the office made a series of recommendations on the Roma and Sinti populations in Europe. Given the office's limited mandate and small operational budget, it concentrated its efforts on those interethnic disputes that were perceived as potentially leading to violence or destabilization, and where the CSCE/OSCE was likely to make a difference. The first HCNM tried to abide by the rules of "quiet diplomacy," visiting countries frequently and talking with state leaders and members of minority populations without fanfare. Early on, the high commissioner identified recurrent problems that exacerbated ethnic tensions; thus, his mediation attempts tended to focus on citizenship, language policy, education, and political participation.

The high commissioner used the CSCE/OSCE's weaknesses—its vague mandate, its underdeveloped instruments, and its paltry resources—to his office's benefit by acting more like a representative of an NGO than a governmental bureaucrat. The office, which was not bound by formal diplomatic procedures, responded quickly to mounting crises. The high commissioner's office worked to diffuse ethnic conflicts by identifying specific issues considered objectionable to the West because of their potential to inflame tensions. The point was not to tell Eastern European countries what to do or to try to impose a specific solution, but to have them arrive at a similar conclusion on their own. Falk Lange, a current adviser to the HCNM, explains the strategy this way: "After identifying a specific problem, the HCNM's office would launch an idea or a concept (as a way of responding to the problem). . . . Quite often the same idea was later presented and used by academics, NGO officials, or even elites. . . . This is how Western ideas were adopted and then eventually implemented in Eastern Europe. . . . When enough people talk about them enough, they become part of the local discussion." [138]

The HCNM's work did not end there; the small staff also worked behind the scenes to persuade governments and intergovernmental organizations to get important groups within these countries to listen to CSCE/OSCE evaluations and recommendations. As Walter Kemp, a former adviser to the HCNM, explains: "In 1993 and especially after the EU's Copenhagen criteria were developed, the HCNM used his close relationship with the EU and influence with CSCE/OSCE government leaders as leverage in Eastern European countries experiencing ethnic tensions." [139]

Discussing the effects of the HCNM's work, van der Stoel sees the relationships of the high commissioner's office with other organizations, mainly the EU but also with the U.S. government, as crucial to the success of its mediation efforts; the HCNM office's greatest source of power came from states and intergovernmental organizations that supported its mandate and attempts to manage ethnic differences.[140] Since the HCNM office was, for a long time, the prime mechanism by which the situation of minorities in candidate countries was measured, the high commissioner was able to use the carrot of EU or NATO membership and wield the stick of exclusion while his office worked to push Eastern European leaders and minority leaders internally to undertake certain actions. As van der Stoel admits: "Frankly, I don't think that I would have had much of an impact if I was just Mr. X with a nice title, with recommendations. . . . Instead, my influence came from the days spent in Vienna, Brussels, and DC talking to government representatives."[141]

The sway of the HCNM office lies in other areas, the first being its narrow focus on ethnic conflict prevention and its knowledge of minority issues. Since it was often the only actor with representatives on the ground, governments and intergovernmental organizations naturally deferred to the HCNM office for recommendations. Second, despite the CSCE/OSCE's intergovernmental structure, the HCNM office was fairly autonomous and thus could respond at the earliest stages of a conflict. If, for example, the HCNM had been required to request permission from the CSCE/OSCE Permanent Council to enter a country experiencing rising ethnic tension, his role in the transnational network would have been very different. Indeed, his ability to prevent violence might have been lost, and, by having to work through official channels, his more high-profile actions might have unintentionally intensified the ethnic crisis. Finally, the unique and even-handed way the first high commissioner interpreted and carried out his mission meant that even when actors in the East did not like van der Stoel's ideas (and they often did not), they still believed that he was generally acting in good faith as a neutral party.[142]

Through "quiet diplomacy," the HCNM proceeded as an independent and impartial actor working largely behind the scenes with governments and ethnic minorities. Its depoliticized, multilateral approach, seeking the support of both governments and nongovernmental actors, allowed the high commissioner to employ cooperative, noncoercive, problem-solving techniques.[143] Its work, moreover, was compliant with CSCE/OSCE principles, particularly the notion of comprehensive security that connects peace, security, and prosperity directly to democracy and shared values. As van der Stoel states, ethnic conflict prevention requires, most urgently, the development of democratic institutions to challenge and resolve communal differences internally.[144] Although the HCNM used both carrots and sticks to get compliance, the ideal situation occurs when states themselves seek solutions.

Most of the literature that addresses the CSCE/OSCE's involvement in ethnic conflict focuses on the efforts of the HCNM's office and Max van der Stoel's individual contributions. Without diminishing the importance of the HCNM's efforts, government officials and NGO representatives in Latvia in particular pointed to the role played by the CSCE/OSCE missions (as well as other CSCE/OSCE offices) in untangling ethnic tensions.[145] This is because the mediation efforts of the HCNM's office were supported by other CSCE/OSCE offices that directly or indirectly addressed social problems, including the Vienna Mechanism of 1989, the Moscow Mechanism of 1990, and the Review Meetings of the Human Dimension. These instruments allowed the CSCE/OSCE to request information from member states regarding ethnic issues and minority rights, to send independent experts to countries to investigate alleged abuses, and to establish in-country missions to monitor and help diffuse interethnic issues. The development of missions of long or short duration was significant because this meant that independent experts or reporters could be dispatched to a CSCE/OSCE state without the state's consent to provide early warning of an emerging crisis. In the 1990s, there were fifteen long-term missions established as well as fifteen additional CSCE/OSCE field activities and/or initiatives.[146]

Missions performed different tasks depending on the country and the conflict. Most field activities gathered information, facilitated communication between local and international actors, and served as forces for domestic moderation. At the same time, they encouraged other international actors to help nurture the atmosphere necessary for conflict management by identifying specific needs. Some CSCE/OSCE missions worked to promote conflict prevention by developing democratic institutions and building civil societies, while many sought to prevent the escalation of conflicts through diplomatic intervention, and a few were actively involved in mediating ongoing conflicts. Responsible to the chairman-in-office, missions were fine-tuned to each situation and regularly collaborated with the HCNM, governments, and other intergovernmental organizations. While some performed an array of functions, as in Latvia, their most important and consistent function was their "insider third party" role, which combined some of the characteristics of traditional mediation with those of an insider to the conflict working closely with domestic partners for peaceful change.[147]

Normative Pressure

Characterizing the CSCE/OSCE's strategies are not clear-cut because, as Steven Ratner points out, the HCNM's unique approach to conflict prevention relied extensively on translating, establishing, and disseminating international standards related to conflict prevention and minority rights.[148] Thus, although these functions had not been envisioned when the HCNM office was established, van der Stoel's personality and inclinations allowed this European official to serve as a "normative entrepreneur," shaping and preventing ethnic conflicts in the East by relying on international norms to settle certain ethnic quandaries. John Packer, a former legal adviser to the HCNM, explains that the use of international standards had not been foreseen when the office's mandate was established, but such norms became part of the HCNM's strategy for containing ethnic conflict, and when normative pressure was used, its primary purpose was to prevent and manage ethnic disputes.[149]

Certainly, the 1990 Copenhagen document, the Charter of Paris, and several other CSCE/OSCE documents offer the earliest and most extensive elaborations of collective or group rights. Overlaid on earlier CSCE/OSCE statements that emphasized the principles necessary for comprehensive security, these documents allowed the HCNM office to rely on standards and norms as ways to diffuse ethnic crises.[150] On three separate occasions in the 1990s, the HCNM brought together international experts to establish specific international standards associated with ethnic disputes, yielding the Hague Recommendations regarding Education Rights of National Minorities (1996), the Oslo Recommendations regarding the Linguistic Rights of National Minorities (1998), and the Lund Recommendations on the Effective Participation of National Minorities in Public Life (1999).[151] While never believing that these recommendations would instantly change states' behavior, the HCNM expected these international standards to help set the parameters for international and domestic solutions.

The Council of Europe (CoE): In terms of standard-setting and normative pressure to shape ethnic politics, one cannot look only at the CSCE/OSCE. In fact, the success and implementation of CSCE/OSCE standards related to ethnic conflict prevention and minority rights depended on other organizations, specifically the Council of Europe. As the leader of the human rights regime in Europe, the use of normative pressure and international law was a well-established practice of this organization. After significant debate, with critics claiming that the council was merely "guarding the temple" rather than meeting the challenges of the new Europe, the council brought its legal expertise and decades of experience in establishing European standards to bear on the problem of ethnic conflict management.[152]

In early 1993, council representatives declared that they were "determined to do everything they could to buttress the peace" in Europe.[153] The general secretary insisted that the new Europe necessitated "democractic security," which required the council to reform its structure and design mechanisms to help ensure *both* democracy and stability.[154] Since the CoE's involvement in ethnic conflict management was somewhat delayed, it often took its cues from the normative agenda already laid out by the CSCE/OSCE. Instead of trying to replace CSCE/OSCE principles or usurp its activities, it overlaid its principles and laws on those of the CSCE/OSCE, directing its legal expertise on efforts to support and reinforce human rights and conflict-management objectives in Eastern Europe. According to Frank Schimmelfennig, the CSCE/OSCE provided the "basic liberal norms" that would later become imbued in all international organizations, serving as the foundation for evaluating the legitimacy and identity of Eastern European states and, in essence, ratifying the "cultural hegemony" of the West in the East.[155] This layering of norms and standards yielded significant progress in multilevel minority protection.[156]

The Vienna Declaration of 1992, for example, affirmed the CoE's desire to become a tool to foster stability, paving the way for a variety of council standard-setting activities in this area. The council then passed the Charter on European Regional and Minority Languages, which did not enter into force until 1998. The Council of Europe also tried, without success, to establish an Additional Protocol to the Convention for the Protection of Human Rights and Fundamental Freedoms concerning minority rights. Despite the rejection of this proposal, the text, which was adopted through Recommendation 1201 (although not without controversy), was significant because it defined national minorities and introduced their right to autonomy. As the council recommendation explained: "The Assembly asked the Council of Ministers to provide the Council of Europe with a suitable mediation instrument. . . . [because] only the recognition of the rights of persons belonging to a national minority within a state, and the international protection of those rights, are capable of putting a lasting end to ethnic confrontations, and thus of helping to guarantee justice, democracy, stability and peace."[157]

In June 1993 (coinciding with the adoption of the EU's Copenhagen criteria), the council took another important step that altered and extended its activities in this area, deciding that the Parliamentary Affairs Committee and the Committee of Legal Affairs and Human Rights would be entrusted with the task of monitoring states' compliance with council legislation.[158] At the council's summit in October 1993, it followed the lead of the EU and other governmental actors by adopting conditionality as a strategy to shape new members' behavior. It declared that states seeking membership in the CoE must promise in advance to comply with certain international minority standards, initiating the plan for the Framework Convention for the Protection of National Minorities.[159] Passed in November 1994 (opened for signature in February 1995), the so-called framework departed significantly from previous policies. It not only spelled out principles related to the protection of national minorities, but it was opened to nonmember states, hoping to spur changes throughout Eastern Europe. Emphasizing its significance, the council declared that the framework "was the first legally binding multilateral instrument concerned with the protection of national minorities."[160]

One scholar notes that despite the spearheading efforts of the CSCE/OSCE, the CoE's framework was a milestone in international law.[161] Importantly, the council had also developed crucial monitoring mechanisms that other organizations lacked. By April 1995, it introduced two permanent mechanisms to monitor compliance with its laws. These two procedures were meant to complement each other, pushing countries that had defaulted on their commitments in the right direction without undue public condemnation.[162] Thus, although the EU and NATO had made the protection of minorities a condition for future members in the East, their effectiveness was "seriously hampered" by their lack of experience in this area and the absence of a permanent monitoring mechanism. This is precisely where the Council of Europe's efforts proved most useful in the transnational network.[163]

As its normative efforts intensified, the council became more collaborative and its own strategy more multifaceted; it increasingly worked with regional organizations and NGOs to push states to manage ethnic conflict peacefully and implement human rights, including the rights of minorities. As the council emphasized in 1997, the actions taken by international organizations to ensure the protection of national minorities have largely been complementary.[164] It specifically welcomed the fact that in carrying out its work, the CSCE/OSCE relied on council instruments and its legal expertise for many of its conflict-prevention recommendations and policies.[165]

It simply cannot be overlooked that both CoE and CSCE/OSCE standards were referenced (often verbatim) in the bilateral treaties that were signed throughout the 1990s and meant primarily to ensure regional stability. Following the clear message sent by the European Union, NATO, and the Western states, postcommunist countries signed bilateral treaties with their neighbors. The agreement between Poland and Germany, heralded as a key instrument for settling the historical ethnic animosity between these countries, proved to be a model for future agreements.[166] Unlike previous bilateral treaties, those signed in the 1990s incorporated a variety of standards established by the CoE as well as the CSCE/OSCE, reflecting what had become a European catalogue of human—and minority-rights norms. Thus, even those who focus on the causal significance of bilateral agreements in settling ethnic conflicts between states in Eastern Europe mention the obvious fact that certain norm-generating international organizations such as the CSCE/OSCE and the CoE directly informed the substance of these treaties. Most bilateral agreements include references to CSCE/OSCE documents relevant to minority protection and, in fact, one can find treaty provisions that quote almost word-for-word the UN Declaration on Minorities, the CSCE/OSCE Copenhagen document as well as the Council of Europe's Framework Convention.[167] Other scholars put the specific relationship between bilateral treaties and the CSCE/OSCE this way: "There has been an intensive one-way interaction between the two levels in that multilateral standards drafted within international organizations have strongly influenced the drafting of standards in bilateral minority treaties; bilateral minority treaties commonly contain express reference to phrases that are evidently borrowed from CSCE/OSCE standards."[168]

Although it is difficult to estimate the exact role bilateral agreements played in quelling ethnic disputes, it is worthwhile to note how common they had become by the late 1990s throughout the region. This is because all candidates for EU accession had to solve any unresolved border issues and address minority problems. One indication of a state's willingness was the conclusion of a bilateral agreement, which usually contained CSCE/OSCE-inspired multilateral standards related to minority protection.[169] Thus, bilateral agreements were, at the same time, a product of EU and NATO conditionality and an extension of CSCE/OSCE and CoE normative pressure, thereby highlighting the layering of influences aiming to manage ethnic conflict.

Cooperation from the Bottom Up

These top-down strategies only tell part of the story of how this transnational network sought to quell ethnic tensions. The other notable component included bottom-up strategies that were initiated even earlier by governments, intergovernmental, and nongovernmental organizations, and were based on the belief that democracy promotion would inherently and inevitably help manage tense majority-minority relations.[170] Many have written on democracy promotion in general and on the region in particular; others have theorized on the direct and indirect ways democracy promotion can contain nationalism and decrease ethnic conflict.[171] This section focuses briefly on how this strategy was practiced in Eastern Europe to encourage stability and ethnic peace.

The cold war produced a wave of optimism in the West regarding democracy's ability to resolve a range of domestic and international problems. As the transitions in Eastern Europe started to falter, one of the ills targeted by democracy-promotion rhetoric and policy was the revival of ethnic tensions. Liberal democracy, as Daniel Byman explains, was believed to be an apt cure for ethnic conflicts because "liberal democracy fosters civility, a common domain of values, institutions and identity. . . . It equals nationalism with citizenship and state with civil society." [172] The U.S. government had long maintained the power of liberal democracy to untangle ethnic knots, but it was only after 1992 that transnational actors, both governmental and nongovernmental, used democracy promotion as an explicit way of countering ethnic tensions. This is because, as Larry Diamond explains, "Overwhelmingly, theory and evidence show that the path to the peaceful management of ethnic pluralism lies in institutional provisions and protections . . . and these are only possible with some considerable degree of democracy." [173] Although public and private actors were motivated by a range of specific concerns in Eastern Europe, democracy promotion became an international priority because, at least to some extent, "it was seen as the best way to manage ethnic conflict and promote regional stability." [174]

Democracy promotion did not begin with Communism's demise in Eastern Europe; what was unique about the 1990s, however, was the large number of actors engaged explicitly in this activity. Early in the decade, democracy promotion was placed on the formal agendas of the EU, the UN, the CoE, and the CSCE/OSCE. It also became a foreign-policy priority for numerous governments and a leading imperative for a growing pool of NGOs. [175] Any attempt to track the actors involved in some aspect of democracy promotion in Eastern Europe would easily produce a list of over a hundred public and private organizations, foundations, think tanks, and associations. [176] Indeed, as Communism collapsed, numerous transnational actors made their way to the former Warsaw Pact countries with the ambitious but ambiguous goal of using their financial resources and powers of normative suasion to promote democracy in formerly Communist countries, based on the assumption that democracy would inherently promote stability within and between countries.

Historically, democracy promotion focused on three main areas: helping to develop the formal political institutions of democracy; assisting in the preparation, conduct, and monitoring of elections; and strengthening independent organizations in civil society. In theory, changes in each one of these areas would diminish ethnic tensions because minority groups would develop ways to organize and channel their interests to policy leaders and would be treated the same as majority members of society. In reality, events in Eastern Europe, as well as research findings on the connections between democratizing states and ethnic conflict, complicated these theoretical assumptions as well as the international community's agenda in Eastern Europe.[177] Put differently, while democracy may be the best system for managing ethnic disputes in the long run, it might intensify ethnopolitical disputes in the short term. Expanding participation, alongside weak institutions that are unable to deal with growing demands and challenges, is a formula for instability.

With standard democracy-promotion activities proving unable to stem the tide of ethnic violence in the Balkans in the early 1990s, transnational actors recalibrated their efforts, focusing instead on actors outside the reach of the state. Strengthening civil society, largely through the promotion of local NGOs, suddenly gained cachet as one, if not *the* key to stability and democratic consolidation.[178] Consequently, if new political institutions and elections did not smooth ethnic relations, investments might be better spent on transforming attitudes from the bottom up. Based largely on the strategies and success of private donors working in the region, support for the associational sphere of interest groups, which stand between private and public spheres, became a leading trait of transnational involvement in post-communist countries because of civil society's perceived ability to cultivate democracy, stability, and even ethnic cooperation.[179]

David Chandler explains this strategy's underpinnings in Bosnia; a strong civil society, often measured in terms of the number of NGOs, was believed to generate a range of interests, mitigate the polarities of conflict, and help develop a culture of compromise.[180] Consequently, support for the creation of a "third-sector" recognized that while both the public and private sectors are necessary components of stable democracies, "they are not sufficient to address all of societies' needs and concerns."[181] To some, the best way to promote long-term peace in the East was to work at the intermediate and grassroots levels to undercut the capacity of those who manipulate and perpetuate conflict, and that is best achieved through developing civil society groups or NGOs.[182] Such a strategy, regardless of its impact, was appealing for several reasons, not the least of which was that it was relatively inexpensive.

When it came to bottom-up ways of preventing and managing ethnic conflicts, members of the transnational network cast their net wide, providing financial, technical, and in-kind assistance to influence institutions. Democracy promotion included assistance for legal and judicial reform and the training of officials, and it also encouraged independent voices and empowered grassroots institutions through education initiatives and infrastructure assistance. The thinking that united these varied initiatives was the recognition of the limits of direct international intervention and the need for domestic answers and local people to work internally. Simply put, while interethnic politics can be influenced by external actors, aid providers, and democracy-promotion activities, there is no standard formula, and transforming the domestic context is crucial to the long-term prospects for ethnic peace.[183] Although numerous transnational actors used the strategy of democracy promotion to counter ethnicity's revival, it is worthwhile to look closely at two actors in particular, the European Union and the United States, given their disproportionate influence in the region, as well as the more scattered involvement of international NGOs.

The EU: The European Union's democracy-promotion efforts in the East started almost immediately. Although the primary aim of the EU's Phare assistance package to Eastern Europe was to facilitate economic reform, this program did not ignore political change completely and, from the very beginning, the EU recognized the importance of strengthening democracy and civil society.[184] However, it took Yugoslavia to drive the point home; that is, instead of leading by example and assuming that democracy and stability would naturally ensue once markets were in place, the EU needed to consciously direct its influence and resources to counter nationalism and promote democracy.[185]

The European Parliament induced this hitherto economic organization to become involved in democracy promotion and conflict—prevention activities, and in 1993, the EU started to fund the projects of the European Human Rights Foundation (the European Foundation) that were broadly aimed at democracy and conflict prevention.[186] The European Foundation provided material and technical assistance to groups in the East while it tried to link Eastern NGOs with similar organizations in the West; the goal was not just to prevent conflict but to strengthen the pan-European human rights network of NGOs.[187] By the mid-1990s, EU-sponsored democracy programs were concentrated in eight areas and included initiatives focused on minority rights, human rights, and the development of equal opportunity. While evaluations of the EU democracy programs in 1997 highlight the challenges involved in assessing the impact of these programs, the report concluded that there were tangible signs of progress. Of significance, these evaluations advocated for more money, particularly for NGO development, because of Western Europe's experiences with NGOs, their ability to spread ideas and values, and their role in drawing attention to governments' weaknesses.[188] In short, independent voices and institutions within states, evaluators contended, were critical to monitoring states' behavior and thus to democracy and stability.

However, one needs to be clear about the EU's democracy-related activities, which were not exhaustive or even well-funded. Even though the EU and its member countries provided the largest share of financial assistance to Eastern Europe, only a small portion of these funds were allotted for democracy promotion and civil society. In 1998, for example, the EU spent less than one percent of its total aid for the region on democracy assistance.[189] This miniscule amount cannot capture the other, less direct ways the EU supported democracy and conflict prevention in Eastern Europe, including member states' bilateral assistance programs, assistance to enable Western NGOs to work with Eastern NGOs, and the EU numerous financial incentives for transborder cooperation and the creation of "euro regions."[190] Likewise, one cannot discount the extent to which EU development incentives for economic reform diminished the potential for conflict in the region.[191]

The EU's Stability Pact for South Eastern Europe, established in 1999, provides insight into the EU's growing appreciation of bottom-up strategies and NGOs to promote regional stability. While at the beginning of the 1990s the EU focused exclusively on economic reform and influencing states' behavior, the Stability Pact embraces the principle of comprehensive security and thus the importance of political as well as economic development. More than anything else, it evidences an appreciation of the need for many governmental organizations to work together and to cultivate organizations outside the reach of the state.[192] Thus, the take-home point of this pact is: Ethnic peace in South Eastern Europe will arise as much from governments as from local nongovernmental initiatives and transfrontier cooperation.

Often the EU promoted democracy by lending its financial support to other regional organizations, such as the CoE and the CSCE/OSCE, which also engaged in a variety of democracy-promotion activities. Given the council's legal expertise but limited resources, it approached ethnic conflict prevention largely by providing technical assistance and training programs while the CSCE/OSCE, through its Office on Democratic Institutions and Human Rights, focused on elections and fostering an environment for democratic development.[193] A main responsibility assumed by both the CoE and the CSCE/OSCE was providing technical assistance to these states to help them create the necessary institutions that would allow them to fulfill their commitments related to democracy, human and minority rights. Democracy-promotion activities were often directly linked to states' accession, and discussions among the EU, the CoE, and the CSCE/OSCE furnished the ongoing reports that were used by the EU commission to evaluate a state's readiness for accession.

The United States: Singling out the U.S. government and its democracy-promotion activities in Eastern Europe is warranted not only because of its long-standing faith in the effectiveness of democracy as a strategy to prevent ethnic conflict but because it spends about five hundred million dollars annually on democracy-related programs. Moreover, in the 1990s, the United States increasingly relied on democracy promotion and civil society development as means of dealing with burgeoning ethnic conflicts.[194] In December 1990, the Democracy Initiative was established, which reoriented the government's policies and made the promotion of democracy one of the country's central foreign policy goals.[195] Initially, the paltry funding was funneled through USAID and was used to support local groups in transitioning countries. The Clinton administration adopted a different tack, increasing assistance to civil society development and using NGOs as intermediaries. In 1994, the Democracy Network (or DemNet) was established, providing $30 million over a three-year period to American NGOs to work with indigenous NGOs in Eastern Europe.

At the time, and partly because of the inability of other actors and strategies to tame the spread of ethnic conflict in Yugoslavia, USAID focused more attention on ethnic conflict management.[196] In Eastern Europe, the Clinton policy rested "on the view that U.S. interests in democracy, market economies, and security work together."[197] Thus, even as top foreign policy advisers and officials, such as President Clinton's administrator of USAID, recognized the growing threat of ethnic-based conflict, the United States opted to emphasize democracy promotion rather than construct specific strategies to contain ethnic conflicts; instead, small, ad hoc initiatives to manage ethnic disputes were put under the umbrella of democracy promotion.[198]

Despite some minor adjustments in the 1990s, the thrust of the U.S. strategy for coping with ethnic conflict in Eastern Europe retained its traditional emphasis; that is to say, democracy and the market would push ethnic tensions aside and everything would fall into place.[199] The United States thus supported peaceful change in Eastern Europe by encouraging market reform, first and foremost, but also by bolstering effective political organizations, designing better schools, and encouraging decentralization.[200] Put differently by a current USAID official, although the U.S. government never identified ethnic conflict in Eastern Europe as a top priority, it was aware of the importance of making multiethnic participation and interethnic cooperation an implicit and unchanging principle of its involvement in Eastern Europe.[201] Development programs, while not making interethnic cooperation an exclusive goal, tried to structure programs to encourage appropriate, peaceful behavior.

The U.S. government extols the virtues and effectiveness of its democracy-promotion activities in the postcommunist region, claiming, for instance, that since 1989 it has created more than fifty thousand NGOs throughout Eastern Europe and the former Soviet Union. Yet, it is also true that it only set aside a small amount of its assistance for democracy promotion, though its commitment to democracy promotion compares favorably with other actors (such as the EU).[202] Nonetheless, the United States still devoted no more than 10 percent of its aid to democracy assistance—despite its belief in the calming power of democracy to ethnic conflict.[203]

International Nongovernmental Organizations (NGOs): While governments and intergovernmental organizations were generally slower and gave less attention to the connections between democracy, civil society, and ethnic conflict management, international NGOs (including public and private foundations) had made an early and explicit link between the need for grassroots change and stability in the region. Strengthening civil societies and empowering individuals was part and parcel of NGO efforts to undermine nationalists and attenuate aggressive sentiment. Moreover, many NGOs recognized the symbolic, intangible aspects of ethnic tensions and thus the need for Eastern European societies, at long last, to come to terms with the past and deep-rooted ethnic problems. Part of their appreciation for grassroots initiatives grew from the fact that most NGOs had neither the resources to leverage governments nor the experience to mediate between parties. Thus, they used their autonomy, expertise, and assets to foster ethnic cooperation in a different way.

As mentioned earlier, it is difficult to know the number of NGOs that engaged in democracy promotion as a strategy to tame ethnic conflict because NGOs often failed to label their activities as such. Indeed, in places such as Bosnia and Romania, NGOs considered effective by locals tended to avoid any references to ethnicity or conflict prevention and claimed a focus on the broader goals of reconstruction, education, or strengthening of civil society.[204] Interviews with officers of several U.S.-based foundations, including the Soros foundations, the German Marshall Fund, the East-West Institute, and the Search for Common Ground, reinforce this point, especially as it relates to the general strategies of international NGOs. In other words, while NGOs might not have had specific programs defined in terms of ethnic conflict or minority rights, the management of ethnic conflict was always an explicit or implicit goal, and they assumed that engagement in civil society would indirectly quell these conflicts.[205] Eran Fraenkel of the Search for Common Ground's office in Brussels concurs, claiming that this NGO develops very basic programs, such as bilingual kindergarten programs, that are meant to change the fundamental conditions in these societies.[206]

Jonas Rolett, an officer of the Soros foundation network in Washinton, D.C., put the foundation's strategy this way: Despite the lack of specific programs bearing the words *ethnic* or *conflict prevention*, it was never indifferent to ethnic conflict; in fact, he contends that every plan undertaken by the foundation somehow related to ethnic cooperation and regional stability. Ethnic-conflict prevention directly or indirectly shaped all of the network's programs.[207] The Soros foundation network's involvement in democracy promotion in Eastern Europe will be remembered as unique and historic, even if it remains difficult to measure its independent influence on conflict management. It is important to note that for several years, this single U.S.-based foundation provided 30 percent of all public and private foundation support to Eastern Europe.[208]

In some countries, Soros contributed more democracy-related aid than any single government. From the beginning, George Soros had an abiding interest in human and minority rights, and concern for violent conflict shaped many of his largest and most ambitious projects, including the Central European University and the Institute for Local Government. Soros's human rights interest is also evident in the network's national foundations, located in almost every postcommunist country. Until the mid-1990s, Soros's money provided more than half of all foundation assistance for human rights activities, and every national Soros foundation provided significant support to indigenous human rights NGOs or groups broadly aimed at conflict management.[209]

By the beginning of the 1990s, a variety of nonstate actors were also focused on the situation of ethnic minorities in Eastern Europe and on the need for democratizing governments to alter their behavior to evade violent conflict. Depending on the country, NGOs approached ethnic conflict management in a variety of ways and relied on numerous, overlapping tools. They might, for example, work with national governments or local authorities (as did the East-West Institute, with its Transborder Cooperation Program); provide information and monitor events (as the International Crisis Group did in Bosnia and Kosovo); address conflict through high-level, confidential mediation and dialogue (as the Project on Ethnic Relations did in Romania); fund education programs (the Soros foundation network did this extensively throughout the region); or help strengthen local institutions (as Catholic Relief Services did in Bosnia).[210]

From the start, international NGOs emphasized regional initiatives as well as national ones to both promote democracy and nurture regional stability; for example, from 1989 through 1994, almost half of all money provided by public and private foundations went to regional—rather than country-specific—programs.[211] Regional initiatives as well as the explicit strategy of regionalization were also supported by governmental actors such as the European Union. According to EU commissioner Hans van den Broek, by the middle of the 1990s, the message to countries in the East, particularly those troubled by security concerns, was clear: "For fruitful cooperation with us you will need fruitful cooperation among yourselves."[212] Consequently, regional cooperation by local officials and NGOs became an implicit precondition for cooperation with Western governments, regional organizations, and NGOs.[213] The basic thinking behind this approach was based on the "relativization of the state"; that is, the state could and should be composed of a diverse range of autonomous decision-making centers; these centers of power could be nation-states or networks of states that include regions, subnational entities, or transnational communities.[214]

What was evident by the second half of the decade was the recognition of and reliance on democracy promotion and other bottom-up initiatives aimed to transform society and groups outside the states as well as individuals within the state itself. At the same time, these initiatives were characterized by high levels of cooperation and overlap among governments, governmental organizations, and NGOs. In sum, the belief was that democracy promotion would increase the nodes of power within Eastern Europe, help strengthen rule of law, and empower individuals to hold their states accountable. In this way, individuals and groups outside the states would directly and indirectly tame ethnic conflicts.[215]

Conclusion

This chapter explained how different organizations adapted their mission and behavior in the 1990s. While governmental and nongovernmental organizations developed their own strategies to prevent ethnic violence, they were reliant on each other for information, resources, and monitoring support. The relationships, nonetheless, remained relatively equal and nonhierarchical, with actors' interests and unique capabilities informing their position in a transnational network bent on ethnic cooperation in Eastern Europe. Therefore, the question is no longer *how* the international community responded to ethnic conflict. Gathering strength in the early 1990s, a network response was blatant by the middle of the decade. The question then is: To *what extent* did this network response and its top-down and bottom-up strategies affect ethnic conflicts in Eastern Europe?

On the face of it, one could argue that the power imbalance between the West and the East was so significant that it was inevitable that, in time, Eastern European countries would fall in line and adopt Western-inspired norms and behavior. Or, as others imply, since ethnic cooperation was the preferred outcome for the majority and minority groups, accommodation would have occurred even without these elaborate transnational strategies. Both of these contentions are unsatisfying and incomplete because of the bumpy road to ethnic cooperation in the 1990s, and the variation in ethnic politics throughout the region.

The complex reality explored in the following case studies is one that international relations scholars have only recently started to address and is rooted in several sources: It is the notion that ethnic conflict was managed not by a single actor or one strategy but by a transnational network of governments and NGOs. As explained here, public and private actors relied on complementary, reinforcing strategies that worked from the top down and bottom up to achieve what no one actor could accomplish on its own.

FOUR

Triumph in Transylvania
Interethnic Cooperation in Romania

> "Who is going to define the future of this part of the world. . . ? Will it be Mr.
> Milosevic? Or will it be a nation like Romania, which is building democracy and
> respecting the rights of ethnic minorities?"
>
> —PRESIDENT BILL CLINTON, April 15, 1999

In 1990, there were almost as many similarities as differences between Illiescu's Romania and Milosevic's Yugoslavia. Both countries were ruled by former Communists struggling for legitimacy. Both had large concentrations of ethnic minorities who took the blame for their countries' problems. But the most significant resemblance was the decision to use "forces of a paramilitary nature against those who opposed their policies."[1] With Yugoslavia's implosion in 1992, eyes turned to the plight of ethnic Hungarians dispersed throughout the seven countries that surround the Hungarian state. Events in Romania were particularly troubling; it was home to the largest Hungarian population outside of Hungary, and most were concentrated in the north central region of Transylvania. The country's bloody democratic revolution, as well as interethnic violence in the spring of 1990, appeared to lay the foundation for an intensification of a conflict with inter- and intrastate dimensions.

By the decade's end, Westerners grappling with the diversity of outcomes in the East were regularly referring to Romania as a model of ethnic cooperation. Even those who take issue with such claims agree that interethnic relations had deviated significantly from expectations: In short, they were more cooperative than conflictual.[2] Writings on Romanian politics in the postcommunist era emphasize different aspects of the country's transition; while many assume or contend that the international community played an important role in transforming the country's ethnic strife, few explain what international actors did or how their actions made a difference in this Balkan conflict. Given understandable concerns about ethnicity, what strategies were used to calm this conflict? What impact, if any, did transnational involvement have on Romanian-Hungarian relations?

This chapter argues that although domestic politics and leadership were casually important to the timing of specific accommodating policies and outcomes, transnational involvement was critical to ethnic accommodation in Romania. This is because of the number and nature of transnational involvement in Romania in the 1990s, which consciously sought to nurture grassroots activity and empower civil society. Indeed, interviews with politicians, NGO representatives, and academics from Romania confirm that only transnational involvement can explain the timing and way ethnic relations there were transformed. For some elites, a change in majority-minority relations occurred almost immediately, but most Romanians and Hungarians were so distrustful of each other that they even refused invitations to meet to discuss their differences.[3] By 1993, with Western governments and regional organizations making interethnic relations and conflict management priorities in their relations with Romania, the path of ethnic cooperation was established. Transnational involvement shaped the way local actors perceived ethnopolitical problems and how they crafted their policies. Domestic institutions in Romania now bear the distinct mark of international instruments and Western discourse. Moreover, although Romanian society does not yet play a significant role in making public policies, there are positive signs that, because of transnational support, Romanian society has evolved in quantitative and qualitative ways.[4] Together, top-down and bottom-up transnational pressures have made a direct impression on interethnic politics.

This argument is based on primary and secondary sources and more than two dozen interviews conducted in Cluj and Bucharest, Romania. I also interviewed former and current officials from regional organizations, including the former high commissioner on national minorities. In addition, I corresponded with Hungarians, Romanians, and Americans who were closely involved in ethnic politics in the region in the 1990s.[5] Since regional experts and historians have written extensively on the history of Transylvania and Romanian-Hungarian relations, this chapter does not repeat the effort. Instead, it first provides a summary of interethnic relations in Romania. It then identifies the transnational actors and the strategies used in the 1990s, highlighting the activities of the U.S. government, the CoE, the CSCE/OSCE, the EU, and NATO. It also discusses the work of the International Helsinki Foundation, the Project on Ethnic Relations (PER), and the Soros foundations network. Given my expectations about transnational networks, the third section examines evidence of interethnic accommodation in Romania, parceling out the unique contributions of its actors. The central contention of the following is that ethnic relations in Romania were positively affected by transnational actors—both public and private—that increasingly coordinated their behavior and provided reinforcing messages for internal change.

Ethnic Politics in Romania

The modern state of Romania dates back to 1859, but Romania only obtained the Transylvanian region after World War I.[6] The Treaty of Trianon in 1920 ceded more than two-thirds of Hungary's territory and almost 60 percent of its population to its neighbors.[7] While not the sole beginning to origins of Romanian-Hungarian animosity, it is an acceptable point of departure for the purpose of understanding contemporary ethnic relations. The following provides an overview of this ethnic conflict to illustrate its complex, historical roots.

Hungarians have never made up more than one-tenth of Romania's population.[8] Yet, since most were concentrated in the north central part of the country (but away from the Romanian-Hungarian border), their presence has always been difficult to ignore.[9] Language, Roman Catholicism, and a tenacious sense of national identity made it impractical to try to assimilate the Magyars. Nonetheless, like other countries during the interwar period, this is exactly what the Romanian government attempted, in spite of promises made to the Hungarians for political autonomy.[10]

The Communist revolution in Romania brought notable progress for the country's minority populations, at least for a while. Hungarians enjoyed extensive political and cultural privileges, as Hungarian secondary schools were created and the Hungarian Bolyai University in Cluj was reopened. Pressured by the Soviet Union, the Romanian government established the "Autonomous Hungarian Province" in 1952, situated in the eastern part of Transylvania, but still distanced from the Hungarian border. Romania's leader used this and other policies as evidence of interethnic cooperation, claiming in 1953 that the country's national question "had been solved for good."[11] When Nicolae Ceausescu came to power in 1965, the rights afforded Hungarians and other minorities were already shrinking. Under Ceausescu, Hungarians experienced the usual abuses doled out by arguably the most repressive regime in Eastern Europe, but they also suffered attacks on their culture as a "harmonization" campaign was launched. The situation for Hungarians changed for the worse in the 1970s, as Ceausescu aimed to eliminate any vestiges of ethnic generosity. The Hungarian Bolyai University was merged with the Romanian Babes University, eliminating the Hungarian institution of higher learning, and the

Hungarian Autonomous Province became the Mures Autonomous Hungarian Region, which included fewer Hungarians.

A 1989 Helsinki Report noted that the so-called "process of assimilation" in Romania was not new but merely accelerated during the mid-1980s with population transfers, the restriction and eventual extinguishing of the Hungarian language, the liquidation of cultural institutions, and an explicit campaign to create in Hungarians a sense of shame about their own identity.[12] By the end of the Communist period, most public signs of Hungarian culture and language were gone, even in towns dominated by Hungarians. Nonetheless, the Communist government in Hungary maintained the illusion of socialist solidarity, choosing not to criticize the minority policies of its neighbors. In 1988, however, Hungary broke with tradition at a meeting of the CSCE, cosponsoring a major Western human rights proposal with Canada that challenged Romania's crushing minority policies.[13]

Opportunities and Obstacles after 1989

With Communism and Ceausescu as their mutual enemy, Romanians and Hungarians banded together to overthrow the repressive regime. Protests in December 1989 evolved quickly into a mass movement. The National Salvation Front (NSF), an unlikely conglomeration of opposition groups, replaced the Communist authorities after Ceausescu was executed. In courting the Hungarian minority, leaders of the Romanian opposition pledged that once in power, the new government would adopt generous policies toward the country's minorities.[14] Although well-known Hungarian intellectuals were included in the front's leadership, this did not stop Hungarians from creating their own ethnic-based associations, namely, the Democratic Alliance of Hungarians in Romania (DAHR). DAHR was an umbrella organization of various Hungarian groups that was established with the twin objective of representing Romania's Hungarian population and assisting the country's move toward democracy.[15]

Romanian-Hungarian reconciliation quickly dissolved. By March 1990, violent clashes erupted as several thousand Hungarians celebrated Hungary's national holiday in the Transylvanian city of Tirgu Mures. Although members of a Romanian nationalist party closely bound to the government were known to have been involved in attacks on Hungarians, the government instead scapegoated "the Hungarian provocateurs from across the border."[16] Within a month, Hungarian groups had severed their ties to the front and interethnic tensions intensified. With the connection to the Hungarian minority and many Romanian dissidents ruptured, President Iliescu's government moved even closer to Romanian nationalist groups. By the end of 1990, the Romanian government decided to resurrect the Secret Police to deal with what it called the perils of the country's dangerous minorities.

Within a year, Romania's nationalizing agenda was institutionalized in the country's new constitution, which had declared Romania a sovereign, independent, and unitary state.[17] To the Hungarian minority, this suggested that members of national minorities were cast as inferior, second-class citizens.[18] The 1992 parliamentary elections illustrated, if nothing else, the growing popularity of extreme nationalist groups such as the Party of Romanian National Unity, which was then headed by Gheorghe Funar, Transylvania's most outspoken nationalist.[19] Given that President Illiescu's party had won only a third of the votes in the election, it maintained its close contact with nationalist parties, and in Transylvania, interethnic relations steadily decayed.

Emboldened by the country's constitution and vague, toothless laws pertaining to minority rights, Funar launched a nationalist, anti-Hungarian campaign in his bid to become the mayor of Cluj-Napoca, in the heart of Transylvania.[20] Once elected mayor in early 1993, he ordered the removal of all Hungarian-language signs, banned the use of Hungarian in public schools, and forbade gatherings of Hungarian organizations. All of this was to ensure, as Funar put it, that Romanians were "the masters in their own house."[21] Throughout the same period, a separate nationalist rhetoric was on the rise within the Hungarian minority living in Romania and among politicians in Hungary. Responding boldly to Funar's policies and rhetoric, Bishop Lazlo Tokes, a leader of the Hungarian minority, drew international attention when he proclaimed that Romania was attempting to assimilate its Hungarian population.[22] Some Hungarians even made territorial autonomy and self-government a priority for the Hungarian minority, if only as a ploy to improve its bargaining position with the Romanian government for concessions in other areas.[23]

Although both Hungary and Romania were intent on joining Euro-Atlantic organizations, ethnic friction in Transylvania stood in the way of Hungarian-Romanian relations; by 1994, it hindered both countries' relations with the West.[24] The emerging contradictions between Romania's stated foreign policy goals and its nationalistic mindset resulted in the adoption of a series of policies deemed by Hungarians to be discriminatory, including proposals for restrictive laws on the use of Hungarian in schools. By the summer of 1994, ethnic tensions ran so high that the Romanian government stepped in, calling for calm and moderation.[25] By this point, Rogers Brubaker's model, which purports to explain the dynamics of interethnic disputes in terms of the "triadic nexus"—or the relationships between the home, host, and minority population—provided essential, though not heartening, insight into the politics of postcommunist Romania.[26]

Model Cooperation?

Despite the intensification of ethnic strife in Romania by the middle of the decade, the subsequent years brought sudden and surprising improvements. By September 1996, Romania and Hungary signed a bilateral treaty, which had been delayed for several years but laid down a number of essential principles regarding borders and the treatment of minorities. For Hungary, the treaty was pivotal because it recognized that national minorities constituted an integral part of the society of the state in which they live, and both states committed to promoting a climate of tolerance and to applying international standards for the protection of national minorities.[27] For Romania, the treaty recognized the permanence of the existing borders and signaled Hungary's refusal to support any secessionist initiatives in Transylvania.

In Romania, the November 1996 elections proved to be a turning point, representing, as one scholar put it, "not merely a change of government common in any democratic political system, but an actual change in regime, a democratic breakthrough after six years of proto democratic institutionalization under the tenure of President Iliescu and his Party of Social Democracy in Romania."[28] The election indeed proved crucial to pushing nationalist rhetoric aside in favor of practical ways of reaching ethnic accommodation. Case in point: The opposition parties invited the Hungarian party to join the governing coalition. This "revolution within a revolution" meant that in exchange for the government's pledge to minority rights and institutional change, Hungarians suspended calls for territorial autonomy.[29] As one observer of interethnic relations in Romania put it, the presence of Hungarians in the government elicited profound effects that are difficult to gauge.[30] Certainly, it is true that the period from 1996 to 2000 heralded the first time in Romania's history that Hungarians participated in ruling the country.

During the four years that the Hungarian party was present in government, there were prominent successes, including the establishment of a series of political and civil arrangements that either recognized or sought to implement minority rights.[31] A longstanding demand of the Hungarian minority had been the inception of a department for national minorities, and in early 1997 such a body was established, with a Hungarian in charge.[32] These attainments, as many Romanians would admit, were often more superficial than substantial, and there were many problems during these four years.[33] By the winter of 1997–98, for example, a crisis loomed within the coalition, ostensibly over a draft bill calling for the separation of the Babes-Bolyai and the formation of a separate, state-supported Hungarian university.

The 2000 elections put the Social Democracy Party and Iliescu back in office. However, four years had done a great deal for the party's attitude toward the country's national minorities; instead of relying on nationalist rhetoric to rally supporters, as President Iliescu had done in the first half of the 1990s, the government emphasized the value of ethnocultural diversity, reaching out specifically to the Hungarian minority. Nationalist parties had not faded among party collaborators, but they were noticeably shouldered to the sidelines. It did not surprise many in Romania that the Social Democratic Party had repackaged itself, given the population's foreign policy goals and the need to appease the international community. However, Romanians were taken aback by the government decision to maintain cooperation with the Hungarian party, which was not an explicit requirement of the international community. A formal agreement expressed common objectives and the desire to solve problems related to local administration, schools, and historical monuments.[34]

Transnational Involvement in the 1990s

Unlike its neighbors in the north, Romania was not flooded with Western assistance or international NGOs seeking to help the country transition to democracy and the market. When it came to ethnic politics in particular, Romanian leaders were not shy about their resistance to international "interference" in what they considered to be exclusively domestic issues. At an OSCE-sponsored conference in 1991, Romanian delegates flatly objected to the internationalization of minority issues, arguing that ethnic politics should remain states' responsibility and any international instruments should be adopted only on a voluntary basis.[35] Yet, Yugoslavia's unraveling and fears that ethnic conflict might engulf the rest of the Balkans pushed transnational actors to further internationalize these issues, specifically targeting potentially violent ethnic conflicts on Yugoslavia's borders. After crucial years and spiraling ethnic tensions, Western government and regional organizations acknowledged the importance of ethnic cooperation within Romania to regional stability.[36] The following discusses transnational efforts to mediate what President Carter once referred to as one of Eastern Europe's most intractable and long-running ethnic disputes.[37]

Marginalization and Neglect

Gabriel Andreescu, former dissident and director of the Romanian Helsinki Committee, divides transnational involvement in Romania into three distinct phases.[38] In the first phase, from roughly 1990 through 1992, only a few transnational actors became active in Romania, and even for them, ethnic politics was not a high priority. This is because no clear "ethnic agenda" had been established by the West. Romania's precarious political environment, specifically the success of former Communists in the elections of 1990 and 1992, meant that the army of internationals clearly present in other Eastern European countries was nearly visible in Romania. The predominant strategy employed most intensively by the U.S. government and the European Union was democracy promotion, but it was tacked on to largely economic reform efforts. Bottom-up initiatives to support opposition groups in civil society were geared largely toward purging former Communists from office. Although some U.S.-based foundations and European governments realized the potential for ethnic conflict in the wake of Communism's collapse, it was hard to convince the U.S. government or intergovernmental organizations that they needed to apply proactive methods in order to avoid ethnic violence.[39]

Thomas Carothers details the significant involvement of the U.S. government in the first six months after the fall of Ceausescu, nothing that the United States "moved with alacrity to support the first elections and the newly emergent groups and associations that represented the seeds of a new independent sector in the country."[40] However, it was clear that the U.S. focus was squarely on human rights. Human Rights Watch confirms the importance of the United States in 1990–91 in elevating human rights by pressuring the Romanian government to abide by international human rights standards.[41] At the same time, and in the face of violent confrontations between Romanians and Hungarians in 1990, this involvement did not culminate in specific programs designed to address the country's long-standing ethnic dispute. On several occasions both before and after Romania's first presidential election, the U.S. government drew attention to Romania's human rights abuses, sending several top U.S. officials to Romania, but it made no major fuss about ethnic issues. The United States condemned the newly elected Illiescu government's decision in June 1990 to call on "miners and conscientious people" to come to Bucharest to restore order during an antigovernment rally, but it did little to develop a plan for averting such behavior in the future.[42] Although both the United States and Western Europe watched events in Romania closely, no country took a genuine interest in it because all saw Romania as being out of its "zone of influence."[43] The United States did continue to provide significant assistance to Romania's opposition, investing in civil society to indirectly encourage democratic change and stability.[44]

Hungary's behavior was arguably as important as any other transnational actor in the early post-Ceausescu years, and its focus was squarely on Romania's Hungarian population and escalating ethnic tensions. In spite of Hungary's commitment to democracy and joining Euro-Atlantic institutions, the fate of ethnic kin abroad was undeniably a concern for the new democracy. Some Hungarians mused that if Yalta was now passé, why not Trianon, too?[45] In 1989, as a response to this new climate and unresolved national problem, a clause was inserted in Hungary's constitution noting that "the country feels responsible for the fate of the Hungarians living beyond its borders and promotes the cultivation of contacts with Hungarians."[46] President Jozsef Antall further encouraged Hungarian organizations and projects in Romania, Slovakia, and Vojvodina, where the largest Hungarian populations resided. In 1991, he disturbed many in both the East and West when he highlighted the legal difference between the promises made after World War I and World War II, suggesting that, with the Soviet Union and Communism gone, Hungary might favor some revision of its borders.[47] Yet, even while such bombastic nationalist statements were made, the Hungarian government's position on its ethnic kin abroad was complicated by the strong consensus that had emerged within the country: Hungary was looking to the future, not to its aggressive irredentist past, and its future rested with Euro-Atlantic institutions.

Despite significant nationalist rhetoric in the early 1990s, the Hungarian government never made any unilateral, aggressive moves. Instead, its leaders looked to international organizations, hoping to put ethnic conflict management and minority rights on the international agenda. In October 1990, just after Hungary was admitted to the Council of Europe, President Antall drew the attention of the CoE's Assembly to a problem that the council had just "discussed in depth for the first time and which would, in the next few years, become one of the major political issues in Europe after the Berlin Wall's disappearance: the protection of minorities."[48] According to Antall, Hungarians hoped that "its ethnic brethren living abroad would be able, while remaining Hungarian, to be loyal citizens of the country in which they live."[49]

Hungary did not rely solely on regional organizations and the power of normative pressure to affect outcomes in Romania; its "trans-sovereign nationalism" meant that the Hungarian government helped establish a range of public and private organizations to help link Hungarians abroad to those in Hungary, working bilaterally and through grassroots, nongovernmental organizations to provide material support.[50] These bottom-up initiatives started as early as 1992, when Hungary established a Government Office for Hungarian Minorities Abroad, tasked with coordinating governmental activities related to Hungarians abroad and building a handful of Hungarian foundations that would work on small, discrete projects with Hungarians living in neighboring countries.[51]

Renata Weber, a former dissident and director of the Open Society Foundation in Bucharest, claims that from the very beginning transnational organizations from the West were crucial to the promotion of positive changes in Romania.[52] Her training as a lawyer and her involvement in human rights issues may perhaps account for why she highlights the numerous, but often overlooked, activities of the Council of Europe during these early years. Representatives of the CoE indeed began visiting Romania in early 1990, and the council sent a delegation to observe Romania's first presidential elections.[53] Human Rights Watch confirms that already by 1991, the council's importance was evidenced by the number of Romanian officials seeking council attention and approval.[54] Like the United States, the Council of Europe's involvement during these years focused exclusively on human rights. For instance, at a January 1991 Parliamentary Assembly meeting of the council, Romania's prime minister received a cool reception by the council because of the restrictions put on the media and trade unions, as well the government's treatment of national minorities. Nonetheless, the Parliamentary Assembly meeting discussed economic reforms, general council policies, and the Gulf crisis—not emerging ethnic tensions in the East.[55] Three days later and based only on promises, the CoE granted Romania special guest status. As Weber herself admits, in the first few years of the decade, the Council of Europe acted like other international organizations; it ignored ethnic politics as its focus was elsewhere.[56]

Although Western governments did not shower Romania with financial assistance, international NGOs and private citizens from the West did travel there with the ambitious goal of trying to rebuild its shattered society, a fact often overlooked in estimating the international community's involvement.[57] The first human rights organization to visit Romania was the International Helsinki Federation (IHF), arriving in Bucharest on January 3, 1990—the very day that Romania's airport reopened after the coup.[58] In its first phase of involvement, IHF representatives conferred with Romanian dissidents to establish a national committee, initiated a dialogue with authorities, and gathered information on civil rights and the rights of minorities to present to national and international organizations.[59] Working with a thin staff and little money, the IHF was unable to diversify its activities or become a professional NGO until late 1993, when it received what it refers to as important financial support from abroad.[60]

The Project on Ethnic Relations (PER) also made inroads in Romania by 1991, but its mission and approach were quite different.[61]

> PER is dedicated to preventing ethnic conflict in Central and Eastern Europe, the Balkans and the former Soviet Union. PER was founded in 1991 in anticipation of the serious interethnic conflicts that were to erupt following the collapse of Communism. PER conducts programs of high-level intervention and dialogue, and it serves as a neutral mediator in several major disputes in the region. PER also conducts programs of training, education, and research at international, national, and community levels.[62]

While its mission seems simple, its strategies are tricky to categorize. They are neither strictly "second track" nor solely intergovernmental, yet this international NGO worked with government officials and nonstate actors to allay ethnic conflict in Romania. Allen Kassof, PER's former director, characterizes its activities appropriately as "track one and a half"; it is "diplomatic activity carried out by private persons dealing with decision makers."[63] From the start, this international NGO opted for a policy of promoting quiet contacts to urge the peaceful resolution of conflict in Romania.[64] After the violence in Transylvania in 1990, PER initiated what it refers to as "an intensive effort" to bring Romanian officials and Hungarian ethnic leaders together. Sponsoring its first conference in June 1992, PER invited the leaders of Romania's fourteen main ethnic communities. What Livia Plaks, PER's current director, recalls from this early period is that PER was largely working alone; while the Carnegie Corporation of New York approached PER in 1990 about becoming involved in the field of ethnic relations, and while the Swiss government later showed interest in their activities, Plaks explains that in these early years, PER was one of the very few international actors interested in ethnic relations in Romania.[65]

A Transnational Campaign Begins

As illustrated, transnational actors had some presence in Romania in the first few years after Communism's collapse; yet, ethnic conflict had not yet emerged as a chief concern. Only in 1993, as the region plunged into instability, did a transnational campaign focused on ethnic conflict management start to gather momentum. In this phase, several actors simultaneously focused on Romanian-Hungarian relations and majority-minority relations within Romania. Although the United States remained active in Romania, its strategies and prominence in the region did shift. Pressing international concerns in other parts of the world, such as Yugoslavia's bloody demise as well as the disappointing results of Romania's 1992 elections, resulted in a marked swing in the U.S. attitude toward this country. In part, the United States had to acknowledge the shortcomings of its reliance on democracy promotion alone to oust former Communist leaders from power. It registered its disappointment with Romania's political choices by reducing its aid substantially in 1993, 1994, and even into the second half of the 1990s.[66]

At the same time, U.S.-Romanian relations were not occurring in a vacuum and were part of larger international framework of relationships that began to hinge on developments in Yugoslavia. Despite the obvious weakness of Romania's political and economic transition, it suddenly began to be seen—rather unexpectedly—"as an island of stability in the Balkan maelstrom."[67] Instead of investing in partisan programs meant to oppose the government, the United States opted to cultivate closer relations with the government and focus on structural and institutional change.[68] During this second phase of involvement, U.S. activities were scattered and unfocused, relying on a combination of top-down and bottom-up strategies, and only sometimes did it make an explicit connection between aid, ethnic conflict, and minority rights. Human Rights Watch observed that in 1994 the United States in fact seemed to deemphasize human rights policies, even as tensions between Romanians and Hungarians intensified.[69] When it did notice ethnic problems, U.S. government officials referenced the activities and the principles of the CSCE/OSCE and the ongoing need for Romania to abide by international obligations.[70]

During this period, the evidence suggests that while the United States showed some interest in keeping ethnic tensions at bay, it eschewed a leadership role. In other words, while it lent its support to the activities of European regional organizations that were drawing attention to ethnic conflict and minority rights, the United States was reluctant to be a central player. However, by 1995, and coinciding with its military involvement in Bosnia, any indecision or hesitation over how to deal with ethnic conflicts in Romania was gone, and it adopted a clear message about the importance of ethnic conflict management and minority rights.

In contrast, Hungary's interest in its ethnic kin living in Romania never flagged, and its strategy continued to evolve. By 1993, Hungary had become an active participant in emerging transnational activities, prodding international organizations to make ethnic conflict and minority rights priorities. When Prime Minister Gyula Horn took office in 1994, he declared that Hungary's top priority was integration into Euro-Atlantic institutions. However, this did not mean the abandonment of fellow Hungarians living in neighboring countries; instead, Hungary used its new-found influence to underscore the call for states to adopt CSCE/OSCE and CoE standards to diffuse ethnic conflict and guard minority rights. Thanks largely to Hungary's efforts, the CoE passed Recommendation 1201, which called for the ad-dition of minority rights to the European Convention on Human Rights and in-cluded a nonbinding reference to collective rights. Meanwhile, the Hungarian government declared that it would become a model of interethnic accommodation, adopting generous legislation for its Roma minority (which comprised some 6 per-cent of its population).

The CSCE/OSCE was better positioned to take a leading role in ethnic conflict management. The new HCNM made the fate of the Hungarian minority a top pri-ority, and Max van der Stoel visited Romania several times beginning in August 1993. During these visits, van der Stoel not only met with government representa-tives, but he also made his way to Transylvania, talking with minority representa-tives and encouraging moderation on both sides of the conflict. The thrust of his strategy during these years lay in deepening and institutionalizing communication between Hungarians and Romanians in an effort to bolster moderate constituencies within both groups. This office also developed the West's message, emphasizing the need for compromise to secure international financial assistance.

Istvan Horvath, a sociologist at the Babes-Bolayai University (BBU) in Cluj, ex-plained that the high commissioner's visits to Transylvania were followed closely by ethnic Hungarians who considered van der Stoel the "Father of Minorities."[71] Part of the reason for this was that up until this point, the international community had not been represented by a single organization—let alone one influential person—who focused exclusively on this issue. Addressing Romania's Council for National Minorities in August 1993, van der Stoel detailed the CSCE/OSCE's evolution, the principles underpinning the Copenhagen document, and the organization's ap-proach to ethnic conflict prevention.[72] Indeed, this was the first time a major figure broached Romania's ethnic problems and connected them to the West's budding agenda. During his visits, the high commissioner met with an array of officials from different ideological positions. A human rights activist at the time recalls fondly the intensity of van der Stoel's engagement in these years, which came well before the EU and NATO became entangled in these issues. In Weber's eyes, the high commis-sioner's knowledge of the challenges facing Hungarian-Romanian relations and his willingness to communicate the concerns of Romania's human rights community to Romanian officials made him a crucial cog in the country's unfolding ethnic drama.[73] Ironically, van der Stoel was not only the messenger from the West, but he was also the link connecting Romanian government officials with the country's Hungarian minority and human rights activists.[74]

CSCE/OSCE involvement, as well as activities undertaken by the CoE, assumed an essential, normative dimension in Romania, as both organizations went to great lengths to bring international standards into view to resolve specific crises that had reared up in Romania.[75] The high commissioner repeatedly cautioned the Romanians that they were party to several international instruments related to minority rights and the peaceful resolution of conflict, including the 1992 treaty between Romania and the Federal Republic of Germany. He did not fail to emphasize that the CSCE/OSCE principles cited in this bilateral treaty concerning national minorities were now part of domestic law in Romania and thus needed enforcement for both international and domestic reasons. The HCNM's normative strategy not only referenced CSCE/OSCE principles and standards but appealed to the umbrella of international laws and norms to which Romania had committed itself. Van der Stoel pointed to Romania's promises to the CoE and its acceptance of the European Convention for the Protection of Human Rights and Fundamental Freedoms as well as lesser but additional protocols, including Recommendation 1201.[76]

During these years, from roughly 1993 through 1995, when the EU, NATO, and the U.S. government were just starting to narrow on ethnic politics, the OSCE/CSCE, the CoE, PER, and the IHF were working independently and in different ways to push this conflict toward resolution. The HCNM provided the official message of CSCE/OSCE governments and served as a go-between Romania and the European Union while PER brought Romanians and Hungarians to the table on a regular basis to bargain specific points of contention. All the while, CoE representatives were working behind the scenes to develop a comprehensive list of legal changes necessary for Romania to conform to its standards. Although emphasizing different aspects of the conflict, they crafted a similar message: Pragmatism, compromise, and interethnic accommodation were necessary for Western approval and financial support.

Coordination and Overlap

In the second half of the decade, with transnational actors declaring that the "job was done" in countries such as Poland and Hungary, and with Yugoslavia's violence still underway, international attention turned south and to other potential Balkan conflicts. Peace efforts in Bosnia made governments such as the United States and intergovernmental organizations such as the EU and NATO organizations take interethnic relations on Bosnia's borders more seriously.[77] Put differently, the transnational campaign to manage ethnic conflicts settled squarely on Romania, and by 1995 networking behavior ensued. Toni Niculescu, executive vice president of DAHR, states: "International influence in the second half of the 1990s went from implicit and indirect to blatant. . . . Even if Romanian officials did not agree with what the international community said or wanted, there was by this point no doubt about Romania's desire to join Euro-Atlantic institutions and its willingness to do what was necessary."[78]

What was noticeably different about the second half of the 1990s was the number of actors engaged in similar actions to avert ethnic conflict. They united the financial and military muscle of the EU and NATO with the legal expertise of the CoE and the firsthand knowledge and mediation efforts of the CSCE/OSCE. In addition to the more pronounced governmental efforts, a handful of international NGOs already active in Romania adjusted their focus to interethnic relations, providing the resources to support and implement governmental actors' focus.[79] Transnational involvement during the last years of the 1990s included an untold hodgepodge of top-down and bottom-up strategies, which were employed simultaneously, and the resources of governments, intergovernmental organizations, and international NGOs were—at long last—brought to bear on the problem of ethnic conflict in Romania.

It is true that the European Union responded to events in Romania almost immediately, and through its Phare assistance program it eventually became the largest donor to Romania in the 1990s. Despite these early efforts, ethnic issues and minority rights were a sidebar concern for this economic organization. The EU's Copenhagen criteria and Stability Pact, indeed, sent a message to Romania about the importance of regional stability and minority rights, but it was not clear how these general statements would translate in practice. When the EU signed an Associated Agreement with Romania, which initiated negotiations for future membership, it notably referenced the principles and provisions contained in several CSCE/OSCE documents and stressed the necessity of stability in Europe.[80] However, even at this point, the EU made no specific demands on Romania, and it had no actors on the ground involved in mediating ethnic tensions. Instead, its involvement in this area was linked to the activities of the HCNM and the CoE.

The EU's strategy for molding Romania's ethnic policies was almost identical to NATO's evolving policy of conditionality. In September 1995, NATO developed guidelines similar to those of the EU for its enlargement, which member governments could use to measure the "suitability of states" seeking NATO membership.[81] Among the conditions for new members included states displaying an observable commitment to the norms established by the CSCE/OSCE and the Council of Europe, specifically their intention to resolve ethnic conflicts and territorial disputes with neighboring countries.[82] While there was no fixed criterion for inviting new member states to join the alliance, it was clear that NATO was quite unwilling to import security problems. By December, after the NATO-led intervention in Bosnia produced the Dayton Peace Accords, Romania's strategic importance and, thus, its ability to manage its own ethnic conflict took on greater urgency. With a strong push coming from the United States, NATO separately started to press both Romania and Hungary to resolve their problems, dangling the carrot of NATO membership close for greater impetus. Even after NATO overlooked Romania in its first wave of expansion (in 1997), it maintained an active focus on developments in Romania, pushing the country to make necessary political changes and, in exchange, promising that NATO membership would inevitably be granted.

With NATO, the EU, and the U.S. government making ethnic conflict, borders, and minority rights priorities, and all referencing CSCE/OSCE-defined criteria to evaluate states' behavior, the role of the HCNM took on a new, more practical dimension. As Walter Kemp explains, once the European Union and NATO were "on board" and focused on interethnic conflict management, the HCNM used his influence and connections within these institutions to garner support for his recommendations.[83] Moreover, since neither the EU nor NATO possessed much expertise in the area of national minorities or human rights, they deferred questions related to ethnic politics and national minorities to the HCNM. As van der Stoel himself admits, when he wanted to be sure that the Romanians were listening to him, he would go to Brussels or to Washington to appeal to these powerful actors to support his cause.[84]

In the second half of the 1990s, as Romania at last made a clear break with its Communist past and transnational actors adjusted their focus, international NGOs, including several private foundations, also adopted a more active ethnic agenda. While the PER had always worked in this area, other NGOs such as the Open Society Institute Romania (OSI-Romania), the Foundation on Interethnic Relations, and the East-West Institute began to address the previously taboo issue of ethnic relations in Romania. Most NGOs tended to address ethnopolitical relations indirectly and from the bottom up, supporting research, education, and/or interethnic cooperation in civil society, but the work of PER was different and not strictly "second track." PER continued sponsoring conferences and forums with local elites, but its audience broadened as representatives of NATO, the OSCE, the EU, and the CoE joined these meetings. Thus, while PER once had brought Romanian officials and Hungarian representatives together in the early 1990s to air their grievances, by 1998, with NATO and EU membership almost an obsession for the Romanians, PER meetings became an international affair.[85]

It is hard to summarize, let alone detail the activities of all the international NGOs involved in Romania in the 1990s, because so many of the initiatives were small, geographically fixed in one city, or because they only indirectly hoped to smooth ethnic tensions. The Open Society Institute Romania (part of the Soros foundations network) was a notable exception; although this NGO was among the first international organizations to establish a presence in Romania by opening OSI-Romania in Bucharest in 1990, with an initial budget of about $1.5 million, it did not deal directly with interethnic issues until the late 1990s.[86] As its current director points out, given that George Soros, the foundation's founder, was born in Hungary, "the foundation was extremely careful about becoming involved directly in preventing ethnic conflict or managing Hungarian-Romanian relations."[87] Instead, the Open Society Institute Romania became a major player in more diffuse democracy-assistance efforts, opening the first grant-giving facility for domestic NGOs, providing money for numerous projects in civil and political culture, and funding a range of other educational, cultural, and public policy initiatives.[88]

Nonetheless, the problems posed by ethnic pluralism clearly informed its early decisions; when the foundation opened branch offices throughout the country, it did so in regions deemed crucial to the country's development and stability, including Cluj and Timosiara, because of the ethnic diversity there. After focusing on broadly defined "civic initiatives" for about four years, OSI-Romania staff started to prioritize public administration and legislative and justice reform. It was not until 1997, with the coming of a more tolerant political environment, that foundation officials felt comfortable taking on ethnic issues directly, providing the bulk of the funding to establish the Ethnocultural Diversity Resource Center (EDRC) with a goal to "contribute to the construction of democracy in Romania by improving the country's interethnic climate and promoting principles of ethnocultural peace and justice based on institutional solutions accepted by both the majority and minorities."[89] Based in Cluj, the EDRC is a grant-giving organization that provides funding for local initiatives seeking to promote tolerance and interethnic relations, publishes studies on interethnic issues, provides scholarships, and engages in training programs as ways to educate the population and promote grassroots change.

The Origins of the Romanian Model

Despite some backpedaling in 1994–95, by the decade's end, interethnic relations in Romania were on the mend and Romanian-Hungarian cooperation a reality. Romania did more than just sign international treaties and seek membership in Euro-Atlantic organizations. The country's desire to become part of the European Union, requiring it to adopt EU laws and regulations, meant that domestic laws, institutions, and notions of national interest were increasingly shaped by external actors. Prime Minister Adrian Nastase put it differently, claiming that, given Romania's foreign policy goals, international factors should be considered an internal factor in its domestic development.[90] The gradual institutionalization of international standards, through the creation of domestic instruments and the adoption of minority-friendly legislation, indeed demonstrates the ability of transnational actors to penetrate domestic politics.[91] Romania's progress and its move toward "rule-consistent behavior" is evidenced by, among other indicators, the European Council's December 1999 decision to begin accession negotiations with Romania as well as Freedom House's 1999–2000 favorable rating of its democracy.[92] The question is: To what extent did transnational actors influence these outcomes and thus interethnic cooperation in Romania?

U.S. diplomats who worked in the U.S. consulate in Cluj at different points throughout the 1990s confirm that by 1993, there was a noticeable turn within Romania; integration into Euro-Atlantic institutions became a top priority. Consequently, they do not accord international-level variables much significance in shaping ethnic relations. Instead, they highlight the bottom-up activities that took place throughout the country, acknowledging the role played by international NGOs such as the Soros foundations network, in funding grassroots initiatives. These diplomats also credit moderate politicians, underscoring the importance of Romanian leadership to changes in Romanian-Hungarian relations. Put another way, in order for transnational actors to affect outcomes, transnational preferences had to correspond to the preferences of Romanian elites and their definitions of national interest.[93]

In contrast, Romanian politicians, NGO activists, and academics I interviewed in Romania see the country's move toward interethnic accommodation differently, maintaining that *only* transnational involvement—with its increasing specificity about conflict management, stability, and minority rights, and the tangible and intangible benefits of yielding to international rules—can explain the preferences of

Romanian politicians and the increasingly tolerant behavior in the 1990s. Thus, the causal arrow flows from transnational actors to domestic ones through the multi-level strategies and normative pressure coming from Western governments as well as the CSCE/OSCE, the CoE, the U.S. government, and scores of NGOs. Toni Niculescu explains the differing perspectives this way:

> It doesn't surprise me that people from the West downplay the role of the international community while those of us sitting in Romania know very well its importance. In fact, there is no contradiction here; big, important actors never realize how important they are in shaping the domestic and foreign policies of smaller, weaker states. Just as elephants, they do not know their weight; powerful members of the international community do not realize the effect of their influence.[94]

Shifting Foreign Policies

Chapters 2 and 3 highlighted 1993 and 1995 as turning-point years for the transnational network that emerged to manage ethnic conflicts in Eastern Europe. These dates also help illuminate important developments in the Hungarian-Romanian conflict. We cannot forget that although there was some transnational involvement in Romania in the early 1990s, ethnic conflict was not a priority for any governmental actor until 1993. In 1990, when Allen Kassof (then director of the International Research and Exchanges Board [IREX]) started talking about the potential for ethnic violence in Eastern Europe in 1990, his warnings fell on deaf ears.[95] The U.S. ambassador in Romania and private foundations realized the urgency of this issue, but it was nearly impossible to get governments to adopt proactive policies. What was even more apparent in the initial post-Ceausescu period was the international community's tacit acceptance of ethnic cleansing, given its half-hearted response to events in Yugoslavia. A Hungarian sociologist from Cluj ventures that the international community's unwillingness to do more in Yugoslavia sent a clear message to nationalists in Romania: Ethnic issues were still a matter of domestic, not international, concern.[96]

In this context, Romania's nationalistic behavior in the early 1990s is hardly surprising, as international actors provided neither the pull nor the push for ethnic cooperation, and playing the nationalist card was an easy way for former Communists to gather supporters. During this period, Romania's leaders were clearly of two minds regarding the country's relationship with the West. They wanted and clearly needed economic assistance and favorable trading arrangements, but they strongly opposed internationalizing minority rights. Tellingly in 1991, as CSCE/OSCE representatives and experts opened a discussion about ethnic conflict, hoping to create a multilayered international regime, the Romanian delegation flatly objected, claiming that "intrusive international mechanisms" would only disrupt states' national unity and territorial integrity.[97] Yet, with every year, as a transnational campaign took shape and Romanian leaders embraced the goal of integration with Euro-Atlantic institutions, Romania's denial of the legitimacy of international involvement slowly gave way to tacit acceptance, then to cosmetic change, and finally, by the second half of the 1990s, the institutionalization of international laws and standards.

It is true that in 1993, the Romanian government adopted a more pro-Western attitude, declaring early in the year that CoE membership had become a top foreign policy goal. Despite the government's more conciliatory tone toward the West, it still maintained a close relationship with Russia, hoping that it could remain between the East and West. The hope for an independent path in its ethnic relations began to fade by the beginning of 1993, as certain, albeit still not well-defined messages began to emerge from the West: The road to Europe was through the CoE.

Although Romania's government depended upon the support of extreme nationalist parties, whose "hostility toward ethnic minorities" had become notorious, it nonetheless sought council membership for the symbolism it represented, and the eventual benefits that it believed would follow.[98] It is difficult to establish the precise cause for Iliescu's turn toward the West in 1993; in all likelihood, his behavior was probably due to a number of factors.[99] The desire for council membership was perhaps driven by souring of U.S.-Romanian relations in 1992 as well as Romania's dire economic situation. After the 1992 elections, in which former Communists beat opposition candidates, U.S. government assistance declined substantially.[100] The EU, also in the midst of concocting some ways to prevent violent ethnic conflict, had decided that it was time for the EU to gather some tools to deal with European security and to help prepare Eastern European countries for future EU membership.[101] In April 1992, it recommended that the European Agreements with Romania and Bulgaria contain a clause mentioning the states' commitment to human rights, democracy, and the recognition of minority rights. This was an important sign since such a clause was not contained in other European Agreements. Given Romania's desperate economic position and its lack of alternatives, the government's Western emphasis is not surprising. As the former minister of foreign affairs confirmed in 1996, in these very difficult years of transition, there has been no other objective that gathered "such a unanimity of views—which has actually been proven by every opinion poll organized in the last six years—from both the political forces and public opinion, than the idea of Romania's integration into Europe." [102]

In 1993, the only international organization that could help Romania start to realize its symbolic "return to Europe" was the CoE, even though it appeared to offer little material rewards. The council did not have funds for large amounts of economic assistance, and it certainly provided no guarantee that membership in it would lead to membership in any other regional body. At the same time, the bar for admittance was not high, and in the early 1990s, states only needed to agree in principle to council recommendations. Within six months of submitting an application for membership, Romania became a council member. Despite the fact that the binding character of council recommendations were questioned by some Romanian politicians, the country's leadership did not hesitate to accede to several CoE recommendations impinging on ethnic relations, including the Framework for the Protection of National Minorities, which it signed on the very first day it was opened in February 1995. (It was ratified by Romania in May 1995.) The Charter for Regional or Minority Languages, another recommended instrument, was signed in July 1995.

There is hardly a consensus on the impact of Council of Europe membership on Romania's domestic behavior. However, it is true that once Romania gained entry into this organization, there was no turning back; the international community now had the right to be involved in Romania's internal affairs, and Romanian politicians could not credibly debate the validity of council laws. With this said, ethnic relations appeared—at least on the surface—to go on as they did before, and ethnic tensions even escalated. By 1995, Milada Vachudova confirms that domestic political discourse in Romania was so steeped in ethnic nationalism aimed against the Hungarian minority that not only did Illiescu's party engage in such behavior, but so did virtually every opposition party. [103] On the legislative front, Romania did its best to avoid implementing CoE laws. For example, Romania signed the Council of Europe's Recommendation 1201, which added a protocol related to the rights of national minorities to the European Convention on Human Rights. Nonetheless, the inclusion of this provision into a bilateral agreement with Hungary was the leading obstacle for the Romanians because it included the delegation of administrative autonomy, a special political status for ethnic minorities, and the granting of collective rights to minority groups, which were viewed by nationalist politicians as "stepping stones" to the country's dissolution.

Given these domestic realities, it is easy for some to discount the CoE's role in Romania. Yet, the history and evolution of debates within Romania related to ethnic politics conform surprisingly well to expectations laid out by constructivists about how states become socialized and internalize international norms.[104] The point is not limited to social mechanisms. Members of this transnational network used a combination of material and normative resources to push ethnic cooperation to fore, hoping to change the incentives of elites and the balance of power among groups in society. Without trying to impose anything specific, transnational actors instead put the burden on local leaders to arrive at their own solutions.

As witnessed elsewhere with other transnational networks, after first accepting the legitimacy of international involvement, governments often sign or adopt international instruments, but they do so for thinly veiled manipulative reasons, believing that they will placate their international audience and evade genuine change. However, the disjuncture between words and deeds cannot last forever; as transnational networks work from the top down and bottom up and domestic-international connections multiply, the domestic political environment opens up. As others writing on democracy promotion and the effects of the EU have explained, as the Romanian government opened itself up to the international community, it simultaneously allowed a variety of public and private actors with unlimited access to its population. The effects of these numerous interactions on Romania are difficult to track, but bottom-up efforts to engage and empower members of the opposition in the substance of democracy paid off in the 1996 election, where opposition candidates competed with the government over the party that could best bring Romania closer to Europe.

Those who were closely involved in Romania's legal reforms and human rights policies in the early 1990s maintain an important process began to transpire once Romania became a member of the CoE.[105] Within a matter of a few years, Romanian leaders went from rejecting international involvement completely, to recognizing the existence of international standards, to referencing these standards publicly, and finally to explaining and justifying their behavior in light of these standards. The council's legal procedures, which tend to be seen as objective and nonpartisan and identify the deficiencies of a state's laws in light of European laws helped create a different legal framework in Romania. One cannot forget, moreover, that because of Romania's membership in the CoE, national and local laws were, for the first time, legitimately subject to foreign scrutiny and discussion. This meant that if Romanian behavior was at odds with CoE laws and recommendations—which it was at many points in the 1990s—its leaders had to, at least, pay lip service to the concerns of this European organization. In other words, by the mid-1990s Romania had to account for its behavior—even if there was no immediate and direct punishment. Such accountability for the Romanian government was both new and significant, because council norms gained what scholars call "prescriptive status," and Romanian leaders could no longer argue their validity. Instead, they had to justify the country's leadership in adhering to or trying to implement council laws.[106]

Membership in the CoE moreover provided a direct but often overlooked link for Romanian politicians and bureaucrats to similarly situated individuals from the rest of Europe. This contributed to the growth of a community of politicians who could independently assess the gap in Romania's foreign policy goals with its domestic behavior.[107] The infusion of training programs, seminars, and practical assistance for politicians and emerging leaders no doubt helped Romania surmount the numerous problems associated with implementing council laws. By 1993, such initiatives, often carried out by international NGOs, had become a standard practice for several transnational actors, including the CoE, the CSCE/OSCE, the EU, and the U.S. government.[108] Istvan Horvath claims that by the end of 1993, one could already discern the impact of transnational actors such as the CoE, the CSCE/OSCE, and the PER by a close reading of the changes in discourse related to majority-minority relations.[109] Almost overnight, the vocabulary for talking about the interethnic conflict and possible solutions changed.

In 1990, for example, Romanians and Hungarians each talked about the conflict in terms of the past and their particular ethnic group's historical claims to Transylvania. Just a few years later, the debate shifted to "a rights discourse," as each group realized the need to couch their arguments and demands in legalistic terms of rights based on different international instruments and norms. Horvath further explains that the CoE was a crucial actor for two additional reasons. First, council reports, usually written in neutral, legalistic language, explained in clear, nonpolitical terms the deficiencies of Romanian laws (it did not accuse or judge). At the same time, since the council did not have any way of enforcing existing standards, it put the burden on local officials.[110] Put differently, the lack of an enforcement mechanism encouraged change without the bite of coercion.

In all likelihood, the Romanian government thought that its membership in the council would not significantly affect its behavior toward its national minorities; it could "have its cake and eat it too." What it could not envision, however, were the challenges that would ensue, both domestically and internationally, when the country did not live up to its commitments, which ultimately became a thorny issue with Western actors. Domestically, local actors bent on reform and integration with Euro-Atlantic institutions provided a check on government claims. Internationally, more governmental and nongovernmental organizations began to narrow on Romania's promises and the threat of ethnic conflict. Foreshadowing the eventual split within Romania between the moderates (who realized early on the need for compromise and pragmatism and follow through) and conservatives (who maintained the fiction that ethnic nationalism could be sustained concurrently with a pro-Western orientation), President Iliescu described Romania's membership in the council as "historical," signifying a decisive endpoint. At the same time, moderate Romanians and Hungarians also saw the membership as a historic event; however, they emphasized that this was only the beginning of change.[111]

One of the most significant shifts in Romania's foreign policy behavior, with clear implications for interethnic and intraethnic relations with Hungarians, was the conclusion of a bilateral treaty with Hungary. The general impetus for the bilateral treaties signed by Eastern European countries in the 1990s is not in dispute; the importance of bilateral agreements, as a means of promoting regional stability, came from outside the region.[112] The question is: Which international actor pushed these countries toward this significant foreign policy? The answer is clearly several actors, all of which saw such a treaty as a requirement for continued Western involvement. In reality, the treaties were impacted by the overlapping, complementary strategies and signals emanating from several transnational actors—all pushing Romania and Hungary into signing a treaty that, in addition to other issues, addressed minority rights.

By March 1995, with the EU-sponsored Stability Pact signed, high on the list of necessary requirements for future member states was the conclusion of bilateral treaties that settled border issues and protected the "rights of persons belonging to national minorities."[113] At virtually the same time, NATO made bilateral treaties a requirement for its future members. In 1994 the CoE passed its Framework Convention, which called for the political commitments of the CSCE/OSCE to be transformed into legal obligations between states to protect the rights of individuals belonging to minority groups.[114] However, much earlier, in 1991, the CSCE/OSCE emphasized the importance of transfrontier cooperation and bilateral and multilateral agreements as ways of resolving border issues, especially when an ethnic group straddles a political frontier. Thus, the same objective, for the same reason, was sought by several transnational actors, and each worked in its own way to push for this outcome. Ultimately, a treaty was signed in 1996 between Romania and Hungary, with profound effects on the countries' relationship. In the year following, twenty ministerial arrangements were made with the two countries, including plans for joint military units.[115] As hoped, it also helped smooth internal majority-minority problems within Romania.

Although nationalists within Romania and Hungary opposed the treaty's conclusion, moderates were eager to gain Western approval, realizing the importance of the treaty to international actors bent on regional stability. After missteps in 1993–94, Hungarian leaders realized that their concern for their ethnic kin abroad was coming into direct conflict with its foreign policy ambitions. U.S. Defense Secretary William Perry warned Hungary and Romania that "NATO was not willing to import security problems."[116] Some Romanian politicians credit domestic leadership with the treaty's conclusion, but they still mention the EU *and* NATO because the treaty's conclusion was "vital to, if not a precondition for, their membership in these organizations."[117] The timing of the treaty was auspicious because the following summer both the EU and NATO were deciding on the states that would be included in the first wave of enlargement.

Although the carrot of EU and NATO membership was important for providing the necessary incentive structure to get Hungarian and Romanian leaders to finalize the treaty, other transnational actors and a confluence of top-down and bottom-up strategies helped foster the necessary environment that allowed moderates to prevail. The CSCE/OSCE and the CoE, for instance, were important because of their intimate knowledge of Romanian-Hungarian relations and their respective efforts to help finalize the language of the treaty. In fact, Romanians and Hungarians knew full well that neither the EU nor NATO dealt with the details of ethnic relations; instead, they rightly assumed that the EU and NATO looked to the CSCE/OSCE, and particularly the HCNM for his insight.[118] Renata Weber confirms that by 1996, with the EU's and NATO's enlargement meetings on the horizon, Romanian leaders were beginning to realize that mere promises would not be enough and that to gain admission into these organizations, they each needed to prove why they should be chosen (over their neighbors). With deadlines looming and moderate politicians in both countries eager for success on this issue, van der Stoel kept the pressure on, engaging in "shuttle diplomacy" to the region to help develop a formula that would allow the treaty's conclusion to move forward.[119]

Nonetheless, one cannot overlook the ongoing, sustaining efforts of the Project on Ethnic Relations, which had been working behind the scenes to keep the lines of communication open, providing regular opportunities for Hungarians and Romanians to negotiate their demands. This is perhaps why President Iliescu singled this organization out, claiming that the elite-level discussions it initiated in the early 1990s represented "pioneering activities" in Romania and helped launch the diplomatic negotiations between Romania and Hungary.[120] After a series of meetings in the early 1990s, PER invited Romanian officials and Hungarian leaders to the

United States in early 1995, where prominent diplomats, including President Carter, were on hand to help Romanians and Hungarians discover solutions to ethnopolitical problems in Transylvania.[121] The involvement of such prominent American leaders no doubt sent a clear sign to Romania and Hungary: The United States wanted a compromise; benefits would result for appropriate behavior and consequences for intolerant, uncooperative behavior. Steven Burg concludes that because of PER's unique contacts and approach, it contributed a good deal to mediating Romanian-Hungarian tensions.[122]

While PER might have been instrumental in initiating and sustaining the dialogue between the parties, the HCNM assumed a different role in mediating the crisis over the bilateral treaty. The main impediment for the conclusion of the treaty was the CoE's Parliamentary Assembly Recommendation 1201, which the Hungarian government insisted on inserting into the treaty. Although Romania had signed and ratified this council recommendation, it did so with reservations because of a clause that referred to a minority's right to autonomous authority. Throughout the summer of 1996, the high commissioner labored, in his words, to clarify each party's views and intentions.[123] According to Gabriel Andreescu, van der Stoel played a critical role as the chief, if not the sole representative of the international community, keeping the official dialogue going and shining the international spotlight squarely on the issue.[124] Working closely with the CoE, the HCNM facilitated its issuance of a new interpretation of Recommendation 1201. Thus, the Romanian-Hungarian treaty included a footnote that says that "The Contracting Parties agree that Recommendation 1201 does not refer to collective rights, nor does it impose upon them the obligation to grant to the concerned persons any right to the special status of territorial autonomy based on ethnic criteria."[125] Crucial then was the HCNM's ability to help the parties arrive at a solution that was more palatable to the Romanians without upsetting the Hungarians. This explains why Teodor Melescanu, Romania's foreign minister from 1992 to 1996, stated that the activities of the HCNM were a catalyst to the conclusion of these negotiations.[126]

These simultaneous activities and overlapping influences explain why it is difficult to identify a single actor that was casually important to the success of the treaty. As Daniel Nelson puts it:

> With increasing urgency in 1995 and '96, the EU, NATO, and American politicians, diplomats and analysts urged the countries to complete the bilateral treaty as a necessary, albeit symbolic step towards full entry into Western institutions. For the US,

the message was carried to Budapest and Bucharest in many visits by State and Defense Department Officials, senior National Council staff members and members of congress, and the business and academic community.[127]

Even if the United States took the lead in trying to convince the parties to conclude a bilateral treaty, it did not take the credit. Instead, it explained the successful outcome in terms of broader trends and Western influence. U.S. ambassadors to Bucharest and Budapest later acknowledged that "both sides are committed because they know that the treaty clears an important hurdle to an even more historic goal: integration with the West." [128]

These same transnational influences affected more than the conclusion of specific treaties. The sway of this transnational network in fact shaped Romania's general foreign-policy orientation in the 1990s. Its turn to the West thus made it more willing to look to the East and South, cooperating economically, politically, and socially at various levels with its neighbors. Romania's interest in regional cooperation was undoubtedly motivated by its wish to improve its reputation with the West. Since 1989, Western countries had encouraged transitioning countries in the East to cooperate with each other as a way of resolving historical ethnic differences and promoting stability and reform. Romania's participation in regional initiatives steadily increased throughout the decade. Many of these arrangements are not strictly governmental but are grassroots initiatives sponsored or initiated by regional actors and implemented by international NGOs seeking to promote transborder cooperation from the bottom up.[129] The EU-inspired Stability Pact is the regional initiative that is most often cited, but Romania participates in a number of other regional initiatives, including the Southeast Europe Cooperation Process, the Central European Initiative, the South-East Europe Defense Ministers, the South-Eastern Cooperation Process, and NATO's Southeast Europe Regional Initiative.[130] For Romania, this outreach to its neighbors to the east and south was never seen as an alternative to closer relations with the West; rather, it was an opportunity to introduce trade rules, economic instruments, and practices that were consistent with European norms and would facilitate Romania's preparation for joining the European Union.[131]

By 1999, Romania's foreign policy behavior betrayed not only a clear Western orientation but also an Eastern direction, embodied in both governmental and nongovernmental initiatives that impinged on interstate and intrastate ethnic relations. There could not be a single purpose for Romania's Eastern turn; clearly such a shift in foreign policy served many objectives. However, there is little doubt that

Romania's participation was part of a larger pattern of behavior. Simply, Romania wanted to integrate with the West, and good relations with its neighbors and, in particular, with Hungarians at home and abroad was a step toward this goal.

Institutionalizing Ethnic Accommodation

Seeking membership in Euro-Atlantic organizations, signing treaties, and participating in regional organizations, all of which implicitly or explicitly address ethnic relations, says something about the lure of the West and the potential of transnational actors to influence outcomes. However, a more important sign of influence is the presence of internationally inspired domestic instruments to mediate ethnic conflict. In this respect, the imprint of transnationalism is evidenced in domestic legislation, which often quotes international instruments verbatim, and in government bodies modeled on those in West and meant to channel ethnic demands and monitor government behavior. To be clear, the existence of domestic mechanisms does not say anything about their implementation or the socialization of new norms, but—parallel to changes in society and the development of grassroots organizations—they make it more difficult for the government to disregard its commitments. Domestic debates over legislation related to education and language in the second half of the 1990s illustrate that by this juncture, contestation shifted from transnational actors rallying for change to the domestic ones debating the urgency of reform—a process that increasingly divided Romanians and Hungarians into moderates and conservatives.

Romania's constitution betrays the country's initial ambivalence toward its ethnic minorities, as well as the delicate path it needed to negotiate with the international community. Like most of the countries in Eastern Europe, Romania's 1991 constitution guarantees fundamental rights and freedoms for *all* its citizens. The rub for the Hungarian minority are the articles that assert that Romania is a unitary, national state where Romanian must be spoken. It provides for the rights of national minorities to preserve and nurture their identity, but the thrust of this document, according to national minorities, signals the majority's desire to protect the Romanian nation and exclude its minority population.[132] However, the constitution also notes that "where any inconsistencies exist between the convents and treaties on fundamental human rights Romania is a party to, and internal laws, international regulation shall take precedence," which is not insignificant. The International Helsinki Federation considers the inclusion of this article an indication of the importance however unspecified of the international community's influence.

Members of the National Salvation Front made a series of promises to the Hungarian minority in 1989–90, but there were few concrete efforts to diffuse ethnic conflict until President Illiescu sought to upgrade the country's guest status to permanent membership in the CoE. In March 1993, the Council for National Minorities was established, even though the idea for such a body was discussed as early as 1991.[133] Michael Shafir credits the Project on Ethnic Relations for this accomplishment, claiming that its officials had proposed such a body as a compromise between the Hungarian minority's demand for a national ministry and the Romanians' outright refusal to create one.[134] Rather than arising from domestic inspiration, the timing of the council's creation and its structure reflect Romania's desire to repair its image in the West; as the Austrian daily *Die Press* noted, it seems clear that in light of other behavior in Romania, the council was set up with an eye to the forthcoming deliberations on Romania's admission to the Council of Europe.[135]

The structure and declared purpose of the Council for National Minorities indicate Romania's facile attempt to inspire the illusion of change. Although the council was created as an advisory group for the president's office, the government did not even consult with minority representatives prior to establishing it. The specific legislation explains: "The Council for National Minorities *ratifies* government decisions concerning the problems of the national minorities."[136] Finally, despite significant differences among Romania's minority populations, the council provided equal (rather than proportional) representation for the country's eighteen national minorities. This "egalitarian" structure provoked Dan Oprescu of Romania's Department for the Protection of National Minorities to admit that rather than giving minorities a voice in governance, this was an attempt to water down their influence, attempting to buy them off to gain their support.[137]

Transnational actors were not fooled by this simulated change; when the high commissioner on national minorities visited Romania for the first time in June 1993, he addressed the council and noted the importance of such a body that acts as an agency to promote regular discussion about minority issues and interethnic dialogue.[138] Obviously realizing the problems with the Council for National Minorities, van der Stoel recommended that the government strengthen its infrastructural capability and resources and give it more authority by allowing it to initiate legislation.[139] The council's weaknesses were not masked for long; six months after it was created, the Hungarian minority withdrew from it because of the government's unwillingness to implement council recommendations. Although transnational attempts to bolster the council may have failed in the short term, they were not ignored completely. As anticipated by Michael Shafir, the adoption of the rhetoric of participation and instrumental change could not forestall genuine change, as it was only the beginning and not the end of the transformation of ethnic relations.[140] As democratization continued and moderates on both sides gathered strength, they shouldered the government into providing more authentic channels for minority participation.

The most significant domestic changes came in late 1996, once the new government invited the Hungarian party to become part of the coalition government. While Hungarian presence might appear to preclude the influence of transnational actors, it instead demonstrates the cumulative effect of the transnational actors that had been pushing for such domestic changes in Romania. No one predicted precisely what the Romanian Democratic Convention would do, but it was clear by this point that despite the enormous diversity of political parties within this coalition and among the Romanian populace, there was one focal point where objectives merged: a desire to integrate into Euro-Atlantic institutions. It was also apparent by 1996 that "the West"—whether it was the EU, NATO, the CSCE/OSCE, or Western governments—was not satisfied with Illiescu's government and was increasingly focused on regional stability and ethnic cooperation. Put differently, the push and pull of transnational pressures did not coerce Romanian actors to change, nor did they specify what elites needed to do. Instead, various actors made ethnic conflict management a priority, establishing material and ideational reasons for compromise. Given this environment, domestic debates centered on how to realize Romania's foreign policy goals.

In explaining the "revolution within a revolution" that happened when the Hungarian minority was invited into the coalition, some Hungarians in Transylvania, in fact, trace the birth of this coalition to the PER's activities in the early 1990s. From the beginning, this NGO identified its strategy and goal: to work with elites to stimulate dialogue and foster moderation and trust in the hope that domestic actors would find a way to improve ethnic relations.[141] Thanks in part to this NGO's discreet but groundbreaking efforts, moderates had emerged by the end of 1996, elbowing out conservatives and bringing together groups that seemed so unlikely just a year earlier. In explaining the origins of this turning point in Romania's history, others point to the mediation of the HCNM office and its "sustaining efforts," because its leader, Max van der Stoel, worked diligently to cultivate relationships and support pragmatism. But, as PER official Livia Plaks notes, what may have been most important was that by the mid-1990s, a handful of international organizations were working along similar lines. "PER was doing its work and the HCNM was doing its work, as was the CoE; they all invited each other to meetings and kept each other informed, because they sought the same outcomes."[142]

The flurry of activities and aspirations that had developed among Western actors had finally reached Romania. Max van der Stoel agrees, confirming that, by the second half of the 1990s, Romania was a clear model of overlapping decentralized governance: Several important international actors (including NATO, the EU, the CoE, and PER) each performed a role but, most importantly, all were shoring Romania in the same direction—toward the peaceful resolution of its ethnic problems.[143]

Transnational involvement not only fostered this moderation, which set the stage for the new government to invite the Hungarian party into the coalition, but it also helped to bind the fragile coalition together. In this regard, the HCNM was indispensable in keeping the coalition government from fracturing from 1996 to 2000. The tenuous coalition was threatened again and again "by the inability of the government to find parliamentary majorities for its minority-related legislation and the subsequent threats by the Hungarian minority. During all these years, the high commissioner closely followed the process and was instrumental in keeping the Hungarians in the government."[144] It was not as though the CSCE/OSCE had the power or resources to coerce anyone, but it played a crucial role in connecting interested players, keeping the light bright on Romania, and providing the overarching normative framework for ethnic conflict management.

In 1997, the Romanian government established the Department for the Protection of National Minorities, which was a longstanding demand of the Hungarian minority. However, the structure and function of the department were almost identical to the expectations and recommendations made by the HCNM in August 1993 with regard to the Council of National Minorities.[145] As the HCNM specifically called for, the department had the right to initiate legislation and supervise the initiatives of other branches of the government on issues affecting national minorities. It was also granted the authority to monitor the implementation of relevant legislation. In other words, by 1997 most of the HCNM's 1993 recommendations were fulfilled. While not without its problems, the department was better regarded than the Council for National Minorities, and it was effective for precisely the tasks for which the HCNM had originally advocated on behalf of the council. With a larger budget and genuine power, the department became a forum for dialogue and a locus for ethnic-related legislation and activities.[146]

As critical as minority participation was, Romania's ethnic friction with its Hungarian minority was closely bound to debates over legislation related to language and education. It may be easier to demonstrate the power of transnational actors in the area of education policy, since domestic actors often reached an impasse and the high commissioner's input was sought to resolve stalemates. The passage of the Law on Education in June 1995, seen by Hungarians as restrictive and discriminatory, is often referenced to demonstrate the helplessness of transnational actors in the face of domestic opposition. This is because the European Parliament, the U.S. government, and the HCNM, among other transnational actors, all criticized it and tried to dissuade Romania from adopting it. Its passage certainly indicates the dilemmas encountered, and it exposes the reality that transnational influence is neither certain nor immediate. Yet, the passage of this law did not mean the end of transnational involvement; on the contrary, in the years that followed, several transnational actors urged Romania to revise this law while they encouraged the Hungarian minority to travel through domestic and international channels to reduce its impact.

After the Law on Education was passed, the Hungarian minority threatened acts of civil disobedience, but it also lobbied the CoE, the European Parliament, the CSCE/OSCE, and Western governments to try to force Romania into reversing this law. Van der Stoel was instrumental in identifying a compromise and deflating tensions, shifting the emphasis from the law itself to its implementation. Traveling to Romania several times after the law had passed, van der Stoel proclaimed that the Romanian government had clarified and explained to him the law's intentions. Given the Romanian government's promises internationally and domestically, there was, in his opinion, significant flexibility in the law's implementation that would allow Romania to abide by its legal commitments.[147] The involvement of the HCNM had the immediate effect of reassuring the minority population of the international community's ongoing interest, because van der Stoel was the only individual Hungarians associated with this issue. At the same time, the high commissioner reminded Romanians that even though the international community could not prevent governments from adopting legislation that it opposed, it would not sit by idly. As a representative of the largest intergovernmental organization with ties to the EU and the CoE, the HCNM stayed involved to ensure that this issue stayed on the international radar screen. In effect, what the HCNM was able to do, with the help of other transnational actors, was to shine the light brightly on Romania's ethnic troubles while offering a way to soften the blow of this harsh legislation.

In early 1996, the HCNM recommended a revision of the law.[148] It took more than a year, and only when the Hungarian party threatened to withdraw from the government, did the government approve an "urgent ordinance" that would allow for the implementation of amendments to this law. Basically, the amendments did away with the provisions that were most problematic for the Hungarians; they allowed for instruction in one's mother tongue at all levels of education and abolished the provision stating that subjects such as history and geography had to be studied in Romanian.[149] Two years later, and with the combined pressure coming from domestic and transnational actors, the Romanian government approved an amendment to the law, doing away with its most of its discriminatory provisions. Significantly, this final version met all of the major recommendations made by the HCNM since the beginning of his involvement in 1993. As van der Stoel admits, the Romanians did not respond immediately to his recommendations and the international community's concerns, mostly because domestic opposition prevented it; nonetheless, by the end of the 1990s, his office's influence, particularly on domestic legislation related to education, was quite apparent.[150]

Transnational actors' ability to deescalate ethnopolitical crises was evident later in the 1990s, as a debate raged over the fate of the Babes-Bolyai University. In 1998, a crisis within the governing coalition loomed as Hungarian party representatives threatened to withdraw if some resolution over the university could not be reached. According to Salat Levente, the vice rector of Babes-Bolyai University, the HCNM and the CoE, as well as the U.S. government, were all embroiled in resolving this issue.[151] Yet, it was the HCNM's input and opinion that domestic political leaders sought to resolve this issue, because he was the West's point-person, the expert who could understand this issue the best and elaborate the West's message. Van der Stoel visited Romania at least seven times between 1999 and 2000 to focus on this crisis.[152] Ultimately, he backed the creation of a multicultural university with instruction in both Hungarian and German, which did not please either the Romanians or the Hungarians. The so-called Petofi-Schiller University never came to pass, but van der Stoel's involvement went a long way to placate both sides while forcing them toward a domestically inspired compromise.

Promoting a Civil Society

Transnational networks also seek to increase the number and strength of independent groups that can monitor the government, advocate for interethnic cooperation, and engender social tolerance.[153] Tracing the specific effect of such initiatives is not easy, but Tom Gallagher asserts that there is "no shortage of evidence" that links grassroots attempts to transform Romanian society to the growth of democratic values in the second half of the 1990s.[154] The prominent role played by civil society in the 1996 election suggests that a domestic constituency committed to democracy and peace, while still relatively weak, had started to form.

In 1990, there were only a few NGOs in Romania; by the decade's end, there was—thanks to foreign support—an impressive number involved in myriad tasks, from health-care provision, to education programs, to human rights advocacy.[155] USAID estimated that in 2000, some twenty-three thousand NGOs were registered in Romania, though significantly fewer were considered active in public life.[156] The majority of these were involved in service provision, but numerous others were busy with a variety of activities that impinged on ethnic relations, including ones involved in promoting human and minority rights, governance, and economic development. Some of the earliest NGOs were part of the National Salvation Front and were instrumental in thwarting ethnic violence in 1990–91.[157] According to the vice president of the Civic Alliance, an umbrella organization that included human rights and prodemocracy organizations, civil society organizations were pivotal to preventing violence in the fall of 1991 when the "Covasna-Harghita Report" was brought to the public's attention.[158] When the Transylvanian city of Miercurea Ciuc was besieged by soldiers, police, and a crowd of between three and five thousand, NGO activists from the Civil Alliance appealed for negotiation and reconciliation, succeeding in the most dangerous of moments to prevent bloodshed.[159] At other points in the 1990s, a handful of NGOs were credited with improving Hungarian-Romanian relations in at least three multiethnic cities in the 1990s.[160]

Nongovernmental organizations need not focus specifically on conflict prevention or minority issues to play a positive role, since most are more broadly interested in strengthening democracy, improving transparency, and promoting tolerance. Research conducted on civil society in Romania does indicate that Romanian NGOs have played a role in placing a number of issues, not discussed under the previous regime, on the public agenda, including human and minority rights.[161] Moreover, since nongovernmental actors are strongly identified with a commitment to democracy and tolerance, by association and reputation, there is reason to believe that even the presence of NGOs—regardless of their specific focus—indirectly promotes and sustains interethnic cooperation.

The evolution of the Hungarian Alliance, which was initially established as an NGO to both promote democracy and to represent the Hungarian minority, is instructive of the positive transformation of Romanian society in the 1990s. DAHR was locally inspired, but it quickly became part of the transnational community of public and private actors seeking to manage interethnic relations in Romania. Its own evolution, from a NGO to a political party seeking to participate in the political system, demonstrates not only the importance of these transnational linkages to enhancing the legitimacy of domestic groups but also of their role in socializing elites on how to best pursue their goals. A one-time adviser to the president of the Hungarian party admits that from the very beginning, Hungarians in Romania were concerned with and connected to the international community. Although this organization was bent on improving the situation of the Hungarian population in Romania, its members realized and depended upon members of the international community to achieve its goal.[162]

By late 1993, the Hungarian party had institutionalized its international connections, joining international organizations, working with Western human rights NGOs, and lobbying Western governments and regional organizations for change in Romania. Put differently, it exercised its voice in Romanian politics instead of trying to exit or undermine the Romanian state. Although the Hungarian minority initially felt betrayed by the conclusion of a Romanian-Hungarian treaty, the party's leadership immediately revamped its tactics and rhetoric, further elbowing aside radical elements within the party. In the 1996 elections, the party nominated the moderate senator, Gyorgy Frunda, to stand as a candidate in the presidential elections.[163] In doing so, the Hungarian minority hoped to both strengthen its image with the West and increase its legitimacy among Romanians as a political party with an interest in reforming Romania from within.

Once a part of the governmental coalition, Hungarians suspended their claims for territorial autonomy and rejected the tactics it had used in the early 1990s. Instead, the party worked with Romanian parties while still appealing to international organizations for support. For example, after the restrictive Law on Education was passed, DAHR members continuously lobbied the CoE, the European Parliament, the CSCE/OSCE, as well as Western governments to keep pressure on the Romanian government to reverse or amend this law. The relationship between this one-time NGO-turned-political-party and the international community was complex. As one Romanian expert explained, EU discourse and Western ideas shaped its goals and strategies while, at the same time, it used EU policies and other institutions to legitimate its own demands.[164] Given that ethnic conflict resolution is ultimately about changes in attitudes and the adoption of new norms, the transformation of the Hungarian minority is telling. In a few short years, this opposition group went from being perceived as a dangerous traitor to becoming a legitimate political party and partner in Romania's transformation.

U.S. diplomats provide anecdotal support for the contention that grassroots, bottom-up initiatives had a positive effect on ethnic relations in Romania. As Michael Mates of the U.S. Information Office in Cluj put it: "The Open Society Institute Romania is definitely a player, and even though the organization did not get involved in ethnic issues until the late 1990s, this foundation empowered so many people and started dozens of nongovernmental organizations throughout the country, it is easy to think that it has directly and indirectly encouraged peaceful change."[165]

In effect, NGO development not only enabled individuals and created organizations, but it distracted people from concentrating on ethnic tensions. Mates further ventures that the ethnic peace in the multiethnic city of Timisoara is related to the large number of NGOs, nurturing democracy, tolerance, and interethnic relations. Others, including a former Open Society Institute official in Romania, believe that while transnational attempts to build civil society have undoubtedly helped many people and produced a professional NGO sector, the evidence linking civil-society organizations to interethnic peace is still difficult to gauge.[166]

It is true that despite an impressive surge in the number of NGOs in the 1990s, Romanian NGOs were never central players in public life, and they did not become the primary agents of change that transnational network members aspired to create—at least at the national level. As in other postcommunist countries, Romanians' NGOs suffered a high mortality rate; most lacked domestic support, and they possessed a limited capacity for affecting public policies. Moreover, most of the country's NGOs relied heavily on foreign funding, and the majority of them lived from project to project with few able to make long-term strategic or financial plans.[167] However, this was not universally true, and in many cities, including Cluj, Timiosoara, and Bucharest, NGOs have been quite active, enjoying notable success. By the end of the 1990s, the conclusions about Romania's civil society were quite mixed. Although there was significantly less funding from abroad, many indigenous groups had cropped up spontaneously to respond to local needs.

Given the success of Romania's annual NGO conferences, the country's ability to attract local, regional, and international NGO attention, and its participation in an array of regional and international initiatives, it is fair to say that Romanian society is linked to the broader transnational community of actors interested in the management of ethnic conflicts. Romania not only receives some financial benefits from these connections, but these ties strengthen the legitimacy of local groups and their demands on the government. As Dan Petrescu observers, an active civil society—regardless of the focus of its activities—has helped Romanians through tough times and economic hardship and, perhaps most importantly, educated citizens on how democracies work.[168] Romania's civil society played a decisive role in the 1996 election, driving home the deficiencies of the governing coalition in light of the country's European aspirations. It is not hard to see how this behavior and the populace's foreign policy goals simultaneously affected the peaceful trajectory of interethnic relations.

Conclusion

Romania may not be the shining model of interethnic accommodation, but as the president of PER put it in 2001, Romania "can be considered a good example of ethnic understanding and progress."[169] One of the most persuasive indications of the country's progress was demonstrated after the 2000 elections, when President Illiescu was returned to office and the government pledged to work closely with the Hungarian party to select mutually agreeable candidates for the leadership of several counties and city councils.[170] In January 2002, a formal agreement was signed with the Hungarian minority aimed at solving, in a top-down way, problems related to schools and historical monuments.[171] Both acts suggest that Romanian leaders saw the Hungarian minority as a legitimate, and even central, domestic player. Thus, although the troubles in Transylvania have not disappeared, there are many reasons for optimism, and the peaceful trajectory of the 1990s is likely to continue, not because of the constraints and incentives emanating from the international community, but because practical politicians realized the necessity of compromise, and because certain values associated with conflict management and ethnic tolerance are being internalized.

I have not attempted in this chapter to discount the primary importance of domestic actors; early on, politicians in Romania acknowledged the need—however difficult the process might be—for dialogue and compromise with the Hungarian minority. However, I assert that without the progressive, reinforcing strategies used by members of a transnational network to steer actors toward ethnic peace, ethnic politics in Romania in the 1990s would have looked quite different, and perhaps become more violent. While specific international organizations may have affected outcomes in discrete ways, no single government or intergovernmental organization played a dominant role in pushing Romania to resolve its ethnic problems. Moreover, while conditionality—often touted as *the* reason why Eastern Europeans changed their behavior and ethnic relations improved—was undeniably important, this strategy was never used in isolation or by a single actor. In fact, conditionality, as employed by NATO and Western governments as well as the EU, was used in conjunction with mediation, normative pressures, and bottom-up attempts to promote democracy and strengthen civil society.

In sum, ethnic cooperation in Romania in the 1990s was encouraged by a transnational network of public and private actors that coordinated policies and made decisions interdependently because they were working toward the same goal. Iulian Chifu, director of the Center for the Prevention of Conflict and Early Warning, explains the relative importance of transnational actors this way: "There was no one international actor that pushed Romania toward dealing with ethnic issues. The relative influence of transnational actors depended on the particular 'pull of the moment'; that is, the country's proximity to membership in a specific regional organization determined its overall impact, but influence neither started nor ended there."[172]

Consequently, the CoE's presence in Romania was important in 1992–93, as was the nudge from the CSCE/OSCE from 1993 on, because the high commissioner's visits to the region, in which he elaborated the West's agenda and priorities in Romania. By 1995, NATO—first and foremost—provided the motivation for the replacement of cosmetic changes because it, more than the EU, demonstrated both an interest in managing ethnic conflicts on Bosnia's borders and the possibility of membership in the short-term. Yet, what is important to emphasize is that these organizations never worked in a vacuum; instead, their strategies and behavior were linked to and dependent upon the evaluations and recommendations of other actors, namely the HCNM and the CoE. Thus, by the second half of the 1990s, with several transnational actors involved in and sending similar messages to Romanian leaders about what was necessary for membership into Euro-Atlantic organizations, it is impossible to discern which actor or strategy prevailed and led to accommodating behavior in Romania.

The evolution of ethnic relations in Romania suggests that although a variety of transnational actors and both top-down and bottom-up strategies had discrete effects on Romania's model of interethnic cooperation, what was more important was the synergy among transnational actors, how their strategies overlapped, and how their objectives for the country reinforced each others' activities.[173] The triumph in Transylvania thus speaks to the role played by transnational actors but, more importantly, it highlights both the reality and transformative potential of networks.

FIVE

Quiet on the Russian Front

The Evolution of Ethnic Politics in Latvia

By 1990, the Baltic republics of Latvia, Estonia, and Lithuania had already initiated what would become their eventual liberation from Communism and Soviet domination. Languages long displaced by Russian were heard again, and exiled dissidents returned home to become political leaders. Although these countries, with a total population of fewer than 10 million, were firmly committed to democracy and desirous of membership in Euro-Atlantic institutions, ethnic nationalism challenged these goals and the region's stability. Latvia's situation was especially problematic; ethnic Latvians represented barely half of the country's population of 2.6 million and remained a minority in seven out of eight of the country's largest cities. In Riga, the country's capital, Russian speakers edged out those speaking Latvian.[1] The Russian diaspora was considered to be the crucial source of instability in the post-cold war era, but the potential for ethnic strife was believed to be particularly great in Latvia because of its unbalanced ethnic composition and its leaders' strident nationalizing agenda.[2]

Grave predictions aside, the country's ethnic dilemmas never erupted in violence, and by the decade's end, ethnic policies related to citizenship, language use, and education were in line with European standards. Several government offices had been established to monitor human rights practices and help peacefully integrate the Russian-speaking population, and national discourse notably eschewed terms such as "occupation" and "repatriation" in favor of "naturalization" and "ethnic pluralism." To be sure, Latvia's ethnic knots were not untangled entirely, but interethnic coexistence and Russia's acceptance of the status quo gave reason for optimism.[3] Given the nationalist rhetoric and exclusionary policies of the early 1990s, how did transnational strategies seek to moderate Latvian ethnic politics? Did strategies and transnational involvement make a difference in this interethnic conflict?

Latvia is a small country with a relatively short modern history, but because of its potential for instability and its conflict with Russia, a substantial amount has been written about this state.[4] A few scholars acknowledge the absence of interethnic violence in Latvia, but they do not explore its origins in any depth. For example, Paul Goble mentions the similar economic status of the Latvian and non-Latvian populations as a possible hypothesis for ethnic peace.[5] Michael Mandelbaum emphasizes the importance of the international environment to the trajectory of majority-minority relations in places such as Latvia, but he does so without providing details about specific organizations, mechanisms, or policies that are likely to affect these relations.[6] Several other scholars, including Judith Kelley, Heather Grabbe, David Smith, and Jekaterina Dorodnova, seek to understand the evolution of ethnic politics in the Baltic states, but they are largely interested in demonstrating the causal significance of one organization or strategy.[7]

Latvian scholars such as Nils Muiznieks and Ilze Brands Kehris instead recognize and highlight the emergence of what they define as "a transnational network"; this network of European-oriented Latvian officials worked hand in hand with Western governments and organizations to inform interethnic relations in the 1990s.[8] Their views are particularly relevant given that Muiznieks is currently the minister for national integration and Brands Kehris is the director of the Latvian Center for Human Rights, and both have worked extensively on ethnic politics and with members of the international community.

As well as secondary sources, my own research into Latvian ethnic politics benefited from access to restricted CSCE/OSCE mission documents.[9] Since the CSCE/OSCE's Latvian mission was on the ground working throughout the country from 1993–2002, providing monthly reports to its members, these reports are used extensively. In addition, I conducted more than a dozen interviews in Latvia in 2004, as well as others conducted in other parts of Europe. A one-on-one interview with Max van der Stoel regarding his activities in Latvia strengthened my argument concerning Western intentions and strategies for dealing with Latvia's ethnic difficulties.

I do not attempt here to delve into the history of Latvia's ethnic dilemmas; there are plenty of thorough accounts of the country's history elsewhere. Instead, my aims are, first, to summarize the nature of interethnic politics in Latvia and explain its large minority population, and, second, to identify the transnational actors seeking to guide Latvia's transition and describe their efforts to contain ethnic tensions. Although concerns developed earlier, it was not until Latvia's first independent elections in 1993 that transnational actors directly focused on the country's ethnic dilemmas. In particular, I explore the activities of the CSCE/OSCE, the CoE, the HCNM, and the UN Development Program (UNDP), which had all made ethnic relations in Latvia a priority. As the decade progressed, the U.S. government, the

Council on Baltic Sea States (CBSS), the European Union, NATO, and the Open Society Institute (OSI)–Latvia formed a transnational network to prevent ethnic-based conflict in Latvia. My third aim is to closely examine evidence of ethnic cooperation in order to isolate the contributions of transnational actors. This analysis demonstrates that in Latvia, as in Romania, 1993 and 1995 were significant turning points for ethnic policies. Although members of the international community started to prod Latvia about interethnic relations in 1993, only two years later were transnational actors in prime network mode, sharing information, making interdependent decisions, and providing overlapping messages to Latvian politicians in an effort to restrain escalating ethnic tensions.

From National Oppression to Ethnic Conflict

If Artis Pabriks is correct in asserting that the ethnic policy of a government is determined not only by its immediate interests and outside influences but also by the population's historically developed understanding of nationhood, Latvia's history of foreign domination is at least worth mentioning.[10] Before conquest by the Russians in the eighteenth century, Latvians had already been subjected to the rule of the Germans, the Swedes, and the Poles. As one scholar put it, years before Latvia was occupied by the Soviet Union, its people were the target of at least two strong drives of assimilation: a weak, spontaneous infiltration drive from Germany, and the clear, more systematic Russification policy.[11] If forced to characterize the history of this small nation wedged between Estonia and Lithuania in two words, they would be domination and subjugation.

An independent Latvian state emerged in 1918 with the conclusion of World War I. One undeniable characteristic was its multiethnic composition; although ethnic Latvians represented about 75 percent of the population, there were significant German and Russian populations.[12] Given its ethnic diversity and the international community's concern over the situation of minorities, the Latvian interim government developed an array of liberal ethnic policies to ensure peace and stability. (Case in point: the Law on Nationality granted Latvian citizenship to everyone, regardless of ethnic origin; all Latvian citizens were given equal rights, and minorities were guaranteed a voice in government.) Latvia's 1922 constitution reversed some of these policies, but its general language still declared that all citizens in Latvia were equal. Later in the 1930s, authoritarian leaders claimed that the constitution's progressive and generous ethnic polices deprived the country of its unity and the creative forces of nationalism.[13] Nonetheless, for most of the country's interwar history, not only did ethnic harmony prevail, but Latvia became a haven for Russians fleeing Communism in their homeland. In contrast to Latvian-Russian relations, ethnic discomfort with Latvia's small German minority was disproportionately intense, since Germans represented less than four percent of the population.

In 1940, twenty-two years after Latvia achieved independence, Soviet tanks rolled into Latvia, initiating the brutal process that transformed the country into a compliant Soviet republic. The Soviet hold was interrupted briefly by the German occupation of Latvia from 1941 through 1944. When the Soviet Union regained its hold, it continued (if not intensified) its stranglehold on the country, resuming deportation of Latvians and the execution of those deemed threatening to Soviet power. As elsewhere, the Soviet Union's "national question" was resolved not through accommodating institutions and policies but by the imposition of Communist ideology and the indoctrination of the population. The myth of the "new Soviet man," unencumbered by primitive ethnic identities, allowed Soviet interests and loyalties to transcend national loyalties.[14] Massive industrialization programs in the Baltic States not only put the Soviet Union on the fast track for economic development, but it simultaneously served to dilute Latvia's ethnic identity. As native Latvians were pushed from their land, Russian speakers from other parts of the Soviet Union were urged to settle in the country's strategic north.

Like other union republics in the Soviet Union, Latvia was autonomous in name only. Although led by indigenous Latvians, those in power received their marching orders from the Communist party in Moscow. Since Latvia's industrial growth exceeded the rest of the Soviet Union, it required a consistent level of migration to the republic to fulfill the increasing demand for labor. As migrants settled and Russification policies continued, the Russian language replaced Latvian in schools and in public life. At the same time, Russians enjoyed a privileged status vis-à-vis Latvians, and since Russian was spoken in all public institutions throughout the Soviet Union, only about a quarter of non-Latvians could claim even proficiency in Latvian.[15] The oppressive Soviet-language policy and superior attitude aimed at other ethnic groups meant that non-Latvians had neither the need nor the desire to learn Latvian.[16] In spite of these policies, however, the Latvian nation remained among the least Sovietized of the republics.

Mikhail Gorbachev's call for *openness* and *reconstruction* as ways of reforming the Soviet Union had a significant (if unintended) effect on national revival, especially among the Baltic peoples. In June 1987, an anti-Soviet demonstration in Riga culminated in Latvia's "atmoda" or "awakening," which united about 250,000 Latvians under the Latvian Popular Front and provided a firm foundation for the country's independence movement.

Independence and Latvian Nationalism

Even before independence was declared, debates in Latvia concentrated on the question of citizenship. The so-called "zero option," heralded by the Latvian Popular Front in 1989, which promised that all inhabitants of Latvia would become citizens, quickly lost to arguments supporting the principle of legal continuity. Legal continuity meant that since recent changes in Latvia did not lead to the establishment of a *new* state but instead signalled the end of the state's unlawful occupation, all laws prior to the Soviet occupation were reinstated. In March 1991, these discussions were stymied by a nonbinding referendum on independence where almost three-quarters of Latvia's population voted in favor of restoring Latvia's independence. With more than 30 percent of the non-Latvian population supporting secession from the Soviet Union, there appeared to be considerable room for interethnic cooperation with the country's large Russian-speaking population.

However, the sudden collapse of the Soviet Union five months later pushed citizenship debates in Latvia toward an immediate but untimely closure. The head of the Bureau of Legal Affairs of the Parliament of the Republic of Latvia at that time put it this way: "After the collapse of the Soviet Union, there was a real need to define the citizenry as a whole." [17] Later in 1991, the Latvian Supreme Council passed a resolution with the force of law, opting to abide by the principle of legal continuity, and the laws created by the prewar Latvian state were officially reinstated. For the Russian-speaking population, this was a tremendous setback and cause for concern because it meant that only those citizens or descendants of citizens of pre-1940 Latvia could receive citizenship. While these policies were largely in accordance with international law and human rights norms, the politics and discourse in Latvia was unmistakably nationalizing, and given concurrent developments elsewhere in the postcommunist space, inherently problematic.

As the head of the Latvian National Independent Movement declared, Russians in Latvia "are not even second class citizens; they are 'nobodies' having rights no greater than a Russian would have travelling to Sweden." [18] The radical politics blossoming in Latvia further led the government to issue deportation orders to segments of the Russian population, and thousands of non-Latvians began to emigrate, fearing that they would have no place in an independent Latvia. In a seem-

ingly pointed message levelled at the non-Latvian population, the government announced that the naturalization process would include residency, basic knowledge
of the constitution, and proficiency in Latvian. Naturalization, moreover, would not
be made available until mid-1992. To contribute to the anxiety of non-Latvians desiring citizenship, officials added that only a new parliament could revise this restrictive law.[19] With these decisions, nearly a quarter of the country's population was
left stateless, with no chance for smooth and timely naturalization, and only those
who were citizens in 1940 (and their descendants) would be allowed to vote in the
country's first post-Soviet elections.

In other attempts to restore the country's national identity, Latvian politicians
adopted laws on language and education meant to return Latvian language to public life. The 1992 amendments to the 1989 Law on Languages tightened requirements that the Latvian language be used in official documents, government offices,
and public facilities.[20] The amendments also created the State Language Center,
which allowed government representatives to conduct random inspections and
issue fines to those not adhering to these tenets. For ethnic Russians the changes in
Latvia were dramatic and paralyzing, but given their political status and their lack of
opportunities, there was little they could do short of emigration.

These nationalizing policies, alongside the continued presence of Soviet troops
in Latvia and the existence of the Soviet Skrunda radar station (the Soviet Union's
most westerly radar station and a prominent, if imposing, presence in Latvia since
1971) exacerbated interethnic tensions in Latvia and complicated Latvian-Soviet
and then Latvian-Russian relations. A bilateral treaty between Latvia and the Russian Federation was signed in 1991 that laid the foundations for interstate relations,
but its content and intentions were left unclear for several years. A series of encounters with Russian troops in 1991 and 1992, during which the Russian military essentially resisted efforts by the Latvian government to establish authority over them,
contributed to the deterioration in Latvian-Russian relations and an intensification
of intraethnic relations.

From the very beginning of Latvia's move toward independence, Latvians
maintained a two-pronged campaign to guarantee sovereignty without engender-
ing inter- or intrastate conflict. While one prong was aimed at Moscow, the other focused on obtaining the diplomatic support and financial assistance of Western
governments and international organizations.[21] As tensions mounted in 1992–93,
Russia adopted a similar strategy, looking to the international community for help
in resolving Latvia's ethnic dilemmas and, more specifically, protecting the rights of
Russians living there. Although Latvian-Russian relations improved significantly by

the middle of the decade, ethnic tensions again escalated in 1998 after a group of Russian pensioners held an unsanctioned rally in Riga. The Latvian police responded with force; although there were no injuries, within two days the Russian government reacted so strongly to the "oppression" of the Russian minority in Latvia that Russian-Latvian relations sank to an all-time low.[22] Ethnic relations waxed and waned, and not until 1999, with the EU's decision to open negotiations for Latvia's eventual accession, were there clear signs that the progress made would not be reversed.

Transnational Involvement in the 1990s

By the time Latvia regained independence in 1991, its leaders had already indicated their commitment to joining the community of democratic European states, signalling a strong desire for membership in Euro-Atlantic institutions. From the beginning, certain members of the international community such as the U.S. government, the Russian Federation, and the CSCE played a crucial role in solidifying the country's sovereignty. The following is not intended to provide an exhaustive account of transnational initiatives in the 1990s; instead, it details the strategies used by important intergovernmental organizations and NGOs to contain ethnic tensions in Latvia.

Several external actors involved themselves in Latvia's transition in the early 1990 by supporting political and economic reform, but in Latvia, as in Romania, ethnic politics only became a significant concern in 1993, and not until 1995 did transnational strategies become noticeably overlapping and reinforcing. This is because the violent ethnic strife in Bosnia had pushed the EU and NATO into creating their own tools to counter ethnic conflict, and their strategies of conditionality worked alongside the strategies of mediation, normative pressure, and democracy promotion. Although the effectiveness of conditionality is taken for granted, this strategy was never used in isolation and was always part of a broader package of top-down and bottom-up transnational efforts to encourage accommodating behavior by the Latvian and Russian governments and Latvia's Russian-speaking population.

In the Empire's Wake

Given the unique situation of Latvia and its relationship to the Soviet Union, it is fair to say that one of the most important influences in the first few years was the Soviet Union and then its legal successor, the Russian Federation. During the fall and winter of 1990, relations between Moscow and Riga deteriorated, as the Kremlin increased its pressure on the Baltic republics to abandon their drive for independence. Until the Soviet Union's collapse in August 1991, its involvement in Latvian ethnic relations can only be characterized as negative and destabilizing. Beginning in late 1990, a spate of explosions shook Latvia, and in February 1991, a blast shattered the windows of the Latvian Communist Party headquarters in Riga, thereby continuing low-level acts of violence throughout the year. In January 1991, for instance, in an attempt to reassert its control over the country, the Latvian Communist Party asked Moscow to intervene to bring down the government and disband the legislature.[23] From February until its own disintegration that August, the Soviet Union maintained an ongoing campaign to halt Latvian attempts at independence by fomenting instability and interethnic tension.

During these years, Boris Yeltsin was driven by his desire to push Gorbachev out of office and was relatively unconcerned with the need to strengthen the position of the Russian Federation within the changing configuration of sovereign states. As such, the fate of Russian speakers living in Latvia had yet to emerge as an important priority. To distance himself further from Gorbachev and the Soviet Union's policies, Yeltsin even cheered on the Baltic States' bid for independence. Consequently, Russia was one of the first countries to recognize Latvia's independence, hinting that if the Soviet Union disappeared, Russian-Baltic relations might assume a different, cooperative course. Within two years of the Soviet Union's dissolution, the Russian Foreign Ministry had concluded eight bilateral treaties with former republics, all of which contained a standard section on minority rights and were based on international human rights standards of the UN and the CSCE/OSCE.[24] Yet, since Russia was designated the legal successor of the Soviet Union, it also inherited many of its extant problems and national concerns, and the fate of Russians abroad was pushed onto the domestic agenda. With 250,000 ethnic Russians living outside the country's borders, the question of the "near abroad" and the cultural discomfort of Russians living in the Baltic States took on great urgency.[25]

By late 1991, Vladimir Zhirinovsky, leader of the ultranationalist Liberal Democratic Party, successfully tapped into nationalist concerns in the presidential elections and garnered a surprising number of supporters. By early 1992, and largely because of his inability to find another way of unifying Russia's highly polarized society, Yeltsin too began to exploit the issue of ethnic Russians abroad.[26] For Latvians, Russia's growing nationalist rhetoric was particularly disconcerting because Russian troops in Latvia constituted the largest number of foreign troops of any country in Europe. Intent on the immediate withdrawal of the Northwestern Group of

Forces (NWGF), which was estimated at between 48,000 and 60,000, Latvians made eliminating this foreign militia a top priority with the Russian government. Latvia's demands, however, were increasingly blocked by growing nationalist sentiment in Russia. By early 1993 Roman Szplorluk claims that "the Russian question became the most important problem facing Moscow's diplomacy."[27] Meanwhile, the opposition continued to use the question of Russian speakers in the Baltics against President Yeltsin with unfailing success. Although no aggressive foreign policy action was ever taken, the unqualified Westernism displayed by President Yeltsin and Foreign Minister Andrei Kozyrev ended, as tensions between Yeltsin and conservative members of parliament bled into foreign policy issues.[28]

By the summer of 1993, a rift within the Yeltsin government was clear, producing schizophrenic tendencies within the government over what should be done about ethnic kin living outside Russia's borders. The president and the foreign minister maintained a cautious but concerned attitude, while the vice president adopted a more aggressive tone, even questioning the legitimacy of the new post-Soviet borders, arguing that it was time to steer policy away from its Western orientation, which was decimating Russia's identity.[29] Similarly, the minster of defense contended that it was time for Russia to "do more for its people abroad," declaring his readiness to fight for the honor and dignity of the Russian people.[30] With similar passion, he even told one Russian newspaper that "only the army is in a position to defend Russians."[31] Rhetoric aside, the Russian government showed tremendous restraint, developing what Heather Hurlburt calls a "multilateral track approach" to deal with its compatriots abroad.[32] That is to say, instead of relying on a single strategy to influence interethnic relations in Latvia, Russia created what Hurlburt refers to as a "network of ties" with governments and intergovernmental organizations, working primarily through the CSCE/OSCE to ensure the peaceful resolution of the ethnic problems facing Russian speakers in Latvia.[33]

Russia was not the only neighboring country to weigh in on Latvian politics. From the beginning of the country's transformation, Latvia's Baltic neighbors tried to ensure the country's peaceful secession while bolstering democracy and human rights. Burdened by many of the same concerns, post-Soviet Baltic States created the Baltic Assembly in November 1991 to stimulate cooperation between parliament representatives from the three republics and encourage consultation on domestic policies. Although only a consultative body, the assembly played an important role in getting national parliaments to coordinate their responses to common dilemmas, including problematic relations with Moscow and the management of large minority populations. The Baltic Assembly led to the establishment of

the Baltic Council in October 1993, which provided a legal framework for cooperation between the Baltic States and the Baltic Assembly. Together these intra-Baltic
influences not only helped build regional standards and affirm common responses
to ethnic problems, but they pushed Latvian leaders to harmonize their policies
with their Baltic neighbors.[34]

In March 1992, a third organization, the Council of Baltic Sea States (CBSS),
was born, embracing a dozen states plus the Europe Union. Among the central issues this regional security organization focused on was human rights, including the
rights of persons belonging to national minorities. Two years later in 1994, the Office of the Commissioner on Democratic Institutions and Human Rights was
founded. Known as the Baltic States high commissioner, Ole Espersen was perceived
by some as a regional ombudsman. Espersen worked in tandem with the
CSCE/OSCE's high commissioner, the EU, the CoE, and the UN to motivate the
region's promotion of human rights and to help countries manage the difficulties
inherent in majority-minority relations.

After Latvia passed the October 1991 resolution that left so many inhabitants
stateless, intergovernmental organizations such as the UN and the CSCE/OSCE
started to comment on the country's ethnic situation. Although neither organization debated the legal bases of Latvia's policies, they could ill afford to ignore Russia
completely, and the exclusion of the Russian-speaking community was a boldly legislated reality. The UN sent a fact-finding mission to Latvia, which pointed out that
while no gross human rights injustices had taken place, the decisions of the Latvian
government and other events had given rise to anxiety.[35] At the CSCE/OSCE's
Helsinki Summit in June 1992, Russia agreed to internationalize its problems with
the Baltic States and to allow the CSCE/OSCE to monitor troop withdrawals from
the region.[36] Perhaps in exchange for Russia's acquiescence, the CSCE/OSCE
adopted a declaration on aggressive nationalism, racism, chauvinism, and anti-
Semitism in an attempt to influence the behavior of the Baltic States.[37]

While the CSCE/OSCE was directly involved in mediating Latvian-Russian relations in these initial years, the CoE also weighed in on the legal implications of
Latvia's October 1991 resolution, claiming that even if this decision was uncomfort-
able for Russian speakers in Latvia, it was not illegal. Latvia applied for membership
in the CoE almost immediately after declaring its independence, and by early 1992,
representatives of the council started to make regular visits to Latvia, focusing in
particular on Latvia's citizenship law and policies related to national minorities.[38]
The council initially maintained that there was no legal problem with the country's
citizenship law because "international law leaves ample leeway for states to enumer-

ate conditions for granting citizenship."[39] After several visits, and in the atmosphere of Russia's vigorous attempts to internationalize this issue by drawing parallels to ethnic conflicts elsewhere, the CoE adopted a markedly different tone and message in late 1992: Even if the 1991 citizenship law was not illegal, Latvia's membership would be delayed because the law was not well-defined.[40]

By this point in time, officials from other regional European organizations were taking note of the developing problems. For example, EBRD observed that while the October resolution did not violate any specific rules, it strongly countered a number of basic principles of human rights.[41] It was clear that although foreign governments, international organizations, and nongovernmental organizations consistently rejected Russia's self-serving assertions of human rights violations in Latvia, there was cause for concern. Transnational actors were increasingly troubled by Latvia's nationalizing, exclusionary policies, which openly complicated its relations with the West. To make matters more urgent, developments in Latvia seemed headed for international violence. The CSCE/OSCE's creation of a high commissioner on national minorities, together with Russia's aggressive, nationalistic attitude, steered international attention toward a direct focus on Latvia's ethnic tangles.

Under the International Spotlight

Although Latvia's road to independence started in the spring of 1990, the transition from a Soviet republic to an independent state became technically complete only after its first parliamentary elections in the summer of 1993.[42] These elections coincided with the West's growing concern with the political exclusion and social isolation of the country's Russian-speaking population, and with the development of new tools to adapt to the post-cold war security environment. As Russia stoked the West's fears of ethnic violence, making specific demands on Latvia's leaders before it would complete the withdrawal of Russian troops and using phrases such as "ethnic cleansing" to characterize Latvia's behavior, a transnational campaign bent on containing ethnic conflict in this Baltic State took hold.

Regardless of the validity of Russia's claims, transnational actors needed to take notice because of the potential effect of these tensions on regional stability.[43] They also responded because of Russia's newfound attitude in 1993 and based on its conscious attempt to lure international support to its side of the conflict. Almost overnight, the Russian government redirected its concerns over Latvia's treatment of its Russian minority toward Western governments and regional organizations, and it noticeably repackaged its strident rhetoric. Like the Latvian leadership, Russian leaders too seemed to appreciate the importance of adhering to, at the least, the discourse of this transnational network. Russia thus stressed its appreciation of the role international organizations could play in helping Russians remain in Latvia and their ability to resolve this foreign policy dilemma. Instead of relying on inflammatory statements to describe developments in Latvia, Russia reached out to the international community, using "rights discourse" and emphasizing its "intention to employ all methods, *acknowledged by international law,* to prevent any violation of the rights of compatriots abroad."[44] Throughout 1994, Russia's "Western campaign" continued, with its foreign minister making a special appeal to CSCE representatives and leaders of international organizations to acknowledge the laws in Latvia that "didn't correspond either to Latvian realities or the norms of international law."[45]

The CSCE/OSCE was involved in Latvia's transition from the beginning, but after 1993 its involvement increased in both scope and domain, helping focus international attention squarely on the troubling implications of its ethnic policies. Although the CSCE/OSCE lacked the traditional forms of power that would allow it to coerce states or direct other organizations, it was clearly well-positioned to lead transnational efforts in this issue area. Because of its unique historical role during the cold war, some note that the CSCE/OSCE was the only international organization with a significant political presence in the region until 1997.[46] Latvia was one of the first places the CSCE/OSCE's newly installed HCNM visited. The high commissioner not only visited Latvia several times in early 1993, but he visited Russia to reassure the former superpower of the office's neutrality and interest in conflict prevention as well as its concern with the protection and promotion of human rights. Van der Stoel contends that the Baltic States were at the top of his agenda when he took office in January 1993, and he hurried there to allay the intensity of intraethnic relations and what he saw as the fomentation of hatred fixed upon the Soviet Union.[47]

As in other ethnically charged places, the HCNM used a mixture of direct mediation and normative arguments to persuade Latvian politicians to amend laws and practices to manage ethnic tensions. In an April letter to the minister for foreign affairs of the republics of Estonia, Latvia, and Lithuania, the HCNM laid out some concerns regarding the countries' ethnic minorities.[48] At the same time, he confirmed what other international experts and governments would later admit—that there was not any evidence of persecution among national minorities in Latvia, and there was no real prospect for violence in the country. Nonetheless, he defended transnational involvement, asserting that the CSCE/OSCE not only worked to prevent ethnic-based violence but it would contribute to harmony and dialogue among various groups.[49] Thus, the goal became galvanizing Latvia's national identity while nurturing harmonious relations with its large non-Latvian population.

Initially, van der Stoel made more than a dozen recommendations, most of which focused broadly on citizenship issues, including the need for the adoption of a new citizenship law that provided rules for naturalization, more lenient language and residency requirements, exclusions for stateless children, and exceptions from language tests for individuals over sixty.[50] During these early visits, the HCNM office concentrated its energies on drafts of Latvia's proposed citizenship law, in particular on provisions related to the government's intention to create a quota system and demanding qualifications for naturalization. Even at this early stage of establishing the West's interests in Latvia, the HCNM and the CSCE/OSCE did not work alone; they coordinated their responses and recommendations with other regional organizations, namely the CoE.

By 1993, the CoE, like the HCNM, took issue with the inclusion of strict naturalization quotas in Latvia's citizenship law.[51] In step with the HCNM's recommendations and in contrast to its earlier statements, its message to Latvia was that the country would be denied membership in the CoE if changes were not made to its citizenship law—in light of the high commissioner's recommendations.[52] Already, Latvian leaders seemed to sense the incipient coordination and overlap between these groups' intentions and requests. In October 1994, the chairman of Latvia's parliament sent a letter to the parliament heads of all CoE member countries "urging them to support Latvia's early admission and stressing that Latvia had in fact developed its citizenship legislation in compliance with CSCE norms."[53]

At the same time, the CSCE/OSCE did not rely solely on the HCNM's office to contain ethnic tensions in Latvia. After a fact-finding mission in September 1993, the chairman in office argued that Latvia needed further CSCE/OSCE engagement because of the country's large number of alien residents and how these stateless people might affect Latvia's future, as well as the issue of Russian troop withdrawal. Within two months, a CSCE/OSCE mission was established in Latvia with a broad-based mandate to address citizenship issues, monitor interethnic relations, and provide a reliable source of information for CSCE/OSCE member states. Like the HCNM, the mission was intended to function as a conflict-prevention instrument, gathering information and supplying early warning to member states if conflict escalated. As the decade progressed, the mission's duties expanded as needed. For example, mission representatives monitored the dismantling of the Skrunda Radar, which had long been an obvious and wounding sign of Soviet domination; mediated issues related to Russian military pensioners; and supported the naturalization process, working hand-in-hand with the naturalization board and other domestic actors to stimulate healthy ethnic dialogue and integration.[54]

Dr. Ilze Brands Kehris of the Latvian Center for Human Rights and Ethnic Studies claims that the CSCE/OSCE mission performed a number of functions that are generally overlooked and underestimated.[55] Unlike other international actors, the mission had a sustained presence in Latvia and its representatives developed credible relationships with government officials and members of civil society. Mission representatives also travelled throughout the country providing "visiting hours" to hear and record the complaints of Latvian residents. Thus, the mission acted like a kind of international ombudsman. Explicitly or implicitly, representatives relayed to Latvian society European principles and standards related to democracy, human rights, and conflict management. As Falk Lange, of the Office of the HCNM, explained, "The HCNM's office would work with the Mission's staff, trying to discreetly convey to Latvian government officials and NGO activists what needed to happen in Latvia and what the international community expected, rather than pushing for specific changes."[56]

As "insider third parties," mission representatives engaged in "quiet diplomacy"; they worked with members of friendly NGOs to strategize about the best way to deal with the country's unique ethnic problems. The expectation was that the mission would last six months, but because of its achievements and ongoing international and domestic support, it remained active until for almost a decade, closing its doors in 2002.

Without a doubt, the U.S. government was actively supporting the Baltic states' bid for independence. However, like other external actors, it did not turn its energies to ethnic politics until 1993, and then largely because of security concerns generated by Russia. U.S. concern with Latvian ethnic politics was neatly summarized by two former U.S. presidents, Jimmy Carter and Richard Nixon. Carter warned that U.S. relations with the Baltic States would be complicated by what he considered "to be mistreatment of Soviet minorities in Latvia and Estonia."[57] Shortly after Carter made these remarks, Nixon wrote an article that appeared in the *New York Times*. Taking a different angle, Nixon claimed that U.S. support of Russia's current leadership was crucial, and that one of the most effective ways of helping Yeltsin domestically would be to champion the rights of the 25 million Russian speakers in the Baltics and other post-Soviet states bilaterally and in international forms.[58] Secretary of State Warren Christopher's 1993 visit to Latvia reflected these concerns, and he pointedly linked the withdrawal of Russian troops to the behavior of the Latvian government toward its Russian population, urging the Latvian government to "act generously" regarding the adoption of a naturalization law.[59]

During this period, the United States relied on economic incentives and bottom-up, broad-based democracy-promotion initiatives to influence outcomes in Latvia. Its economic assistance and democracy-promotion programs were announced with much international fanfare, as evidenced clearly by President Clinton's historical trip to Riga in the summer of 1994. Nonetheless, the United States tended to rely on a more discreet strategy when it came to containing ethnic conflict, privately informing Latvian politicians of its concerns and position on specific issues. Olafs Bruvers, director of the Latvian National Human Rights Office and a former member of parliament, recalls that although regional actors such as the HCNM, the CSCE/OSCE mission, and the CoE had a high profile in interethnic issues, this did not mean that they in fact affected Latvia's behavior; Latvia was very concerned with what the United States had to say.[60] Like Bruvers, Igor Pimenov, the former director of the Latvian Association of Schools of Russian and a Russian human rights activist, asserts that when it came to setting the agenda in Latvia, the United States and NATO should not be ignored.[61] This is because by 1993, the U.S. government not only emphasized the importance of human rights, but it identified the need for a different and generous naturalization law, wanting Latvia to pursue this issue vigorously.[62]

Although the United States did not assert leadership in the transnational campaign, it provided ongoing support for the CSCE/OSCE and other multilateral involvement, nominating a top-level Eastern European specialist from the State Department to join the CSCE mission to Latvia. It also demonstrated its concerns by providing monies for programs geared to draw attention to the imperative of national harmony, including funding a national forum, which included governmental representatives, minority representations, and NGOs. During his visit to Riga, President Clinton reiterated U.S. alarm over the state of Latvian-Russian relations. To ensure the withdrawal of Russian troops, the United States promised to double financial assistance to Latvia, and offered to provide up to $4 million for the dismantling of the Skrunda "monster."[63] Yet, its support for Latvia and its economic assistance were not extended without stipulations, and President Clinton underscored the need for a tolerant Latvia characterized by an inclusive approach toward minorities.

Transnational Saturation

During the second half of the 1990s, a handful of regional organizations were diligently working alongside national governments and private foundations to transform interethnic relations in Latvia. The intensity of transnational involvement was partly due to the CoE's decision in 1995 to make Latvia a full member. By this point, other Euro-Atlantic institutions had decided to enlarge their memberships, and Latvians were intent on making this political success a stepping stone for entry into other international organizations. Latvia's foreign minister proclaimed that Latvia would immediately sign the European Convention on Ethnic Ministries, while the prime minister noted that since "Latvia had politically joined Europe, its next task is to join the EU."[64]

Given the supportive signals coming from Brussels in 1995, EU membership was becoming a definite possibility. In 1991, the EU began providing unilateral trade concessions and financial assistance to Latvia as part of its Technical Assistance to the Community of Impendent States program (TACIS). In May 1992, a Trade and Cooperation Agreement was signed that entered into force in 1993; the agreement notably included a clause on the importance of democracy and human rights. Only in 1995, however, did Latvia sign a European Agreement, which provided the framework to support its integration into the EU; by April 1997, the EU had opened an office in Riga to deliver closer involvement in Latvia.[65] It was clear from the beginning of the EU's intense involvement in ethnic issues that this organization followed the CSCE/OSCE's and the CoE's lead, aligning itself with the HCNM's recommendations and using CSCE/OSCE standards as benchmarks for EU decisions related to a country's fulfillment of the Copenhagen criteria.[66] Although the EU's presence and involvement in ethnic issues was important, what was more significant, according to Nils Muiznieks, Latvia's integration minister, was the networking behavior that started in the second half of the 1990s and the unique role of the CSCE/OSCE: "The game started earlier. . . . The EU and NATO plugged in later . . . [but] the OSCE was the only institution on the ground, had the best people, and could use its clout with the EU to great effect."[67]

Within two years of Latvia's application to the EU, the European Commission concluded that accession negotiations should be opened as soon as Latvia had made sufficient progress in satisfying membership conditions. In its assessment, the EU confirmed that Latvia was fulfilling the political criteria for admission in general, but it was still concerned about interethnic relations, and its concerns mirrored those of the high commissioner. For example, one of the issues highlighted by van der Stoel was the need to eliminate the so-called "windows system," an idea developed by van der Stoel himself and adopted with the country's 1994 Citizenship Law. Like NATO, the EU reinforced the HCNM's message, asserting that the window system was too restrictive and needed to change. The July 1997 Opinion on

Latvia's Application for Membership in the EU stated that for Latvia to fulfill the EU's political criteria, it needed to take measures to accelerate the naturalization process to enable Russian-speaking noncitizens to become better integrated into Latvian society.[68]

After 1995, when Latvia became a member of NATO's Partnership for Peace program, this security organization started to weigh in on ethnic issues, becoming a crucial member of the transnational network. In 1996, the presidents of the Baltic States signed a resolution on the security of the Baltic region that mentioned the need for more activities with NATO-member countries. NATO did not yet offer Latvia membership, but it was close at hand, given the Baltic States' friendship with the United States, which was solidified with a security agreement in January 1998 (the U.S.-Baltic Partnership Charter). The Latvian president pointed out that the charter would facilitate cooperation on security and economic issues, adding that cooperation with the United States is an essential component in the country's evolving portfolio of relations with the EU, NATO, and Russia.[69] Despite the United States' close relations with the Baltic states, the U.S. maintained its link with the CSCE/OSCE and its principles related to ethnic conflict management and minority rights. Speeches by President Clinton and Secretary of Defense William Perry are peppered with mention of OSCE norms and principles involving the treatment of ethnic minorities, resolving territorial disputes, and the importance of multilateral organizations.[70] Yet, despite the U.S. interest in Latvia's political environment and Latvian-Russian relations, it remained largely passive in this area, deferring to other organizations to evaluate countries' behavior and develop ways to overcome these problems.

Even though both the EU and NATO had become active players in the emerging network, pushing the CoE and the CSCE/OSCE out of the limelight, the roles and responsibilities of the latter organizations remained central to the success of this network. For one, the HCNM was persistently proactive, keeping difficult issues on Latvia's radar screen. In March 1996, van der Stoel reminded Latvian officials of the problems posed by its citizenship law.[71] Several months later, the HCNM office sent a letter to the Latvian government, registering its concern with the slow pace of naturalization and, as in previous citing, its reliance on European standards for its evaluations and recommendations.[72] Throughout 1996–97, the HCNM continued to focus on unresolved issues related to naturalization and Latvia's unwillingness to develop a comprehensive program for national integration.[73] By early 1998, the HCNM was intent on getting Latvia to abolish its window system because of the low number of Russian speakers who had applied for citizenship.[74]

By the decade's end, van der Stoel alone had made over a dozen trips to Latvia, written numerous letters to Latvian officials, and issued a series of public statements outlining the steps Latvia needed to take to attenuate ethnic tensions and to earn approval from the West.[75] Deviating from his mandate of quiet diplomacy, van der Stoel publicized his visits to Latvia in a specific attempt to make the Latvian public aware of the contradictions in its domestic and foreign policies and the West's concerns over interethnic relations. Since no other Western actor had the experience or the on-the-ground resources of the CSCE/OSCE, the HCNM held regular briefings with ambassadors of Western countries and heads of international organizations on Latvian-Russian relations.[76]

By this point in time, regional and governmental actors were joined by NGOs that had also begun to focus centrally on interethnic issues. Vita Terauda, director of Providus and former director of the Open Society Institute-Latvia, explains that although George Soros had established a foundation in Latvia in 1992, it did not become directly involved in ethnic issues until it helped establish the Latvian Center for Human Rights in 1993. (Later in 1996 it established a Human Rights and Tolerance Program.)[77] Andris Aukmanis, the current director of the foundation, explains that initially OSI-Latvia did not have a set agenda; unsure of how to proceed, it adopted a "planting-a-thousand-seeds" approach to see what would take root in Latvia.[78] Over a ten-year period, the foundation invested approximately $6 million annually in Latvia, a total of nearly $50 million. Much of this went to individuals for travel and exchange programs, but by the middle of the 1990s, as Western governments and international organizations firmly clarified the need for both changes in legislation and corresponding changes in society, OSI-Latvia concentrated its resources on key public policy issues, including rule of law, human rights, and ethnic tolerance.

Given its unique position as an NGO with significant resources, OSI-Latvia worked closely with intergovernmental actors to "fill in the gaps" in Latvia, particularly those that existed between the Latvian majority and the Russian-speaking minority. For OSI-Latvia, public-private partnerships discouraged duplication and allowed international actors with complementary objectives to make the most of scarce resources. The foundation provided funds for local NGOs while it worked with the UNDP and other intergovernmental organizations to develop Latvian-language-training programs for Russian-language speakers, thereby underwriting the promotion of national integration. Daigma Holma, a representative of the UNDP, claims that the UNDP has been engaged in Latvia in a number of ways, but its approach always leaned toward working with international and domestic groups to overcome the stiffest challenges of interethnic relations.[79] As elsewhere in the world, the UNDP worked with social groups and Latvian leaders to establish programs aimed at ethnic tolerance and national integration; once it did this, it went to foreign embassies and intergovernmental organizations to support these programs.

Overlapping, complementary objectives and public-private partnerships were certainly evident in the Baltic American Partnership Fund (BAPF), established in 1998 and funded by USAID-OSI-Latvia to develop civil society, philanthropy, and advocacy in the Baltic region. Like other public-private initiatives, BAPF assumed that Latvia's future depended upon the empowerment of individuals who would suppport changes within the state and encourage Latvians to find their own way of resolving the country's ethnic dilemmas.

The Lure of Europe

By 2000, interethnic relations in Latvia shifted from tension to accommodation, but only in fits and starts as the international community calculated what was necessary not only to prevent violence but to foster interethnic harmony. By 1999, the success of these efforts was revealed by the similar attitudes taken by the EU and NATO to Latvia's accession potential. In February of the following year, formal negotiations were underway with the EU, and Latvia's accession to NATO seemed secure in light of close U.S.-Latvian cooperation and the conclusion of the U.S.-Baltic Partnership Charter. Domestically, changes in legislation and the presence of monitoring bodies, alongside civil initiatives, augured not only a movement toward accommodation and tolerance, but solid evidence of transnational effectiveness. Given the potency of transnational engagement, particularly in the second half of the 1990s, how and to what extent did transnational initiatives affect domestic political choices in Latvia and thus the dynamics of interethnic relations?

Others writing on Latvian ethnic politics readily point out that although transnational actors did not always accomplish their objectives in the short run, their influence was undeniable and cannot be underestimated.[80] As Valdis Birkavs, a former prime minister and foreign minister, confirms, "There is no doubt about it . . . the opinions of intergovernmental organizations and foreign governments affected the calculations of Latvian politicians who were intent on becoming members of the EU and NATO."[81]

Although Birkavs talks about the positive impact of transnational actors, such as the HCNM, on the trajectory of ethnic politics in Latvia, I should emphasize that not all Latvians see transnational involvement in the 1990s as either positive or necessary to the management of the country's ethnic problems. For example, a representative of the Ministry of Foreign Affairs acknowledged the power of the West to affect politicians' behavior, but he maintained that this international "interference" was not positive for Latvia or for majority-minority relations.[82]

Opinions of the effects of transnational involvement varied somewhat, but representatives of Latvia's NGO community and most government officials maintained that the international community provided the necessary pressure to move these matters forward, acknowledging that without it, "Latvians would not have addressed the concerns of its minority population."[83] Admitting to the occasional problem with foreign involvement, Birkavs concedes that "international pressure, even when clumsy and ambitious . . . and thus problematic . . . was still better than without."[84] By hounding Latvia to come to terms with ethnic problems and manage these matters peacefully and in accordance with European standards, transnational actors helped pave the way for Latvia's symbolic return to Europe.

Eizenija Aldermane, the head of Latvia's naturalization board, confirms the crucial role of Western governments, regional organizations, and NGOs to her office's success. As Aldermane puts it: "International involvement in this issue [naturalization] is evident on many levels throughout the country; internationals helped set up government offices, they provided advice and funding. . . . Without international cooperation, Latvia would not have done any integration activities . . . and my office would not be regarded as successful as it is."[85]

Opinions do vary when it comes to identifying which international organization or actor was most significant in affecting ethnic relations. Like secondary sources focusing on ethnic politics in Latvia, most Latvians identified several actors that played a role in spawning domestic change, depending on the year and specific issue area. As one government representative noted: "It is impossible to know who or what actor was most important. As an adviser to the President's Office from 1995–99, I did not distinguish among the international actors and I don't think that most Latvians did either. . . . all Western organizations were lumped together as the West."[86]

Just as the West had once seen Eastern Europe as a unified, homogenous bloc, some Latvian government officials adopted a similar attitude toward the international community. This perception was fostered in large part by the overlapping strategies of the international actors. According to Nils Muiznieks and Ilze Brands Kehris, "one organization cannot be seen in isolation from that of other organizations," because it was the coordination among these actors that led to a significantly greater policy impact than when action was taken separately.[87]

Fulfilling Foreign Policy Goals

Even before the country's independence was assured, Latvians made it clear that they were eager to make their "return to Europe" by joining Euro-Atlantic organizations. Given that CoE membership was an unwritten first step in this process, Latvia reached out to the council almost immediately. Membership proved elusive for more than three years, largely because of the absence of a well-defined citizenship law. Ultimately, and *only* because of the push from the HCNM and the pull of council membership, Latvia adopted such a law in the summer of 1994. In early 1995, Latvia received its reward of admission to the council, which was a critical first step toward realizing its foreign policy goals. The adoption of this law demonstrated that nearly from the conception of Latvia's independence, a connection was made between the country's foreign policy goals and domestic ethnic issues. This was because of the HCNM's "agenda-setting" role and the CoE's stipulation that a citizen law was necessary for membership. It also illustrates that although many of the concerns of these transnational actors were not addressed in the 1994 law, their recommendations did not expire and instead became part of ongoing discussions about Latvia's future. Van der Stoel admits that many of the ideas and suggestions he made in 1993–94 were not welcomed immediately or uniformly in Latvia; they were simply "not possible at the time."[88] Indeed, domestic politics in the Latvian state were defensive about policies toward its Russian-speaking minority and about international involvement in the area, given recent history and experience in the Soviet Union. However, with time and the concentrated effort of this transnational network to encourage peaceful change, these obstacles were overcome.

Latvian politicians began discussions of a citizenship law in 1992, in the context of a heated dialogue aimed at Russia's withdrawal of troops from Latvia. In early 1993, Max van der Stoel joined the CoE in identifying the specific issues Latvians needed to address (from the standpoint of the West), including the need to provide rights to noncitizens. Even at this early point, the HCNM sought out and worked with other transnational organizations, recognizing the nascent division of responsibilities among transnational actors. In fact, he explained that he was not covering all aspects of the Latvian draft law on citizenship because he was aware that the CoE had been asked to make its comments on specific issues.[89] Latvian politicians sent drafts of the Citizenship Law to both the CoE and the HCNM's office for comment.[90] In the spring of 1993, after van der Stoel made a number of precise recommendations, Latvia's foreign minister explained that most of the HCNM's conclusions and recommendations seemed "reasonably grounded," but because of constitutional limitations, the government would not be able to adopt a citizenship law until the parliament was elected that June.[91]

As domestic debates intensified throughout 1993, it became clear how important this legislation was to other regional organizations and national governments, and thus to realizing Latvia's foreign policy ambitions. The U.S. government even weighed in on this issue; the secretary of state sent the Latvian ambassador a note emphasizing the government's concerns about the rights of Russian-speaking residents who were not permitted to vote. International pressure "pushed nationalist politicians to criticize what they considered to be crude and overt pressure and interference in Latvian internal affairs."[92] Moderates adopted a markedly different take, and following the HCNM's assertions oncs that bound his recommendations to Latvia's foreign policy priorities—they emphasized that such legislation was a key step toward integration with Western Europe, specifically linking the HCNM's recommendations to Latvia's future membership in the EU.[93] According to Birkavs: "This was a very delicate time in Latvian history and politicians were sensitive to this issue. . . . [Moreover,] many in Latvia initially wanted international involvement but without any strings attached. Perhaps it was that Latvians were too inexperienced and the international community too ambitious and unrealistic."[94]

Throughout this period, the input of both the HCNM and the CoE was regularly solicited, with the former providing input on the content of the law while the latter evaluated its fit with European laws. In a telling gesture of the priority given the CoE in 1993, Latvia's foreign minister assured the CSCE's high commissioner that his recommendations would be taken into account, but that an expert opinion from the CoE was also anticipated. Nonetheless, many in Latvia, particularly those working in civil society, credit the HCNM's office for its anticipatory, proactive approach. "Van der Stoel was the first and most consistent, systematic person from the international community following these issues," Birkvas said. "He followed them closely."[95]

The Citizenship Law, passed by Latvia's Saeima in June 1994, generally ignored the recommendations made by the HCNM and the CoE. However, transnational pressure had more an effect on President Guntis Ulmanis, who used his presidential powers to return the law to parliament for revision, citing legal imperfections and the opposition expressed by experts from *both* the OSCE and the CoE.[96] As if to explain the president's decision, the prime minister connected the evaluations of the HCNM and the CoE to further integration with the West, specifically the EU and NATO.[97] Only after highly publicized talks with members of the CoE was a revised Citizenship Law passed a month later. The revision did not embrace all of the

HCNM's recommendations, but it did eliminate the quota system, which had been a major worry identified by the HCNM.[98] Instead of quotas for naturalization, a timetable or "window system" was established that allowed naturalization based on years of residency, rather than limiting the overall number of those naturalized. The establishment of this system (as well as its elimination) are cited as shining examples of the CSCE/OSCE's ability to shape ethnic policies in Latvia.

Despite the failure of transnational actors to influence every aspect of the Citizenship Law, it was a start. As the CSCE mission noted, the law "goes a long way toward accommodating recommendations by both the CSCE and the CoE, and appears to consolidate Latvia's continued integration into regional organizations."[99] The CSCE/OSCE touted the passage of the law as evidence of Latvia's desire for ethnic accommodation, the sway of international actors, as well as the cooperation between CSCE/OSCE and the CoE.[100] Latvian politicians concurred, claiming that many authorities in both the HCNM's office and the CoE worked in consultation with its parliament to create this law. The EU not only welcomed the fact that the law accepted some of the recommendations of regional organizations, but claimed that its adoption was "a good basis for progress in the integration of ethnic minorities and the development of inter-community relations."[101] In spite of its concerns that the citizenship law was still too restrictive and did not fully resolve the problems Latvia's minority population faced, the CoE granted Latvia full membership. That is to say, membership was granted in exchange for the Latvian government's willingness to continue cooperating with the CoE and the CSCE in implementing the law and in drafting a separate law on noncitizens.[102]

Whether Latvians liked it or not, fulfilling the country's primary foreign policy goal—integration with the West—depended upon more than positive interactions with regional organizations and the adoption of what some saw as symbolic pieces of legislation. Latvia needed to nurture compatibility with Moscow and convince its potentially irredentist neighbor that it would adequately protect the rights of its Russian-speaking population. In light of Latvia's exclusionary policies and nationalist rhetoric in the early 1990s, this was a daunting task, one that it did not relish undertaking alone. Moreover, other issues, such as the withdrawal of Russian forces and the dismantling of the Skrunda Radar Station, complicated Latvian-Russian relations and intensified domestic interethnic relations. However, in these cases, both Latvia and Russia came to accept—if not prefer—working through international, multilateral organizations to manage their complicated and fragile relations. Instead of focusing on the promises made to each other, they both referred to international documents and agreements, engaging in "referencing" to demonstrate the legitimacy of their claims. In each area of these struggles, the CSCE/OSCE (particularly the mission and the HCNM) played an important role in mediating and cultivating peaceful relations. To be sure, neither side was always happy with the position taken by outsiders; this was especially true regarding the HCNM. While Latvians occasionally accused the HCNM of being Russia's envoy, Russians noted their displeasure with van der Stoel and his recommendations. Nonetheless, the even-handedness of this organization effectively fostered positive Latvian-Russian relations.

Ethnic Latvians were eager to facilitate the quick and peaceful withdrawal of the 150,000 Russian troops stationed in their country. Regarding their presence as well as other delicate matters related to the stationing of Russian troops, Latvians regularly sought out and consulted the international community for help. It is impossible to know what prompted Yeltsin's behavior in the summer of 1992—namely, his sudden decision to withdraw completely from the Baltics—but there is significant evidence that his change at heart was linked to pressure coming from the West and the transnational campaign that started to take root to manage ethnic tensions. For example, on a visit to North America in 1992, Yeltsin was made aware of the link between the withdrawal of troops from the Baltics and U.S. aid. In July, American lawmakers tied aid directly to Russian troop withdrawal from the Baltic States, voting to restrict funds to Russia after one year if significant progress had not been made toward pulling its military out of the Baltic region. Later that month—pointedly on the eve of a CSCE meeting and a G-7 conference—Russia promised to vacate eighty-four military bases and pull out of Latvia completely by the end of 1992. The timing was auspicious and obviously a response to the message emerging from the West and its "support of Baltic demands for a complete withdrawal of foreign troops."[103]

Some amount of conditionality was obviously at play because, after Yeltsin's announcement, the G-7 countries agreed to reschedule Russia's debt and granted it $1.5 billion in new credits. At a news conference, Yeltsin acknowledged that this assistance was not without conditions and was bound to the expeditious withdrawal of troops from the Baltic region. These thorny issues and Yeltsin's concessions pushed the CSCE to further internationalize ethnic problems in 1993. The compromise that was struck between the Baltic States and Russia resulted in a joint resolution for troop withdrawals and additional tools for the CSCE to help manage ethnic conflicts. Significantly, this joint resolution made Russia accountable to the CSCE, a point rejected earlier by Russia.

When interstate problems developed, both countries looked to the CSCE/

OSCE and other international mechanisms for resolution. For example, at a CSCE/OSCE meeting in late 1992, the Latvian delegation warned members: "Russia is not fulfilling its international obligations to withdraw its troops from the Baltic States, which have been clearly stated in CSCE and UN documents."[104] Like Latvia, Russia tried to use transnational actors to its own advantage, hoping that the CSCE/OSCE, the United States, and the CoE would pressure the country to change its behavior. Adopting the rhetoric of transnational actors, Russia changed its tack, couching its concerns and demands in terms of discrimination and human rights. In October 1992, President Yeltsin's adviser Sergei Stankevich wrote to the CoE complaining that 900,000 ethnic Russians in Latvia had been deprived of the possibility of becoming loyal citizens.[105] Russia's campaign was partially successful; by the beginning of 1993, the United States narrowed its attention to ethnic politics in Latvia. It also linked Russia's withdrawal of its troops in Latvia to that country's nationalizing politics. After the passage of a citizenship law, Russia's minister of foreign affairs was careful to point out Latvia's shortcomings and its willful disregard of international opinion. Latvians had not only deliberately ignored Russia, but it overlooked the appeals of the CSCE/OSCE, the CoE, the EU, and heads of state of Europe and America.[106]

Later in the 1990s, when Russian-Latvian relations again deteriorated, transnational actors, specifically the HCNM, were welcomed to smooth feathers. Despite a focus on different issues, transnational actors encouraged a quick resolution without taking sides. Realizing the problems that could surface in a close relationship between the CSCE/OSCE and Russia, the HCNM office worked diligently to obtain Russian support for its efforts without cultivating what might look like a partnership. The key was cooperation rather than collusion. Thus, as the HCNM office worked to get the EU and Western actors on board for recommendations it made to revise Latvia's citizenship law in 1997–98, it actively discouraged the Russians from joining the bandwagon. For example, in an April 1998 letter to Russia's foreign minister, van der Stoel urged Russia not to link the normalization of relations with the full implementation of the HCNM's recommendations, believing that this would put Latvian politicians in a corner from which it would be hard to escape.[107]

What was obvious was not just Latvia's desire to integrate with the West but Russia's too; thus, when Russia's concerns were adequately addressed by members of the international community, its leaders were quick to give credit to international organizations. At a OSCE Permanent Council meeting, the head of the Russian delegation, Ambassador V. Shustov, stated that due to the efforts of international organizations and the OSCE specifically, "Latvian authorities are trying to mitigate the practices of the Law on Citizenship and introduce some amendments to the legislation." [108] Importantly, instead of developing their own recommendations or list of concerns with regard to the situation in Latvia, the Russian government linked its concerns with those of the HCNM. As the HCNM saw it, although Latvia's citizenship law did conform to international standards, individual articles contradicted the spirit of European standards and thus discouraged interethnic harmony in Latvia.

Establishing Domestic Legislation

Better relations with Russia may have diminished the likelihood of ethnic-based violence in Latvia, but it did little to help the large non-Latvian population. The long-term resolution of ethnic dilemmas necessitated the formation of new laws and governmental bodies to protect and preserve minority rights. As with Latvia's citizenship law, transnational involvement did not always affect outcomes immediately or completely, but there is sufficient evidence to indicate that transnational actors helped shape many of the laws and offices established to manage Latvia's ethnic tensions and improve the future of the Russian-speaking population.

Inga Reina, Latvia's representative before international human rights organizations, explains that while many tend to overlook the influence of the CoE because its activities are less well-known and its expert opinions are delivered without much fanfare, its effect on Latvian legislation and "the rules of the game" cannot be exaggerated. [109] To extend its reach, the council sponsored "orientation trips" to Strasbourg for Latvian politicians to acquaint them with the council's activities, hoping to impress upon them its power and ability to promote democracy and human rights. It is unclear if these trips made much impact on what the politicians believed, but it is true that in time, Latvians realized that by joining the council, they had to accept "the whole package," which meant that they had to respond regularly to international concerns.

Once Latvia became a member of the CoE, it had to create specific offices within the government to harmonize its laws with the CoE. The office of the representative before international human rights organizations sits at the nexus of international and domestic politics; its explicit purpose is to explain and translate international laws to Latvian politicians while it explains and justifies Latvia's behavior to international organizations. Reina explains that a major responsibility of her office is to explain how Latvia has implemented various international treaties and standards. International organizations then evaluate the country's behavior and provide this office with recommendations to address the shortcomings and ways for it to better meet international and European legislation. International organizations have some different requirements, but in the 1990s, their messages were similar and overlapping. As Reina notes, organizations such as the CoE have not solved Latvia's ethnic problems, but because of its involvement, Russia has been appeased and ethnic situations have been dealt with expeditiously, while Latvia has simultaneously achieved its goal of moving closer to Europe.[110]

When it came to shaping Latvian legislation, transnational actors did not always work behind the scenes to avoid domestic political debates. Many times representatives of the West had to plea their case with obstinate Latvian politicians. For example, shortly after the citizenship law was passed, the HCNM office again conveyed its concern that the law had not gone far enough to address the country's stateless population. The HCNM pressed leaders to adopt a law on the status of noncitizens.[111] Latvian politicians, many of whom had presumably agreed to the citizenship law for instrumental reasons, thought that once it was passed, transnational actors would disappear and the pressure would subside. Latvians were noticeably disappointed and annoyed that Latvia remained under scrutiny, claiming that international organizations were placing unfair, new conditions on it.[112] Undeterred by comments from politicians, the HCNM and the CoE urged Latvia to give some legal status to more than seven hundred thousand residents who entered or were born in Latvia to noncitizen parents after World War II.[113] A draft law for noncitizens was first considered in January 1995 but was rejected by a majority in Latvia's parliament, even after the chairman of the Standing Committee on Legal Affairs linked its adoption to accession in the CoE.[114] In dismissing this legislation, a government representative defended these actions, citing that only seven of the thirty-nine CoE members possessed such a law, and argued that Latvia needed to conform to the "average" image of council members.[115] Thus, even when rejecting external pressures, Latvia appealed to international standards to defend its position.

Despite this failure, transnational actors, led again by the HCNM, concentrated on the slow pace of naturalization and the problems noncitizens faced in trying to naturalize. By 1996, the HCNM started to press the government for a revision of its citizenship legislation. These attempts to amend the citizenship law were a clear demonstration of transnational influence, as several of the HCNM's recommendations were ultimately included in the 1998 legislation. As with other successes, the HCNM's recommendations were able to shape domestic laws because of the support they received from other regional organizations and Western governments. Latvia's window system, which was adopted in the 1994 legislation and which displaced quotas, was the HCNM's idea, but by 1996 this system became a focus of van der Stoel's criticisms of naturalization. The high commissioner claimed that the window system contributed to the country's sluggish progress on naturalization; throughout 1996 and 1997, he sent letters to Latvia's Foreign Ministry urging it to overcome this stagnation and move ahead. To achieve this, the HCNM encouraged Latvia to reduce naturalization fees, simplify applicants' tests, and grant citizenship to stateless children, as well abolish the window system. Valdis Birkavs was initially evasive and defensive about these recommendations, but by 1997 an intense effort was made by several actors, specifically the European Commission, to toss the window system, offering more noncitizens the possibility of naturalization.[116] In early April 1997, the director of the EU Commission for External Relations, Hans van den Broek, pointed out the problems with Latvia's citizenship law, indicating that this was a major issue for the EU. The director explicitly referenced both the HCNM's recommendations and the opinions of the CoE. The overlapping, reinforcing messages of the transnational network had clearly penetrated by the time the Latvian president, Ulmanis, returned from a trip to Finland in April, for in speaking to the Latvian press, he admitted to the need to abolish the window system.

By the spring of 1997, domestic splits within Latvia's Way political party arose; although party members may not have agreed completely with the recommendations of the international community, they called for an evaluation of why naturalization was proceeding at a snail's pace. Those members of Latvia's Way, who perceived themselves as liberal democratic politicians and open to the normative arguments of the international community, began to part ways—at least in discourse—with the party's more nationalistic members and representatives of nationalist parties such as the Freedom Party, who openly scorned what they continued to call international "interference" in Latvia's domestic affairs.[117] The slow progress on naturalization was thus intricately linked to the country's severely fragmented political environment rather than a split between the views of the international community and domestic actors.

As transnational actors hoped, by 1997 the struggle and pressure for change shifted to the domestic realm in Latvia. Birkavs, a central player in the unfolding drama, claims that most of the events of the time were simply posturing on the part of Latvian politicians who were starting to feel as if Latvia was becoming Europe's "whipping boy."[118] Personally, he hoped to depoliticize these issues by allowing time to pass. The problem was that the HCNM, and thus the international community, would not wait. In July 1997, the European Commission's *Opinion on Latvia* was published, highlighting the legal snags of citizenship and the lethargic naturalization process, signalling that these issues would indeed be a problem for Latvia's accession into the EU. A month later, a more nationalistic coalition government took over.

Latvia's new prime minister maintained that the noncitizen issue would not pose an obstacle to EU accession, though this was clearly untrue and the government needed to address sensitive ethnic policies directly. In the spring of 1998, despite the conservative orientation of the government, Latvian politicians approved the idea of abolishing the window system and introduced procedures for granting citizenship to stateless children. In April, the Latvian prime minister's office sent a letter to van der Stoel with proposals to amend the citizenship, education, and language laws with a request for the high commissioner's opinion.[119] There is no visible way to explain these acts other than transnational pressures, especially given the radicalization of Latvian politics during the previous six months. Birkavs admits that these domestic changes were a direct reaction to foreign concerns.[120] Although a number of governments and governmental organizations urged these changes, the greatest weight was given to the EU, which had unequivocally backed the recommendations of the OSCE's high commissioner.[121]

By June 1998, the foreign minister urged Parliament to comply with the OSCE recommendations because Latvia might "otherwise risk losing allies in Europe and the United States as well as the chance to improve relations with Russia."[122] Thus, the pressure came not only from the EU but included the CoE and the CSCE/CSCE. Beyond these primary players, powerful Western governments, including the United States, Sweden, and the UK, were watching closely. Even NATO, which had not taken a conspicuous position on ethnic-related issues earlier, weighed in on this situation, supporting the HCNM and flexing its considerable muscle to convince Latvia to amend this law. The pressure coming from transnational actors, alongside the endorsement of moderate Latvian politicians of CSCE/OSCE recommendations, meant that by late June 1998, the necessary domestic coalition was in place. As Latvia prepared revisions of its citizenship law, it frequently sought opinions and input on the exact wording of legislation from the office of the HCNM. As one analyst put it,

> [W]hether the radicals like it or not, Max van der Stoel is regarded as one of the most authoritative people entitled to give his opinion on Latvia. He is taken seriously in the EU, which even draws its conclusions on whether Latvia is ready to enter the EU using his judgements. . . . Also the CoE . . . recognizes his opinion. . . . In the same way, the U.S. . . . has firmly emphasized its wish that Latvia implement Max van der Stoel's recommendations.[123]

The head of the government's working group emphasized the proposed changes in Article 31, relating to children of stateless persons, an issue which had been raised time and again since 1993. Although the high commissioner welcomed most of the changes proposed, he pushed the issue of the state's obligation to provide opportunities not only for minorities to learn the country's official language but to be taught in their mother tongue.[124]

The amendments were eventually passed, but nationalist politicians were so agitated by the vote that they called for an October referendum, triggering another bout of intense transnational pressure and coordination, with representatives of regional organizations brandishing the stick of exclusion from their organizations. Even the United States joined the fray, with Secretary of State Madeline Albright presenting a letter from President Clinton supporting the HCNM's recommendations. Importantly, the EU's Hans van den Brock indicated in July 1998 that a vote of "no" in the referendum would be seen as quite negative by the EU, thereby explicitly connecting EU membership to the recommendations of the HCNM.[125] Despite the disgruntled cries of nationalists, the referendum did not overturn Parliament's decisions, and the law was revised. Van der Stoel extolled the abolition of the window system of naturalization, claiming that by doing so the Latvian government had increased the opportunities for interethnic harmony.[126]

In October 1998, Latvia's Saeima approved amendments to the constitution of Latvia, ushering in a new chapter on human and minority rights. Significantly, the amendments provided for a broad range of basic human, civil, and social rights to all inhabitants, regardless of their status as citizens.[127] Although processes related to citizenship and naturalization were drawn out for several years, by the end of the 1990s, of the nineteen conclusions or recommendations made by the high commissioner, at least thirteen were adopted by the Latvian government, including his recommendations on naturalization fees, language tests, and stateless children.[128] Interethnic harmony may not have been the instant result of revisions in citizenship, but the amendments made a clear and potent impact. In the following year alone, more people were naturalized than in the previous three.[129]

In contrast to the rally for changes in the country's citizenship laws, in the early 1990s transnational actors remained relatively quiet on legislation related to language use. When the international community turned to this piece of the country's ethnic puzzle in the mid-1990s, it did so only because the HCNM drew international attention to the issue. Latvia's 1989 legislation had made working knowledge of Latvian a perquisite for many positions in the public and private sector. Amendments subsequently made by the Latvian Supreme Council in 1992 took these initiatives a step further, granting the government the right to randomly inspect and regulate language use. Yet during the first half of the 1990s, these restrictions went virtually unnoticed by the international community. For example, a UN fact-finding mission to Latvia in late 1992 concluded that "the language law itself is not incompatible with international law or with generally accepted human rights stands."[130] It was only in 1997, in the context of debates within Latvia, to make this legislation even more restrictive, that the HCNM took up this issue.[131] Once the CsCe took notice, drafts of this legislation were forwarded to the HCNM, the CoE, and the Council of Baltic States for comment. By the spring of 1998, the European "troika"—comprised of the European Commission, the HCNM, and the CoE—were working side by side to persuade the Latvian government to back down on the proposed expansion of its regulatory power.

In the wake of the transnational network's victory with the amendments to the citizenship law, relevant transnational actors again sent Latvia a similar message: The proposed language law was not appropriate and would not be accepted by the international community. By this point, Latvians were clearly frustrated with transnational actors and the HCNM in particular because he kept Latvia under the international spotlight. However, if the HCNM's office wanted Latvia's ear, it needed to ensure that the EU was on board, sending the same message.[132] Muiznieks and Brands Kehris contend that in this case it was clear that "a transnational network" of European-oriented Latvian officials worked hand-in-hand with Western organizations, providing Latvians with the ammunition to face down domestic criticism and opposition.[133] In fact, when the president of Latvia vetoed the law in the summer of 1999, she admitted having received communications from the HCNM and the secretary general of the CoE recommending that she return the law to the parliament for further consideration, and she did just that.[134] A new, more generous language law was finally adopted in December 1999, but only after the HCNM, the CoE, the EU, and numerous governments, including the Danish, Finish, and German, weighed in.[135]

Creating Domestic Instruments

Transnational network members simultaneously provided financial and technical assistance to establish domestic instruments to encourage interethnic harmony. In 1994, the government of Latvia requested the assistance of the UN, the CSCE/OSCE, and CoE to help it map out a multiyear National Program for the Protection and Promotion of Human Rights in Latvia.[136] In the years that followed, and based on the recommendations of key transnational network members, a handful of government bodies were established. For example, the president's Consultative

Council on Nationality Affairs was established, and although only an advisory group, it included a broad range of national minority groups with a mandate to "discuss the most serious problems in order to promote their solution at the level of executive bodies or legislative initiative." [137] Later in the decade, a range of more authoritative groups were created, including a state minister for human rights within the Ministry of Justice, the National Human Rights Office, the Ministry for National Integration, and the Naturalization Board. It is clear that these domestic instruments were built and sustained with significant financial and technical backing from several members of the international community.

The establishment of the Naturalization Board was critical to internal ethnic politics and Latvian-Russian relations. Since Latvia's Ministry of the Interior, which handled these issues initially, had a bad reputation among members of Latvia's Russian-speaking community, transnational actors encouraged the creation of a totally new office. Put together in a matter of months, the Naturalization Board was tasked to assist with the acquisition, revocation, and renewal of citizenship and was intended to function in a nonpolitical way to create a fair system for naturalization. This was an important step forward for majority-minority relations because of the sensitivity of the issue and the chauvinism associated with the Ministry of the Interior, which had previously handled this issue. This institution's legitimacy would be looked at by the international community as evidence of Latvia's intention to deal with its ethnic problems.

The Naturalization Board's achievements and professionalism in the 1990s are noted by Latvians and non-Latvians alike, who see this office as among the most neutral and effective government bodies: Its sound leadership and effective policies have thus made it a crucial instrument of interethnic cooperation and a key member of the transnational network. From the very beginning, according to director Eizenija Aldermane, the Naturalization Board was directly shaped by individuals representing governments and organizations from abroad. [138] Among the board's first visitors were Charles McGee of the CSCE/OSCE and the British ambassador. Right after the board was created, officials from EU states and the CoE travelled to Latvia, holding seminars for board employees and discussing with its director and staff various ways to encourage naturalization. Since the total number of applicants for naturalization was much lower than expected in the first years, the board welcomed the advice and assistance from transnational actors, particularly the CoE. [139] By all accounts, the Naturalization Board has been an effective government body able to naturalize large numbers of noncitizens. In the estimation of the CoE, the

CSCE/OSCE, and various NGOs, the board has sought to apply laws fairly and systematically, and since the removal of the restrictive naturalization windows in November 1998, the number of citizenship applicants has increased significantly.[140]

The HCNM closely followed the problems associated with naturalization, identifying a few simple obstacles: lack of information on becoming a citizen, difficult language requirements, and high testing fees. In a short time, the Naturalization Board addressed each of these issues, receiving substantial assistance from the international community to do so. The CoE provided extensive advice on language examinations and testing methodology, while Western governments and regional organizations assisted the board in staging a series of public-awareness campaigns. Largely because of the ongoing support, the Naturalization Board took on broader responsibilities related to national integration. In 1999, it started to house the Social Integration and Information Center, which was launched with support of USAID and the EU's Phare program. In light of budget constraints in Latvia and the sensitivity of citizenship, the Naturalization Board depended on the cooperation and financial support of the West to help it carry out its tasks. In the 1990s until early 2003, it estimated that almost five hundred different meetings took place with representatives of Western states and public and private organizations.[141] According to Aldermane, it is daunting to keep track of these exchanges and the numerous international donations from abroad, but she estimates that, at the least, nineteen countries and five intergovernmental organizations directly assisted and supported the board's activities.[142]

A second office inspired from abroad was the Latvian National Human Rights Office, created in 1997. President Ulmanis claimed that a national ombudsman was a fundamental step in the country's democratic development and necessary to bring the country's legal system another step closer to European standards.[143] Olafs Bruvers, a former pastor and dissident, became the country's national ombudsman in 1997. Bruvers confirms that the human rights office was created to appease the international community and fulfill European requirements. The CoE, the CSCE/OSCE, the UN Development Program, Nordic countries, and other international actors all supported the creation of a strong and independent ombudsman to address human rights and minority issues.[144] Although one of the intentions of this office was that it would respond to individual complaints associated with ethnic discrimination, this has not been a priority thus far.[145] Instead, its basic task has been to bring Latvia's human rights legislation into compliance with European norms. Regardless of the abandonment of ethnic minorities, the existence of an independent human rights office with the capacity to comment on minority rights was clearly the result of a transnational push.

A significant sign of the Latvian government's determination to institute domestic mechanisms to help the society transform came in the spring of 1998, when an integration council was established and given the task of drafting the framework document of a national program called "Integration of Society in Latvia."[146] The adoption of a national program was premised on the need for a broad, comprehensive, and multisectoral strategy for integrating the country's Russian-speaking minority. As Latvia's minister for national integration admits, the idea for this program was not indigenously inspired; instead, its adoption came only after much prodding from the international community.[147] While it is too soon to evaluate its long-term effects, its adoption has resulted in significant tangible outcomes, including the establishment of a Ministry for Integration. Yet even this important organization does not appear to have domestic roots; Daigma Holma claims that the UN had been pushing for the creation of such a ministry for at least three or four years.[148]

According to Reinis Aboltins, director of the Department of Social Integration within the Ministry for Integration, the role of the ministry is to coordinate social integration policy, work with minority groups, and promote the development of civil society in Latvia.[149] The appointment of Nils Muiznieks as the minister for this office should be seen as an unambiguously positive development and evidence of the government's sincerity, given Muiznieks's unique position and experience. Previously, he worked with the Latvian Center for Human Rights and Ethnic Studies and the Open Socity Institute-Latvia, and several Latvian and European officials noted that Muiznieks is a key person, if not *the* key person, in Latvia working on these issues. He is intricately involved in ethnic issues; given his work experience and international connections, one can say that for quite some time he personally has been at the nexus between domestic and international politics, understanding what is both necessary and feasible given the expectations of the international community and the Latvian reality.

The national plan also instituted the Society Integration Foundation. Committed to fulfilling the goals of the program for national integration, this government-initiated NGO opened its doors in 2001 with almost an equal number of government ministers, representatives of municipal government, and NGO officials, but was funded largely by the European Union. The idea for such a foundation first came up in the late 1990s, and while it is generally agreed that its inspiration came from the international community, it is not clear whether the UNDP or some foreign embassy initially proposed the idea. Nils Sakss, its current director, explains that the idea was that Latvia needed to develop a mechanism for governments, private donors, and international organizations to help fund NGOs and civil society.[150] Acknowledging the importance of creating an environment conducive to interethnic cooperation, the foundation encourages bottom-up initiatives based on the belief that civil society development and integration should be society-driven. The foundation's primary goal is to promote ethnic integration in Latvia through grassroots initiatives that elevate individual empowerment and teach democratic skills.

Bridging the Ethnic Divide

Almost from the beginning of Latvia's transition, the UNDP and the Soros Foundation-Latvia acknowledged that Latvia's ethnic tensions existed in a broader political, economic, and social context. Along with other actors, they worked to alter this milieu through "soft initiatives" or projects that worked with and through the government toward ethnic peace from the bottom up. Daigma Holma explains that when the UN established an office in Latvia, it used its experience and fundraising abilities to develop (among its several initiatives) an extensive and comprehensive Latvian-language program as a way to promote ethnic cooperation.[151] Working closely with the Latvian government and members of the Russian-speaking population, the UNDP initiated a National Program for Latvian Language Training (NPLLT) in 1995.[152] The goal of NPLLT was to bolster the consolidation of Latvian society while decreasing the linguistic divide, thereby stimulating common values through the increase of Latvian-language speakers.[153] This strategy for containing ethnic conflict was so successful that by 1998, its second phase was sponsored by the EU, Sweden, Finland, Norway, Denmark, the Netherlands, and Canada.[154]

Igor Pimenov, former director of the Latvian Association of Schools of Russian and an advocate for the Russian minority, credits the UNDP with focusing on this issue because it caused such a fundamental split among Latvians and Russian speakers.[155] Pimenov also acknowledged the role played by the HCNM, the CoE, and the CSCE/OSCE mission in fostering dialogue with Latvia's Russian community and responding to its needs. Part of the problem was that Latvian legislation expected Russian speakers to learn Latvian instantly; yet, there was little money and few programs to teach Latvian to nonspeakers. Without the international community's involvement, the needs of the Russian population would have been ignored by Latvian politicians. Yet, it was not only that the UN realized the importance of Latvian-language instruction and made it a priority, but it, along with the United States and

European governments, provided the funding for these programs. As elsewhere in the world, once the UN develops a strategy to manage a complex problem such as interethnic tensions, it seeks funding from various sources. In Holma's opinion, the U.S. government was instrumental in a couple of ways: "While the U.S. was not involved in the day-to-day activities in Latvia . . . and it really did not even influence a lot of its substance, the U.S. . . . had a lot of money and it really wanted to use it efficiently. . . . They genuinely cared about people and the situation on the ground and when it came to human rights, minority rights and ethnic issues, they did not let them die."[156]

The Soros Foundation-Latvia dabbled in Latvian-language training programs as well, but it only filled in the gaps left by the UNDP. In 1999, for example, it helped establish twenty-eight bilingual schools. The Open Schools Project is just one example of the foundation's involvement in ethnic relations. Soros's main contribution to Latvian society and to interethnic relations, according to its current director, Andris Aukmanis, is evidenced by the number of successful NGOs sponsored by the foundation; these NGOs have helped create an institutionally rich environment in Latvia and pushed traditionally marginalized issues to fore.[157] Aukmanis mentions a range of NGOs created with Soros funding, including the NGO Center, the Judicial Center, the Educational Center, and Providus (Center for Public Policy). However, its shining example of a local NGO committed to conflict prevention and able to affect government policy is the Latvian Center for Human Rights and Ethnic Studies. Established in 1993, it has become a crucial domestic member of the transnational network working to promote human rights and ethnic tolerance in Latvia.[158]

The center conducts research, monitors policies, and provides legal assistance. Two years after its creation, it had developed such a good reputation that its staff was regularly providing opinions to local and international authorities on interethnic relations and human rights in Latvia.[159] Its close collaboration with international NGOs meant that it had to be taken seriously by Latvian politicians. In May 1996, the center worked with the Hague-based Foundation for Interethnic Relations (created to support the work of the HCNM) and the Soros Foundation-Latvia to host a seminar on government-minority dialogue with members of the Latvian government and the HCNM. Behind closed doors, senior government officials, minority NGO representatives, and prominent researchers discussed the future of the country's ethnic relations.[160] If the center has been effective, as its current director attests, this success is the result, at least in part, of its international partnerships and its contacts with Westerners who have not only provided the bulk of funding to support its activities but have legitimized its position domestically, preventing the government from dismissing it completely.[161]

The presence of a few, well-respected Latvian NGOs working on interethnic relations and minority rights, although still supported by funds from abroad, provides some promising avenues for social change. What is equally important, as U.S. State Department reports note, is the Latvian government's recognition of NGOs and its willingness to engage in dialogue with those working on human rights issues.[162] The problem in Latvia, as elsewhere in Eastern Europe, is that the number of NGOs focused on these issues is not large, and the programs are not extensive. With this said, the number of Latvian NGOs are on the rise; in 1994, a forum in Latvia attracted just over forty NGOs involved in broadly defined ethnic or human-rights activities.[163] By 2001, the number had skyrocketed, and there were more than 3,000 NGOs, about 150 of which had "ethnic attributes" or were involved in ethnic issues broadly defined.[164]

Yet, a focus on numbers alone is insufficient to illustrate the vibrancy or strength of civil society. In Latvia (as elsewhere in the region) at least some of these organizations exist only on paper or are active intermittently. Second, a large number of NGOs often says more about the interests of the international community than local actors. As director of the Baltic American Partnership Program (BAPP), Ieva Morica admits that while BAPP was created in 1998 with funding from USAID and Soros money, with the goal of developing philanthropy and encouraging advocacy, there is little demonstrated interest in ethnic issues or any kind of advocacy in Latvia.[165] Third, even if many of these organizations are active, it is not clear that these activities either affect government behavior or ethnopolitical relations. Finally, as even members of Latvia's civil society readily admit, for these and other reasons it is nearly impossible to know the impact of bottom-up initiatives in affecting interethnic cooperation.[166]

Conclusion

By the decade's end, it is fair to say that the ethnic crisis in the Baltics was over. There was no threat of inter- or intrastate violence; Russia's involvement in these countries' internal affairs was marginal. In Latvia, a variety of governmental and nongovernmental initiatives had been adopted to calm tensions and encourage peace. Signs of success aside, this did not mean that Latvia's ethnic dilemmas were resolved. In fact, the fate of almost a quarter of the country remained ambiguous; stateless non-Latvians could not yet vote, run for public office, or hold state-sector jobs.[167] And although the ethnic conflict was transformed in the 1990s, it is impossible to conclude definitively that transnational efforts prevented ethnic violence. It is fair to assert, however, that the cumulative actions of a transnational network of public and private actors contributed significantly to the deescalation of ethnic tensions and to the promotion of interethnic accommodation within this state. One of the strongest statements that can be made, based on primary research and on secondary sources, is that there is no evidence—none at all—to suggest that Latvians would have adopted *any* accommodating measures without the push and pull coming from the international community.

In this chapter, I did not try to discount the significance of domestic politics or moderate politicians. It is important to emphasize that in spite of Latvia's size and small population, its politicians, especially in the early 1990s, successfully resisted transnational pressure and pursued a nationalist, exclusionary agenda. Latvia's citizenship law is a good example of how impervious Latvian politicians could be to transnational recommendations because it only incorporated a few of the HCNM and CoE recommendations. However, by taking a longer view of the 1990s, I demonstrated how transnational actors were not only able to set the agenda, influence domestic debates and ultimately Latvian legislation, but they sent similar and overlapping messages to the Latvian government. Recommendations from transnational network members were rarely adopted within a short period of time, and all entailed a great deal of political discussion and often-heated debated, but by the end of the 1990s, the majority of international recommendations had been adopted and implemented.[168]

In the early 1990s, the role of the HCNM and the CoE was clearly issue-identification, crafting the West's response to the most troubling aspects of Latvian politics. By 1995, with the EU, NATO, and the United States closely following ethnic conflicts and Latvian-Russian relations, added constraints and incentives pushed Latvian politicians to establish a range of domestic instruments to manage majority-minority relations and promote ethnic harmony. By 1998, a climate of ethnic accommodation had arrived, largely because of the complementary strategies of transnational actors and the synergy that ensued. Transnational involvement shaped elite decisions, informed domestic instruments, and inspired the creation of civil initiatives meant to give voice to minority concerns and foster ethnic tolerance. Thus, the quiet on this part of Russia's front was not the result of one government or a single conflict-management strategy but was instead affected by the interaction and coordination of several governmental and nongovernmental organizations seeking stability and interethnic accommodation in Latvia.

SIX

Transnational Networks and Ethnic Cooperation

The Lessons Learned

As Inus Claude reminds us, "the relationship between majorities and minorities is a perennial problem of politics."[1] In this book, I have sought to show that this "perennial problem" need not culminate in ethnic violence, and in addition, that it is a problem with a multitude of solutions.

Given the prevalence of the literature on violent ethnic conflict, and the under-theorized role of the international community's involvement in ethnic politics in Eastern Europe, my research goals were twofold. First, I examined *how* the international community responded to rising ethnic tensions in the 1990s. Second, I explored the effects of these actions on ethnic politics in Romania and Latvia. These investigations yielded a straightforward central conclusion: The trajectory of majority-minority relations in Eastern Europe was positively affected by a transnational network of public and private actors that exchanged information, adhered to common principles, and developed overlapping strategies to achieve together what none could accomplish on its own.

Most research on Eastern Europe either draws attention to the problem of ethnic conflict or attempts to separate the causal effects of various international actors on policies friendly to ethnic minorities, pitting materially based strategies against normative pressures.[2] This book argued that the similar goals of governments, multilateral organizations, and NGOs, together with their use of complementary strategies—often employed simultaneously—make this exercise futile when trying to explain the broader outcome of ethnic cooperation. At the same time, concentrating on a single actor or one strategy in isolation overlooks transformative trends in international relations and the changes in state-societal relations. In both Romania and Latvia, ethnic cooperation was achieved through the efforts of a jumble of transnational organizations working closely with like-minded domestic actors to pressure governments from above and below the state to pursue a path of peace.

Managing Ethnicity in Eastern Europe

In chapter 2, I discussed historical efforts by the international community to manage interethnic relations. I explained that in the past, the international community either charged one organization to be responsible for ethnic conflict management or it marginalized ethnic issues and minorities in favor of a focus on human rights. The strategies employed in the 1990s were different from those used in the aftermaths of the two world wars. In a sentence, strategies were both multilateral and multileveled. Although the international community did little to stop the spread of ethnic violence in Yugoslavia, this was neither a precedent for the region nor an accurate portrayal of how the international community grappled with ethnic conflict in other contexts. Often below the radar screen, the effects of Bosnia proved to be an effective vaccination against bloody ethnic violence elsewhere.[3]

At the same time, the eruption of violence in the Balkans did a great deal to revive long-standing stereotypes of Eastern Europe: of the backwardness of the region and the virulence of Eastern nationalism. It also reinforced the notion that the international community was incapable of containing what are often seen as age-old ethnic hatreds. By 1993, with violence intensifying, indifference and indecision gave way to a multiplicity of separate, uncoordinated initiatives. Regional organizations shifted their missions, and governments started to focus squarely on the problem of ethnic violence. As organizational theorists would predict, the institutionally fragmented environment in this area, alongside a consensus-oriented political culture, resulted in a form of arrangement best described as a decentralized network.

In chapter 3, I explained the concept of networks, elaborating on their characteristics and behavior in international politics. Although the term *network* is used in a variety of disciplines and in political science by those studying public policy, I asserted that this concept could be usefully applied to the international community's response to the shared problem of ethnic conflict in Eastern Europe. The term *network*, however, is not a synonym for many actors but instead characterizes unique, nonhierarchical relationships and cooperative behavior among public and private actors. In the second half of the 1990s, the relationships among the international and domestic actors seeking to quell potential ethnic conflict had indeed become so dense and intertwined that a transnational network formed. Organizations remained separate and independent, but they came to voice the same principles regarding ethnic conflict management, democracy, and minority rights. Relying on each other for information and expertise while using different but overlapping strategies, they pushed for the same outcome: stability and the management of ethnic conflict in the East.

The second purpose of my research, to specify the effects of this transnational network, are addressed in chapters 3, 4, and 5, where I detailed how transnational actors provided the *message, motivation,* and *means* to facilitate this peaceful trajectory. The CSCE/OSCE and the CoE performed crucial duties for ethnic peace, focusing on the common hurdles to interethnic cooperation (with a focus on citizenship, language, education, and participation). Working separately and together, they established the West's *message,* which asserted the need for ethnic conflict management and the protection of minority rights. The CSCE/OSCE's broad-based membership and focus on conflict prevention and human rights meant that this organization's principles became the standards by which other multilateral organizations discussed ethnic conflict and minority rights and later evaluated outcomes in Eastern Europe.

Despite the CSCE/OSCE's spearheading role in ethnic conflict management and its loose management of the network structure, it readily shared this responsibility with other regional organizations, governments, and NGOs. In particular, the CSCE/OSCE interfaced regularly with the CoE, exchanging information and discussing potential solutions to ethnic tangles, crafting the West's normative objectives related to ethnic conflict management. Importantly, these institutions were the stepping stones to other, more powerful Euro-Atlantic clubs, as they were able to link ideas and international norms in this area to the resources of the EU and NATO. Indeed, they were crucial parts of what one author refers to as "the accession constellation."[4]

There is little doubt that the involvement of the EU and NATO provided the *motivation* for the most difficult policy decisions made in the second half of the decade because they had the resources to sanction and reward transitioning states in the East. In this respect, the EU is a leading reason for the region's political and economic stabilization. Although a significant literature exists to support this claim, its involvement in conflict management did not start to take shape until the middle of the decade. This is not to say that its passive leverage (from 1989–94) did nothing, but that it became focused on ethnic conflict management only in the second half of the decade.[5] The EU's response to the Kosovo crisis and the creation of the Stability Pact for South Eastern Europe is a clear demonstration of the EU's more active stance toward conflict management but, more importantly, an acknowledgment of the need for other governmental and nongovernmental actors to be involved to ensure stability.[6] It cannot be overlooked, moreover, that by the time the EU and NATO were active in this issue, ethnopolitical conflicts in the East were already on the mend. Thus, rather than setting the agenda or shining the international spotlight on the problems of national minorities or the potential for ethnic conflict, they were instead responsible for driving home the urgency of the resolution of these issues.

The objectives and *means* of most NGOs are modest, and they tend to target players outside the state, relying on bottom-up strategies to help implement policies or supply the resources necessary to shift societal relations. In Eastern Europe, the proliferation of NGOs and foundations involved in guiding the region politically toward democracy and economically toward the market meant that a handful of NGOs, such the Project on Ethnic Relations, Human Rights Watch, and the Soros foundations, worked alongside governmental actors to help push ethnic peace forward. To different degrees, NGOs provided significant financial, technical, and moral support for interethnic dialogue, education, and training programs, and, in the process, they spawned a host of local NGOs committed to democracy and ethnic cooperation. Although NGOs tend to operate on the margins or behind the scenes, and their efforts are hard to quantify, understanding ethnic cooperation in Eastern Europe requires not only an acknowledgment of the material incentives and ideational pressures coming from outside these states but also the different roles played by transnational actors with unique capabilities.

Evaluating the Effects

Some practitioners involved in ethnic conflict management recognize the often circuitous ways the international community affects outcomes. For example, in discussing the effects of the HCNM's involvement on ethnic conflict in Eastern Europe, Max van der Stoel admits that its recommendations often fell on deaf ears—at least in the short term—but he maintains that this did not mean that the CSCE/OSCE or the HCNM's office had no effect at all.[7] Perhaps surprisingly, most practitioners involved in ethnic conflict management do not go to great lengths to evaluate their programs or to prove their organization's impact. A EU report on its democracy-promotion projects from 1992 to 1997, for example, considers the methodological problems inherent in evaluating these projects, acknowledging that although one is never sure of the "exact" impact of a single project, it does not logically follow that democracy-promotion programs are unimportant and do not, at least indirectly, encourage stability within these countries. The report concludes that the EU needs to continue its support for democracy-promotion activities and particularly for local NGOs.[8] This conclusion is not based on the proven ability of bottom-up initiatives in Eastern Europe but instead on the historical development of Western European democracies and academic research, which both point to the importance of civil society development and NGOs to help spread democratic ideas and ethnic tolerance. The point is that while the EU cannot prove that its strategies for peaceful change make a difference, funding should continue and rely heavily on NGOs.

Similarly, despite the U.S. government's concerns over ethnic-based conflict in Eastern Europe, this neither translated into a comprehensive strategy for managing ethnic conflicts nor thorough evaluations of its policies. According to Nancy Lubin, questions related to ethnic conflict have "long been in the background" of U.S. assistance efforts in Eastern Europe and the former Soviet Union, but few, if any, U.S. government-sponsored assistance programs were designed to explicitly analyze ethnic conflict.[9] Instead of developing a comprehensive plan as a part of its assistance strategy, U.S. efforts were confined to a handful of projects implemented by NGOs or were the byproduct of other programs placed under the rubric of democracy promotion. To some extent, international NGOs and U.S.-based private foundations filled in this gap, providing significant financial and technical assistance for ethnic conflict management and the promotion of minority rights. The fact remains, however, that since most NGOs do not even have the money for sustained, comprehensive programs, they have even fewer resources to devote to evaluation.[10]

What was indeed evident in the interviews that I conducted in Europe and in the United States was the lack of systematic thought given to the strategies employed to contain ethnic conflict or how their activities impacted ethnic conflicts in Eastern Europe. Tellingly, when I questioned policymakers or NGO officials about evaluation and how they knew their organization's efforts had "made [a] difference" to ethnic conflict or minority rights in Eastern Europe, there was often a pregnant pause. An official from EuropeAid explained the EU's knack for dealing with these challenges, admitting that "evaluating the impact of our democracy or conflict prevention activities is hard, and in the end, our attempts have not always been fruitful. We [EU officials] just assume that we make a difference."[11]

Another adviser to the EU and the former director of the European Human Rights Foundation (the organization initially charged with managing the EU's Democracy Program) admitted that the foundation did not aim to be scientific, but evaluating the impact of the West's influence on Eastern Europe in this area was not that difficult.[12] By comparing the objectives of transnational actors with the changes associated with ethnic politics within these countries, one can acquire some sense of cause and effect. Moreover, while evaluating outcomes was never a major preoccupation for the EU, it did fund yearly evaluations of its programs, and it compared changes in Eastern Europe in light of the EU's objectives in specific issue areas (such as ethnic politics and minority rights) as well as its broader goals for the country and region. The absence of more evaluations of international initiatives is indeed regrettable, especially given the substantial financial resources devoted to ethnic peace, but it should not come as a surprise. The bottom line for practitioners is simple: They rarely have the time or the money to invest in evaluation. As Thomas Carothers explains, by their nature, practitioners must focus on the future, not on the past.[13]

With some success, academic research has developed ways of evaluating the impact of transnational influence. As Sarah Mendelson and John Glenn suggest, there are ways of approximating influence, considering the goals of transnational network members on one hand and the timing, content, and (if possible) the justification for outcomes within targeted states on the other.[14] To interpret domestic changes and the role of transnational actors, I relied on Thomas Risse and Kathyrn Sikkink's "spiral model" that lays out the effects of transnational involvement and how states are socialized into the international system.[15] Although this book examined both material and normative strategies for ethnic conflict management, the spiral model helped to both discern and interpret effects. In fact, the model proved quite illuminating in explaining, if not predicting, changes in the trajectory of ethnic relations. As it suggests, as transnational actors from abroad advocated for changes in the East, states went from denying the right of international actors a say in these issues, to tactical concessions associated with ethnic conflict management, to establishing domestic instruments and allowing norms and standards of behavior to gain prescriptive status, and finally, to changes in policies and social behavior.

To be sure, the transformation of ethnic politics in Eastern Europe was affected by a combination of material and normative-based influences, and there is little evidence to suggest that normative strategies alone would have led to the important changes of the second half of the 1990s. Fieldwork in Bosnia, Romania, and Latvia reinforced the complex reality of ethnic cooperation as well as the importance of different actors and material-based incentives. Interviews with representatives of intergovernmental organizations, politicians, and NGO representatives in the West and East, alongside secondary research, evoked a tangled picture of governmental and nongovernmental organizations, relying on material *and* normative resources to foster stability in Eastern Europe. This is because governmental and nongovernmental organizations consciously used multiple strategies concurrently, accepting that ethnic conflict prevention requires many actors and multilevel responses.[16]

More confounding still for evaluation purposes was that the same strategy is often used by different actors. For example, although here I highlighted the fact that both the EU and NATO had nudged toward a policy of conditionality by 1995, it is also true that by this point, several Western governments (such as the United States) and other intergovernmental organizations (including international financial institutions) were also engaging this strategy (implicitly or explicitly) to quell ethnic tensions and shape outcomes in Eastern Europe. Moreover, as important as EU membership was to transitioning states in Eastern Europe, few would deny the importance of security to these states. Thus, U.S. support and NATO membership cannot be underrated.

Transnational networks seek changes in the short term, but they are ultimately engaged in a long-term incremental process of permanently shifting behavior and perceptions, and often this process is neither linear nor quantifiable. Like scholars who have struggled to demonstrate the impact of a multitude of transnational influences on domestic outcomes and international relations, I illustrated how transnational influences shaped outcomes in three ways. First, transnational actors helped set the ethnic agenda for countries in the West and East. To different degrees and depending on the domestic context, transnational actors were crucial to identifying the problems and providing support and legitimacy to moderate domestic actors committed to change. Second, transnational actors informed domestic debates and decisions, directly and indirectly shaping domestic bodies and instruments that were created to manage ethnic conflict and protect minority rights. Finally, financial and in-kind support from abroad significantly altered the density and content of civil society, creating an untold number of local NGOs and regional initiatives. It also empowered individuals within Eastern Europe to monitor the government's behavior and contain ethnic conflict.[17]

Ethnic Cooperation in Romania and Latvia

In the past, most literature took for granted the negative effects of transnational relations on ethnic conflicts, particularly in situations where an ethnic group straddled a political border, such as in Romania and Latvia. Given the history of divided nations in Eastern Europe, such an assumption is not totally unwarranted. Rogers Brubaker's concept of a triadic nexus of relations went a long way to explicate the problems and potential dangers associated with such a configuration. At the same time, its narrow focus and outdated assumptions, which overlooked the role of other actors and the changes in international relations in the last decade of the twentieth century, led to the mistaken belief that the divided nations in these coun-tries were inherently destabilizing and prone to violence. Contemporary transna-tional literature tends to err in the other direction, assuming an inherently positive and influential role for transnational actors, because of their geographic origin and resources or the perceived effects of what is often referred to as a "transnational civil society."[18]

This research on transnational networks and their effects on Romania and Latvia demonstrates that international involvement is sometimes indeterminate, and outcomes depend not only on the transnational actor, its goals, and the strate-gies it used, but also on the broader international environment and the attention paid to ethnic politics. Transnational involvement can intensify nationalist agendas (as was true in Romania and Latvia from 1989 to 1992), or it can skirt ethnic politics by failing to adopt a clear message on the importance of ethnic cooperation (as evi-denced by U.S. actions in these countries at the beginning of the decade). Although a host of governmental and nongovernmental organizations started to flood East-ern Europe after 1989, little attention was paid to ethnic relations, minority rights, or the importance of conflict prevention in these first few years. The West's eupho-ria over Communism's collapse tended to gloss over emerging ethnic tensions. The U.S. government reacted swiftly to changes in the East, but it was clearly concerned with human rights violations.

Since American leaders tended to ignore the advice of analysts who warned of the potential for ethnic conflict, minority rights and ethnic politics were never a pri-ority. Instead, the United States focused the lion's share of its resources in the former Communist bloc on economic reform and, to a lesser extent, democracy promo-tion, based on the imprudent hope that these strategies would be sufficient to keep nationalist agendas at bay. Such diffuse, ill-specified support for broad economic and political goals, while important on some levels, not surprisingly did little to smooth ethnic relations in Romania and Latvia. In fact, partly because of the im-plicit message coming from the international community at the time—that minor-ity issues were an internal matter—ethnic relations in these countries became more contentious between 1990 and 1993.

Only with Yugoslavia's bloody implosion did the international community wake to the fact that nationalizing agendas and minority rights in these countries could not be ignored, lest they provoke similar crises. By 1993, a minimal interventionist agenda was in place in both countries, reflecting the similar policies of regional or-ganizations, national governments, and NGOs. More than any other transnational actor, the HCNM unpacked the problem of ethnic conflict in Romania and Latvia, exposing the policies that stood in the way of better majority-minority relations. Because of its unique position, history, and expertise, the CSCE/OSCE was at the center of international efforts to management these ethnic conflicts.[19] With this said, the HCNM's role and relative influence was different in these countries. In Latvia, the CSCE/OSCE separated symbolic aspects of the ethnic conflict from tangible problems in need of compromise (such as minority participation in governance, access to education, and language use). In this case, the CSCE/OSCE truly set and defined the ethnic agenda. In Romania, the HCNM reinforced and gave legitimacy to domestic leaders and NGOs that were already actively working in this direction.[20] Perhaps as a consequence, in Latvia the HCNM's efforts assumed a much higher profile and attracted a good deal of public attention, and in the eyes of some Latvian nationalists, Max van der Stoel embodied the imposing, patronizing West that was interfering in issues it did clearly did not understand. In contrast, in Romania the HCNM's efforts instead gave focus to the West's message and expectations and supported the agendas of moderate Romanians and Hungarians.

Inspired by the same set of tragic events, other transnational actors such as the CoE weighed in on interethnic relations in Romania and Latvia. By 1993, with a number of public and private actors starting to put a name to the problem and pointing to the urgency of involvement, a transnational campaign of largely uncoordinated activities emerged to discourage nationalism's ascent in Romania and Latvia. Gradually, through CSCE/OSCE recommendations and the CoE's legal focus, they crafted the West's position on ethnopolitical conflicts in the East, emphasizing the importance of European norms related to democracy, the peaceful resolution of disputes, and human rights—including the rights of minorities.

By this point, although both Romania and Latvia had committed themselves publicly to joining the West, an obvious disjuncture between their stated foreign policy goals and domestic behavior was evident. As expected by Risse and Sikkink's spiral model, both went from denying the right of international actors a say in these matters to adopting legislation and using the language of the international community for their own purposes. It was becoming clear that token legislation and the international community's vocabulary were meant largely to simulate change. However, by the middle of the 1990s, with the goals and strategies of the EU and NATO in place and overlapping, the locus of ethnic-related activity increasingly shifted from the international arena to the domestic one. After 1995, Latvian and Romanian moderates were publicly debating with nationalists the importance of bringing domestic policies in line with international goals and commitments. In very different environments, moderate politicians in both countries used this network to bolster their own positions and validate their claims.

While the CSCE/OSCE and the CoE were both essential to unpacking the problem of ethnic conflict and clarifying how these issues were interpreted by the West and should be handled in the East, the CoE's role and effects are more elusive, and are often overlooked entirely. Part of this is because lawyers and seemingly innocuous laws made in Strasbourg rarely made for front-page coverage, and delegations from the council or local politicians' visits to France did not have an immediate impact on policy or debate. While more subtle, in both Romania and Latvia, locals indicated that the council's impact was incisive because of its effect on domestic legislation. The CoE also eventually established two mechanisms to monitor compliance with its laws. Importantly, these procedures were not meant to shame countries for not living up to their commitments but instead identified "problem areas" and, by this identification, helped garner resources and expertise to assist each country with the implementation of necessary legal reforms.[21] As Anne Marie Slaughter puts it, a transnational network of lawyers and government officials works behind the scenes in Europe to improve compliance with international laws.[22] Together, the CSCE/OSCE and the CoE not only identified the obstacles to closer relations with the West, but, in the process, they translated the meaning of these concerns into viable legal, political, and social solutions.

In the early 1990s, these messengers, or in the words of Steven Ratner, "normative entrepreneurs," often failed to gain the ear of nationalist politicians—at least immediately.[23] In Romania, for example, a law on nationalities was never adopted while a restrictive Law on Education was passed in 1995—despite the strong opposition of the CSCE/OSCE and the CoE. In Latvia, the 1994 Law on Citizenship was passed, which the CSCE/OSCE and CoE had urged, yet it barely reflected the recommendations of these Western envoys. Clearly, normative pressures and the sway of international norms were insufficient to get states to adopt and implement sensitive legislation. Thus, their efforts alone cannot explain ethnic cooperation in either Romania or Latvia. Instead, by the middle of 1990s, with the most precarious phase underway, and as domestic groups argued the meaning and implications of their international promises, other actors, namely the EU and NATO, took a more active role in ethnic conflict management and minority rights, using materially based incentives to drive home the message of change.

What was evident by about 1995 in both Romania and Latvia—despite significantly different governments—was the way transnational actors behaved and the similar effects of their involvement. That is to say, the West's minimalist activities gave way to a clear ethnic agenda and to a comprehensive, interventionist position. Coinciding with NATO-led military action in Bosnia, ethnic issues were given consistent attention by the EU, NATO, and the United States as well as other transnational actors. The EU's policy of membership conditionality was no doubt important in gaining the ear of moderate and nationalist governments alike, directly affecting the Hungarian-Romanian bilateral treaty in 1996 and the adoption of amendments to the citizenship law in Latvia in 1998. Although the EU's role is crucial, one should not overlook NATO and the U.S. government, as both were consistently weighing in on the issue in the second half of the 1990s.

Membership in the EU and NATO were important to both Romanians and Latvians, but it is difficult to say which organizations had more influence over the management of ethnic conflict, and it appears that their influence was not the same in these countries. For example, in Romania, while there was a surprising consensus on the desire to become "part of Europe" and enjoy its benefits, perceptions and understandings of what different regional organizations did suggests a different causal effect. A statement signed by all of Romania's political parties in June 1995 illustrated the country's unified vision: Romania would integrate into the EU and adopt the Western value system.[24] However, later versions of this document discussed the differences between the EU, which is largely economic, and NATO expansion, which is more political. For Romania, EU integration was seen as largely symbolic and ambiguous while membership in NATO would fulfill immediate and clear goals, namely, it would provide long-awaited security guarantees for Romania. Given that even in 1998 many Romanian politicians were confused by the implications of EU membership, it may be true that NATO had more of immediate bearing on Romanian-Hungarian relations.[25] In contrast, when difficult decisions were proposed and passed in Latvia, they were tied publicly to the EU or the country's chances for membership in the EU. Privately, however, Latvian government officials and NGO leaders reinforced the importance of NATO's security guarantees and U.S. support. Nonetheless, in both countries, as the EU and NATO linked membership to ethnic politics, these international institutions and their strategy of conditionality often had the intended effects—in spite of domestic opposition.

Yet the use of membership conditionality, mediation, and normative pressure—what might be called "structuralist" approaches to conflict prevention—were combined with a broad array of instruments based on a "social-psychological" approach to conflict prevention that emphasizes the intangible, symbolic aspects of ethnic conflict and highlights the importance of reaching out to actors beyond the state.[26] A survey of USAID practices related to ethnic conflict explained that bottom-up strategies were consciously used as a blanket method for encouraging interethnic stability, since promoting effective legal systems and third-sector organizations provided outlets to ethnic communities to express their concerns.[27] Investments in actors outside the state, in what is referred to as "civil society development," were fostered through the establishment of local NGO. In this regard, international NGOs like the Soros foundations network, the Project on Ethnic Relations, and the Helsinki Committee (to name just a few) were crucial to providing the means for the construction of open, tolerant, and democratic societies.

In Latvia, internationally funded NGOs such as the Latvian Language Program, the Latvian Center for Human Rights, and the Integration Fund were all part of broader efforts to transform Latvian society from the bottom up. In Romania, transnational actors provided the funding for domestic NGOs such as the Ethnocultural Diversity Center in Cluj and the Euroregional Center for Democracy in Timisoara which enabled Romanian citizens to encourage interethnic cooperation within Romania and throughout the region. Individually, these efforts do not appear to make much of a difference. However, as a U.S. diplomat suggested, together they may have empowered people enough that ethnic tensions faded and new identities were constructed.[28] The point is that these social-psychological projects can be narrowly focused on ethnic conflict or minority rights, but they need not be; in fact, the goal of bottom-up initiatives is not to resolve specific ethnic conflicts but to establish and cultivate channels of communication between different groups in society, "creating an understanding of the kinds of decision making processes that can lead parties out of a conflict."[29] In the two cases of ethnic cooperation this book explored, this transnational network assembled different but crucial components for the promotion of ethnic peace.

The Limits of These Findings

Just as there are many justifications for a book, there are also as many limitations; the most obvious of which is this book's narrow geographic scope and its case selection. Not only have other regions seen a revival in ethnic conflict, but some might observe that despite the existence of this transnational network, it did not deter the spread of violence in Kosovo. The point was not to conclude that the existence of a transnational network of public and private actors committed to ethnic conflict management affected all ethnic disputes in the same way. Indeed, a central assertion made by this research is that the effectiveness of transnational actors is a function of their ability to elicit and sustain domestic support, and thereby shift the locus of activity from the international to the domestic realm.

Just as this book did not attempt to embrace all interethnic relationships in Eastern Europe, it did not seek to develop an exhaustive compendium of transnational influences that directly or indirectly shaped ethnic relations in the East. Even a larger study could not incorporate all the numerous political, economic, and social influences weighing on interethnic relations. Instead, the goal was to explain how leading international actors responded to ethnicity's revival in the East and to probe the effects on majority-minority relations in Romania and Latvia. However, research that looks closely at other ethnic conflicts in the region suggests that a similar transnational conglomeration of public and private actors weighed in on these conflicts.

For example, research that addresses the EU's stabilization plan in the Balkans draws attention to its efforts to bring together an extraordinary range of states, regional organizations, and NGOs; this is because a main objective of the Stability Pact for South Eastern Europe was to develop a "shared strategy" toward the region.[30] Without attaching the label of network, they note the significant shift in organizational culture that occurred after the Bosnian conflict and the importance of coordination and synergy to encourage stability, development, and integration.[31] Yet, Gaetano Pentassuglia's research is not limited to the Balkans but instead confirms that that an upsurge of minority problems and social tensions resulted in a dense network of strategies meant both to protect minorities and to prevent conflict.[32]

Others highlight the unique role played by NGOs (in conjunction with governments and regional organizations) throughout Europe and Eurasia, in places like Montenegro, which has managed to avoid violent ethnic conflict.[33] As in the cases explored here, the OSCE, the EU, the U.S. government, and a broad range of NGOs worked together to keep violence at bay in this former Yugoslav republic. At the end of 2000, according to the Center for the Development of Nongovernmental Organizations, there were more than eight-hundred registered NGOs. While only a handful were involved in ethnic issues directly, they embraced a range of strategies.[34] In Macedonia as well, numerous international NGOs joined official conflict management activities, which started in 1992 when the United Nations Preventive Deployment Force was relocated from Croatia to Macedonia. As elsewhere in the region, these initiatives paralleled and reinforced the efforts of the EU, OSCE, the CoE, and NATO.[35]

Moreover, although this book looked at the politics of "divided nations" and at situations where internal ethnic conflicts had the potential to become interstate conflicts, studies of the Roma minority in Eastern Europe suggest that a similar transnational network of public and private actors developed in the 1990s in response to the challenges facing this group. The Roma are a difficult minority to categorize or quantify, but the problems of discrimination they face throughout Europe are well documented.[36] The political and economic changes in Eastern Europe made the Roma even more vulnerable; because of the unique challenges facing this minority group, the CSCE/OSCE asked the HCNM to prepare a report on the situation of the Roma and to consider the international dimensions of this majority-minority problem.[37] Noting the grave challenges facing this extremely vulnerable population, the HCNM observed that every CSCE/OSCE document since 1990 had highlighted the situation of the Roma and that several other multilateral bodies, including the CoE, various UN agencies, and the EU, had taken notice.[38] Although majority rights per se were not within the HCNM's narrow mandate, by 1993 various governmental and philanthropic sources in Western Europe and North America were funneling money to study and address Roma issues. Importantly, this transnational campaign focused on the Roma involved intergovernmental organizations working closely with NGOs and philanthropic organizations.

Scholars indeed note a dramatic change in the scale and nature of the transnational initiatives targeting the Roma people and communities throughout the decade.[39] Peter Vermeersch, for example, traces the growth and impact of these public and private activities, referring to the "transnational advocacy network" that developed around this situation. Highlighting the work of several international NGOs, Vermeersch argues that international attention was generally positive for Romani advocacy organizations and political participation, raising awareness of the problems, giving voice to the population, and, most urgently, providing the tools and resources to address these issues.[40] Without minimizing the "marked and immediate effects" of NGOs, Vermeersch explains that intergovernmental organizations, including the UN, the EU, the CSCE/OSCE, and the CoE, also put Roma issues high on their list of priorities, establishing specific programs and bodies for Roma affairs and increasing financial and technical resources to this group.[41]

Paralleling the developments in Romanian-Hungarian and Latvian-Russian relations in the second half of the 1990s, the region witnessed a "clear increase in special government programs targeted at Romani communities."[42] While no one suggests that programs or declarations necessarily add up to significant improvements for this group, the sudden and dramatic increase in attention to the Roma is closely tied to transnational involvement and the activities of several actors, both public and private. Future research should thus examine in more depth the potential role of transnational actors and networks in other ethnic conflicts in the region, including both those with the potential for interstate conflict and those with only intrastate consequences.

Problems and Unintended Consequences

In spite of the effectiveness of this transnational network in transforming ethnic politics in Romania and Latvia, I cannot conclude with the suggestion that its impact was wholly positive. It was not, and rarely are international influences one-sided. Interwar attempts to manage ethnicity in Eastern Europe provided numerous lessons for ethnic conflict management in the 1990s, but it appears that members of this network did not always heed historical warnings. Moreover, despite the ability of networks to bring the resources of many actors to bear on problem of ethnic conflict, networks are no panacea, and a few downsides warrant mention.

The most common criticism of this transnational network is its narrow focus on potentially violent ethnic conflicts. Consequently, although different actors and strategies were involved, transnationalism in the 1990s was similar in important respects to interwar attempts to manage Eastern nationalism. Both forays were first and foremost about promoting stability in Europe. As important as the post-World War I order was to laying the foundation for a minority-rights regime, international involvement was not about justice or national self-determination for European minorities. Similarly, in the 1990s, bilateral treaties, international standards, and the inclusion of minority rights protections were not in fact meant to create better or even consistent standards to improve the situation of national minorities; instead, these strategies were used on weak states to discourage violence.

This meant that unlike transnational *advocacy* networks, this network was comprised largely of individuals who were advocating policy changes because of rational self-interest.[43] To a great extent, this involvement emerged because of self-interested behavior and a concern over the potential for violence. For example, in explaining his office's mission, van der Stoel would frequently clarify the nuances associated with his title; he was the high commissioner *on* rather than *for* national minorities. This is because despite the CSCE/OSCE's pivotal role in promoting human rights during the cold war, its primary objective in the post-cold war era, especially as it related to the responsibilities of the HCNM, was conflict prevention and management. However, it would be unfair to categorize all transnational efforts as self-interested; in fact, as others have argued, there were many reasons for international involvement in this issue, based on different justifications and a mixture of motivations.[44] Given the number of NGOs and grassroots initiatives focused on the Hungarian and Russian minorities, one cannot conclude that all transnational efforts were focused on preventing violence. In practice, however, it seemed that ethnicity's revival in the East mattered only when violence was a possibility, not because of an explicit desire to improve majority-minority relations or a minority group's situation.

The mistaken assumption that some minorities made—that transnational actors were primarily interested in their rights or ensuring justice for long-oppressed groups—caused significant disillusionment among minority group members who initially looked to the international community for answers, if not salvation. Such disappointment was articulated by members of the Hungarian minority in Romania. The painful logic for minority groups in Eastern Europe is clear: If they are not violent, the international community will not pay attention to them.[45] Thus, to some, transnational actors were clearly uninterested in the problems the Hungarian minority encountered in Romania or if the Romanian government did not fulfill its international commitment—unless these issues were likely to spark interethnic violence. In Latvia, too, Russians were sometimes skeptical of the international community's commitment to minority rights.[46] There is no evidence to suggest that any minority group in Eastern Europe undertook radical measures to attract international attention, but some research does suggest that international norms and economic incentives established by transnational actors unintentionally encouraged ethnic groups such as Moravians in the Czech Republic and Silesians in Poland to transform themselves in order to be acknowledged and to benefit from the protections (and financial assistance) offered by the CSCE/OSCE, the CoE, and the EU.[47]

The double standards inherent in this transnational network's thematic and geographic focus are irrefutable. As Karen Smith confirms with regard to EU enlargement, the EU insisted on European standards, including those related to minority rights, to be applied in states that were not currently members because they hoped that the protection of minority rights would help prevent violent ethnic conflict, and the EU wanted desperately to avoid importing ethnic problems.[48] However, bearing striking similarities to Western efforts in the interwar period and the inequality between the East and the West, transnationalism in the 1990s was a clear sign of the West's attempt to export certain values and behavior to the East without corresponding expectations and behavior for the West. Since Eastern Europe was so desperately dependent on the West economically, politically, and for security, the power of transnational actors was immense. While not always intentionally flexing its financial and political muscle, transnational actors recognized their sway and importance in Eastern Europe, often adopting strategies and wielding ideas related to ethnic conflict management and minority rights that were, as Bruno de Witt put it, for export only, not internal consumption.[49]

The seeds of this double standard were evident by the time the office of a high commissioner on national minorities was established. For almost two years prior to its establishment, several Western countries voiced their concerns over the internationalization of minorities' issues. Turkey, Great Britain, and the United States, for example, claimed that their countries did not have national minorities among their populations; it was also decided that the newly established office would not be able to intervene in cases involving terrorism.[50] In other words, despite the claim of universalism and the application of CSCE/OSCE principles in all member states, efforts related to ethnic politics were viewed as security issues and, thus, focused squarely on the longstanding problems in the East, ignoring similar problems in the West. Latvians in particular grew tired of what some referred to as international interference. In the opinion of some, the West's crude solutions to ethnic tensions betrayed its lack of historical knowledge or its appreciation of Latvia's experiences. In Romania as well, there was often the distinct feeling that the West made excessive or capricious demands on weaker, transitioning states in the East, even though they were quite unwilling to implement them on their own, simply because they knew they could get away with it.[51]

Moreover, the demands placed on Eastern European states sometimes overshadowed other aspects of the transition process. One certainly cannot forget that although ethnic tensions and national minorities were important issues, these states faced myriad political, economic, and social challenges. As one writer notes with regard to the dissolution of Yugoslavia, economic failure did more to set the people of Yugoslavia against each other than most realize.[52] Despite the obvious connection between economics and interethnic conflict, transnational actors often ignored the importance of economics and the need to address both concerns. Many of the same transnational actors involved in ethnic conflict management and which, by extension, encouraged the state to increase its domestic instruments in this area were the very same actors pushing for the state's retreat and for market reform.

Moreover, in Eastern Europe, market reforms contributed to a dramatic, if short-lived economic decline in all postcommunist states, and while such downturn alone does not cause ethnic conflict, economic problems correlate with violent ethnic conflict. Economic development is a key component to ethnic conflict management and to helping countries create the necessary structures to establish multicultural societies. A dearth of government funds to pay for such changes or to monitor legislation puts the burden on struggling states or the minority communities themselves, which can easily render legislated rights or social initiatives meaningless. In Latvia, transnational actors such as the UN, the Soros foundations network, and the Baltic American Partnership seemed to appreciate the importance of filling in the gaps left by the retreating state, initiating language programs and civil society projects to empower minorities and to help integrate Latvian society.

Another problem associated with this transnational network emerged out of the so-called "solutions" advanced by actors to manage ethnic conflicts. Some argue that in an attempt to avert violence, international recommendations entailed an almost imperceptible move away from liberal democracy to what some have defined as liberal nationalism.[53] Liberal nationalism assumes that culture provides individuals with the necessary framework to evaluate options and exercise liberty. This thinking had become so influential among some individuals with European organizations, largely because of their exaggerated fear of nationalism, that Western problem solvers encouraged excessively generous minority policies. In the process, transnational actors encouraged and perhaps reified ethnic differences in Eastern Europe. Early CSCE and CoE documents, in fact, reflect these broad-based conceptions of minority rights, even hinting at an embrace of collective rather than individual rights through ideas like territorial autonomy, consociationalism, federalism, or bilingualism. However, as just as these ideas might be in theory, in practice Eastern Europeans found them totally inappropriate, if not counterproductive, to the long-term management of ethnic conflict given the region's history. As Bruno de Witt puts it, "academic pilgrims" from the West brought their model constitutions to Eastern Europe, but since they did not have a ready-made minority-protection model in their first aid kits, they often promoted or pushed a variety of different and even conflicting ideas on the East.[54] Bosnia serves as the most troubling example of contradictory international solutions for a country's ethnic dilemmas; some "solutions" encouraged multiethnic identities while others separated ethnic groups at the highest levels, thereby not only complicating reconciliation but perhaps even threatening the long-term viability of the Bosnian state.[55] Although the most obvious example, Bosnia is not the only example of good intentions gone awry. Discussions in the CSCE/OSCE and the CoE about territorial autonomy and minority rights related to education and language use may have inadvertently intensified ethnic tensions in Romania and Latvia at some points in the the 1990s. By underscoring the rights of the group, rather than a focus on individual rights, such solutions threatened to open Pandora's box.

At the same time, despite the rhetoric about European standards and the need for East European states to conform to generally accepted norms, transnational efforts failed to produce uniform standards, and they were not even able to clarify fundamental terms like *minority group*. To this day, there is no consensus on the collective rights of minority groups in the Euro-Atlantic community. While Hungary joined Germany, Austria, Italy, the Netherlands, and Canada in supporting the collective rights of groups, countries such as Slovakia, Romania, and Bulgaria joined the position of France and Greece, favoring individual rights.[56] Thus, instead of initiatives that reconciled competing views of liberal democracy with regard to minority rights, transnational initiatives in the 1990s side-stepped the problem, advocating both depending on the country and the intensity of the situation. Critics argue that because of these failures, countries in the West have not in fact taken a serious attitude toward the treatment of minorities or the need for the internationalization of ethnic politics.[57]

A final negative consequence of this transnational network relates to its ineffectiveness and inability to manage ethnic conflicts. Networks emerge because governments are not able (or willing) to accomplish goals on their own, and there is a need for speed and flexibility. Yet, even when a culture of consensus exists and a network forms, this does not mean that it will necessarily be quick, responsive, or efficient. In contrast to the interwar period, in which the League of Nations was *the* intergovernmental organization responsible for containing ethnic conflict, the decentralized nature of the transnational network of the 1990s meant that public and private actors each assumed only part of the burden for ethnic conflict management. In many ways, this division of labor and responsibilities was positive; power was diffused, which allowed actors to engage different constituencies within Eastern European states. By diluting responsibility among actors, no one organization was faced with the overwhelming challenge of conflict management. By implication, however, no one actor was responsible for deterring or responding to violent conflict. Thus, when Milosevic continued his aggression in Kosovo, there was no government or organization charged with a response. Indeed, as international involvement showed, there was even significant disagreement over the right of the international community to intervene militarily in Kosovo.

Given that a network's effectiveness is a function of the engagement of different responses coming from multiple actors, networks are clearly not the best mechanism for avoiding imminent violence. Moreover, since there is no assigned leader to set priorities, to divide responsibilities, or to ensure the efficient use of resources, disorganization and hesitancy are not unlikely. In fact, while the current Stability

Pact recognizes the need for governmental actors, donors, and NGOs to work separately and together, it was consciously crafted to ensure more coordination and greater responsibility. Thus, while helpful in the 1990s in certain Eastern European countries, especially when ethnic violence was not imminent, transnational networks can be woefully inadequate if a quick, decisive policy is needed to avert bloodshed.

Finally, transnational networks by their very nature are not permanent, and they are continually changing to adapt to new circumstances and realities. By the end of the decade, the transnational network described here became too dense with actors' missions overlapping. It became inefficient because too many actors and responses were at work. By the beginning of the twenty-first century, CSCE/OSCE principles and practices were not only evident in other regional organizations, but the EU, the CoE, and NATO had each adopted their own conflict prevention bodies to counter ethnicity's rise and encourage stability in the East. Bosnia's fate in the last years of the 1990s is testimony to what can happen when a large array of governmental and nongovernmental organizations focus on the same problem without sufficient coordination. By 2000, for example, there were so many actors and so little management that efforts were needlessly duplicated while others were painfully neglected, money was wasted, and organizations became unnecessarily competitive.[58]

The Implications of This Research

By 2004, eight Eastern European countries marked their "symbolic return to Europe," becoming full members of the European Union. Of the eight, all had gained membership in NATO, the OSCE, and the CoE. Thus, to varying degrees, the countries of Eastern Europe have, without exception, become part of a dense institutional web of intergovernmental and nongovernmental institutions that inform leaders' preferences, shape state policies, and facilitate social change. As elsewhere in Europe, these changes have allowed suprastate institutions to shape ethnic politics from above while giving rise to substate organizations that seek to transform state-society relations and attitudes from below.[59] While mindful of the problems of generalization and the limited geographical scope of this book, the successes (as well as the shortcomings) of this transnational network contain important lessons for ethnic conflict management elsewhere and perhaps even the management of other transnational security issues.

This book has focused on the transformation of ethnic politics in Eastern Europe, and it is easy to conclude, with the power of hindsight, that the peaceful trajectory of this region was over-determined. One might think that geography, the lure of powerful regional organizations, and large doses of Western assistance guaranteed that all arrows would point in the same direction and thus toward ethnic cooperation and stability. Yet, the extensive literature on ethnic conflict, the pessimistic predictions about Eastern Europe, violent ethnic conflicts in Bosnia and Kosovo, as well as ethnic crises in many Eastern European states in the 1990s serve as correctives to such pedestrian conclusions. The surprising but important transformation of ethnic politics in Eastern Europe reminds us, first and foremost, of the continuum of ethnic relations, but also of the ability of the international community to directly and indirectly push ethnic conflicts away from violence and toward ethnic peace.

Despite the uniqueness of Europe, the strategies used in the 1990s to avert ethnic conflict may be relevant for other contexts. Conflict prevention is about "early warning" and, if necessary, "early action." This should not be interpreted as a call for Western states to intervene militarily to thwart ethnic violence. Instead, what this research suggests is an appeal for governments to work collaboratively with each other and regional organizations, to rely on similar principles to manage ethnic conflicts and to exchange information and expertise. Although the necessary institutions and relationships may not yet exist elsewhere in the world, top-down and bottom-up strategies, derived from local conditions and pursued by complementary, reinforcing relationships, may go a long way to manage ethnic conflicts in other contexts. As in Eastern Europe, this should not happen through government initiatives alone but need to include the support of existing intergovernmental organizations. Indeed, an obvious take-home point of this research is the importance of governments working with and through intergovernmental organizations, employing strategies that are often based on different assumptions of ethnic conflict management.

In regions such as the Middle East or Africa, this might suggest a broadening in the geographical focus of regional organizations such as the OSCE. Indeed, given the OSCE's gradual creep into the former Soviet Union and its involvement in the Caucasus and Central Asia today, an expansion of its principles and practices elsewhere might serve as an important first step to promoting liberal democracy and managing ethnic conflicts. At the same time, NATO has not only enlarged its membership, but it now has an extensive web of relationships short of membership with states around the globe, using security guarantees, training procedures, and other tools to broaden its positive reach and promote stability. The evolution of intergovernmental organizations does not suggest that governments can simply withdraw;

while the roles and responsibilities of regional organizations and NGOs might need to expand to manage interethnic relations, states remain crucial to the formula.

A second implication of this research relates to the other important actors that play a role in preventing ethnic conflict: nongovernmental organizations. The role of NGOs might be even more important in places such as the Middle East and Africa, where states are weak or less legitimate and where regional organizations are not as strong. Margaret Keck and Kathryn Sikkink's work on transnational advocacy networks explains the multifaceted role NGOs' have played in spearheading changes in human rights, women's rights, and the environment. Others claim that NGOs can and have played an important role in conflict prevention in a variety of situations.[60] In Eastern Europe, NGOs, particularly in Romania, were crucial in raising awareness and bringing elites together for dialogue and debate. The hefty financial involvement of public and private foundations such as the Soros foundations network is further evidence of the growing importance of nonstate actors, which can establish a range of institutions outside the state and empower individuals to play a role in transforming societies and their values.

As the 1990s progressed, governments and regional organizations increasingly acknowledged the important role of NGOs and the need for an active civil society to cement ethnic cooperation and regional stability. The Stability Pact embodies this awareness.[61] The pact also reflects this public-private model of conflict management in Europe, funded largely by the EU, and is managed by the OSCE, which coordinates the activities (and financial assistance) of governments and intergovernmental organizations and engages local NGOs and the private sector.[62] Preventing ethnic conflict elsewhere will no doubt include some similar public-private partnership, where governments subcontract to NGOs that are better able to implement programs, promote values, and empower individuals. This trend is already obvious in cases of peace-building and postconflict reconstruction. However, although there are many advantages to the proliferation and involvement of NGOs in ethnic conflict management, putting too much faith in them is unwarranted. NGOs are increasingly a part of the architecture of governance, but that does not mean that they are always the most effective actors or should be seen as a replacement to government involvement.

Third, just as there is no single cause for ethnic conflict, this research indicates that there is no single solution. Indeed, ethnic cooperation emerges from pressures from both above and below. These solutions do not conform to any cookie-cutter model of ethnic conflict management; instead, this research suggests the need for governments and NGO to develop, if not systemize, its toolbox of solutions for averting ethnic conflict. Such a toolbox would further develop its range of instruments with the goal of having top-down and bottom-up initiatives work together closely. This conflict-prevention toolbox would include mediation from the HCNM, security relationships with NATO, legal advice from the CoE, as well democracy promotion initiatives from NGOs with experience in conflict prevention and human rights. More than anything else, this research demonstrates the need for those involved in ethnic conflict management activities to share information, allow actors to exploit their unique expertise and skills, and encourage interdependent behavior. While often confusing and no doubt complicated, there is a need for a baffling variety of actors and instruments to provide the message, motivation, and means to encourage ethnic peace.

At the same time, these tools cannot be used the same way in all ethnic conflicts. The key with this toolbox is ensuring that all arrows point in the same direction—toward ethnic cooperation—without trying to impose specific outcomes on states. Indeed, the clear lesson of Communist Eastern Europe was the problematic way the Soviet Union dictated its approach to ethnic diversity. As social-psychological approaches to conflict prevention claim, a great deal is gained by discussion and dialogue and allowing actors to come to terms with majority-minority relations on their own. In the 1990s, good intentions often went awry because of efforts, though unintentional, that tended to impose certain solutions on ethnic conflicts. This was true even in the area of civil society development, which was largely aimed at encouraging bottom-up, local initiatives. The reality behind many of these Western civil society programs betrayed a hidden attempt to control or unnecessarily craft civil society in Eastern Europe to emulate the West. Just as promoting democracy is a delicate process, managing ethnic conflict is more of an art than a science. If the international community tries to construct ethnic peace for its own self-interest or merely to impose stability, short-term payoffs will ultimately undermine long-term goals.

The final conclusion is that governance by network in international relations has been in the making for a long time. Such decentralized forms of governance have numerous positive attributes, and in the cases examined here, the combined energy of governments, regional organizations, and NGOs reduced the likelihood of ethnic-based violence in Eastern Europe. There are, no doubt, also downsides to this approach, including inefficiency and a lack of accountability. Yet, the effectiveness of preventing ethnic conflict by network behavior provides potentially important insights for the international community as new security concerns emerge.

Perhaps the lessons learned by transnational networks and ethnic cooperation in Eastern Europe could be applied to other foreign policy concerns, namely terrorism and weapons of mass destruction proliferation. For example, Amitai Etizioni recognizes the changing global architecture of governance and its ability to resolve transnational problems, claiming that one of the most positive, but generally overlooked, developments since the terrorist attacks on the United States has been the emergence of a global antiterrorist coalition in which over 140 countries have banded together formally and informally to share intelligence, make arrests, and fight terrorism.[63] Anne Holohan's recent book on Kosovo examines a different arrangement of public and private actors that are devoted to peace making, claiming that when networks are created from independent organizations, outcomes are more successful.[64] The existence of other complex, multilayered structures of global governance working in these areas suggests that other security problems could be (and perhaps already are) effectively managed through transnational networks.

Conclusion

With the cold war's end, some scholars optimistically believed that "the end of history" would inherently mean less violence. Others saw a different world, one of identity conflicts and ethnically inspired bloodshed.[65] This book paints still a different picture of the post-cold war era, one that is challenging and prone to discord but hardly characterized by extremism and bloodshed. It is a world where different ethnic groups are shopping in the same markets and sitting together in cafés, and children are playing in their yards without a thought to the ethnicity of their neighborhood friend. This is the reality in Romania and Latvia today and throughout most of Eastern Europe.

This research thus depicts Eastern Europe in the 1990s and today as a place where there is little ethnic violence but still ethnic difference. In light of Eastern Europe's history and grave predictions to the contrary, the possibility that ethnic conflicts here might be cultivated to remain nonviolent provides important messages and lessons worthy of emulating and encouraging elsewhere. The active participation of governmental and nongovernmental organizations, working side by side in an almost seamless web, does not mean that transnational networks are *the* cure for the all problems posed by ethnic diversity, but it does offer important and successful ways to tame ethnic hatred and advance ethnic cooperation.

APPENDIX

NOTES

BIBLIOGRAPHY

INDEX

Analysis of Books and Articles on Ethnic Cooperation, Conflict, Peace, and War

This analysis was based on the following sources: World Cat, a leading bibliographic database that includes more than fifty million records; Article First, a World Cat database of article listings in English; JSTOR, a scholarly journal archive used by many institutions of higher learning; and InfoTrac, an online database of journal and newspaper articles. The numbers were compiled on August 19, 2003.

1. Academic Books and Articles Published on Ethnic Conflict

	Total Numbers	Before 1990	Before 1990 as a % of total	1991–2000	1991–2000 as a % of total	2001–2003	2001–2003
World Cat-Books in English	2148	447	21	1236	58	465	22
World Cat-Books in other major langs.	2504	491	20	1470	59	543	21
Article First	554	156	39	398	72	0	0
JSTOR	1043	401	38	633	61	9	1
InfoTrac	206	34	17	172	84	0	0

2. Academic Books and Articles Published on Ethnic War

	Total Numbers	Before 1990	Before 1990 as a % of total	1991–2000	1991–2000 as a % of total	2001–2003	2001–2003
World Cat-Books in English	1628	321	20	968	59	339	29
World Cat-Books in other major langs.	2805	656	23	1709	61	440	17
Article First	194	63	32	131	68	0	0
JSTOR	52	6	12	42	81	4	8
InfoTrac	71	17	24	54	76	0	0

3. A Comparison of Academic Books and Articles on Ethnic Cooperation vs. Ethnic Conflict

	All books & articles	Before 1990	1991–2000	2001–2003
World Cat				
-In English on ethnic cooperation	290	93	161	36
-In other major languages on ethnic cooperation	308	98	173	37
-In English on ethnic conflict	2148	447	1236	465
-In other major languages on ethnic conflict	2504	491	1470	543
Article First				
-Ethnic cooperation	25	4	21	0
-Ethnic conflict	554	156	398	0
JSTOR				
-Ethnic cooperation	28	15	13	0
-Ethnic conflict	1043	401	633	9

4. A Comparison of Academic Books and Articles on Ethnic Peace vs. Ethnic War

	All books & articles	Before 1990	1991–2000	2001–2003
World Cat				
-In English on ethnic peace	479	71	297	111
-In other major languages on ethnic peace	539	83	341	115
-In English on ethnic war	1628	321	968	339
-In other major languages on ethnic war	2805	656	1709	440
Article First				
-Ethnic peace	230	111	119	0
-Ethnic war	194	63	131	0
JSTOR				
-Ethnic peace	24	3	21	0
-Ethnic war	52	6	42	4

Notes

1. Ethnic Cooperation in Eastern Europe

1. Will H. Moore and David R. Davis, "Transnational Ethnic Ties and Foreign Policy," in *The International Spread of Ethnic Conflict: Fear, Diffusion and Escalation,* ed. David A. Lake and Donald S. Rothchild (Princeton: Princeton Univ. Press, 1998), 90. Among the best-known proponents of this view are Robert Kaplan, *The Balkan Ghosts: A Journey Through History* (New York: St. Martin's Press, 1993), and Samuel Huntington, *The Clash of Civilizations and the Remaking of World Order* (New York: Simon and Schuster, 1997).

2. See Ted Robert Gurr, *Peoples Versus States* (Washington, D.C.: USIP Press, 2000); Gurr, "Wane of Ethnic Conflict," *Foreign Affairs* 73, no. 3 (2000): 52–64; and studies by the Minorities at Risk Project at the University of Maryland (http://www.cidcm.umd.edu/inscr/mar/). Other studies challenge the conventional wisdom that the world became less secure after the end of the cold war, concluding that at least between 1989 and 1997 global violent conflict decreased. See Peter Wallensteen and Margareta Sollenberge, "Armed Conflict and Regional Conflict Complexes, 1989–1997," *Journal of Peace Research* 35, no. 5 (Sept. 1998): 621–34.

3. See Judith Kelley, *Ethnic Politics in Europe* (Princeton: Princeton Univ. Press, 2004); Steven R. Ratner, "Does International Law Matter in Preventing Ethnic Conflict?" *Journal of International Law and Politics* 32, no. 3 (Spring 2000): 591–642.

4. *Human Security Report 2005* (London: Oxford Univ. Press, 2005).

5. Donald Horowitz, *Ethnic Groups in Conflict* (Berkeley: Univ. of California Press, 1985), 684.

6. David D. Laitin, "Secessionist Rebellion in the Former Soviet Union," *Comparative Political Studies* 34, no. 8 (Oct. 2001): 840.

7. Many believed that the Russian diaspora would constitute a global security problem. See, for example, Walter Laqueur, *Black Hundred: The Rise of the Extreme Right in Russia* (New York: Harper Perennial, 1994), 156–57; Stephen van Evera, "Hypotheses on Nationalism," *International Security* 18, no. 4 (Spring 1994): 5–39; and Rogers Brubaker, *Nationalism Reframed* (Cambridge: Cambridge Univ. Press, 1996).

8. On comparisons between Germany and Russia, see Stephen E. Hanson and Jeffrey S. Kopstein, "The Weimar/Russia Comparison," *Post-Soviet Affairs* 13, no. 3 (1997): 252–83. On post-Soviet Russia's foreign policy, especially as it relates to ethnic Russians abroad, see Michael McFaul, "A Precarious Peace: Domestic Determinants of Russian Foreign Policy," *International Security* 22, no. 3 (1997–98): 5–35; Jeff Chinn and Robert Kaiser, *Russians and the New Minority: Ethnicity and Nationalism in the Soviet Successor States* (Boulder: Westview Press, 1996); and Paul Kolstoe, *Russians in the Former Soviet Republics* (London: Hurst and Company, 1995).

9. On Hungary's historical behavior, see J. F. Brown, *Hope and Shadows: Eastern Europe After Communism* (Durham: Duke Univ. Press, 1994), 192–207. For recent evaluations of Hungary's behavior, especially as it relates to EU norms and standards, see the European Commission's *2002 Regular Report on Hungary's Progress Towards Accession,* 9.102002 SEC, 2002.

10. Carl Bildt, "The Balkans' Second Chance," *Foreign Affairs* 80, no. 1 (2001): 152; and Ivo H. Daalder and Michael B. G. Froman, "Dayton's Incomplete Peace," *Foreign Affairs* 78, no. 6 (1999): 106.

11. On January 1, 1995, the Conference on Security and Cooperation in Europe became the Organization for Security and Cooperation in Europe (OSCE). Unless I am referencing a specific date, policy, or quote, I refer to this organization as the CSCE/OSCE.

12. The Maastricht treaty was signed in February 1992, allowing the European Community to become the European Union in January 1993.

13. Others describe this evolving security architecture in Europe as a "variable geometry," in which different institutions have developed special competencies in particular security activities. See P. Terrence Hopmann, "Building Security in Post-Cold War Eurasia," *Peaceworks,* no. 31 (Sept. 1999): 6.

14. Robert Keohane and Joseph S. Nye, Jr., *Power and Independence* (New York: Longman, 2001), 5–32.

15. See Anne-Marie Slaughter, *A New World Order* (Princeton: Princeton Univ. Press, 2004); Amitai Etizioni, *From Empire to Community* (New York: Palgrave, 2004); and Anne Holohan, *Networks of Democracy Lessons from Kosovo for Afghanistan, Iraq, and Beyond* (Stanford: Stanford Univ. Press, 2005).

16. See David Rieff, *Slaughterhouse: Bosnia and the Failure of the West* (New York: Simon and Schuster, 1995); Ivo H. Daalder, *Getting to Dayton* (Washington, D.C.: The Brookings Institution, 2000); and Richard Holbrooke, *To End a War: From Sarajevo to Dayton—and Beyond* (New York: Random House, 1998).

17. This dynamic is explained in Brubaker, *Nationalism Reframed,* 54.

18. William T. Johnsen, *Pandora's Box Reopened: Ethnic Conflict in Europe and Its Implications* (Carlisle, Pa.: U.S. Army War College, 1994), v.

19. USAID, *A Decade of Change: Profiles of USAID Assistance to Europe and Eurasia,* (Washington, D.C.: Agency for International Development, 2000).

20. For example, there are fewer than five hundred books indexed in English on either ethnic cooperation or ethnic peace, whereas there are almost two thousand books indexed in English on ethnic war or ethnic conflict. See Appendix.

21. Geoffrey Blainey, *The Causes of War,* 3rd ed. (New York: Free Press, 1988).

22. van Evera, "Hypotheses on Nationalism," 5.

23. Daniel P. Moynihan, *Pandemonium: Ethnicity in International Politics* (New York: Oxford Univ. Press, 1993), 5.

24. For discussions of nationalism and ethnic relations in the post-Communist period, see Ben Fowkes, *Ethnicity and Ethnic Conflict in the Post-Communist World* (London: Palgrave, 2002); Brubaker, *Nationalism Reframed;* Charles A. Kupchan, ed., *Nationalism and Nationalities in the New Europe* (Ithaca: Cornell Univ. Press, 1995).

25. George Schopflin, *Nations, Identity and Power* (New York: New York Univ. Press, 2000), 4.

26. For a similar typology, see Donald Rothchild and David Lake, "Spreading Fear: The Genesis of Transnational Ethnic Conflict," in *The International Spread of Ethnic Conflict,* 3–32.

27. For more academic applications as well as modifications of this explanation, see Clifford Geertz, *Old Societies and New States: The Quest for Modernity in Asia and Africa* (New York: Free Press, 1963), and Anthony D. Smith, *The Ethnic Origins of Nations* (Oxford: Basil Blackwell, 1986). On the security dilemma, see Barry Posen, "The Security Dilemma and Ethnic Conflict," in *Ethnic Conflict and International Security,* ed. Michael E. Brown (Princeton: Princeton Univ. Press, 1993), 103–24. For a review of this literature, see Paul Roe, "The Intrastate Security Dilemma: Ethnic Conflict as Tragedy," *Journal of Peace Research* 36, no. 2 (Mar. 1999): 83–202; V. P. Gagnon, "Ethnic Nationalism and Internal Conflict," *International Security* 19, no. 3 (1994–95): 130–66.

28. For an overview of each of these and other explanations for ethnic conflict in Eastern Europe, see, for example, Anthony Oberschall, "The Manipulation of Ethnicity: From Ethnic Cooperation to Violence and War in Yugoslavia," *Ethnic and Racial Studies* 23, no. 6 (Nov. 2000): 982–1001.

29. See Gurr, *Peoples Versus States,* chaps. 1, 3, 7, and 8.

30. Ibid., 275–77.

31. Unlike Ted Gurr and the Minorities at Risk Project, James Fearon and David Laitin did not have a database that would allow for replication, and their conclusions are based on an informal survey of the interethnic scene. See Fearon and Laitin, "Explaining Interethnic Cooperation," *The American Political Science Review* 90, no. 4 (1996): 716.

32. Michael S. Lund, *Preventing Violent Conflicts* (Washington, D.C.: USIP Press, 1996), 4.

33. See Stephen van Evera, "Managing the Eastern Crisis: Managing War in the Former Soviet Empire," *Security Studies* 1, no. 3 (1992): 361–81. On more general suggestions, see Timothy Sisk, *Power Sharing and International Mediation in Ethnic Conflict* (Washington, D.C.: USIP Press, 1996), 87–118.

34. See, for example, Barbara F. Walter and Jack Snyder, eds., *Civil Wars, Insecurity, and Intervention* (New York: Columbia Univ. Press, 1999); Milton J. Esman and Shibley Telhami, eds., *International Organizations and Ethnic Conflict* (Ithaca: Cornell Univ. Press, 1995).

35. There are, of course, exceptions. See Daniel L. Byman, *Keeping the Peace* (Baltimore: The Johns Hopkins Press, 2003); Jay Rothman, *From Confrontation to Cooperation: Resolving Ethnic and Regional Conflict* (Newbury Park: SAGE Publications, 1992).

36. See Jenonne Walker, "International Mediation of Ethnic Conflicts," in *Ethnic Conflict and International Security,* 165.

37. Kelley, *Ethnic Politics,* 179–82.

38. Tanja Borzel, "Organizing Babylon: On the Different Conceptions of Policy Networks," *Public Administration* 76 (Summer 1998): 254.

39. Interview with Armands Gutmanis, Riga, Latvia, July 12, 2004.

40. See Robert Keohane and Joseph S. Nye, Jr., "Transnational Relations and World Politics: An Introduction," *International Organization* 25, no. 3 (Summer 1971): 329–49.

41. Samuel P. Huntington, "Transnational Organizations in World Politics," *World Politics* 25, no. 3 (Apr. 1973): 333.

42. Sidney Tarrow, "Transnational Politics: Contention and Institutions in International Politics," *Annual Review of Political Science* 4 (2002): 5.

43. See Thomas Risse-Kappen, "Bringing Transnational Actors Back In: Introduction," in *Bringing Transnational Relations Back In: Non-State Actors, Domestic Structures and International Institutions,* ed. Thomas Risse-Kappen (Cambridge: Cambridge University Press, 1995), 5–7.

44. Margaret Keck and Kathryn Sikkink, *Activists Beyond Borders: Transnational Advocacy Networks in International Politics* (Ithaca: Cornell Univ. Press, 1998).

45. Ibid., 4.

46. Sidney Tarrow, *Power in Movement* (Cambridge: Cambridge Univ. Press, 1998), 176–89.

47. Thomas Risse and Kathryn Sikkink, "The Socialization of International Human Rights Norms into Domestic Practices, 19.

48. Keck and Sikkink, *Activists Beyond Borders,* 6.

49. Risse and Sikkink, "The Socialization of International Human Rights Norms into Domestic Practices," 21.

50. Michael Freeman, "Liberal Democracy and Human Rights," in *Human Rights, New Perspectives and New Realities,* ed. Adamantia Pollis and Peter Schwab (Boulder: Lynne Rienner, 2000), 31–52.

51. See in particular Section 4 of the Document of the Copenhagen Meeting of the Conference on the Human Dimension of the CSCE, Jan. 5–29, 1990.

52. William D. Coleman, "Policy Networks, Non-state Actors and Internationalize Policy-making: A Case Study of Agricultural Trade," in *Non-State Actors in World Politics,* ed. Daphne Josselin and William Wallace (New York: Palgrave, 2001), 94.

53. See Daalder, *Getting to Dayton*; Holbrooke, *To End a War.*

54. This research was conducted under the auspices of grants from the National Research Council (in 2000 and 2001). In 2002, the research was supported by the U.S. Army and the Nebraska National Guard.

55. Daalder, *Getting to Dayton,* 160–79.

56. For more on the specific strategies and impact in Bosnia, see Patrice C. McMahon, "Rebuilding Bosnia: A Model to Emulate or Avoid?" *Political Science Quarterly* 119, no. 4 (Winter 2004–5): 569–94.

57. In the conflict-prevention literature, bottom-up strategies are also known as Track II diplomacy. See Joseph Montville, ed., *Conflict and Peacemaking in Multiethnic Societies* (Lexington, Mass.: Lexington Books, 1991).

58. This research was supported by a grant from the National Council on East European and Eurasian Research; in the summer of 2004 I was a researcher-in-residence at the OSCE in Prague, the Czech Republic.

59. See Istvan Horvath, "Facilitating Conflict Transformation," in *Comparative Case Studies on the Effectiveness of the OSCE High Commissioner on National Minorities: The Possibilities for Preventive Diplomacy,* ed. Wolfgang Zellner, Randolf Oberschmidt, and Claus Neukirch (Hamburg: Baden-Baden, 2004); and Jekaterina Dorodnova, "Challenging Ethnic Democracy: Implementation of the Recommendations of the OSCE High Commission on National Minorities to Latvia, 1993–2001," both in *Comparative Case Studies on the Effectiveness of the OSCE High Commissioner on National Minorities: The Possibilities for Preventive Diplomacy,* ed. Wolfgang Zellner, Randolf Oberschmidt, and Claus Neukirch (Baden-Baden: University of Hamburg, 2004).

60. Interview with Falk Lange, senior adviser to the OSCE's High Commissioner on National Minorities, The Hague, Netherlands, Mar. 4, 2004.

61. This model of coordination is suggested by Abram Chayes and Antonia Handler Chayes in their introduction to *Preventing Conflict in the Post-Communist World: Mobilizing International and Regional Organizations* (Washington, D.C.: The Brookings Institution, 1996), 1–22.

62. See, for example, Milada Anna Vachudova, *Europe Undivided: Democracy, Leverage and Integration After Communism* (Oxford: Oxford Univ. Press, 2005); Marise Cremona, ed., *The Enlargement of the European Union* (Oxford: Oxford Univ. Press, 2003); Aneta Borislavova Spendzharova, "Bringing Europe In? The Impact of EU Conditionality on Bulgarian and Romanian Politics," *Southeast European Politics* 4, no. 2 (2003): 141–56; Frank Schimmelfennig, Stefan Engert, and Heiko Knobel, "Costs, Commitment and Compliance: The Importance of EU Democratic Conditionality on Latvia, Slovakia, and Turkey," *Journal of Ethnopolitics and Minority Issues in Europe* 3 (2003): 495–518; James Hughes and Gwendolyn Sasse, "Monitoring the Monitors: EU Enlargement, Conditionality and Minority Protection in the CEEC," *Journal of Ethnopolitics and Minority Issues in Europe* 1 (2003): 1–35; Heather Grabbe, "How Does Europeanization Affect CEE Governance? Conditionality, Diffusion and Diversity," *Journal of Europe Public Policy* 8, no. 6 (2001): 1013–31; and Bruno de Witt, "Politics Versus Law in the EU's Approach to Ethnic Minorities," in *Europe Unbound: Enlarging and Restructuring the Borders of the EU,* ed. Jan Zielonka (New York: Routledge, 2002), 137–60.

63. For a similar observation, see Stephen M. Saideman and R. William Ayres, "Pie Crust Promises and Silence Procedures: Understanding the Limited Impact of NATO and EU Membership," unpublished paper presented at the 2005 International Studies Association Conference, Honolulu, Hawaii, March 2–5.

64. Hughes and Sasse, "Monitoring the Monitors," 1–35.

65. Gregory Flynn and Henry Farrell, "Piecing Together the Democratic Peace: The CSCE, Norms, and the 'Construction' of Security in the Post-Cold War Europe," *International Organization* 53, no. 3 (Summer 1999): 505–35; Michael R. Lucas, ed., *The CSCE in the 1990s: Constructing European Security and Cooperation* (Hamburg: Univ. of Hamburg, 1993).

66. See P. Terrence Hopmann, "Regional Security: Institutions and Intervention in Internal Conflicts; The OSCE's Experience in Eurasia," in *Limiting Institutions? The Challenge of Eurasian Security,* ed. Sean Kay, S. Victor Papacosma, and James Sperling (Manchester, Eng.: Manchester Univ. Press, 2003), 144–65. While scores of articles touch on the activities of the CSCE/OSCE, there are only a few good books on this organization. See, for example, Walter Kemp, ed., *Quiet Diplomacy in Action: The OSCE High Commissioner on National Minorities* (Vancouver: Univ. of British Columbia Press, 2003); Jonathan Cohen, *Conflict Prevention in the OSCE: An Assessment of Capacities* (The Hague: Netherlands Institute of International Relations Clingendael, 1999).

67. Ratner, "Does International Law Matter," 591–642.

68. Kelley, *Ethnic Politics,* 6–25.

69. On this relationship and strategy, see Anita Inder Singh, *Democracy, Ethnic Diversity and Security in Post-Communist Europe* (Westport: Praeger, 2001); S. Neil MacFarlane, "The Internationalization of Ethnic Strife," in *Democratic Consolidation in Eastern Europe,* ed. Jan Zielonka and Alex Pravda (Oxford: Oxford Univ. Press, 2001), 139–62.

70. Interviews with Marianna Ginsburg, Senior Program Officer, Environmental Partnerships, The German Marshall Fund, Washington, D.C., June 23, 2003; Jonas Rolett, Director for the Eastern Europe/Former Soviet Union Project, The Open Society Institute, Washington, D.C., June 24, 2003.

71. EU, "Evaluation of the PHARE and TACIS Democracy Programme, 1992–97," PTDP Evaluation Report. Available online at http://ec.europa.ed/comm/europeaid/evaluation/evinfo/1997/951432_ev.pdf, July 1997.

72. Jack Snyder and Edward Mansfield, "Democratization and War," *Foreign Affairs,* May-June 1995: 79–97.

73. Michael Brown, "Causes and Implications of Ethnic Conflict," in *Ethnic Conflict and International Security,* 4.

74. Monty G. Marshall, "Systems at Risk," in *Wars in the Midst of Peace: The International Politics of Ethnic Conflict,* ed. David Carment and Patrick James (Pittsburgh: Univ. of Pittsburgh Press, 1997), 82.

75. Paul A. Goble, "Ethnicity as Explanation, Ethnicity as Excuse," *Ethnic Conflict and Regional Instability: Implications for U.S. Policy and Army Roles and Missions,* ed. Robert L. Pfaltzgraff, Jr., and Richard H. Shultz, Jr. (Washington, D.C.: Strategic Studies Institute, 1994). For similar ideas on the strategic use of words and international intervention, see Samantha Power, *A Problem From Hell: American and the Age of Genocide* (New York: Basic Books, 2002); John Mueller, "The Banality of 'Ethnic War,' " *International Security* 25, no. 1 (Summer 2000): 42–70.

76. For similar definitions, see Gurr, *Peoples Versus States,* 6; and Michael Brown, "Causes and Implications of Ethnic Conflict," 5.

77. This definition is similar to Paul Diehl's definition of conflict management, as opposed to conflict resolution. Conflict management does not mean that fundamental issues have been settled and confrontations, crises, and wars no longer occur. It does mean, in short, reduced hostilities. See "Strategies, Necessary Conditions, and Comparative Effectiveness," in *Regional Conflict Management,* ed. Paul Diehl and Joseph Lepgold (New York: Rowman and Littlefield, 2003), 42.

78. This is a modified definition of international cooperation. See Robert Keohane, "International Institutions: Two Approaches," in *International Organization: A Reader,* ed. Friedrich Kratochwil and Edward Mansfield (New York: Longman, 1994), 45.

79. Risse and Sikkink, "The Socialization of International Human Rights Norms into Domestic Practices," 29.

80. Robert Keohane and Joseph S. Nye, Jr., "Transnational Relations and World Politics: An Introduction," in *Transnational Relations and World Politics,* edited by Robert Keohane and Joseph S. Nye, Jr. (Cambridge: Harvard Univ. Press, 1970), xii.

81. Ibid., xiii.

82. Unless I am explaining the history of this organization, I use this term, rather than *European Community* or the *European Economic Community.*

83. See Lonnie R. Johnson, *Central Europe: Enemies, Neighbors, Friends* (Oxford: Oxford Univ. Press, 2002), 3–12.

84. On defining the region, see ibid., chap. 1.

85. On the problems and the meaning of this term, see Milan Kundera, "The Tragedy of Central

Europe," *The New York Review of Books,* Apr. 26, 1984; Karen Dawisha, *Eastern Europe Gorbachev and Reform: The Great Challenge,* 2d ed. (New York: Cambridge Univ. Press, 1990), chap. 3.

86. Brubaker, *Nationalism Reframed,* 54.

87. See Walker, "International Mediation," 165–80.

88. Robert Zaagman, "Conflict Prevention in the Baltic States," *Journal of Ethnopolitics and Minority Issues* (1999): 1–75.

89. Sarah E. Mendelson and John K. Glenn, "Introduction: "Transnational Networks and NGOs in Postcommunist Societies," in *The Power and Limits of NGOs* (New York: Columbia Univ. Press, 2002), 9–11.

90. On evaluations, see Risse and Sikkink, "The Socialization of International Human Rights Norms into Domestic Practices," 11–35.

91. See, for example, Alexei Arabatov, Abram Chayes, Antonia Handler Chayes, and Lara Olson, eds., *Managing Conflict in the Former Soviet Union: Russian and American Perspectives* (Cambridge: The MIT Press, 1997).

2. Historical Responses to Ethnic Conflict

1. Inaugural address of George Bush, Jan. 20, 1989.

2. Extracted from the European Community, *The European Community and Its Eastern Neighbors* (Luxembourg: Office of the Publications of the European Communities, 1990).

3. Inaugural address of Bill Clinton, Jan. 20, 1993.

4. The consolidated version of the Treaty on European Union, Feb. 7, 1992, is available online at http://www.europa.eu.int/eu-lex/en/treatieis/dat/C_2002325EN.000501.html.

5. See, for example, David Callahan, *Unwinnable Wars: American Power and Ethnic Conflict* (New York: Twentieth Century Fund, 1997); Chayes and Handler Chayes, eds., *Preventing Conflict*; Ted Hopf, "Managing the Post-Soviet Security Space: A Continuing Demand for Behavioral Regimes," *Security Studies* 4, no. 2 (Winter 1994–95): 242–80; van Evera, "Managing the Eastern Crisis," 361–91.

6. For others who link the characterizations of the region to policies in the 1990s, see "Minority Rights and European Union Enlargement to the East," *Report of the First Meeting of the Reflections Group on the Long-Term Implications of EU Enlargement: The Nature of the New Borders,* European Union Institute: RSC Policy Paper no. 98/5 (Sept. 1998).

7. Morton H. Halperin and David J. Scheffer, with Patricia L. Small, *Self Determination in the New World Order* (Washington, D.C.: The Carnegie Endowment for International Peace, 1992), 8–25.

8. For a good review of how the principle of sovereignty has evolved throughout history, see J. Samuel Barkin and Bruce Cronin, "The State and the Nation: Changing Norms and the Rules of Sovereignty in International Relations," *International Organization* 48, no. 1 (Winter 1994): 107–30.

9. Will Kymlicka and Magda Opalski, eds., *Can Liberal Pluralsim Be Exported?: Western Political Theory and Ethnic Relations in Eastern Europe* (Oxford: Oxford Univ. Press, 2002), 14. For a criticism of these views, see Stephen D. Krasner and Daniel T. Froats, "Minority Rights and the Westphalian Model," in *Ethnicity, Nationalism, and Minority Rights,* ed. Stephen May, Tariq Modood, and Judith Squires (Cambridge: Cambridge Univ. Press, 2004), 227–30.

10. For historical accounts, see Inis L. Claude, *National Minorities: An International Problem* (New

York: Greenwood Press, 1955); C. A. Macartney, *National States and National Minorities* (London: Oxford Univ. Press, 1934); Alfred Cobban, *The Nation State and National Self Determination* (New York: Thomas Y. Crowell Company, 1970). For a legal account, see Robert J. Beck and Thomas Ambrosio, eds., *International Law and the Rise of Nations: The State System and the Challenge of Ethnic Groups* (New York: Chatham House Publications, 2002).

11. One could back even further to 1516 and the Treaty of Perpetual Union that protected the linguistic rights of the Swiss, who spoke no language other than German. Fernand de Varennes, "The Linguistic Rights of Minorities in Europe" in *Minority Rights in Europe: European Minorities and Languages,* ed. Snezana Trifunovska, 1st ed. (The Hague: Springer, 2001), 4.

12. Jozsef Galantai, *Trianon and the Protection of Minorities* (Budapest: Corvina Books, 1989), 13.

13. For more on the post-Vienna period, see Piotr Stefan Wandycz, *The Lands of Partitioned Poland, 1795–1918* (Seattle: Univ. of Washington Press, 1993), 65–107.

14. According to Stephen Krasner, an international regimes includes "sets of implicit and explicit principles, norms, rules and decision making procedures around which actors' expectations converge in a given area." See "Structural Causes and Regime Consequences: Regimes as Intervening Variables," in *International Regimes,* ed. Stephen D. Krasner (Ithaca: Cornell Univ. Press, 1983), 2.

15. Johnson, *Central Europe,* 172–80.

16. These are the words of President Wilson in Cobban, *The Nation State,* 53.

17. Frederic S. Pearson, Jonathan Nagle, and Mark Suprun, "Overcoming Wilsonianism: American Conflict Resolution and Ethnic Nationalism in Eastern Europe and the former Soviet Union," in *Reconcilable Differences: Turning Points in Ethnic Conflict,* ed. Sean Byren and Cynthia L. Irvin (Bloomfield: Kumarian Press, 2000), 25.

18. Cobban, *The Nation State,* 53.

19. Dexter, 88.

20. In Upper Silesia, for example, a 1921 vote resulted in more than half of the population voting to become part of Germany, while 40 percent voted in favor of joining Poland. Yet, since this vote had lured some 200,000 Germans to return to the region, opponents argued that these "out-voters" had swayed the outcome. The decision was referred to the league, and two zones created, and industrial areas made into communal German-Polish ownership. For more on plebiscites, see Cobban, *The Nation State,* 70–74.

21. Minority treaties were relevant in Austria, Bulgaria, Czechoslovakia, Greece, Hungary, Poland, and Yugoslavia. Albania, Lithuania, Latvia, Estonia and Iraq made unilateral declarations relating to minority protection upon their admission to the League of Nations.

22. See *The League of Nations and Minorities* (Geneva: League of Nations Secretariat, 1923); and *The League of Nations and the Protection of Minorities of Race, Language and Religion* (Geneva: League of Nations Secretariat, 1927).

23. *The Covenant of the League of Nations,* available online by The Avalon Project at Yale University Law School. See http://www.yale.edu/lawweb/avalon/leagcov.htm#art11, accessed July 28, 2003.

24. Dexter, 113–16.

25. Galantai, *Trianon,* 117.

26. Maynes, 9.

27. Galantai, *Trianon,* 138.

28. Callahan, *Unwinnable Wars,* 10–14.

29. Claude, *National Minorities,* 71.

30. Stephen Ryan, *Ethnic Conflict and International Relations* (Aldershot, England: Dartmouth Publishing Company, 1990), 162.

31. For more on the UN, see Cecilia Thompson, "United Nations: The Protection of Minorities within the UN," in *Minority Rights in Europe,* 115–37.

32. Michael Freeman, "Liberal Democracy and Minority Rights," in *Human Rights: New Perspectives and New Realities,* ed. Adamantia Pollis and Peter Schwab (Boulder: Lynne Rienner, 2000), 31; Krasner and Froats, "Minority Rights and the Westphalian Model," 96–103.

33. Freeman, "Liberal Democracy and Minority Rights," 31; Halperin and Scheffer, *Self Determination,* 48.

34. See Vernon Van Dyke, "Self-Determination and Minority Rights," *International Studies Quarterly* 13, no. 3 (Sept. 3, 1969): 223–53.

35. Halperin and Scheffer, *Self Determination,* 22.

36. Ryan, *Ethnic Conflict,* 162–63.

37. Except taken from Florence Benoit-Rohmer, *The Minority Question in Europe: Text and Commentary* (Strasbourg: Council of Europe Publishing, 1996), 21.

38. On the interpretations of this and legal cases, see Patrick Thornberry, "An Unfinished Story of Minority Rights," *Diversity in Action Local Public Management of Multi-Ethnic Communities in Central and Eastern Europe,* ed. Anna-Maria Biro and Petra Kovacs (Budapest: OSI Publications, 2001), 47–54.

39. For UN involvement in the 1950s and 60s, see Linda B. Miller, *World Order and Local Disorder: The United Nations and Internal Conflicts* (Princeton: Princeton Univ. Press, 1967).

40. For example in S. Tyrol in 1946 and 1969, in Palestine in 1947 and 1950, in Trieste in 1954 and 1974, and in Cyprus in 1960, the UN supported group rights and the need for autonomous self-rule.

41. Halperin and Scheffer, *Self Determination,* 23–24.

42. Schopflin, *Nations, Identity and Power,* 5–13.

43. Philip Payton, "Ethnicity in Western Europe Today," *Ethnicity and Democratisation in the New Europe,* ed. Karl Cordell (London: Routledge, 1999), 24.

44. Council of Europe, "Ad Hoc Committee for the Protection of National Minorities," 7th Meeting, Oct. 10–14, 1994, Strasbourg, *Council of Europe Meeting Reports,* CAHMIN (94)32.

45. Payton, "Ethnicity in Western Europe," 34–35.

46. For a development of this argument, see Singh, *Democracy, Ethnic Diversity and Security.*

47. On the origins and varieties of nationalism, see Benedict Anderson, *Imagined Communities: Reflections on the Origins and Spread of Nationalism* (London: Verso, 1991).

48. Sabrina P. Ramet, *Whose Democracy? Nationalism, Religion and The Doctrine of Collective Rights in Post-1989 Eastern Europe* (Lanham, Md.: Rowman and Littlefield, 1997), 1–16.

49. The essay I am referring to is "Two Types of Nationalism," in *Nationalism: The Nature and Evolution of an Ideal,* ed. E. Kamenka (Canberra: Australian National Press, 1973), 22–36.

50. Ernest Gellner, *Nations and Nationalism* (Ithaca: Cornell Univ. Press, 1983), 99–100.

51. Robin Okey, *Eastern Europe 1740–1980: Feudalism to Communism* (Minneapolis: Univ. of Minnesota Press, 1982), 13–21.

52. See Immanuel Wallerstein, *The Modern World System: Capitalist Agriculture and the Origins of the European World Economy in the Sixteenth Century* (New York: Academic Press, 1974).

53. Daniel Chirot, ed., *The Origins of Backwardness in Eastern Europe: Economics and Politics from the Middle Ages until the Early Twentieth Century* (Berkeley: Univ. of California Press, 1989).

54. Chirot, "Causes and Consequences of Backwardness," in *The Origins of Backwardness,* 11.

55. Johnson, *Central Europe,* 131–34.

56. George W. White, *Nationalism and Territory* (New York: Rowman and Littlefield, 2000), 1–10.

57. These are the ideas of Roman Dmowski, often referred to as the father of modern Polish nationalism. For more on Dmowski, see Wandycz, *The Lands of Partitioned Poland,* 288–95.

58. Ibid., 293.

59. For more on this see Gellner, *Nations and Nationalism,* 97–101.

60. See Joseph Rothschild, *East Central Europe During the Two World Wars* (Seattle: Univ. of Washington Press, 1974).

61. Galantai, *Trianon,* 13.

62. Andre Liebiech, "Ethnic Minorities and Long-Term Implications of EU Enlargement," in *Europe Unbound,* 117.

63. Irredentism is understood as "any political effort on the part of state leaders to redeem territory based on ethnic, historic, religious, cultural, or geographic grounds." See Chazan, "Introduction," 1–10.

64. Rothschild, *East Central Europe,* 14.

65. Ramet, *Whose Democracy?* 22.

66. Liebiech, "Ethnic Minorities and Long-Term Implications," 117.

67. Okey, *Eastern Europe, 1740–1980,* 160.

68. Ramet, *Whose Democracy?* 32–34.

69. Rothschild, *East Central Europe,* 14.

70. This is a conservative estimate according to R. J. Rummel, as German sources calculated about 750,000 and the Serbs estimate somewhere between 600,000 and 800,000. See *Death by Government* (New Brunswick: Transaction Publishers, 1997), 342–47.

71. Johnson, *Central Europe,* 172–180.

72. For more on this see Hugh Seton-Watson, *The East European Revolution* (London: Methuen and Co., Ltd., 1950), 339.

73. Walter Kemp, *Nationalism and Communism in Eastern Europe and the Soviet Union: A Basic Contradiction* (New York: St. Martin's Press, 1999), 32.

74. Dawisha, *Eastern Europe Gorbachev and Reform,* 25.

75. Brubaker, *Nationalism Reframed,* 24–27.

76. Ibid., 36.

77. On the origins and mechanisms of Soviet influence, see Zbigniew K. Brzezinski, *The Soviet Bloc: Unity and Conflict,* 2nd ed. (Cambridge: Harvard Univ. Press, 1967).

78. There were exceptions: see Alex Motyl, *Sovietology, Rationality, Nationalism* (New York: Columbia Univ. Press, 1990); Motyl, *Will the Non-Russians Rebel?* (Ithaca: Cornell Univ. Press, 1987), and Dawisha, *Eastern Europe Gorbachev and Reform,* 47–76.

79. Walker Conner, *The National Question in Marxist-Leninist Theory* (Princeton: Princeton Univ. Press, 1984).

80. As quoted in Graham Smith, ed., *The Nationalities Question in the Soviet Union* (London: Longman, 1990), 10.

81. According to Rummel, Germans were treated brutally into the 1950s. By 1950, he estimates at almost 1.9 million were killed and 15 million were ethnically cleansed. He also has statistics on the number of expulsions and deaths of Germans from 1945–50 from Czechoslovakia, Poland, and Yugoslavia. See Rummel, *Death by Government*, 312.

82. Schopflin, *Nations, Identity and Power*, 8.

83. Sabrina P. Ramet, *Balkan Babel: The Disintegration of Yugoslavia from the Death of Tito to the War for Kosovo* (Boulder: Westview Press, 1999), 250.

84. Ibid., 5. For more on Yugoslav nationalism, see J. F. Brown, *Hope and Shadows*, 229–70. On the late 1980s in particular, Warren Zimmerman, *Origins of a Catastrophe* (New York: Random House, 1996), 3–110.

85. J. F. Brown, *Hope and Shadows*, 173–75.

86. It is important to point out that this region was intentionally set up in Eastern Romania in the Szekler region, not along or near the Hungarian border.

87. The Soviet Union "inherited" Bessarabia and Northern Bukovina from Romania, while the latter retained Transylvania. In exchange, Hungary, considered the least worthy of rewards, was moderately placated with the creation of this autonomous region.

88. CSCE, *Helsinki Final Act,* Aug. 1, 1975.

89. Daniel C. Thomas, "The Helsinki Accords and Political Change in Eastern Europe," in *The Power of Human Rights: International Norms and Domestic Change,* edited by Thomas Risse, Stephen Ropp, and Kathryn Sikkink (Cambridge: Cambridge University Press, 1999), 205–33.

90. CSCE, Concluding Document of the Madrid Meeting 1980, Madrid 1983; CSCE, Concluding Document of the Vienna Meeting 1986, Vienna, 1989.

91. Monty G. Marshall, "States at Risk: Ethnopolitics in the Multinational States of Eastern Europe," in *Minorities at Risk: A Global View of Ethnopolitical Conflicts,* ed. Tedd Gurr (Washington, D.C.: USIP Press, 1993), 171.

92. J. F. Brown, *Hope and Shadows*, 173.

93. Brubaker, *Nationalism Reframed*, especially chaps. 1,4–6.

94. Jacques Rupnik, "Eastern Europe: the International Context," in *Globalization, Power, and Democracy,* ed. Marc F. Plattner and Aleksander Smolar (Baltimore: The Johns Hopkins Press, 2000), 62–68.

95. On the "Balkanization of Europe," see John J. Mearsheimer, "Back to the Future: Instability in Europe After the Cold War," *International Security* 15, no. 1 (Summer 1990): 5–56.

96. David A. Hamburg, "Preventing Contemporary Inter-Group Violence," in *The Handbook of Interethnic Coexistence,* ed. Eugene Weiner (New York: Continuum Publishing, 1998), 27–39.

97. *An Agenda for Peace: Preventive Diplomacy, Peacemaking and Peace-keeping.* UN Doc. A/47/277-S/2411, June 17, 1992.

98. Adopted by the UN General Assembly resolution 47/135, Dec. 18, 1992, see www.unhcr.ch/

html/menu3/b/d-minor.thm. For an explanation and analysis of the UN's instruments for addressing minority rights, see John Packer, "United Nations Protection of Minorities in Time of Public Emergency: The Hard-Core of Minority Rights," in *Non-Derogable Rights and States of Emergency* 36 (Brussels: Etablissements Emile Bruyland, 1996), 502–22.

99. Patrick Thornberry, "International and European Standards on Minority Rights," in *Minority Rights in Europe: The Scope for a Transnational Regime*, ed. Hugh Miall (New York: Council on Foreign Relations, 1994), 15–17.

100. Petra Roter, ed., "Managing the Minority Problem in Post-Cold War Europe within the Framework of a Multilayered Regime for the Protection of National Minorities," *European Yearbook of Minority Issues* 1 (2001–2): 97.

101. Raymond Taras and Rajat Ganguly, *Understanding Ethnic Conflict: The International Dimension* (New York: Longman, 2002), 103.

102. UN, *Supplement to an Agenda for Peace: Position Paper of the Secretary-General on the Occasion of the Fiftieth Anniversary of the University Nations*, Doc. A/50/60-S/1995/1, Jan. 3, 1995.

103. For more on NATO enlargement, see David S. Yost, *NATO Transformed* (Washington, D.C.: USIP Press, 1998); Frank Schimmelfennig, "NATO Enlargement: A Constructivist Explanation," *Security Studies* 8, no. 2–3 (1998–99): 198–234; Lars S. Skalener, "From the Outside In, From the Inside Out: NATO Expansion and International Relations Theory," *Security Studies* 7, no. 4 (1998): 44–87; Karen Fierke and Antje Wiener, "Constructing Institutional Interests: EU and NATO Enlargement," *Journal of European Public Policy* 6, no. 5 (1999): 721–42.

104. John S. Duffield, "International Regimes and Alliance Behavior: Explaining NATO Conventional Force Levels," *International Organization* 46, no. 4 (1992): 819–55.

105. See John Mearsheimer, "The False Promise of International Institutions," *International Security* (Winter 1994–95): 5–49; and Michael E. Brown, "Minimalist NATO," *Foreign Affairs* 78, no. 3 (1999): 203–18.

106. For explanations, see Robert B. McCalla, "NATO's Persistence after the Cold War," *International Organization* 50, no. 3 (Summer 1996): 445–75.

107. "The Alliance's Strategic Concept," Nov. 7–8, 1991, in *NATO Handbook*. Also available at www.nato.int/docu/comm/c911107a.htm.

108. Sean Kay, "NATO Enlargement," in *America's New Allies: Poland, Hungary, and the Czech Republic in NATO*, ed. Andrew A. Michta (Seattle: Univ. of Washington Press, 1999), 149.

109. On this reason and the reality of NATO enlargement, see Dan Reiter, "Why NATO Enlargement Does Not Spread Democracy," *International Security* 25, no. 4 (Spring 2001): 41–67.

110. M. Brown, "Minimalist NATO," 206.

111. Celeste A. Wallander," Institutional Assets and Adaptability: NATO After the Cold War," *International Organization*, 54, no. 4 (Autumn 2000): 720.

112. Hans-Joachim Heintze, "Bilateral Agreements and Their Role in Settling Ethnic Conflicts," in *Managing and Settling Ethnic Conflicts Perspectives on Successes and Failures in Europe, Africa and Asia*, ed. Ulrich Schneckener and Stefan Wolff (London: Hurst and Company, 2004), 191.

113. For CSCE documents and some analysis, see the following edited volumes: A. Bloed, ed., *The Challenges of Change: The Helsinki Summit of the CSCE and Its Aftermath* (Dordrecht: Martinus Nij-

149. Mendelson and Glenn, "Introduction," 1–28.

150. For more on NGOs and the UN, see Pei-neng, *NGOs at the United Nations.*

151. Ann L. Phillips, "Exporting Democracy: German Political Foundations in Central-East Europe," *Democratization* 6, no. 2 (Summer 1999): 81.

152. This was especially true of the early years, from 1989 through 1994, largely because governments were focused on economic reform. See Kevin F. F. Quigley, *For Democracy's Sake: Foundations and Democracy Assistance in Central Europe* (Washington: The Woodrow Wilson Center, 1997).

153. Kevin F. F. Quigley, "Philanthropy's Role in East Europe," *Orbis* 37, no. 4 (1993): 583.

154. For more on U.S. foundations, see Irving Louis Horowitz and Ruth Lenora Horowitz, "Tax-exempt Foundations: Their Effects on National Policy," *Orbis* 37, no. 4 (Fall 1993): 220–28.

155. These figures came from Quigley, *For Democracy's Sake.* He uses the term "Central Europe" to talk about foundation involvement in Hungary, Czechoslovakia, the Czech Republic, Slovakia, and Poland, 3.

156. Ibid., 3–4.

157. Quigley, "Philanthropy's Role," 583.

158. Kevin F. F. Quigley, "Lofty Goals, Modest Results: Assisting Civil Society in Eastern Europe," in *Funding Virtue: Civil Society Aid and Democracy Promotion,* ed. Martina Ottaway and Thomas Carothers (Washington, D.C.: The Carnegie Endowment for International Peace, 2000), 213 n. 1.

159. Quigley, *For Democracy's Sake,* 1. For a full list of the foundations and assistance by country and modality, see Appendix 3, 122–55.

160. For more on their activities, see Chip Gagnon, "INGOs in Bosnia-Herzegovina," in *The Power and Limits of NGOs: A Critical Look at Building Democracy in Eastern Europe and Eurasia,* ed. Sarah E. Mendelson and John K. Glenn (New York: Columbia University Press, 2002), 207–31.

161. Interview with Valdis Birkavs, former prime minister and minister of Foreign Affairs of Latvia, Riga, Latvia, July 15, 2004.

162. Interview with Sasha Havlicek, Deputy Director, East-West Institute, Brussels, Belgium, Mar. 2, 2004.

163. Sarah E. Mendelson and John K. Glenn, eds., *The Power and Limits of NGOs: A Critical Look at Building Democracy in Eastern Europe and Eurasia* (New York: Columbia University Press, 2002), 49–52.

164. Ginsburg, interview.

165. van der Stoel, "Principles and Pragmatism," 25.

3. The Network Response in the 1990s

1. Borzel, "Organizing Babylon," 254.

2. Walter W. Powell, "Neither Market Nor Hierarchy: Network Forms of Organization," *Research in Organizational Behavior* 12 (1990): 303.

3. See Keck and Sikkink, *Activists Beyond Borders,* chap. 1; and Risse-Kappen, "Bringing Transnational Actors Back In." For a review of this literature and "new" transnationalists, see Tarrow, "Transnational Politics," 1–20.

4. For an overview of this literature, see R. A. W. Rhodes, "Policy Network Analysis," in *The Oxford*

Handbook of Public Policy, ed. M. Moran, M. Rein, and R. E. Goodin (Oxford: Oxford Univ. Press, 2006); Grant Jordan, "Sub-Governments, Policy Communities and Networks, Refilling the Old Bottles?" *Journal of Theoretical Politics* 2, no. 3 (1990): 319–39.

5. Adapted from Douglass C. North, *Institutions, Institutional Change and Economic Performance* (Cambridge: Cambridge Univ. Press, 1990), 3. For a review of the institutionalist literature in social science, see Paul J. DiMaggio and Walter L. Powell, *The New Institutionalism* (Chicago: Univ. of Chicago Press, 1991), 1–38. For a discussion of "international" institutions, see Robert Keohane, "International Institutions: Two Approaches," *International Studies Quarterly* 32, no. 4 (1988): 379–96.

6. Jeffrey L. Bradach and Robert G. Eccles, "Price, Authority, and Trust: From Ideal Types to Plural Forms," *Annual Review of Sociology* 15 (1989): 97–118.

7. Powell, "Neither Market Nor Hierarchy," 299.

8. Ibid., 303.

9. Gordenker and Weiss, "Pluralizing Global Governance," 34–37.

10. Jan Johanson and Lars-Gunnar Mattsson, "Interorganizational Relations in Industrial System: A Network Approach Compared with the Transational-Cost Approach," *International Studies of Management and Organization* 17, no. 1 (1987): 34–48.

11. Colette Chaboot, "Development INGOs," in *Constructing World Culture,* 226.

12. On the advantages of INGOs in conflict prevention, see Kenneth Hackett, "The Role of NGOs in Preventing Conflict," in *Preventive Diplomacy: Stopping Wars Before they Start,* ed. Kevin Cahill (New York: Basic Books, 1996), 269–84.

13. There is an extensive and growing literature on NGOs. For recent works, see Boli and Thomas, *Constructing World Culture*; Keck and Sikkink, *Activists Beyond Borders*; Kappen, Roppe, and Sikkink, *The Power of Human Rights*; and Ann Marie Clark, "Non-Governmental Organizations and their Influence on International Society," *Journal of International Affairs* 48, no. 2 (1995): 507–26.

14. Wolfgang H. Reincke and Francis Deng, *Critical Choices: The UN, Networks and the Future of Global Governance* (Ottawa: International Development Research Center, 2000), xi–31.

15. E-mail correspondence with Nate Bluhm, July 26, 2004.

16. Interview with Haralambos Kondonis, Expert on Democratization and Human Rights, Stability Pact for South Eastern Europe, Brussels, Belgium, Mar. 2, 2004.

17. Reincke and Deng, *Critical Choices,* 36.

18. See Slaughter, *A New World Order,* chap. 1.

19. "Annual Report 2000 on Interaction between Organizations and Institutions in the CSCE/OSCE Area," Nov. 1, 1999-Oct. 31, 2000.

20. Powell, "Neither Market Nor Hierarchy," 305.

21. Gordenker and Weiss, "Pluralizing Global Governance," 35.

22. Interview with Walter Kemp, senior CSCE/OSCE adviser and HCNM political officer (1999–2003), Vienna, Austria, June 2004.

23. Interview with Max van der Stoel, The Hague, Netherlands, July 2004.

24. Havlicek, interview; interview with Bjorn Kuhne, political adviser, Stability Pact for South Eastern Europe, Brussels, Belgium, Mar. 3, 2004; Kondonis, interview, Mar. 2, 2004. Kondonis's article reinforces this point, "Civil Society and Multilateral Cooperative Models: The Role of Non-

governmental Organizations in the Stability Pact in South Eastern Europe," *Journal of Southeast Europe and Black Sea Studies,* 2, no. 1 (2002): 43–63.

25. Interview with Ilze Brands Kehris, Riga, Latvia, July 2004.

26. Powell, "Neither Market Nor Hierarchy," 303–6.

27. For similar conclusions in different issue areas, see Holohan, *Networks*; Etzioni, *From Empire to Community;* Slaughter, *A New World Order*; Keck and Sikkink, *Activists Beyond Borders*; and Reincke and Deng, *Critical Choices.*

28. Hussein Kassim, "Policy Networks, Networks and European Union Policy Making: A Skeptical View," *West European Politics* 17, no. 4 (Oct. 1994): 15–27.

29. See Slaughter, *A New World Order,* chap. 1.

30. Several scholars refer to or talk about transnational networks without however any discussion of what a network is or how it operates. In the globalization literature, see Joseph S. Nye and John Donahue, eds., *Governance in a Globalizing World* (Washington, D.C.: The Brookings Institution, 2000). Some use the term to explain policymaking in the European Union only while others use it when taking about governance in Europe more broadly. See, for example, R. A. W. Rhodes, *European Policy-Making: Implementation and Subcentral Governments: A Survey* (Maastricht: European Institute of Public Administration, 1986); Ann Florini, ed., *The Third Force: The Rise of Transnational Civil Society* (Washington, D.C.: The Carnegie Endowment for International Peace, 2000).

31. For similar assertions see Alex Pravda, "Introduction" and Karen E. Smith's "Western Actors and the Promotion of Democracy," in *Democratic Consolidation in Eastern Europe,* 1–27 and 31–57; see also Robert Keohane and Stanley Hoffman, "Conclusion," in *After the Cold War: International Institutions and States Strategies in Europe, 1989–1991,* ed. Robert Keohane, Joseph S. Nye and Stanley Hoffmann (Cambridge: Harvard Univ. Press, 1993), 388.

32. "Relations between the European Communities and the United States," Commission of the European Communities SEC (93) 538 def., Apr. 6, 1993.

33. Keohane and Nye, "Introduction," in *After the Cold War,* 18–19.

34. Larry Diamond, *Promoting Democracy in the 1990s* (New York: The Carnegie Commission on Preventing Deadly Conflict, 1995), 15.

35. This was, moreover, twice as much as the U.S. provided during the same period. See Stephen Haggard and Andrew Moravcsik, "The Political Economy of Financial Assistance to Eastern Europe, 1989–91," in *After the Cold War: International Institutions and States Strategies in Europe, 1989–1991,* ed. Robert Keohane, Joseph S. Nye, and Stanley Hoffmann (Cambridge: Harvard Univ. Press, 1993), 253. On Germany's attitude and involvement, see K. Smith, "Western Actors," 32–33.

36. The U.S. government had provided more assistance at different points during the 1980s, to the tune of almost $50 million in 1981 through the Food for Peace grants. Starting in 1981, the United States provided over $47 million to the region through this USAID program. After peaking in 1981, this assistance stopped in 1988 and began again in 1990 with $140.7 million. USAID Web site, *http://qesdb.cdie.org/gbk/index.html,* accessed Jan. 29, 2004; on private foundations, see Quigley, "Philanthropy's Role," 583.

37. Ann L. Phillips, "Exporting Democracy: German Political Foundations in East-Central Europe," *Democratization* 6, no. 2 (Summer 1999): 77.

38. The G-7 includes France, the U.S., the UK, Germany, Japan, Italy, and Canada, while the G-24

includes these countries plus Australia, Austria, Belgium, Denmark, Finland, Greece, Iceland, Ireland, Luxembourg, the Netherlands, New Zealand, Norway, Portugal, Spain, Sweden, Switzerland, and Turkey.

39. Janine Wedel, *Collision and Collusion: The Strange Case of Western Aid to Eastern Europe, 1989–1998* (New York: St. Martin's Press, 1998), 17–18. For more on this, see Stephen Haggard and Andrew Moravcsik, "The Political Economy of Economic Assistance to Eastern Europe, 1989–91," in *After the Cold War,* 247–61.

40. The countries Phare assisted included Albania, Bosnia and Herzegovina, Bulgaria, the Czech Republic, Estonia, the Former Yugoslav Republic of Macedonia (FYROM), Hungary, Latvia, Lithuania, Poland, Romania, Slovakia, Slovenia, and the former Czechoslovakia; it also aided multicountry and horizontal programmes. See "Total Phare Commitments, Contracts and Payments by Country," *Phare 1998 Annual Report,* Oct. 2000.

41. See USAID, *A Decade of Change.*

42. *The European Community and its Eastern Neighbors* 8/1990, Office of the Publications of the European Communities, 1990. Luxembourg, 18.

43. "Priorities of U.S. Assistance to Central and Eastern Europe," *U.S. Department of State Dispatch* 2, no. 16 (1991).

44. For similar statements and a discussion of the factors, see Reinicke and Deng, *Critical Choices,* 1–28.

45. "Focus on Central and Eastern Europe: Overview of U.S. Assistance," *U.S. Department of State Dispatch* 2, no. 11, Mar. 18, 1991.

46. "Priorities of U.S. Assistance to Central and Eastern Europe," *U.S. Department of State Dispatch* 2, no. 16, Apr. 22, 1991.

47. See Diamond, *Promoting Democracy*; Thomas Carothers, *Assessing Democracy Assistance Abroad* (Washington, D.C.: The Carnegie Endowment for International Peace, 1999); Carothers, *Assessing Democracy Assistance: The Case of Romania* (Washington, D.C.: The Carnegie Endowment for International Peace, 1996); and Quigley, *For Democracy's Sake.* On George Soros's contribution, see Kim Lane Scheppele, "The Soros Empire," in *American and German Cultural Policies in Eastern Europe: Assessing Developments in the 1990s,* ed. Frank Trommler (Washington, D.C.: American Institute for Contemporary German Studies, 1998), 18–26.

48. Callahan, *Unwinnable Wars,* 121.

49. For more on these relationships, see Anne M. Slaughter, "The Real New World Order," *Foreign Affairs* 76, no. 1 (1997): 183–97.

50. See "The CSCE Helsinki Document 1992: The Challenges of Change," specifically the Helsinki Declaration; see also Roter, "Managing the Minority Problem," 96–97.

51. Worner makes similar statements in several other speeches. See *Change and Continuity in the North Atlantic Alliance: Speeches by the Secretary General of NATO Manfred Worner* (Brussels: NATO Office of Information and Press, 1990), 158–63.

52. "Fact Sheet: NATO," U.S. Department of State, 95/11/22.

53. Huber, *Decade,* 68–70.

54. Jacques Poos's comments in *The Times* (London), June 29, 1991, as cited in Steven L. Burg and Paul S. Shoup, *The War in Bosnia-Herzegovina* (New York: M. E. Sharpe, 2000), 201.

55. On the amount of money spent by Europe and the United States on defense and international assistance, see "Relations between the European Communities and the United States," Commission of the European Communities SEC (93) 538 def. Apr. 6, 1993. See also Pond, *Rebirth of Europe,* chap. 4, on U.S. interests in NATO expansion.

56. Only a few of the State Department dispatches from 1990 through 1993 focused on Eastern Europe, and still fewer mentioned the problems of ethnicity. Even in documents specifically about the region and its problems, for example, "Central and Eastern Europe: A Year Later," a talk about the connections between Iraq's invasion of Kuwait and the problems in this region. See *U.S. Department of State Dispatch* 2, no. 20, May 20, 1991. On "tenacious diplomacy" see Secretary of State Designate Warren Christopher's remarks at the Senate Foreign Relations Committee, U.S. Department of State, 93/01/13 Statement at Senate Confirmation Hearing.

57. Pond, *Rebirth of Europe,* 59.

58. John Packer, "On the Content of Minority Rights," in *Do We Need Minority Rights?* ed. J. Raikka (The Hague: Kluwer Law International, 1996), 121–78.

59. On the concept of linking-pin, see Gordenker and Weiss, "Pluralizing Global Governance," 34–36.

60. Patrick Thornberry, "An Unfinished Story of Minority Rights," in *Diversity in Action. Local Public Management of Multi-Ethnic Communities in Central and Eastern Europe,* ed. Anna-Maria Biro and Petra Kovacs (Budapest: Open Society Institute, 2001), 57. See also Arie Bloed and Peter van Dijk, "Bilateral Treaties: A new Landmark in Minority Protection," in *Protection of Minority Rights Through Bilateral Treaties: The Case of Central and Eastern Europe,* ed. Bloed and van Dijk (The Hague: Kluwer Law International, 1999), 1–15.

61. Wolfgang Zellner, "The CSCE/OSCE: Uniquely Qualified for a Conflict-Prevention Role," in *Searching for Peace in Europe and Eurasia,* ed. Paul van Tongeren, Hans van de Veen, and Juliette Verhoeven (Boulder: Lynne Rienner, 2002), 15.

62. "London Declaration on a Transformed North Atlantic Alliance," July 6, 1990.

63. "Partnership with the Countries of Central and Eastern Europe," statement issued by the North Atlantic Council meeting in Ministerial Session, Copenhagen, June 7, 1991.

64. Francis T. Miko, "American Perspectives on the Helsinki Review Conference and the Future Role of the CSCE," in *The CSCE in the 1990s,* 61–71.

65. "Secretary General's Intervention at the CSCE/OSCE Permanent Council," PC.DEL/668/00, Nov. 2, 2000.

66. See Oana C. Popa, "Ethnic Nationalism and Regional Security in Southeast Europe: A Multi-dimensional Perspective," NATO Final Report, Mar. 1999.

67. Janie Leatherman, *From the Cold War to Democratic Peace: Third Parties, Peaceful Change and the CSCE/OSCE* (Syracuse: Syracuse Univ. Press, 2003), 1–23.

68. For a discussion of this, see John Packer, "Making International Law Mattering Preventing Ethnic Conflict: A Practitioner's Perspective," *International Law and Politics* 32 (2000): 715–24.

69. CSCE/OSCE, Lisbon summit, 1996. "Contribution by the North Atlantic Treaty Organization," REF.S/97/96, Nov. 29, 1996.

70. Annual Report 1993 on CSCE Activities, sect. 3, High Commission on National Minorities.

71. Kemp, interview.

72. van der Stoel, interview; Lange, interview; Kemp, interview.

73. On missions, see Chigas, "Preventive Diplomacy," 52–63.

74. CSCE/OSCE Structures and Institutions SEC.GAL/94/02, June 6, 2002.

75. See, for example, the "Second Conference on the Human Dimension of the CSCE," June 5-July 29, 1990, and the "Prague Document on the Further Development of CSCE Institutions and Structures. Declaration on Non-Proliferation and Arms Transfer," January 1992.

76. For forms of cooperation with various organizations and in specific countries, see "Co-operation with International Organizations and Institutions: Selected Documents and Catalogue of Forms of Co-operation," COOP_DRF.DOC/04.11.94.

77. Conference on Security and Cooperation in *Europe Final Act,* Helsinki 1975, 47–51.

78. See Second Meeting of the Council, *Prague Document on Further Development of CSCE Institutions and Structures,* Jan. 30–31, Prague 1992, chap. 9, para. 43–44, and CSCE Communication no. 124, Prague, Apr. 3, 1992.

79. CSCE, "Exchange of Information and Documents," *CSCE Journal,* no. 3, annex 2, Jan. 10, 1992.

80. Niels Moller-Gulland, "The Forum for Security Co-operation and Related Security Issues," in The CSCE in the 1990s, 32. See also Helsinki Follow-up Meeting CSCE/HM-P, De.2, Helsinki, Mar. 20, 1992.

81. *Prague Document on Further Development of CSCE Institutions and Structures,* Declaration on Non-Proliferation and Arms Transfers, January 1992.

82. OSCE, *Annual Report 1998* on CSCE/OSCE Activities.

83. OSCE, *Annual Report 2000* on Interaction Between Organizations and Institutions in the CSCE/OSCE Area.

84. Thomas M. Buchbbauum, "The CSCE and International Organizations: Expanding Cooperation with the Council of Europe," in *The CSCE in the 1990s,* 125–42.

85. See the Helsinki Summit Declaration, Helsinki, June 9–10, 1992, chap. 4, and Third Meeting of the Council, Stockholm, Dec. 14–15, 1992, chap. 8; Fourth Meeting of the Council, Nov. 30-Dec. 1, 1993, chap. 6, contained in "Co-operation with International Organizations and Institutions: Selected Documents and Catalogue of Forms of Co-operation," COOP_DR.DOC/-4.11.94.

86. *Annual Report 2000* on Interaction Between Organizations and Institutions in the CSCE/OSCE Area.

87. Huber, *Decade,* 155.

88. "Secretary General Intervention at CSCE/OSCE Permanent Council," PC.DEL/668–00, Nov. 2, 2000.

89. On the international community's role in Yugoslavia, see Burg and Shoup, *The War in Bosnia-Herzegovina*; and Susan L. Woodward, *Balkan Tragedy: Chaos and Dissolution after the Cold War* (Washington, D.C.: The Brookings Institution, 1995).

90. Tindemans, *Unfinished Peace,* xviii.

91. Phillipe C. Schmitter, "The Influence of the International Context upon the Choice of National Institutions and Policies in Neo-Democracies," in *The International Dimensions of Democratization, Europe and the Americas,* ed. Laurence Whitehead (Oxford: Oxford Univ. Press, 1996), 29–33.

92. George Schopflin alludes to such processes. See *Nations, Identity and Power,* 1–49.

93. Patricia David and Peter Dombrowski, "International Assistance to the Former Soviet Union: Conditions and Transitions," *Policy Studies Journal* 28, no. 1 (Mar. 2000): 68–71.

94. Judith Kelley, "Membership, Management and Enforcement." Unpublished paper presented at 2002 annual meeting of the American Political Science Association, Boston, Mass., Aug. 29-Sept. 1. For discussions of the EU's policy of conditionality as well as its limitations, see Spendzharova, "Bringing Europe In?" 141–56; Schimmelfennig, Engert, and Knobel, "Costs, Commitment," 495–518; Grabbe, "Europeanization," 1013–31; and Milada Anna Vachudova, "Strategies for European Integration and Democratization in the Balkans," *Slovak Foreign Policy Affairs* (2003): 92–105.

95. Indeed, in some studies of post-Communist politics other actors are barely mentioned. See Vachudova, *Europe Undivided.*

96. Paul Eavis and Stuart Kefford, "Conflict Prevention and the EU: A Potential Yet to Be Fully Realized," in *Searching for Peace in Europe and Eurasia,* ed. Paul van Tongeren et al. (Boulder: Lynne Rienner, 2002), 5. See also Vachudova, "Strategies," 147.

97. Karen E. Smith, "The Evolution and Approach of EU Membership Conditionality," in *Enlargement of the European Union,* 122.

98. Kuhne, interview.

99. Council Decision of June 14 on the continuation of the joint action adopted by the Council on the basis of Article J.3 of the Treaty on European Union on the inaugural conference on the Stability Pact. Council Decision of June 14, 1994 (94/367/CFS).

100. See Bruno de Witt, "Politics Versus Law in the EU's Approach to Ethnic Minorities," EUI Working Paper, RSC no. 2000/4.

101. Martin Brusis, "The EU and Interethnic Power-sharing Arrangements in Accession Countries," *Journal of Ethnopolitics and Minority Issues in Europe* 1 (2003): 3.

102. Roter, "Managing the Minority Problem," 97.

103. Brusis, "EU and Interethnic Power-sharing," 3.

104. Lange, interview.

105. Interviews with Franz Cermak, Adviser, Coordination of Negotiations and Pre-accession, Enlargement, Directorate General, European Commission; Franck-Oliver Roux, International Organizations, EuropeAid Co-operation Office, European Commission; both in Brussels, Belgium, Mar. 2004.

106. Cermak, interview.

107. Cermak, interview.

108. See Hughes and Sasse, "Monitoring the Monitors," 1–35.

109. Several EU officials past and present confirmed the important role the CSCE/OSCE, the Council of Europe, and NGOs play in ethnic politics. Interviews with Peter Ashman, senior adviser, EuropeAid and former director, European Human Rights Foundation; Malin Stawe, coordinator of Europe, EuropeAid, European Commission; Franck-Oliver Roux.

110. For the exact term "accession constellation," see Brusis, "EU and Interethnic Power-sharing"; For similar terms and conclusions, see Grabbe, "Europeanization," 1013–31.

111. Kondonis, "Civil Society," 43–63.

112. Kondonis, interview, Mar. 2, 2004.

113. For more on this topic, see Suzanne Baier-Allen, ed., *Synergy in Conflict Management* (Baden-Baden: Nomos: Verlagsgesellschaft, 1998).

114. M. Brown, "Minimalist NATO," 205.

115. See Hugh Miall, ed., *Redefining Europe. New Patterns of Conflict and Cooperation* (London: The Royal Institute of International Affairs, 1994); see also McCalla, "NATO's Persistence," 400.

116. Robert E. Hunter, "Maximizing NATO," *Foreign Affairs* 78, no. 3 (1999): 192.

117. McCalla, "NATO's Persistence," 400.

118. For more on this, see Trevor Taylor, "Security for Europe," in *Redefining Europe,* 166–85.

119. Rupnik, "Eastern Europe," 70–71.

120. See *Report to Congress on the Enlargement of the North Atlantic Treaty Organization: Rationale, Benefits, Costs and Implications* (Feb. 24, 1997), http://www.fas.org/man/nato/offdocs/us_97/wh970224.htm, accessed February 2004.

121. Reiter, "NATO Enlargement," 42.

122. "Declaration of the Heads of State and Government Participating in the Meeting of the North Atlantic Council," Jan. 10–11, 1994. Press Communiqué M-1 (94) 3.

123. "Declaration of the Heads of State and Government Participating in the Meeting of the North Atlantic Council," Jan. 10–11, 1994. Press Communiqué M-1 (94) 3.

124. "Fact Sheet: NATO's Partnership for Peace; A Record of Success" INF/103/95 June 2, 1995.

125. "Talking points by Ambassador Jerzy M. Nowak on the Presentation of the NATO Enlargement Study," REF.PC/730/95 Nov. 24, 1995.

126. Paul E. Gallis, "NATO: Congress Addresses Expansion of the Alliance," *Congressional Research Report for Congress,* July 24, 1997.

127. Klaus-Peter Klauber, "A Cooperative NATO in a Cooperative Europe," *Romanian Journal of International Affairs* 4 (1998): 306–10.

128. Other reasons included their shared border with Germany (for Poland and the Czech Republic), their proximity to Russia, and their support for U.S. operations in Bosnia. See Hunter, 195.

129. The former statements were made by Senators Roth and Lugar. See "NATO: Congress Addresses Expansion of the Alliance," *Congressional Research Service Report for Congress,* updated July 24, 1997.

130. Wallander, 727–29.

131. DiMaggio and Powell, 7.

132. Kay, 152.

133. "Meeting of the North Atlantic Council in Defence Ministers Session on 13th June 1996," Press Communiqué M-NAC (DM)-2(96)89; see also "NATO Contribution to the 1996 CSCE/OSCE Review Meeting," REF.RM/262/96 Nov. 18, 1996.

134. "CSCE/OSCE Ministerial Meeting. Statements by the Assistant Secretary of NATO, Gebhardt van Molke," REF.MC/42/95 Dec. 7, 1995 restricted.

135. "Secretary General's Intervention at the CSCE/OSCE Permanent Council," PC.DEL/668/00 Nov. 2, 2000.

136. For other criticisms of NATO's enlargement, see M. Brown, "Minimalist NATO," 204–18; and M. Brown, "The Flawed Logic of NATO Expansion," *Survival* 37, no. 34 (1995): 34–52.

137. Reiter, "NATO Enlargement," 49–66.

138. Lange, interview.

139. Kemp, interview.

140. van der Stoel, interview.

141. van der Stoel, interview.

142. Max van der Stoel, "The Role of the CSCE/OSCE High Commissioner in Conflict Prevention." Address by the CSCE/OSCE High Commissioner on National Minorities, Skopje, Oct. 18, 1996.

143. van der Stoel, "The Role of the CSCE/OSCE High Commissioner in Conflict Prevention," in *Herding Cats,* 66–68.

144. Max van der Stoel, "International response to ethnic conflicts: Focusing on Prevention," keynote address by the CSCE HCNM to the Fourth International PIOOM Symposium: Ethnic Conflicts and Human Rights Violations in Europe, June 25, 1993, Leiden, The Netherlands.

145. Several individuals in Latvia mentioned this, believing that the CSCE/OSCE mission to Latvia, which was established in September 1993 and closed in December 2001, had been a significant force for interethnic peace. However, little research exists on the role of this mission. For basic information on this mission, see "Survey of CSCE/OSCE Long-Term Missions and other CSCE/OSCE Field Activities," SEC.INF/115/04 June 2, 2004.

146. "Survey of CSCE/OSCE Long-Term Missions and other CSCE/OSCE Field Activates," SEC.INF/115/04 June 2, 2004.

147. Chigas, "Preventive Diplomacy," 47–61.

148. Ratner, "Does International Law Matter," 622–23.

149. Packer, "Making International Law Matter in Preventing Ethnic Conflict," 716; for other discussions by Packer on the HCNM's use of standards and their effect on ethnic politics, see "On the Content of Minority Rights," 121–78; and "Considerations on Procedures to Implement the Right to Self Determination," in *The Implementation of the Right to Self-Determination as a Contribution to Conflict Prevention,* ed. Michael van Walt van Praage, Report of the International Conference of Experts, UNESCEO Division of Human Rights, Nov. 21–27, 1998.

150. I also have in mind the Geneva Report on National Minorities (1991), the Moscow Document (1991), The Helsinki Document (1992), and the Budapest Document (1994).

151. Review conference, Vienna-Istanbul consolidated document. Vienna, Sept. 20-Oct. 1, Nov. 8–10, 1999.

152. On the debates and activities of the council during this period, see Huber, *Decade,* 1–85.

153. Ibid., 152.

154. Council of Europe, order no. 488 of June 29, 1993, which instructs its Political Affairs Committee and Committee on Legal Affairs and Human Rights to monitor closely the honoring commitments entered into by the authorities of new member states and to report to the bureau at regular six-monthly intervals until all undertaking are honored.

155. Frank Schimmelfennig, "Introduction: the Impact of International Organizations on the Central and Eastern European States -Conceptual and Theoretical Issues," in *Norms and Nannies: The Impact of International Organizations on Central and East Europe,* ed. Ron H. Linden (Lanham, Md.: Rowman and Littlefield, 2002), 7.

156. Joachim-Heintze, "Bilateral Agreements," 193–95.

157. This is paraphrased from the Council of Europe's, "Recommendation 1201 on an additional protocol on the rights of national minority to the European Convention on Human Rights," available online at *http://assembly.coe.int/Documents/Adopted TExt/TA93/EREC1201.HTM*, accessed Nov. 3, 2004.

158. Huber, *Decade,* 91.

159. Council of Europe Opinion, no. 174, Oct. 1993; see Roter, "Managing the Minority Problem," 124.

160. For a summary of the Council of Europe's framework, see http://conventions.coe.int/Treaty/en/Summaries/Html/157.htm.

161. See Kinga Gal, "The Council of Europe Framework Convention," in *Minority Governance in Europe,* ed. Kinga Gal (Budapest: The Open Society Institute, 2003), 1–8.

162. Huber, *Decade,* 127.

163. "General policy: Council of Europe and CSCE/OSCE," CIO.GAL/57/98, Sept. 28, 1998.

164. "Recommendation 1345 (1997) 1 on the protection of national minorities," available online at *http://assembly.coe.int/Documents/AdoptedText/TA97/erec1345.htm,* accessed Nov. 10, 2004.

165. "General policy: Council of Europe and CSCE/OSCE," CIO.GAL/57/98, Sept. 28, 1998.

166. On current efforts toward reconciliation, see Joachim-Heintze, "Bilateral Agreements," 189–205.

167. Kinga Gal, "Council of Europe Framework Convention for the Protection of National Minorities and its Impact on Central and Eastern Europe," *Journal on Ethnopolitics and Minority Issues in Europe* (Winter 2000): 5.

168. Bloed and van Dijk, *Protection of Minority Rights Through Bilateral Treaties,* 14.

169. Joachim-Heitze, "Bilateral Agreements," 203.

170. Quigley, *For Democracy's Sake,* 9.

171. For general coverage of democracy promotion in the 1990s, see Diamond, *Promoting Democracy*; K. Smith, "Western Actors," 1–57; Mendelson and Glenn, *The Power and Limits of NGOs,* particularly chaps. 1,8, and 9; on the Council of Europe's initiatives, see Manas, "Council of Europe's Democracy Ideal," 99–144; on the EC and democracy promotion, see John Pinder, "The EC and Democracy in Central and Eastern Europe," in *Preventing Conflict in the Post-Communist World,* ed. Abram Chayes and Antonia Handler Chayes (Washington, D.C.: The Brookings Institution, 1996), 119–43; on the U.S. government's strategy, see Carothers, *Aiding Democracy Abroad* and *Assessing Democracy Assistance.* For a normative look at what the U.S. government should do to prevent nationalism and ethnic conflict, see Steven L. Burg, *War or Peace? Nationalism, Democracy and American Foreign Policy in Post-Communist Europe* (New York: New York Univ. Press, 1996).

172. Byman, *Keeping the Peace,* 125.

173. Diamond, *Promoting Democracy,* 6.

174. Singh, *Democracy, Ethnic Diversity and Security,* xxii.

175. On these actors, see Diamond, *Promoting Democracy,* 12–38.

176. For a list of only the nongovernmental organizations that have received U.S. funding for democracy programs, see ibid., 16–31.

177. See Jack Snyder and Edward Mansfield, "Democratization and the Danger of War," *International Security* 20, no. 1 (Summer 1995): 5–38.

178. Thomas Carothers and Marina Ottaway, "Introduction: The Burgeoning World of Civil Society Aid," in *Funding Virtue: Civil Society Aid and Democracy Promotion,* ed. Ottaway and Carothers (Washington, D.C.: The Carnegie Endowment for International Peace, 2000), 7.

179. On the relationship between private and public funders, see Quigley, *For Democracy's Sake,* 109–18; for this definition, see Marina Ottaway and Theresa Chung in "Toward a New Paradigm," *Journal of Democracy* 10, no. 4 (1999): 106.

180. David Chandler, "Democratization in Bosnia: The Limits of Civil Society Strategies," *Democratization* 5, no. 4 (Winter 1998): 78–83.

181. Quigley, "Philanthropy's Role," 587; for similar conclusions, see Ottaway and Carothers, *Funding Virtue,* 7; Ashutosh Varshney, *Ethnic Conflict and Civic Life: Hindus and Muslims in India* (New Haven: Yale Univ. Press, 2003), esp. chap. 2.

182. Hackett, "Role of NGOs," 275.

183. See Milton J. Esman, "Policy Dimensions: What Can Development Assistance Do?" in *Carrot, Stick and Ethnic Conflict. Rethinking Development Assistance,* ed. Milton J. Esman and Ronald J. Herring (Ann Arbor: Univ. of Michigan Press, 2001), 235–56.

184. See EU, "Evaluation of the PHARE and TACIS Democracy Programme."

185. Pinder, "EC and Democracy," 134–43.

186. Ashman, interview.

187. Pinder, "EC and Democracy," 181.

188. PTDP Evaluation Report; Ashman, interview.

189. K. Smith, "Western Actors," 49.

190. Ibid., 51–56.

191. For more on the potential role of development assistance, see Eavis and Kefford, "Conflict Prevention," 9–11.

192. Kondonis, interview, Mar. 2, 2004; see also Kondonis, "Civil Society"; on the novelty of the Stability Pact, see Eavis and Kefford, "Conflict Prevention," 11–14.

193. Singh, *Democracy, Ethnic Diversity and Security,* 70–75.

194. See Ottaway and Carothers, *Funding Virtue,* 5.

195. On U.S. democracy promotion, see Carothers, *Aiding Democracy Abroad*; Allison and Beschel, "Can the U.S. Promote Democracy?" 88–98.

196. Heather S. McHugh, "USAID and Ethnic Conflict: An Epiphany?" in *Carrot, Stick and Ethnic Conflict: Rethinking Development Assistance,* ed. Milton J. Esman and Ronald J. Herring (Ann Arbor: University of Michigan Press, 2001), 52.

197. Thomas Carothers, *Critical Mission: Essays on Democracy Promotion* (Washington, D.C.: Carnegie, 2004), 41.

198. McHugh, "USAID and Ethnic Conflict," 50.

199. Interviews with David Cowles, Sarah Farnsworth, Susan Fertig-Dyke, Jennifer Stuart, and Peter D. Graves, USAID officials, Washington, D.C., June 2003.

200. McHugh, "USAID and Ethnic Conflict," 71.

201. Stuart, interview.

202. See USAID, *A Decade of Change.*

203. *Lessons in Implementation: The NGO Story,* USAID Report, Oct. 1999. For the U.S. in the

1990s, it was about 10 percent for the EU, civil society and democratization amounted to less than 1 percent of Phare commitments from 1990–1998, though other sector commitments, like education or public institutions, might have been used for democracy-related activities. See Phare 1998 annual report. Ten percent is also used by Quigley and based on USAID figures and information from EBRD, the World Bank and other sources. See Quigley, "Lofty Goals, Modest Results," 192.

204. Mendelson and Glenn, *The Power and Limits of NGOs*, 49–52.

205. Rolett, interview; Ginsberg, interview; Havlicek, interview.

206. Interview with Eran Fraenkel, Brussels, Belgium, Mar. 2, 2004.

207. Rolett, interview.

208. Quigley, *For Democracy's Sake*, 88.

209. For the years 1989–94, see Quigley, *For Democracy's Sake*, 139.

210. See Mendelson and Glenn, *The Power and Limits of NGOs*, chap. 1.

211. Quigley, *For Democracy's Sake*, 73.

212. Tindemans, *Unfinished Peace*, 142.

213. Andrea Witt, "National Borders: Images, Functions, and Their Effects on Cross-Border Cooperation in North America and Europe," in *Caught in the Middle. Border Communities in an Era of Globalization*, ed. Demetrios G. Papademetriou and Deborah Waller Meyers (Washington, D.C.: Carnegie Endowment for International Peace, 2001), 176–77.

214. For more on this, see Iver B. Nuemann, "Regionalization and Consolidation," in *Democratic Consolidation in Eastern Europe*, 60–68.

215. Neumann, 58–75.

4. Triumph in Transylvania: Interethnic Cooperation in Romania

1. Gabriel Andreescu, "Pages from the Romanian-Hungarian Reconciliation, 1989–1999: The Role of Civic Organizations," *Interethnic Relations in Post-Communist Romania. Proceedings of the Conference the Romanian Model of Ethnic Relations. The Last Ten Years, The Next Ten Years,* ed. Lucian Nastase and Levente Salat (Cluj: Ethnocultural Diversity in Romania Series, 2000), 89–122.

2. This statement is supported by opinion polls taken in Romania by the Ethnocultural Diversity Center in Cluj, Romania. See Tables 1–3 from the *Barometer of Ethnic Relations,* Nov. 2001. See also the views of various political leaders and experts from Romania and the U.S. in Nastase and Salat.

3. Allen Kassof, unpublished manuscript, 2005.

4. For such conclusions, see Dan Petrescu, "Civil Society in Romania: From Donor Supply to Citizen Demand," in *Funding Virtue*, 217–40.

5. This chapter was also informed by e-mail communication with Nate Bluhm, a U.S. State Department official who worked in Romania in the early 1990s and helped establish the U.S. consulate in Cluj in 1994; representatives from the Hungarian Laszlo Teleki Institute in Budapest that focuses on Hungarian foreign policy and international relations; Livia Plaks, the Director of the Project on Ethnic Relations based in Princeton, N.J., and Allen Kassof, former director of the Project on Ethnic Relations.

6. Others argue that the conflict stretches back much further. For more on the roots of this conflict, see Barbara Jelavich, *History of the Balkans,* vol. 2 (Cambridge: Cambridge Univ. Press, 1983). On

the rise of nationalist sentiment in Romania, see Kathcrine Verdery, "Nationalism and Nationalism in Post-socialist Romania," *Slavic Review,* 52, no. 2 (Summer 1993): 179–203.

7. The territory went to Austria, Czechoslovakia, Romania, and to the-yet-to-be-established Yugoslav state, which was in 1920 still the Kingdom of Serbs, Croats, and Slovenes. A tiny strip of land was also ceded to Poland.

8. Census figures from 1930, 1956, 1977, and 1992 indicate that the Hungarian population hovered between 7–9 percent. In the 1992 census, the Hungarian population of just over 1.6 million made up 7.1 percent of Romania's population of 22.7 million. See Istvan Horvath, "Facilitating Conflict Transformation," 14.

9. In the regions of Maramures, Crisana, and Banat, and constituting a majority in the Covasna (Kovaszna) and Harghita (Hargita) counties.

10. On the interwar period in Romania, see Joseph Rothschild, *Eastern Europe during the Two World War* (Seattle: Univ. of Washington Press, 1979).

11. Holly Cartner, "Struggling for Ethnic Identity: Ethnic Hungarians in Post-Ceausescu Romania," *Helsinki Watch Report,* Sept. 1993, 9.

12. Janet Heischman, "Destroying Ethnic Identity: The Hungarians of Romania," *Helsinki Watch Report,* February 1989, 2–3.

13. Gabor Kardos, "The Culture of Conflict. Hungary's Role in Resolving Ethnic Disputes," *World Policy Journal* 12 (1995): 103.

14. J. F. Brown, *Hope and Shadows,* 94–104.

15. For more on the organization's history, see Anna-Maria Biro, "International Relations of the Democratic Alliance of Hungarians in Romania (DAHR)," *International Studies* (Romania) 2 (1996): 21–41.

16. Fowkes, *Ethnicity and Ethnic Conflict,* 114–15.

17. For more on state building and constitutions, see Irina Culic, "State Building and Constitution Writing in Central and EE after 1989," *Regio: A Review of Minorities, Politics and Society,* 2003.

18. For an elaboration of the objectionable articles, see "Memorandum by the Democratic Alliance of Hungarians in Romania on Romania's Admission to the Council of Europe," Available online at the Hungarian Human Rights Foundation, at: http://www.hhrf.org/hhrf/index_en.php.

19. J. F. Brown, *Hope and Shadows,* 197–98.

20. Michael Shafir, "The Political Party as National Holding Company: The Hungarian Democratic Federation of Romania," in *The Politics of National Minority Participation in Post-Communist Europe. State-Building, Democracy, and Ethnic Mobilization,* ed. Jonathan P. Stein (Armonk, N.Y.: M. E. Sharpe, 2000), 109.

21. Tom Gallagher, "Tensions in Cluj," *RFE/RL* 2, no. 9, Feb. 26, 1993, 27.

22. Ibid., 31–32.

23. Narcisa Medianu, "Analyzing Political Exchange between Minority and Majority Leaders in Romania," *The Global Review of Ethnopolitics* 1, no. 4 (June 2002): 34.

24. These nationalist parties were PUNR, or the Party of Romanian National Unity, PRM, the Greater Romania Party, and PSM, the Socialist Labour Party.

25. Michael Shafir, "Ethnic Tensions Run High in Romania," *RFE/RL* 3, no. 32, Aug. 19,1994, 29.

26. See Brubaker, *Nationalism Reframed,* 1–10.

27. van der Stoel, "The Role of the OSCE High Commission," 76.

28. Zsusza Csergo, "Beyond Ethnic Division: Majority-Minority Debate," *East European Politics and Societies* 16, no. 1 (2002): 21.

29. Michael Shafir, "Romania's Road to "Normalization," *Journal of Democracy* 8, 2 (1997): 150.

30. "Political Will: Romania's Path to Ethnic Accommodation," *Report by the Project on Ethnic Relations,* Bucharest, Romania, Feb. 22–24, 2001, 6.

31. Shafir, "The Political Party as a National Holding Company," 121.

32. Governmental Decision 17, Jan. 31, 1997.

33. See Dan Oprescu's critical comments in "Public Policies on National Minorities in Romania (1996–98)," in *Interethnic Relations in Post-Communist Romania,* ed. Nastase and Salat, 73–81.

34. Medianu, "Analyzing Political Exchange," 33.

35. Proposal submitted by the Delegation of Romania, "Code of conduct of states relating to international co-operation on minority problems," OSCE Meeting of Experts, Geneva, Switzerland, restricted, CSCE/REMN.7, July 9, 1991.

36. For more on regional stability, see Tindemans, *Unfinished Peace,* 137–74.

37. The words of President Jimmy Carter are taken from Hieko Furth, "Reconstructing Political Order: The High Commissioner on National Minorities in Transylvania," in *South East European Politics* 4, no. 2 (2003), 124.

38. Interview with Gabriel Andreescu, director, Bucharest, Romania, June 2004.

39. Telephone interview with Livia Plaks, January 2005.

40. Carothers, *Aiding Democracy Abroad,* 119.

41. Holly Cartner, "Since the Revolution: Human Rights in Romania," Helsinki Watch Report (New York: Human Rights Watch, 1991), 59.

42. Ibid., 60.

43. Tom Gallagher, "Building Democracy in Romania: Internal Shortcomings and External Neglect," in *Democratic Consolidation in Eastern Europe,* 387.

44. Carothers, *Aiding Democracy Abroad,* 119.

45. J. F. Brown, *Hope and Shadows,* 193.

46. Bennett Kovrig, "Partitioned Nation: Hungarian Minorities in Central Europe," in *The New European Diasporas. National Minorities and Conflict in Eastern Europe,* ed. Mandelbaum (New York: Council on Foreign Relations Press, 2000), 57.

47. Edith Oltay, "Minorities as a Stumbling Block in Relations with Neighbors," *RFE/RL,* May 8, 1992, 28.

48. Huber, *Decade,* 37.

49. Ibid., 37, fn B.

50. See Zsusza Csergo and James Goldeier, "Hungary's 'Status Law': A Post-Territorial Approach to Nation Building?" Paper presented at the annual meeting of the American Association for the Advancement of Slavic Studies, Nov. 21–24, Pittsburgh, Pa., 2002.

51. According to Zoltan Kantor of the Teleki Laszlo Institute in Budapest, the most important Hungarian foundations working in this area include: Illyes Foundation, the New Shake Hands Foundation, Segito Jobb Foundation, Apaczai Foundation, Arany Janos Foundation, Domus Hungarica, and Sapientia Foundation. E-mail communication, May 13 and July 18, 2004.

52. Interview with Renata Weber, Bucharest, Romania, June 2004.

53. After a first mission to monitor electing in the GDR on March 18, the council's Parliamentary Assembly sent delegation to Hungary, Slovenia, Croatia, Czechoslovakia, and Bulgaria from March until June. See Huber, *Decade,* 31, fn A.

54. Cartner, "Since the Revolution."

55. Huber, *Decade,* 42–43.

56. Weber, interview.

57. Gallagher, "Building Democracy in Romania," 388.

58. *1990 Human Rights Watch Report on Romania,* 1991.

59. Andreescu, interview, July 2004. For more information, see the International Helsinki Federation for Human Rights Web site at http://www.ihf-hr.org/index.php. On the Romanian committee, see the Association for the Defense of Human Rights in Romania—the Helsinki Committee Web site at http://www.apador.org/indexe.htm, accessed September 2004.

60. "1993 Report. Aspects of the Evolution of Human Rights in Romania and the Reactions of APADOR-Ch in 1993." Available online, at http://www.apador.org/indexe.htm, accessed September 2004.

61. The Project on Ethnic Relations is supported by the Carnegie Corporation of New York, the William and Flora Hewlett Foundation, the Staff Foundation, the Charles Stewart Mott Foundation, the Ford Foundation, the Rockefeller Brothers Fund, and the German Marshall Fund of the United States.

62. The project has country-based programs, several regional programs (such as the East-East series), the Central European series, and programs that focus specifically on the Roma.

63. This quote from Allen Kassof was taken from Steven L. Burg's report, "NGO Mediation of Ethnic Conflict: A Study of the Project on Ethnic Relations in Romania and Kosovo." Unpublished report prepared for the John D. and Catherine T. MacArthur Foundation, Jan. 2003, 2.

64. Michael Shafir, "Minorities Council Raises Questions," *RFE/RL* 2, no. 24, June 11, 1993, 36.

65. Telephone interview with Livia Plaks, Jan. 2005.

66. See Office of Development Evaluation and Information, U.S. Agency for International Development.

67. Gallagher, "Building Democracy in Romania," 389.

68. For more on U.S. strategies, see Dan Petrescu, "Civil Society in Romania," 217–27.

69. *1994 Human Rights Watch Report on Romania,* 1995.

70. *1995 Human Rights Watch Report on Romania,* 1996.

71. Interview with author, Cluj, Romania, June 2004.

72. "Remarks to the Meeting of Romania's Council for National Minorities by the High Commissioner on National Minorities, Max van der Stoel," Bucharest, Aug. 18, 1993. Available online, http://www.minelres.lv/osce/counrec.htm

73. Weber, interview.

74. This dynamic is similar to the "boomerang" pattern of influence described by Risse and Sikkink in "The Socialization of International Human Rights Norms into Domestic Practices," 18.

75. CSCE Communication no. 253, Sept. 23, 1993.

76. Wojciech Kostecki, "Prevention of Ethnic Conflict. Lessons from Romania," *Berghof Occasional Paper* no. 19 (2002): 35.

77. For more on this, see Tindemans, *Unfinished Peace,* 137–74.

78. Interview with author, Bucharest, Romania, June 2004.

79. According to Dan Petrescu, the private donors involved in democracy and civil society included: German *Stiftungen,* Dutch, and American foundations. See "Civil Society in Romania," 230–31.

80. European Agreement establishing an association between the European Economic Communities and their Member States, of the one part, and Romania, of the other part. OJ L 357, 31/12/1994, 12–18.

81. North Atlantic Treaty Organization, "Study on NATO Enlargement," Sept. 1995, available at http://www.nato.int/docu/basictxt/enl-9502.html, accessed Jan. 28, 2005.

82. "NATO Applicant Status: A Status Report," Report for Congress, Congressional Research Service, RL30168, updated Apr. 25, 2003.

83. Kemp, interview.

84. van der Stoel, interview.

85. Telephone interview with Plaks, January 2005.

86. For information on the foundation, its programs, and budget, see the Open Society Foundation-Romania Web site, www.osf.rom.org. See also Petrescu, "Civil Society in Romania," 230–31.

87. Weber, interview.

88. Petrescu, "Civil Society in Romania," 232.

89. The mission statement is taken from the EDRC's informational pamphlet and from a series of publications, including *Barometer of Ethnic Relations,* Nov. 2001, 91. Although EDRC received money from several Open Society Foundations, including OSI-Romania, the Open Society Institute in Budapest, and the Central European University, it also receives funding from a variety of other donors, including the King Baudouin Foundation, Belgium, the Charles Mott Foundation, U.S., and the Delegation of the European Commission in Romania.

90. As quoted in Melanie H. Ram, "Sub-regional Cooperation and European Integration: Romania's Delicate Balance," unpublished paper presented at the International Studies Association Annual Meeting, Feb. 20–24, 2001, Chicago, Ill., 2.

91. For a list of minority relation national legislation, see the MINELRES Web site, http://www.arts.uwaterloo.ca/MINELRES/count/romania.htm.

92. The Freedom House ratings demonstrate Romania's improvement in political and social areas in particular. Rated on a scale of one to seven, with one being the most free, in 1989–90 Romania was given a seven for political rights and a seven for civil rights and was considered "not free." In 1990–2000 it earned a two for political rights and two for civil rights and was considered "free." The significance of "rule consistent behavior" is discussed in Risse and Sikkink, "The Socialization of International Human Rights Norms into Domestic Practices," 19–38.

93. Csergo, "Beyond Ethnic Division," 2.

94. Interview with Toni Niculescu, executive vice president, Democratic Alliance of Hungarians in Romania, Department for European Integration, Bucharest, Romania, June 2004.

95. Plaks, telephone interview.

96. Interview with Istvan Horvath, Cluj, Romania, June 2004.

97. I am referring to the Romanian ambassador's remarks about World War I and the decision by the experts not to revert to any concepts or policies that proved to be a total failure. See "Concluding Statement by Ambassador Traian Chebelau, Head of the Delegation," July 19, 1991, Geneva.

98. Shafir, "Minorities Council Raises Questions," 35.

99. Dan Oprescu, senior adviser, Government of Romania, Office of Roma Issues focuses on the Bratislava-Bucharest-Belgrade relationship and events in the former Yugoslavia. He contends that because of what was happening in Belgrade and the international community's reaction, Iliescu realized that it was necessary for the country to present itself to the world differently and separate from these other rogue states. Interview in Bucharest, Romania, June 2004.

100. According to USAID's Overseas Loans and Grants (Greenbook), U.S. economic assistance in loans and grants went from a high of 63.8 million in 1990 to just 3 million in 1994. U.S. economic assistance information available online at *http://qesdb.cdie.org/gbk/*.

101. "Towards a Closer Association with the Countries of Central and Eastern Europe," Report by the Commission to the European Council, SEC (92) 2301, Dec. 1992.

102. Theodora Melescanu, "The Accession to the European Union: The Fundamental Option of Romania's Foreign Policy," *Romanian Journal of International Affairs* (English) 2, no. 4 (1996): 26.

103. Vachudova, *Europe Undivided*, 55.

104. These expectations are part of the "spiral model" developed by Risse and Sikkink, "The Socialization of International Human Rights Norms into Domestic Practices," 1–38.

105. Both Renata Weber and Gabriel Andreescu made this point.

106. On the prescriptive status of norms and state socialization, see Risse and Sikkink, "The Socialization of International Human Rights Norms into Domestic Practices," 1–38.

107. This is a central point made by Anne-Marie Slaughter in *A New World Order.*

108. Jenonne Walker, "European Regional Organizations and Ethnic Conflict," in *Central and Eastern Europe: The Challenge of Transition,* ed. Regina Cowen Karp (Oxford: Oxford Univ. Press, 1993), 47–48.

109. Horvath, "Facilitating Conflict Transformation," 42–44.

110. Horvath, interview.

111. Dan Ionescu and Alfred A. Reisch, "Still no breakthrough in Romanian-Hungarian Relations," *RFE/RL* 2, no. 42, Oct. 22, 1993, 32.

112. For more on the similarities and differences between the Romanian-Hungarian bilateral agreement and others signed in the region, see Kinga Gal, "Bilateral Agreements in Central and Eastern Europe: A New Inter-State Framework for Minority Protection," ECMI Working Paper no. 4 (May 1999).

113. See "The Pact on Stability in Europe—Text" in *The Minority Question in Europe: Text and Commentary,* ed. Florence Benoit-Rohmer (Strasbourg: Council of Europe Publishing, 1996), 82.

114. See the "Framework Convention for the Projection of National Minorities and Explanatory Report," in *The Minority Question in Europe,* 121–51.

115. See "The Role of Minorities in International and Transborder Relations in Central and Eastern Europe," Helsinki Foundation for Human Rights, MRK workshop paper, Apr. 30-May 3, 1998.

116. See Michael Shafir, "Radical Politics in East-Central Europe," *RFE/RL East European Perspectives,* Nov. 22, 2000, 2, no. 21.

117. Michael J. Jordan, "Hungary and Romania Get an Offer They Can't Refuse: Make Up," *Christian Science Monitor,* Oct. 4, 1996, 6.

118. Horvath, interview.

119. van der Stoel, interview; for more on Romania, see Kemp, *Quiet Diplomacy,* 239.

120. "Political Will: Romania's Path to Ethnic Accommodation," Predeal, Romania, PER Report, Feb. 22–24, 2001.

121. Andreescu, "Pages from the Romanian-Hungarian Reconciliation," 106–7.

122. See Steven L. Burg, "NGO Mediation of Ethnic Conflict: A Study of the Project on Ethnic Relations in Romania and Kosovo," Report prepared for the John D. and Catherine T. MacArthur Foundation, 2002.

123. van der Stoel, "The Role of the OSCE High Commission," 78.

124. Gabriel Andreescu, *Right Wing Extremism in Romania* (Cluj: Ethnocultural Diversity Resource Center, 2003), 75.

125. "Treaty between the Republic of Hungary and Romania on Understanding, Cooperation and Good Neighborhood," Official Translation by the International Law Department of the Minister of Foreign Affairs of the Republic of Hungary, Annexe: List of documents referred to in Article 15, paragraph (2) b of the treaty.

126. Kemp, *Quiet Diplomacy,* 239.

127. Daniel N. Nelson, "Hungary and Its Neighbors: Security and Ethnic Minorities," *Nationalities Papers* 26, no. 2 (1998): 313–30.

128. Donald M. Blinken and Alfred H. Moses, "Good News From Central Europe," *International Herald Tribune,* Sept. 19, 1996, 8, cited in Pal Dunay, "Hungarian-Romanian Relations: A Changed Paradigm?" in *The Effects of Enlargement on Bilateral Relations in Central and Eastern Europe,* ed. Monika Wohlfeld Chaillot Paper 26 (June 1997).

129. I am thinking specifically, but not exclusively about the Pact on Stability in Europe, which was initiated by the EU but worked closely with the OSCE, NATO, WEU and local partners to coordinate international assistance and work with local partners to encourage stability. For more on the role of NGOs in particular, see Kondonis, "Civil Society," 43–63.

130. For more on this see, Thomas M. Buchsbaum, "The OSCE and the Stability Pact for Southeastern Europe: A Mother-Daughter, Brother-Sister Partner Relationship," *Helsinki Monitor* 2000, no. 4, 62–79.

131. Melanie H. Ram, "Black Sea Cooperation toward European Integration," unpublished paper presented at the Black Sea Regional Policy Symposium, Mar. 29-Apr. 11, 2001, Leesburg, Va., 10.

132. On the wording of this complete article, see the Constitution of Romania. For an analysis, see *Human Rights in Romania after Ceausescu,* International Helsinki Federation for Human Rights Report (Apr. 1994).

133. Plaks, telephone interview. Plaks explained by the summer of 1993 several of the issues that were debated and discussed were finally being acted upon.

134. Michael Shafir, "Minorities Council Raises Questions," *RFE/RL* 2, no. 24, June 11, 1993, 36.

135. Ibid., 36.

136. Ibid., 35.

137. Oprescu, "Public Policies on National Minorities in Romania," 73–74.

138. OSCE Document 1028/93/L, 9 Sept. 9, 1993.

139. Remarks to the Meeting of Romania's Council for National Minorities by the High Commission on National Minorities, Max van der Stoel, Bucharest, Aug. 18, 1993.

140. Shafir, "Minorities Council Raises Questions," 37.

141. In interviews with Istvan Horvath and Gabor Adam both mentioned the importance of PER in creating an environment that allowed these actors to consider cooperation.

142. Plaks, telephone interview.

143. van der Stoel, interview.

144. Horvath, "Facilitating Conflict Transformation," 119.

145. Remarks to the Meeting of Romania's Council for National Minorities by the High Commission on National Minorities, Max van der Stoel, Bucharest, Aug. 18, 1993.

146. Horvath, "Facilitating Conflict Transformation," 70–90.

147. CSCE Communication no. 253, Sept. 23, 1993.

148. HCNM letter to Melescanu, Feb. 26, 1996.

149. Report by the International Helsinki Federation for Human Rights to the United Nations Commission on Human Rights Fifty-Fourth Session Geneva, Mar. 16-Apr. 24, 1998, item no. 16.

150. van der Stoel, interview.

151. Interview with Levente Salat, Cluj, Romania, June 2004.

152. Furst, 122–40.

153. Risse and Sikkink, "The Socialization of International Human Rights Norms into Domestic Practices," 18–20.

154. Gallagher, "Building Democracy in Romania," 388.

155. Petrescu, "Civil Society in Romania," 232.

156. In Romania 30,000 are registered but of these only 2,500 are estimated to be active. See *The 2002 NGO Sustainability Index* Washington, D.C.: USAID Report, May 2003.

157. Andreescu, "Pages from the Romanian-Hungarian Reconciliation," 92–103.

158. Ibid., 92–103.

159. Ibid., 101.

160. Sherrill Stroschein, "NGOs Strategies for Hungarian and Roma Minorities in Central Europe," *Voluntas* 13, no. 1 (Mar. 2002), 1–26.

161. On the values associated with civil society organizations, see CIVICUS Index on Civil Society Occasional Paper Serigves 1, Issue 9 (2000), 8.

162. Anna-Maria Biro, "The International Relations of the Democratic Alliance of Hungarians in Romania (DAHR)," 21–41.

163. See Michael Shafir "The Hungarian Democratic Federation of Romania: Actions, Reactions, and Factions," *Ethnicity Unbound: The Politics of Minority Participation in Post-Communist Europe,* ed. Robert W. Mickey (London: St. Martin's Press, 1996), 120–21.

164. Medianu, "Analyzing Political Exchange," 40.

165. Interview with Michael Mates, Cluj, Romania, June 2004.

166. Interview with Salat, June 2004.

167. The 2000 NGO Sustainability Index. *USAID Report* (May 2001).

168. Petrescu, "Civil Society in Romania," 232.

169. "Political Will: Romania's Path to Ethnic Accommodation," PER Report, Budapest, Feb. 22–24, 2001, 4.

170. Ibid., 9.

171. Medianu, "Analyzing Political Exchange," 33.

172. Interview with Iulian Chifu, Director, Center for Conflict Prevention and Early Warning, Bucharest, Romania, June 10, 2004.

173. A similar statement is made by Gabriel Andreescu in *Right Wing Extremism in Romania* (Cluj: Ethnocultural Center, 2003).

5. Quiet on the Russian Front: The Evolution of Ethnic Politics in Latvia

1. I use the word Russian-speakers rather than Russians because in 2000, 57.4 percent of the country was ethnically Latvian, only 30 percent were of Russian descent. For more statistics, see *The Naturalization Board of the Republic of Latvia* (Riga, 2001).

2. Eric Rudenshield, "Ethnic Dimensions in Contemporary Latvian Politics: Focusing Forces for Change," *Soviet Studies* 44, Issue 4 (1992), 609. On the threat of the Russian diaspora, see Michael Mandelbaum, ed., *The European Diasporas* (New York: Council on Foreign Relations, 2000), 2; Paul Kolstoe, *Russians in the Former Soviet Republics* (Bloomington: Indiana Univ. Press, 1995); and van Evera "Hypotheses on Nationalism," 5–39.

3. For similar conclusions, see Jekaterina Dorodnova, "Challenging Ethnic Democracy: Implementation of the Recommendations of the OSCE High Commission on National Minorities to Latvia, 1993–2001," Center for OSCE Research, Univ. of Hamburg, Working Paper 10. 2003.

4. Most of this research compares and contrasts ethnic policies in the Baltic states, with a particular focus on Estonia and Latvia. See David D. Laitin, *Identity in Formation* (Ithaca: Cornell Univ. Press, 1998). On the role of the international community, see David Smith," Framing the National Question in Central and Eastern Europe: A Quadratic Nexus," *The Global Review of Ethnopolitics* 2, no. 1 (2002), 3–16; Conrad J. Huber, "Averting Interethnic Conflict: An Analysis of the CSCE's HCNM in Estonia," The Carter Center Working Paper, Apr. 1994; Raivo Vetik, "Ethnic Conflict and Accommodation in Post-Communist Estonia," *Journal of Peace Research* 30, no. 3 (1993), 271–80.

5. According to an official from the UNDP's office in Riga, ethnicity does not play a significant role in determining poverty in the country. In fact, Russian speakers have more amenities than Latvia, which at least according to some provides some insight into the country's stability. See Paul Goble, "Latvia's Analysis from Washington: When Ethnicity is not the Explanation," *RFE/RL* January 23, 2001.

6. See Michael Mandelbaum, "Introduction," in *The New European Diasporas*, 1–15.

7. On the role of the EU and conditionality in Latvia, see Judith Kelley, "International Actors on the Domestic Scene: Membership Conditionality and Socialization by International Institutions," *International Organization* 58 (Summer 2004): 425–57; Grabbe, "Europeanization," 1013–31. For an emphasis on the CSCE/OSCE, see Dorodnova, "Challenging Ethnic Democracy."

8. See Nils Muiznieks and Ilze Brands Kehris, "The European Union: Democratization and Minorities in Latvia," in *The European Union and Democratization,* [ED?] Paul. J. Kubicek (London: Rout-

ledge: 2003), 30–50. See also Elmars Svekis, "Latvia's Compliance with the OSCE Principles: Domestic Choices or International Commitments?" MA thesis, The Central European Univ., Budapest, Oct. 30, 2001.

9. Mission documents are housed in the OSCE's library in Prague, the Czech Republic. They were accessed in the summer of 2004 with the help of Martina Steiner and Maartje Breakman. Among others, Nils Muiznieks and Ilze Brands Kehris point to the important role of the CSCE/OSCE mission but also the dearth of information on its activities.

10. Artis Pabriks, *From Nationalism to Ethnic Policy: The Latvian Nation in the Present and Past* (Berlin: Berliner Interuniversitare Abreitns gruppe Baltische Staaten, 1999), Nr. 17, 73.

11. See Gershon Shafir, *Immigrants and Nationalists: Ethnic Conflict and Accommodation in the Basque, Country, Latvia and Estonia* (Albany: State University of New York Press, 1995), 140–44.

12. John Ginkel, "Identity Construction in Latvia's Singing Revolution: Why Interethnic Conflict Failed to Occur," *Nationalities Papers* 30, no. 3 (2002): 416.

13. I thank Michael Johns for this point.

14. Aurel Braun, "All Quiet on the Russian Front? Russia, Its Neighbors, and the Russian Diaspora," in *The New European Diasporas,* by Mandelbaum, 83–85.

15. Dzintra Bungs, "Latvia: Toward Full Independence," *RFE/RL* 2, no. 1, Jan. 1, 1993, 98.

16. Dorodnova, "Challenging Ethnic Democracy," 15.

17. Svekis, "Latvia's Compliance," 10.

18. Laitin, "Secessionist Rebellion," 97.

19. The Naturalization Board of the Republic of Latvia, 1994–99.

20. Ulf Hansson, "The Latvian Language and the Involvement of the OSCE-HCNM. The Developments 2000–2002," *The Global Review of Ethnopolitics* 2, no. 1 (Sept. 2002): 17–28.

21. Dzintra Bungs, "Soviet Troops in Latvia," *RFE/RL,* 1, no. 24, Aug. 28, 1992, 23–24.

22. For more on this, see Aivars Stranga, "The End Product: A Crisis in Latvian-Russian Relations," NATO Academic Affairs Unit, (Mar.-Aug. 1998), http://www.nato.int/acad/fellow/ 96–98/stranga.pdf.

23. Dzintra Bungs, "The Latvian-Russian Treaty of the Vicissitudes of Interstate Relations," *RFE/RL,* Feb. 28, 1992, 29–30.

24. Heather F. Hurlburt, "Russian Bilateral Treaties and Minority Policy," in *Protection of Minority Rights Through Bilateral Treaties,* 59.

25. Braum, 83.

26. Vera Tolz, "Russia: Westernizers Continue to Challenge National Patriots," *RFE/RL* 1, no. 29, Dec. 11, 1992, 3.

27. Roman Szplorluk, "Belarus, Ukraine, and The Russian Question," *Post-Soviet Affairs* 9, no. 4 (1993): 368.

28. For more on these issues, see Neil Malcolm, Alex Pravda, Roy Allison, and Margot Light, eds., *Internal Factors in Russian Foreign Policy* (New York: Oxford Univ. Press, 1996).

29. Peter Shearman, "Introduction," in *Russian Foreign Policy since 1990,* ed. Peter Shearman (Boulder: Westview Press, 1995), 5.

30. Andrei Edemsky and Paul Kolstoe, "Russian Policy towards the Diaspora," in *Russian Policy,* 273.

31. Ibid., 273.

32. Hurlburt, "Russian Bilateral Treaties," 55–57.

33. Ibid., 57.

34. Interview with Olafs Bruvers, Director, Latvian National Human Rights Office, Riga, Latvia, July 2004.

35. Dorodnova, "Challenging Ethnic Democracy," 29.

36. Svekis, "Latvia's Compliance," 27–89.

37. Hurlburt, "Russian Bilateral Treaties," 61.

38. Opinion no. 183 (1995) on the application by Latvia for membership of the Council of Europe.

39. Svekis, "Latvia's Compliance," 12.

40. Muiznieks and Brands Kehris, "European Union," 33.

41. Dorodnova, "Challenging Ethnic Democracy," 29.

42. Dzintra Bungs, "Latvia: Transition to Independence Completed," *RFE/RL,* 3, no. 6, Jan. 17, 1994, 96.

43. CSCE Mission to Latvia, Activity Report (hereafter AR), no. 2, Jan. 14, 1994.

44. Italics are mine to emphasize its attention to international law; for more, see Hurlburt, "Russian Bilateral Treaties," 56.

45. Excerpts from the Press Conference of Vialy Churkin, Deputy Minister of Foreign Affairs of Russia, Jan. 27, 1994, regarding relations between Russia and Baltic States, CSCE correspondence (unofficial translation).

46. See Michael Johns, "The Responsibility to Interject? The Impact of European Organizations on Minority Rights," unpublished paper presented at the International Studies Association Annual Conference, Honolulu, Hawaii, Mar. 1–5, 2005.

47. van der Stoel, interview.

48. CSCE Communication no. 124 and 125/Add 1, "Letters dated 6 April 1993 to the Ministers for Foreign Affairs of the Republic of Estonia, Latvia, Lithuania" (Letters of reply and Comments on the Conclusions and Recommendations of the Mission of the CSCE High Commissioner on National Minorities").

49. Kemp, *Nationalism and Communism,* 155.

50. CSCE Communication no. 8, "Letter of the CSCE High Commissioner on National Minorities to the Minister for Foreign Affairs of the Republic of Latvia, dated 10 December 1993," as well as the letter of republic, dated Jan. 25, 1994, from the Minister of Foreign Affairs of Latvia.

51. 1994 Human Rights Watch Report, 1995.

52. Schimmelfennig, Engert and Knobel, "Costs, Commitment," 510.

53. CSCE Mission to Latvia, AR, no. 9, Oct. 10, 1994.

54. CSCE Mission to Latvia, Spot Report no. 12, Nov. 29, 1994.

55. Brands Kehris, interview.

56. Lange, interview.

57. Richard J. Krickus, "Latvia's "Russian Question," *RFE/RL* 2, no. 18, Apr. 30, 1993, 29.

58. Ibid., p. 29.

59. 1993 Human Rights Watch Report, 1994.

60. Bruvers, interview.

61. Interview with Bruvers and Igor Pimenov, former director of LASHOR, Latvian Association of Schools of Russian, July 2004.

62. 1993 Human Rights Watch Report, 1994.

63. "The U.S. Delegation to the CSCE Office of the Public Affairs Advisor," Joint News Conference by the President of the U.S. with the Presidents of Latvia, Lithuania, and Estonia July 6, 1994," OSCE Doc. 469, July 7, 1994.

64. OSCE Mission to Latvia, AR, no. 13, Feb. 28, 1995.

65. Agenda 2000—Commission Opinion on Latvia's Application for Membership of the European Union DOC/97/14, Brussels, July 15, 1997.

66. Schimmelfennig, Engert and Knobel, "Costs, Commitment," 510–11.

67. E-mail correspondence, July 8 2005.

68. Dorodnova, "Challenging Ethnic Democracy," 49.

69. "Presidents of Estonia, Latvia, Lithuania Hold Briefing," USIS Washington File, Jan. 15, 1998. Available online, http://www.fas.org/man/nato/national/98011503_wpo.html, accessed February 2004.

70. Grazina Miniotaite, "Lithuania and NATO Enlargement, "*Baltic Defence Review* 2, no. 6 (2001): 30–35.

71. "Letter dated 15 March 1996 to the Minister for Foreign Affairs of the Republic of Latvia," REF.HC/5/96, Apr. 22, 1996.

72. "Letter dated 28 October 1996 to the Minister for Foreign Affairs of the Republic of Latvia, REF.HC/2/77, Dec. 10, 1996.

73. "Letter of 21 November 1996 to the Minister for Foreign Affairs of the Republic of Latvia," Mr. V. Birkavs, as well as the letter of republic, dated Feb. 27, 1997, REF.HC/3/97.

74. Press Release of the OSCE HCNM in Riga, Apr. 17, 1998 on the abolition of the so-called "window" system for naturalization."

75. Dorodnova, "Challenging Ethnic Democracy," 136.

76. Max van der Stoel made this point when I interviewed him but so did many EU officials.

77. Interview with Vita Morica, director of Providus and former OSI director (1992–96), Riga, Latvia, July 2004.

78. Interview with Andris Aukmanis, director of the Open Society Institute, Riga, Latvia, July 2004.

79. Interview with Daigma Holma, head of Programme Unit, United Nations Development Program, Riga, Latvia, July 2004.

80. See Muiznieks and Brands Kehris, "European Union"; Dorodnova, Svekes, and Smith for similar conclusions.

81. Birkavs, interview.

82. Confidential interview with representative of the Ministry of Foreign Affairs, Riga, Latvia, July 2004.

83. Morica, interview.

84. Birkavs, interview.

85. Interview with Eizenija Aldermane, Head of the Naturalization Board, Riga, Latvia, July 2004.

86. Gutmanis, interview.

87. Muizniek and Brands Kehris, "European Union," 30.

88. van der Stoel, interview.

89. CSCE Communication no. 8 Vienna, 312 January 1994/Reference: NO. 1463/93/L.

90. Bungs, "Latvia: Transition to Independence Completed," 98.

91. "Letter of April 18, 1993, to Max van der Stoel from Georgs Andrejevs."

92. Muiznieks and Brands Kehris, "European Union," 35–36.

93. Dobrodovna, 136–37.

94. Birkavs, interview.

95. Birkavs, interview; similar comments were made by Brands Kehris about the HCNM.

96. Kemp, *Quiet Diplomacy,* 156.

97. Dorodnova, "Challenging Ethnic Democracy," 33.

98. The Naturalization Board of the Republic of Latvia, 1994–99, 10.

99. CSCE Mission to Latvia, AR, no. 7, Aug. 2, 1994.

100. "Press Release of the CSCE Chairmanship-in Office of the CSCE with regard to the adoption of the Law on Citizenship by the Latvian Parliament On 22 July 1994" Doc. 575/94 Aug. 16, 1994.

101. "Statement by the Minister of Foreign Affairs of the Republic of Latvia," Aug. 4, 1994 unofficial translation.

102. CSCE Mission to Latvia, AR, no. 10 Nov. 2, 1994.

103. Dzintra Bungs, "Soviet Troops in Latvia," 25.

104. Republic of Latvia information about the Implementation of Paragraph 5 of the Helsinki Summit Declaration 1992, CSCE Document, Stockholm Council Meeting of Dec. 1992.

105. Dzintra Bungs, "Russian Troop Withdrawal from Latvia: An Update," *RFE/RL* 1, no. 49, Dec. 11, 1992, 31.

106. "Appeal of the Minister of Foreign Affairs of the Russian Federation to Ministers of Foreign of the CSCE Participating States and Heads of International Organizations in Connection with the Adoption of the Law on Citizens of the Latvian Republic," CSCE unofficial document, Aug. 23, 1994.

107. Dorodnova, "Challenging Ethnic Democracy," 140.

108. "Statement by Ambassador V. Shustov, Head of Delegation of Russian Federation at a Meeting of the OSCE Permanent Council," CSCE unofficial translation, May 14 1996.

109. Interview with Inga Reina, Representative of the Government of Latvia before International Human Rights Organizations, Riga, Latvia, July 2004.

110. Interview with Reina, July 2004.

111. OSCE Mission to Latvia, AR, no. 12, Jan. 30, 1995.

112. CSCE Mission to Latvia, AR, no. 9, Oct. 10, 1994.

113. OSCE Mission to Latvia, AR, no. 15, Apr. 24, 1995.

114. OSCE Mission to Latvia, AR, no. 12, Jan. 30, 1995.

115. OSCE Mission to Latvia, AR, no. 26, Apr. 26, 1996, restricted.

116. Schimmelfennig, Engert and Knobel, "Costs, Commitment," 513.

117. OSCE Mission to Latvia, AR, no. 39, July 7, 1997, restricted.

118. Birkavs, interview.

119. "Letter from the Prime Minister of Latvia, Mr. Guntars Krasts," April 24, 1998, to the HCNM and his letter of reply, April 30, 1998, HCNM.GAL/3/98.

120. Birkavs, interview.

121. Dorodnova, "Challenging Ethnic Democracy," 50.

122. Schimmelfennig, Engert and Knobel, "Costs, Commitment," 513.

123. Dorodnova, "Challenging Ethnic Democracy," 50.

124. Reference No 984/98/L, "Letter from the HCNM, Max van der Stoel, dated 30 April 1998, to Guntars Krasts."

125. Muizenks and Brands Kehris, "European Union," 41.

126. Press Statement of the OSCE HCNM, Mr. Max van der Stoel, Riga, Apr. 17, 1998. INF./1/98 Apr. 20, 1998.

127. OSCE Mission to Latvia, AR, no. 52, Nov. 1, 1998, restricted.

128. Svekis, "Latvia's Compliance," 49; Kemp, *Quiet Diplomacy,* 159; and Dorodnova, "Challenging Ethnic Democracy," 55–57.

129. OSCE Mission to Latvia, Background report: Background information for Ambassador Orns' Permanent Council Appearance," 15 Mar. 2000, restricted.

130. Nils Muiznieks and Brands Kehris, "European Union," 44.

131. Dobrodnova, "Challenging Ethnic Democracy," 140.

132. Birkavs, interview.

133. Muinzieks and Brands Kehris, 45.

134. OSCE Mission to Latvia, AR, No 37, July 16, 1999, restricted.

135. For more on this issue evolved subsequently, see Hansson, 17–28.

136. CSCE Mission to Latvia, AR, no. 7, Aug. 2, 1994, restricted; See also Country Reports on Human Rights Practices for 1996, U.S. Department of State, Jan. 30, 1997.

137. 1996 Country Reports on Human Rights Practices, U.S. Department of State, Jan. 30, 1997.

138. Interview with Aldermane, July 2004.

139. According to the Naturalization Board, in 1996, 2,627 applications were submitted and 3,016 persons were naturalized; in 1997, 3,075 applications were submitted and 2,992 persons were naturalized; in 1998 5,608 applications were submitted and 4,439 persons were naturalized. In 1999 the applications submitted jumped to 15,183 and persons naturalized to 12,427 and in 2000, 10,692 applications were submitted and 14,900 persons were naturalized. Naturalization Board 2002, 66.

140. 1999 Country Reports on Human Rights Practices, U.S. Department of State, Feb. 25, 2000.

141. *Cooperation of the Naturalization Board with Foreign Institutions and International Organizations, 1994–2004.* (Riga: Naturalization Board Foreign Relations Department, 2004), 5.

142. Interview with Aldermane, July 2004.

143. OSCE Mission to Latvia, AR, no. 34, Jan. 10, 1997, restricted.

144. Bruvers, interview.

145. Bruvers admitted this, explaining that there were simply too many other issues for his office to address.

146. For more on this, see www.no.gov.lv/en/fjas

147. E-mail correspondence from Nils Muizniek, July 8, 2004.

148. Holma, interview.

149. Interview with Reinos Alboltins, Riga, Latvia, July 2004.

150. Interview with Nils Sakks, Riga, Latvia, July 2004.

151. Holma, interview.

152. OSCE Mission to Latvia, AR, no. 21, Nov. 20, 1995, restricted.

153. OSCE Mission to Latvia, AR, no. 51, Oct. 13, 1998, restricted.

154. OSCE Mission to Latvia, AR, no. 53, Dec. 18, 1998, restricted.

155. Pimenov, interview.

156. Holma, interview.

157. Aukmanis, interview.

158. In 2003, for example, it received the van der Stoel prize by the CSCE/OSCE for its timely and informed research and commentary on ethnic politics.

159. Latvian Center for Human Rights and Ethnic Studies pamphlet; Brands Kehris, interview.

160. OSCE mission to Latvia, AR, no. 27, June 3, 1996.

161. Brands Kehris, interview.

162. U.S. Department of State, Human Rights Reports for 1999, Latvia, Feb. 25, 2000.

163. Final Report: "High-Level Mission for the Formulation of a National Program for the Protection and Promotion of Human Rights in Latvia," Riga, Latvia, July 25-Aug. 1, 1994.

164. Vadim Poleshchuk, "Accession to the EU and National Integration in Estonia and Latvia" (Baltic seminar 2000, Dec. 7–10, 2000), ECMI Report no. 8, Mar. 2001.

165. Morica, interview.

166. Interview with Vita Terauda, director, PROVIDUS, Center for Public Policy, former director of Soros Foundation Latvia, Riga, Latvia, July 13, 2004.

167. Fred Weir, "Latvia gives Russia Cold Shoulder," *The Christian Science Monitor.* Nov. 26, 2002.

168. See Svekis, "Latvia's Compliance," 49.

6. Transnational Networks and Ethnic Cooperation: The Lessons Learned

1. Claude, *National Minorities,* 1.

2. While Judith Kelley does try to separate and compare the relative influence of different strategies, she too notes the inherent difficulties of doing this, see "International Actors," 450–51.

3. As suggested by Abram Chayes and Antonia Handler Chayes, "Transition and Conflict: Russian and American Perspectives on the Former Soviet Union," in *Managing Conflict in the Former Soviet Union,* 12.

4. For similar conclusions, see Grabbe, "Europeanization," 1013–31.

5. Smith, "The Evolution and Approach," 113–22.

6. Vachudova, "Strategies," 158.

7. van der Stoel, interview.

8. See EU, "Evaluation of the PHARE and TACIS Democracy Programme."

9. Nancy Lubin, "Ethnic Conflict Resolution and U.S. Assistance," a report for the Eisenhower Institute (2004).

10. This is not to say that no evaluations of NGOs have been done. In fact, Steven L. Burg does an

evaluation of the impact of PER programs, and Soros has conducted evaluations of its programs in Eastern Europe. See Burg's "NGO Mediation of Ethnic Conflict."

11. Interview with Franck Oliver Roux, EuropeAid Co-operation Office, European Commission, Brussels, Belgium, Mar. 3, 2004.

12. Ashman, interview.

13. Thomas Carothers, "Democracy Assistance: The Question of Strategy," *Democratization* 4, no. 3 (Autumn 1997): 117–19.

14. Mendelson and Glenn, *The Power and Limits of NGOs,* 9–11.

15. For more on the spiral model, see Risse and Sikkink, "The Socialization of International Human Rights Norms into Domestic Practices," 1–38.

16. See the recommendations made in Tindemans, *Unfinished Peace,* 137–72.

17. On evaluations, see Risse and Sikkink, "The Socialization of International Human Rights Norms into Domestic Practices," 11–35.

18. Alexander Cooley and James Ron, "The NGO Scramble: Organizational Insecurity and the Political Economy of Transnational Action," *International Security* 27, no. 1 (Summer 2002): 5–39.

19. Hopmann, "Building Security," 5–6.

20. I thank Allen Kassof for this point. E-mail correspondence Nov. 5, 2005.

21. C. Huber, "Averting Interethnic Conflict," 127.

22. Slaughter, *A New World Order,* 24.

23. Ratner, "Does International Law Matter," 591–642.

24. Alina Mungiu-Pippidi, "Identity Crisis," *Transitions* (Apr. 1998): 79. See also Peter Gross and Vladimir Tismaneanu, "No NATO Shelter for Romania," *Transitions* (Apr. 1998): 26–31.

25. Mungiu-Pippidi, "Identity Crisis," 79.

26. See Chester A. Crocker, Fen Osler-Hampson and Pamela Aall, "Multiparty Mediation and the Conflict Cycle," in *Herding Cats,* 19–45.

27. McHugh, "USAID and Ethnic Conflict," 71.

28. Mates, interview.

29. Crocker, Osler-Hampson, and Aall, "Multiparty Mediation," 24.

30. Marise Cremona, "Creating the New Europe: The Stability Pact for South-Eastern Europe in the Context of EUI-SEE Relations," in *Cambridge Yearbook of European Legal Studies,* A. Dashwood and A. Ward, eds. (Oxford: Hart Publishing, 2000), 466.

31. Cremona, "Creating the New Europe," 463–506; Smith, "Evolution and Approach," 105–40; and Vachudova, "Strategies," 141–60.

32. Gaetano Pentassuglia, "On the Models of Minority Rights Supervision in Europe and How They Affect a Changing Concept of Sovereignty," *European Yearbook of Minority Issues* 1 (2001–2): 29–64.

33. Allen Kassof, unpublished paper on PER Activities in Eastern Europe 2005.

34. For more on prevention activities in the Balkans, see van Tongeren, van de Veen, and Verhoeven, *Searching for Peace in Europe and Eurasia,* especially 309–21 on Montenegro.

35. Sally Broughton and Eran Franenkel, "Macedonia: Extreme Challenges for the 'Model' of Multiculturalism," in *Searching for Peace in Europe and Eurasia,* 264–79; Fraenkel, interview.

36. While Roma is the most common way to describe this group, *Romani, Sinti,* and *Gypsy* are also

used. The total number of Roma in Europe is somewhere between 6 and 8 million. Official numbers based on self-identification are much lower and amount to about 2.5 million.

37. "Statement of the HCNM on his study of the Roma in CSCE region," Sept. 21, 1993, available online at: http://www.osce.org/hcnm/documents.html.

38. CSCE Communication no. 240, Sept. 14, 1993.

39. Martin Kovats, "Problems of Intellectual and Political Accountability in Respect of Emerging European Roma Policy," *Journal on Ethnopolitics and Minority Issues in Europe* (Autumn 2001): 2.

40. He also discusses some of unintended consequences of transnational involvement and the new divisions that have emerged between officially acknowledged Romani Advisors and Romani activists." See Peter Vermeersch, "Advocacy Networks and Romani Politics in Central and Eastern Europe," *Journal of Ethnopolitics and Minority Issues in Europe* (2001): 1–19.

41. On the conditions of Roma in Eastern Europe, see Jo Martin Goodman and Ana Revenga, *Poverty and Ethnicity: A Cross-Country Study of Roma Poverty in Central Europe* (New York: World Bank 2002).

42. Vermeersch, "Advocacy Networks," 12.

43. Keck and Sikkink, *Activists Beyond Borders,* 8–9.

44. Pentassuglia, "Minority Rights Supervision," 30.

45. Confidential interview, Cluj, Romania, June 2004.

46. See Boris Tsilevich, "EU Enlargement and the Protection of National Minorities: Opportunities, Myths and Prospects," available at http://www.eumap.org/journal/features/2001/oct/euenlarge.

47. Lynn M. Tesser, "The Geopolitics of Tolerance: Minority Rights under EU Expansion in East-Central Europe," *East European Politics and Societies* 17, no. 3 (2003): 493–95.

48. Smith, "Evolution and Approach," 120.

49. de Witt, "Politics Versus Law," 137–60.

50. See David Chandler, "The OSCE and the Internationalization of National Minority Rights," in *Ethnicity and Democratisation in the New Europe,* ed. Karl Cordell (London: Routledge, 1999), 67.

51. Ibid., 71.

52. Mandelbaum, *The New European Diasporas,* 296.

53. Stephen Deets, "Reconsidering Eastern European Minority Policy: Liberal Theory and European Norms," *Eastern European Politics and Society* 16, no. 1 (2002): 30–53.

54. de Witt, "Politics Versus Law," 144.

55. Susan L. Woodward, "Bosnia and Herzegovina: How Not to End Civil War," in *Civil Wars, Insecurity, and Intervention,* 88.

56. Hughes and Sasse, "Monitoring the Monitors," 6.

57. Boris Tsilevich, "New Democracies in the Old World: Remarks on Will Kymlicka's Approach to Nation-building in post-Communist Europe," in *Can Liberal Pluralism be Exported?* ed. Will Kymlicka and Magda Opalski (Oxford: Oxford Univ. Press, 2001), 168.

58. See "Bosnia: Reshaping the International Machinery," *International Crisis Report,* no. 121, Nov. 29, 2001.

59. Peter Schwab and Adamantia Pollis, "Globalization's Impact on Human Rights," in *Human Rights,* 216.

60. For similar claims, see Vermeersch, "Advocacy Networks"; van Tongeren, van de Veen, and

Verhoeven, *Searching for Peace in Europe and Eurasia*; John Paul Lederach, *Building Peace: Sustainable Reconciliation in Divided Societies,* 5th ed. (Washington, D.C.: USIP Press, 2002).

61. Kondonis, "Civil Society," 43–63.

62. Ibid., 44–45.

63. See Etizioni, *From Empire to Community.*

64. See Holohan, *Networks.*

65. Francis Fukuyama, "The End of History," *National Interest* (Summer 1989): 3–18; Huntington, *The Clash of Civilizations*, esp. chap. 1; and John J. Mearsheimer, "Why We Will Soon Miss the Cold War," *The Atlantic Monthly* 266, no. 2 (Aug. 1990): 35–50.

Bibliography

Allison, Graham T., Jr., and Robert P. Bescehel, Jr. "Can the U.S. Promote Democracy?" *Political Science Quarterly* 107, no. 1 (1992): 81–101.

Anderson, Benedict. *Imagined Communities: Reflections on the Origins and Spread of Nationalism.* London: Verso, 1991.

Andreescu, Gabriel. "Pages from the Romanian-Hungarian Reconciliation, 1989–1999: The Role of Civic Organizations." In *Interethnic Relations in Post-Communist Romania: Proceedings of the Conference the Romanian Model of Ethnic Relations, The Last Ten Years, The Next Ten Years,* edited by Lucian Nastase and Levente Salat, 89–122. Cluj: Ethnocultural Diversity in Romania Series, 2000.

———. *Right Wing Extremism in Romania.* Cluj: Ethnocultural Center, 2003.

Baier-Allen, Suzanne, ed. *Synergy in Conflict Management.* Baden-Baden: Verlagsgesellschaft, 1998.

Barkin, J. Samuel, and Bruce Cronin. "The State and the Nation: Changing Norms and the Rules of Sovereignty in International Relations." *International Organization* 48, no. 1 (1994): 107–30.

Barry, Robert L. "Priorities of U.S. Assistance to Central and Eastern Europe." U.S. Department of State Dispatch 2, no. 16 (April 22, 1991).

Beck, Robert J., and Thomas Ambrosio, eds. *International Law and the Rise of Nations: The State System and the Challenge of Ethnic Groups.* New York: Chatham House Publications, 2002.

Benoit-Rohmer, Florence. *The Minority Question in Europe: Text and Commentary.* Strasbourg: Council of Europe Publishing, 1996.

Bieber, Florian. "Consociationalism-Prerequisite or Hurdle for Democratization in Bosnia? The Case of Belgium as a Possible Example." *South-East Europe Review* 2, no. 3 (1999): 79–94.

Bildt, Carl. "The Balkans' Second Chance." *Foreign Affairs* 80, no. 1 (2001): 148–58.

———. *Peace Journey: The Search for Peace in Bosnia.* London: Weidenfeld and Nicolson, 1998.

Biro, Anna-Maria. "International Relations of the Democratic Alliance of Hungarians in Romania (DAHR)." *International Studies* (Romania) 2 (1996): 21–41.

Biro, Anna-Maria, and Petra Kovacs, eds. *Local Public Management of Multi-Ethnic Communities in Central and Eastern Europe.* Budapest: Open Society Institute, 2001.

Blainey, Geoffrey. *The Causes of War.* 3d ed. New York: Free Press, 1988.

Bloed, Arie, ed. *The Challenges of Change: The Helsinki Summit of the CSCE and Its Aftermath.* Dordrecht: Martinus Nijhoff, 1994.

———, ed. *The Conference on Security and Cooperation in Europe: Analysis and Basic Documents, 1972–1993.* The Hague: Kluwer Academic Publishers, 1993.

———, ed. *From Helsinki to Vienna: Basic Documents of the Helsinki Process.* Dordrecht: Martinus Nijhoff, 1990.

Bloed, Arie, and P. Van Dijk, eds. *The Human Dimension of the Helsinki Process: The Vienna Follow-Up Meeting and its Aftermath.* Dordrecht: Martinus Nijhoff, 1991.

———, eds. *Protection of Minority Rights Through Bilateral Treaties: The Case of Central and Eastern Europe.* The Hague: Kluwer Law International, 1999.

Boli, John, and George M. Thomas, eds. *Constructing World Culture: International Nongovernmental Organizations Since 1875.* Stanford: Stanford Univ. Press, 1999.

Borzel, Tanja. "Organizing Babylon: On the Different Conceptions of Policy Networks." *Public Administration* 76 (1998): 253–73.

Bowen, John R. "The Myth of Global Ethnic Conflict." *Journal of Democracy* 7, no. 4 (1996): 3–15.

Bradach, Jeffrey L., and Robert G. Eccles. "Price, Authority, and Trust: From Ideal Types to Plural Forms." *Annual Review of Sociology* 15 (1989): 97–118.

Broughton, Sally, and Eran Fraenkel. "Macedonia: Extreme Challenges for the "Model" of Multiculturalism." In *Searching for Peace in Europe and Eurasia,* edited by Paul van Tongeren, Hans van de Veen, and Juliette Verhoeven, 264–79. Boulder: Lynne Rienner, 2002.

Brown, J. F. *Hope and Shadows: Eastern Europe After Communism.* Durham: Duke Univ. Press, 1994.

Brown, Michael E. "The Flawed Logic of Nato Expansion." *Survival* 37, no. 34 (1995): 34–52.

———. "Minimalist NATO." *Foreign Affairs* 78, no. 3 (1999): 203–18.

———, ed. *Ethnic Conflict and International Security.* Princeton: Princeton Univ. Press, 1993.

———, ed. *Nationalism and Ethnic Conflict.* Cambridge: MIT Press, 2001.

Brubaker, Rogers. *Nationalism Reframed.* Cambridge: Cambridge Univ. Press, 1996.

Brusis, Martin. "The EU and Interethnic Power-sharing Arrangements in Accession Countries." *Journal of Ethnopolitics and Minority Issues in Europe* 1 (2003): 1–12.

Brzezinski, Zbigniew. "Post-Communist Nationalism." *Foreign Affairs* 68, no. 5 (1989–90): 1–25.

———. *The Soviet Bloc: Unity and Conflict.* 2d edition. Cambridge: Harvard Univ. Press, 1967.

Buchsbaum, Thomas M. "The Osce and the Stability Pact for Southeastern Europe: A

Mother-Daughter, Brother-Sister Partner Relationship." *Helsinki Monitor,* no. 4 (2000): 62–79.

Bungs, Dzintra. "Latvia: Toward Full Independence," *RFE/RL* 2, no. 1, Jan. 1, 1993.

———. "Latvia: Transition to Independence Completed." *RFE/RL,* 3, no. 6, Jan. 17, 1994.

———. "The Latvian-Russian Treaty of the Vicissitudes of Interstate Relations." *Radio Free Europe/Radio Liberty* (hereafter *RFE/RL*), Feb. 28, 1992.

———. "Russian Troop Withdrawal from Latvia: An Update." *RFE/RL* 1, no. 49, Dec. 11, 1992.

———. "Soviet Troops in Latvia." *RFE/RL* 1, no. 24, Aug. 28, 1992.

Burg, Steven L. "NGO Mediation of Ethnic Conflict: A Study of the Project on Ethnic Relations in Romania and Kosovo." Report prepared for the John D. and Catherine T. MacArthur Foundation, 2002.

———. *War or Peace? Nationalism, Democracy and American Foreign Policy in Post-Communist Europe.* New York: New York Univ. Press, 1996.

Burg, Steven L., and Paul S. Shoup. *The War in Bosnia-Herzegovina.* New York: M. E. Sharpe, 2000.

Bush, George. Inaugural Address of George Bush, Jan. 20, 1989.

Byman, Daniel L. *Keeping the Peace.* Baltimore: The Johns Hopkins Press, 2003.

Callahan, David. *Unwinnable Wars: American Power and Ethnic Conflict.* New York: Twentieth Century Fund, 1997.

Carment, David, and Patrick James, eds. *The International Politics of Ethnic Conflict: The Neglected Interstate Dimension.* Pittsburgh: Univ. of Pittsburgh Press, 1997.

Carothers, Thomas. *Aiding Democracy Abroad: The Learning Curve.* Washington, D.C.: Carnegie Endowment for International Peace, 1999.

———. *Assessing Democracy Assistance: The Case of Romania.* Washington, D.C.: Carnegie Endowment for International Peace, 1996.

———. *Assessing Democracy Assistance Abroad.* Washington, D.C.: Carnegie Endowment for International Peace, 1999.

———. *Critical Mission. Essays on Democracy Promotion.* Washington: Carnegie Endowment for International Peace, 2004.

———. "Democracy Assistance: The Question of Strategy." *Democratization* 4, no. 3 (1997): 109–32.

Carothers, Thomas, and Marina Ottaway. "Introduction: The Burgeoning World of Civil Society Aid," in *Funding Virtue: Civil Society Aid and Democracy Promotion,* ed. Ottaway and Carothers. Washington, D.C.: Carnegie Endowment for International Peace, 2000.

Cartner, Holly. "Since the Revolution: Human Rights in Romania." Helsinki Watch Report. New York: Human Rights Watch, 1991.

————. "Struggling for Ethnic Identity: Ethnic Hungarians in Post-Ceausescu Romania." Helsinki Watch Report. New York, N.Y.: Human Rights Watch, 1993.

Chandler, David. "Democratization in Bosnia: The Limits of Civil Society Strategies." *Democratization* 5, no. 4 (1998): 78–102.

————. "The OSCE and the Internationalization of National Minority Rights." In *Ethnicity and Democratisation in the New Europe,* edited by Karl Cordell, 61–76. London: Routledge, 1999.

Chayes, Abram, and Antonia Handler Chayes,ed. *Preventing Conflict in the Post-Communist World: Mobilizing International and Regional Organizations.* Washington, D.C.: The Brookings Institution, 1996.

Chayes, Abram, and Antonia Handler Chayes. "Transition and Conflict: Russian and American Perspectives on the Former Soviet Union." In *Managing Conflict in the Former Soviet Union: Russian and American Perspectives,* edited by Alexei Arbatov, Abram Chayes, Antonia Handler Chayes, and Laura Olson, 1–20. Cambridge: MIT Press, 1994.

Chazan, Naomi, ed. *Irredentism and International Politics.* Boulder: Lynne Rienner, 1991.

Checkel, Jeffrey T. "International Norms and Domestic Politics: Bridging the Rationalist-Constructive Divide." *European Journal of International Relations* 3, no. 4 (1997): 473–95.

————. "Norms, Institutions, and National Identity in Contemporary Europe." *International Studies Quarterly* 43 (1999): 83–114.

Chigas, Diana, with Elizabeth McClintock and Christophe Kamp. "Preventive Diplomacy and the Organization for Security and Cooperation Europe: Creating Incentives for Dialogue and Cooperation." In *Preventing Conflict in the Post-Communist World,* edited by Abram Chayes and Antonia Handler Chayes, 47–63. Washington, D.C.: The Brookings Institution, 1996.

Chinn, Jeff, and Robert Kaiser. *Russians and the New Minority: Ethnicity and Nationalism in the Soviet Successor States.* Boulder: Westview Press, 1996.

Chirot, Daniel, ed. *The Origins of Backwardness in Eastern Europe: Economics and Politics from the Middle Ages until the Early Twentieth Century.* Berkeley: Univ. of California Press, 1989.

Clark, Ann Marie. "Non-Governmental Organizations and Their Influence on International Society." *Journal of International Affairs* 48, no. 2 (1995): 507–26.

Claude, Inis L. *National Minorities: An International Problem.* New York: Greenwood Press, 1955.

Clinton, William Jefferson. Inaugural Address of Bill Clinton, Jan. 20, 1993.

Cobban, Alfred. *The Nation State and National Self Determination.* New York: Thomas Y. Crowell Company, 1970.

Cohen, Jonathan. *Conflict Prevention in the OSCE: An Assessment of Capacities.* The Hague: Netherlands Institute of International Relations Clingendael, (1999).

Coleman, William D. "Policy Networks, Non-State Actors and Internationalize Policy-Making: A Case Study of Agricultural Trade." In *Non-State Actors in World Politics,* edited by Daphne Josselin and William Wallace, 93–112. New York: Palgrave, 2001.

Conner, Walker. *The National Question in Marxist-Leninist Theory.* Princeton: Princeton Univ. Press, 1984.

Cooley, Alexander and James Ron. "The NGO Scramble: Organizational Insecurity and the Political Economy of Transnational Action." *International Security* 27, no. 1 (2002): 5–39.

Council of Europe. "Ad Hoc Committee for the Protection of National Minorities," 7th Meeting, Oct. 10–14, Strasbourg, *Council of Europe Meeting Reports,* CAHMIN (94) 32, 1994.

———. Council Decision of 14 June 1994 (94/367/CFS), 1994.

———. *The Declaration on Eastern Europe by the European Council,* Strasbourg, Dec. 8–9, 1989.

———. Opinion No. 183 on the application by Latvia for membership of the Council of Europe, 1995.

Conference on Security and Cooperation in Europe. *Annual Report 1993 on CSCE Activities, Section 3 by High Commission on National Minorities,* 1993.

———. "Appeal of the Minister of Foreign Affairs of the Russian Federation to Ministers of Foreign of the CSCE Participating States and Heads of International Organizations in Connection with the Adoption of the Law on Citizens of the Latvian Republic." CSCE unofficial document, Aug. 23, 1994.

———. Charter of Paris for a New Europe, Nov. 19–21, 1990.

———. Communication no. 8: "Letter of the CSCE High Commissioner on National Minorities to the Minister for Foreign Affairs of the Republic of Latvia, dated 10 December 1993, as well as the letter of republic, dated 25 January 1994, from the Minister of Foreign Affairs of Latvia," 1994.

———. Communication no. 8. Vienna, 12 January 1994, no. 1463/93/L, 1994.

———. Communication nos. 124 and 125/Add 1. "Letters dated 6 April 1993 to the Ministers for Foreign Affairs of the Republic of Estonia, Latvia, Lithuania," 1993. (Letters of reply and Comments on the Conclusions and Recommendations of the Mission of the CSCE High Commissioner on National Minorities.)

———. Communication no. 253, Sept. 23, 1993.

———. Concluding Document of the Madrid Meeting 1980, 1983.

———. Concluding Document of the Vienna Meeting 1986, 1989.

———. Copenhagen Document of the Second Conference on the Human Dimension of the CSCE. June 5-July 29, 1990.

———. Council Decision of 14 June on the continuation of the joint action adopted by the Council on the basis of Article J.3 of the Treaty on European Union on the inaugural conference on the Stability Pact, 1990.

———. Document of the Copenhagen Meeting of the Conference on the Human Dimension of the CSCE, 1990.

———. Excerpts from the Press Conference of Vialy Churkin, Deputy Minister of Foreign Affairs of Russia, regarding relations between Russia and Baltic States, Jan. 27, 1994. CSCE correspondence, 1994. Unofficial translation.

———. "Exchange of Information and Documents," *CSCE Journal,* no. 3, annex 2, Jan. 10, 1992.

———. Helsinki Final Act, 1 August 1975.

———. *Prague Document on the Further Development of CSCE Institutions and Structures: Declaration on Non-Proliferation and Arms Transfer,* January 1992.

———. "Press Release of the CSCE Chairmanship-in Office of the CSCE with regard to the adoption of the Law on Citizenship by the Latvian Parliament on 22 July 1994." Doc. 575/94, Aug. 16, 1994.

———. Proposal submitted by the Delegation of Romania, "Code of conduct of states relating to international co-operation on minority problems," CSCE Meeting of Experts, Geneva, Switzerland, Restricted, CSCE/REMN 7. July 9, 1991.

———. "Remarks to the Meeting of Romania's Council for National Minorities by the High Commissioner on National Minorities, Max van der Stoel," Bucharest. Aug. 18, 1993. http://www.minelres.lv/osce/counrec.htm.

———. *Report of the CSCE Meeting of Experts on National Minorities,* Geneva, 1991, restricted, CSCE/REMN 20. July 1991.

———. Republic of Latvia information about the Implementation of Paragraph 5 of the Helsinki Summit Declaration 1992, CSCE Document, Stockholm Council Meeting of December 1992.

———. "Statement by Ambassador V. Shustov, Head of Delegation of Russian Federation at a Meeting of the OSCE Permanent Council," May 14, 1996. Unofficial translation.

———. "Statement by the Minister of Foreign Affairs of the Republic of Latvia," Aug. 4, 1994. Unofficial translation.

———. "Statement of the HCNM on his study of the Roma in CSCE region," Sept. 21, 1993. Available online at: http://www.osce.org/hcnm/documents.html.

The Covenant of the League of Nations. http://www.yale.edu/lawweb/avalon/leagcov .htm#art11.

Cremona, Marise. "Creating the New Europe: The Stability Pact for South-Eastern Europe in the Context of EUI-SEE Relations." In *Cambridge Yearbook of European Legal Studies,* edited by A. Dashwood and A. Ward, 463–506. Oxford: Hart Publishing, 2000.

———, ed. *The Enlargement of the European Union.* Oxford: Oxford Univ. Press, 2003.

Crocker, Chester A., Fen Osler-Hampson, and Pamela Aall. "Multiparty Mediation and the Conflict Cycle." In *Herding Cats: Multiparty Mediation in a Complex World,* edited by

Chester A. Crocker, Fen Osler-Hampson, Pamela Aall, 19–46. Washington, D.C.: U.S. Institute of Peace, 1999.

Csergo, Zsusza. "Beyond Ethnic Division: Majority-Minority Debate." *East European Politics and Societies* 16, no. 1 (2002): 1–29.

Csergo, Zsusza, and James Goldeier. "Hungary's 'Status Law': A Post-Territorial Approach to Nation Building?" Paper presented at the annual meeting of the American Association for the Advancement of Slavic Studies, Pittsburgh, Pa., 2002.

Culic, Irina. "State Building and Constitution Writing in Central and Eastern Europe after 1989." *Regio: Minorities, Politics, Society* 3 (2003): 38–58.

Daalder, Ivo H. *Getting to Dayton.* Washington, D.C.: The Brookings Institution, 2000.

Daalder, Ivo H., and Michael B. G. Froman. "Dayton's Incomplete Peace." *Foreign Affairs* 78, no. 6 (1999): 106–13.

Davis, Patricia, and Peter Dombrowski. "International Assistance to the Former Soviet Union: Conditions and Transitions." *Policy Studies Journal* 28, no. 1 (2000): 68–95.

Dawisha, Karen. *Eastern Europe Gorbachev and Reform: The Great Challenge,* 2d edition. New York: Cambridge Univ. Press, 1990.

Deets, Stephen. "Reconsidering Eastern European Minority Policy: Liberal Theory and European Norms." *Eastern European Politics and Society* 16, no. 1 (2002): 30–53.

Deutsch, Karl W. *Political Community and the North Atlantic Area: International Organization in the Light of Historical Experience.* Princeton: Princeton Univ. Press, 1957.

de Varennes, Fernand. "The Linguistic Rights of Minorities in Europe." In *Minority Rights in Europe: European Minorities and Languages,* edited by Snezana Trifunovska, 255–318. The Hague: Springer, 2001.

de Witt, Bruno. "Politics Versus Law in the EU's Approach to Ethnic Minorities." EUI Working Paper RSC no. 2000/4 (2000): 1–28.

———. "Politics Versus Law in the EU's Approach to Ethnic Minorities." In *Europe Unbound: Enlarging and Restructuring the Borders of the EU,* edited by Jan Zielonka, 137–60. New York: Routledge, 2002.

Diamond, Larry. 1995. *Promoting Democracy in the 1990s.* New York: The Carnegie Commission on Preventing Deadly Conflict.

Diehl, Paul, and Joseph Lepgold, eds. *Regional Conflict Management.* New York: Rowman and Littlefield, 2003.

DiMaggio, Paul J., and Walter L. Powell. 1991. *The New Institutionalism.* Chicago: Univ. of Chicago Press, 1991.

Dorodnova, Jekaterina. "Challenging Ethnic Democracy: Implementation of the Recommendations of the OSCE High Commission on National Minorities to Latvia, 1993–2001." Working Paper 10, Center for OSCE Research, Univ. of Hamburg, 2003. Also in *Comparative Case Studies on the Effectiveness of the OSCE High Commissioner on*

National Minorities: The Possibilities for Preventive Diplomacy, edited by Wolfgang Zell-ner, Randolf Oberschmidt, and Claus Neukirch. Baden-Baden: University of Hamburg, 2004.

Duffield, John S. "International Regimes and Alliance Behavior: Explaining NATO Conventional Force Levels." *International Organization* 46, no. 4 (1992): 819–55.

———. "NATO's Functions after the Cold War." *Political Science Quarterly* 190, no. 5 (1994–95): 763–89.

Dunay, Pál. "Hungarian-Romanian Relations: A Changed Paradigm?" In *The Effects of Enlargement on Bilateral Relations in Central and Eastern Europe,* edited by Monika Wohlfeld. EU-ISS Chaillot Paper 26, June 1997.

Eavis, Paul, and Stuart Kefford. "Conflict Prevention and the EU: A Potential Yet to Be Fully Realized." In *Searching for Peace in Europe and Eurasia,* edited by Paul van Tongeren, Hans van de Veen, and Juliette Verhoeven, 3–15. Boulder: Lynne Rienner, 2002.

Esman, Milton J., and Ronald J. Herring, eds. *Carrot, Stick and Ethnic Conflict: Rethinking Development Assistance.* Ann Arbor: Univ. of Michigan Press, 2001.

Esman, Milton J., and Shibley Telhami, eds. *International Organizations and Ethnic Conflict.* Ithaca: Cornell Univ. Press, 1995.

Etizioni, Amitai. *From Empire to Community.* New York: Palgrave, 2004.

European Commission. "2002 Regular Report on Hungary's Progress Towards Accession." Brussels: European Commission, 2002.

European Community. "Association Agreements with Countries of Central and Eastern Europe: A General Outline." Commission of the European Communities, COM (90) 398, Aug. 27, 1990.

———. *The European Community and Its Eastern Neighbors.* Luxembourg: Office of the Publications of the European Communities, 1990.

———. "Towards a Closer Association with the Countries of Central and Eastern Europe." Report by the Commission to the European Council, SEC (92) 2301, December 11–12, 1992.

European Union. Agenda 2000-Commission Opinion on Latvia's Application for Membership of the European Union DOC/97/14 Brussels, July 15, 1997.

———. European Agreement Establishing an Association Between the European Economic Communities and Their Member States, of the One Part, and Romania, of the Other Part. OJ L 357, Dec. 31, 1994.

———. "Evaluation of the PHARE and TACIS Democracy Programme, 1992–97." PTDP Evaluation Report. Available online at http://ec.europa.ed/comm/europeaid/evaluation/evinfo/1997/951432_ev.pdf, July 1997.

———. "Relations between the European Communities and the United States." Commission of the European Communities SEC (93) 538 def., Apr. 6, 1993.

———. "Total Phare Commitments, Contracts and Payments by Country." Phare 1998 Annual Report, 2000.

———. Treaty on European Union. http://www.europa.eu.int/eu-lex/en/treatieis/dat/C_2002325EN.000501.html, 1997.

Fearon, James D., and David D. Laitin. 1996. "Explaining Interethnic Cooperation." *American Political Science Review* 90, no. 4 (1996): 715–36.

Florini, Ann, ed. *The Third Force: The Rise of Transnational Civil Society.* Washington, D.C.: The Carnegie Endowment for International Peace, 2000.

Flynn, Gregory, and Henry Farrell. "Piecing Together the Democratic Peace: The CSCE, Norms, and the 'Construction' of Security in the Post-Cold War Europe." *International Organization* 53, no. 3 (1999): 505–35.

Fowkes, Ben. 2002. *Ethnicity and Ethnic Conflict in the Post-Communist World.* London: Palgrave.

Freeman, Michael. "Liberal Democracy and Minority Rights." In *Human Rights, New Perspectives and New Realities,* edited by Adamantia Pollis and Peter Schwab, 31–52. Boulder: Lynne Rienner, 2000.

Fukuyama, Francis. "The End of History." *National Interest,* 3–18, 1989.

Gagnon, Chip. "INGOs in Bosnia-Herzegovina," in *The Power and Limits of NGOs: A Critical Look at Building Democracy in Eastern Europe and Eurasia,* edited by Sarah Mendelson and John K. Glenn, 207–31. New York: Columbia University Press, 2002.

Gagnon, V. P. "Ethnic Nationalism and Internal Conflict." *International Security* 19, no. 3 (1994–95): 130–66.

Gal, Kinga. "Bilateral Agreements in Central and Eastern Europe: A New Inter-State Framework for Minority Protection," ECMI Working Paper no. 4, 1999.

———, ed. "Council of Europe Framework Convention for the Protection of National Minorities and its Impact on Central and Eastern Europe." *Journal on Ethnopolitics and Minority Issues in Europe* 1, no. 4 (2000): 1–17.

———, ed. *Minority Governance in Europe.* Budapest: The Open Society Institute, 2003.

Galantai, Jozsef. *Trianon and the Protection of Minorities.* Budapest: Corvina Books, 1989.

Gallagher, Tom. "Building Democracy in Romania: Internal Shortcomings and External Neglect." In *Democratic Consolidation in Eastern Europe,* edited by Jan Zielonka and Alex Pravda, 383–412. Oxford: Oxford Univ. Press, 2001.

———. "Tensions in Cluj." *RFE/RL* 2, no. 9, February 26, 1993.

Gallis, Paul E. "NATO: Congress Addresses Expansion of the Alliance." *Congressional Research Report for Congress,* July 24, 1997.

Geertz, Clifford. *Old Societies and New States: The Quest for Modernity in Asia and Africa.* New York: Free Press, 1963.

Gellner, Ernest. *Nations and Nationalism.* Ithaca: Cornell Univ. Press, 1983.

Ginkel, John. "Identity Construction in Latvia's Singing Revolution: Why Interethnic Conflict Failed to Occur." *Nationalities Papers* 30, no. 3 (2002): 403–33.

Goble, Paul. "Ethnicity as Explanation, Ethnicity as Excuse." In *Ethnic Conflict and Regional Instability: Implications for US Policy and Army Roles and Missions,* edited by Robert L. Pfaltzgraff, Jr., and Richard H. Shultz, Jr., 45–65. Washington, D.C.: Strategic Studies Institute, 1994.

———. "Latvia's Analysis from Washington: When Ethnicity is not the Explanation." *RFE/RL,* Jan. 23, 2001.

Goodman, Jo Martin, and Ana Revenga. *Poverty and Ethnicity: A Cross-Country Study of Roma Poverty in Central Europe.* New York: World Bank, 2002.

Grabbe, Heather. "How Does Europeanization Affect CEE Governance? Conditionality, Diffusion and Diversity." *Journal of Europe Public Policy* 8, no. 6 (2001): 1013–31.

Gross, Peter, and Vladimir Tismaneanu. 1998. "No NATO Shelter for Romania." *Transitions* 4, no. 7 (December 1997): 26–31.

Gurr, Ted Robert. *Peoples Versus States.* Washington, D.C.: USIP Press, 2000.

———. "Wane of Ethnic Conflict." *Foreign Affairs* 73, no. 3 (2000): 52–64.

Hackett, Kenneth. "The Role of NGOs in Preventing Conflict." In *Preventive Diplomacy. Stopping Wars Before they Start,* edited by Kevin Cahill, 269–84. New York: Basic Books, 1996.

Haggard, Stephen, and Andrew Moravcsik. "The Political Economy of Financial Assistance to Eastern Europe, 1989–91." In *After the Cold War: International Institutions and States Strategies in Europe, 1989–1991,* edited by Robert Keohane, Joseph S. Nye, and Stanley Hoffmann, 247–61. Cambridge: Harvard Univ. Press, 1993.

Halperin, Morton H., and David J. Scheffer with Patricia L. Small. *Self Determination in the New World Order.* Washington, D.C.: The Carnegie Endowment for International Peace, 1992.

Hamburg, David A. "Preventing Contemporary Inter-group Violence." In *The Handbook of Interethnic Coexistence,* edited by Eugene Weiner, 27–39. New York: Continuum Publishing, 1998.

Hanson, Stephen E., and Jeffrey S. Kopstein. "The Weimar/Russia Comparison." *Post-Soviet Affairs* 13, no. 3 (1997): 252–84.

Hansson, Ulf. "The Latvian Language and the Involvement of the OSCE-HCNM: The Developments, 2000–2002." *The Global Review of Ethnopolitics* 2, no. 1 (2002): 17–28.

Heintze, Hans-Joachim. "Bilateral Agreements and Their Role in Settling Ethnic Conflicts." In *Managing and Settling Ethnic Conflicts Perspectives on Successes and Failures in Europe, Africa and Asia,* edited by Ulrich Schneckener and Stefan Wolff, 189–205. London: Hurst and Company, 2004.

Heischman, Janet. "Destroying Ethnic Identity: The Hungarians of Romania." *Helsinki Watch Report,* 1989.

Helsinki Foundation for Human Rights. "The Role of Minorities in International and Trans-border Relations in Central and Eastern Europe." Helsinki Foundation for Human Rights, MRG workshop. April 30-May 3, 1998.

Herring, Eric. "International Security and Democracy in Eastern Europe." In *Building Democracy? The International Dimensions of Democratisation in Eastern Europe,* edited by Geoffrey Pridham, Eric Herring, and George Sanford, 87–118. London: Leicester Univ. Press, 1994.

Hobsbawm, Eric J. *Nations and Nationalism since 1780.* Cambridge: Cambridge Univ. Press, 1992.

Holbrooke, Richard. *To End a War: From Sarajevo to Dayton and Beyond.* New York: Random House, 1998.

Holohan, Anne. *Networks of Democracy Lessons from Kosovo for Afghanistan, Iraq, and Beyond.* Stanford: Stanford Univ. Press, 2005.

Hopf, Ted. 1994–95. "Managing the Post-Soviet Security Space: A Continuing Demand for Behavioral Regimes." *Security Studies* 4, no. 2 (1994–95): 242–80.

Hopmann, P. Terrence. "Building Security in Post-Cold War Eurasia." *Peaceworks* 31, no. 3 (1999). USIP Publication.

———. "Regional Security. Institutions and Intervention in Internal Conflicts. The OSCE's Experience in Eurasia." In *Limiting Institutions? The Challenge of Eurasian Security,* edited by Sean Kay, Victor Papacosma, and James Sperling, 144–65. Manchester: Manchester Univ. Press, 2003.

Horowitz, Donald. *Ethnic Groups in Conflict.* Berkeley: Univ. of California Press, 1985.

Horowitz, Ruth Lenora. 1993. "Tax-exempt Foundations: Their Effects on National Policy." *Orbis* 37, no. 3 (1993): 220–28.

Horvath, Istvan. "Facilitating Conflict Transformation." In *Comparative Case Studies on the Effectiveness of the OSCE High Commissioner on National Minorities: The Possibilities for Preventive Diplomacy,* edited by Wolfgang Zellner, Randolf Oberschmidt, and Claus Neukirch. Baden-Baden: University of Hamburg, 2004.

Huber, Conrad J. "Averting Interethnic Conflict: An Analysis of the CSCE's HCNM in Estonia." Working Paper. Atlanta, Ga.: The Carter Center, 1994.

Huber, Denis. *A Decade Which Made History: The Council of Europe, 1989–1999.* Strasbourg: Council of Europe Press, 1999.

Hughes, James, and Gwendolyn Sasse. "Monitoring the Monitors: EU Enlargement, Conditionality and Minority Protection in the CEEC." *Journal of Ethnopolitics and Minority Issues in Europe* 1 (2003): 1–35.

Human Security Report 2005. London: Oxford Univ. Press, 2005.

Hunter, Robert E. "Maximizing NATO." *Foreign Affairs* 78, no. 3 (1999): 190–203.

Huntington, Samuel. *The Clash of Civilizations and the Remaking of World Order.* New York: Simon and Schuster, 1997.

———. *The Third Wave.* Norman: Univ. of Oklahoma Press, 1991.

———. "Transnational Organizations in World Politics." *World Politics* 25, no. 3 (1973): 333–68.

Ionescu, Dan, and Alfred A. Reisch. "Still No Breakthrough in Romanian-Hungarian Relations." *RFE/RL* 2, no. 42 (1993).

Ishiyama, John T., and Marijke Breuning. *Ethnopolitics in the New Europe.* Boulder: Lynne Rienner, 1998.

Johanson, Jan, and Lars-Gunnar Mattsson. "Interorganizational Relations in Industrial System: A Network Approach Compared with the Transational-Cost Approach." *International Studies of Management and Organization* 17, no. 1 (1987): 34–48.

Johns, Michael. 2005. "The Responsibility to Interject? The Impact of European Organizations on Minority Rights." Unpublished paper presented at the International Studies Association Annual Conference, Honolulu, Hawaii, March 1–5.

Johnsen, William T. *Pandora's Box Reopened: Ethnic Conflict in Europe and Its Implications.* Carlisle, Pa.: U.S. Army War College, 1994.

Johnson, Lonnie R. *Central Europe: Enemies, Neighbors, Friends.* Oxford: Oxford Univ. Press, 2002.

Jordan, Grant. 1990. "Sub-Governments, Policy Communities and Networks: Refilling the Old Bottles?" *Journal of Theoretical Politics* 2, no. 3 (1990): 319–39.

Josselin, Daphne, and William Wallace. *Non-State Actors in World Politics.* New York: Palgrave, 2001.

Kaplan, Robert. *Balkan Ghosts: A Journey Through History.* New York: St. Martin's Press, 1993.

Kardos, Gabor. "The Culture of Conflict: Hungary's Role in Resolving Ethnic Disputes." *World Policy Journal* 12, no. 1 (1995): 102–7.

Kassim, Hussein. "Policy Networks, Networks and European Union Policy Making: A Skeptical View." *West European Politics* 17, no. 4 (1994): 15–27.

Kay, Sean. "NATO Enlargement." In *America's New Allies: Poland, Hungary, and the Czech Republic in NATO,* edited by Andrew A. Michta, 149–84. Seattle: Univ. of Washington Press, 1999.

Keck, Margaret, and Kathryn Sikkink. *Activists Beyond Borders: Transnational Advocacy Networks in International Politics.* Ithaca: Cornell Univ. Press, 1998.

Kelley, Judith. *Ethnic Politics in Europe.* Princeton: Princeton Univ. Press, 2004.

———. "International Actors on the Domestic Scene: Membership Conditionality and Socialization by International Institutions." *International Organization* 58 (2004): 425–57.

———. "Membership, Management and Enforcement." Unpublished paper presented at the annual meeting of the American Political Science Association, Boston, Massachusetts, 2002.

Kemp, Walter. *Nationalism and Communism in Eastern Europe and the Soviet Union: A Basic Contradiction.* New York: St. Martin's Press, 1999.

———, ed. *Quiet Diplomacy in Action: The OSCE High Commissioner on National Minorities.* Vancouver: Univ. of British Columbia Press, 2003.

Keohane, Robert. "International Institutions: Two Approaches." *International Studies Quarterly* 32, no. 4 (1988), 379–96.

———. *International Institutions and State Power.* Boulder: Westview Press, 1989.

Keohane, Robert, and Stanley Hoffman. "Conclusion." In *After the Cold War: International Institutions and States Strategies in Europe, 1989–1991,* edited by Robert Keohane, Joseph S. Nye, and Stanley Hoffmann, 381–406. Cambridge: Harvard Univ. Press, 1993.

Keohane, Robert, and Joseph S. Nye, Jr. "Transnational Relations and World Politics." *International Organization* 25, no. 3 (Summer 1971): 329–49. Also in *Transnational Relations and World Politics,* edited by Robert Keohane and Joseph S. Nye, Jr. Cambridge: Harvard Univ. Press, 1970.

———, eds. *Power and Independence.* New York: Longman, 2001.

———, eds. *Transnational Relations and World Politics.* Cambridge: Harvard Univ. Press, 1970.

Keohane, Robert, Joseph S. Nye, and Stanley Hoffman, eds. *After the Cold War: International Institutions and States Strategies in Europe, 1989–1991.* Cambridge: Harvard Univ. Press, 1993.

Klauber, Klaus-Peter. "A Cooperative NATO in a Cooperative Europe." *Romanian Journal of International Affairs* 4 (1998): 306–10.

Kolstoe, Paul. *Russians in the Former Soviet Republics.* Bloomington: Indiana Univ. Press, 1995.

Kondonis, Haralambos. "Civil Society and Multilateral Cooperative Models: The Role of Non-governmental Organizations in the Stability Pact in South Eastern Europe." *Journal of Southeast Europe and Black Sea Studies* 2, no. 1 (2002): 43–63.

Kostecki, Wojciech. "Prevention of Ethnic Conflict: Lessons from Romania," *Berghof Occasional Paper* no. 19 (2002).

Kovats, Martin. "Problems of Intellectual and Political Accountability in Respect of Emerging European Roma Policy." *Journal on Ethnopolitics and Minority Issues in Europe* 2, no. 1 (2001): 1–10.

Kovrig, Bennett. "Partitioned Nation: Hungarian Minorities in Central Europe." In *The New European Diasporas: National Minorites and Conflict in Eastern Europe,* edited by Michael Mandelbaum, 19–80. New York: Council on Foreign Relations Press, 2000.

Krasner, Stephen D., ed. *International Regimes.* Ithaca: Cornell Univ. Press, 1983.

Krasner, Stephen D., and Daniel T. Froats. "Minority Rights and the Westphalian Model." In

Ethnicity, Nationalism, and Minority Rights, edited by Stephen May, Tariq Modood, and Judith Squires, 227–50. Cambridge: Cambridge Univ. Press, 2004.

Krickus, Richard J. "Latvia's "Russian Question," *RFE/RL* 2, no. 18 (April 30, 1993).

Kundera, Milan. "The Tragedy of Central Europe." *The New York Review of Books,* April 26, 1984.

Kupchan, Charles A., ed. *Nationalism and Nationalities in the New Europe.* Ithaca: Cornell Univ. Press, 1995.

Kymlicka, Will. *Multicultural Citizenship. A Liberal Theory of Minority Rights.* Oxford: Oxford Univ. Press, 1995.

Kymlicka, Will, and Magda Opalski, ed. *Can Liberal Pluralism Be Exported? Western Political Theory and Ethnic Relations in Eastern Europe.* Oxford: Oxford Univ. Press, 2002.

Laitin, David D. *Identity in Formation.* Ithaca: Cornell Univ. Press, 1998.

———. "Secessionist Rebellion in the Former Soviet Union." *Comparative Political Studies* 34, no. 8 (2001): 839–62.

Lake, David A., and Donald S. Rothchild, eds. *The International Spread of Ethnic Conflict: Fear, Diffusion, and Escalation.* Princeton, N.J.: Princeton Univ. Press, 1998.

Laqueur, Walter. *Black Hundred: The Rise of the Extreme Right in Russia.* New York: Harper Perennial, 1994.

The League of Nations and Minorities. Geneva: League of Nations Secretariat, 1923.

The League of Nations and the Protection of Minorities of Race, Language and Religion. Geneva: League of Nations Secretariat, 1927.

Leatherman, Janine. *From the Cold War to Democratic Peace: Third Parties, Peaceful Change and the CSCE/OSCE.* Syracuse: Syracuse Univ. Press, 2003.

Lederach, John Paul. *Building Peace: Sustainable Reconciliation in Divided Societies.* 5th edition. Washington, D.C.: The U.S. Institute of Peace, 2002.

Liebiech, Andre. "Ethnic Minorities and Long-Term Implications of EU Enlargement." In *Europe Unbound,* edited by Jan Zielonka, 117–36. New York: Routledge, 2002.

Linde, Robyn. "Norm Compliance: The European Union, Accession Partners, and the Roma." Unpublished paper presented at the ISA Annual Convention, New Orleans, La., 2002.

Lipschultz, Ronnie, and Beverly Crawford, eds. *The Myth of "Ethnic Conflict" Politics, Economics, and "Cultural" Violence.* Berkeley: Univ. of California Press, 1998.

Lubin, Nancy. "Ethnic Conflict Resolution and U.S. Assistance." A Report for the Eisenhower Institute, 2004.

Lucas, Michael R., ed. *The CSCE in the 1990s: Constructing European Security and Cooperation.* Hamburg: Univ. of Hamburg, 1993.

Lund, Michael S. *Preventing Violent Conflicts.* Washington, D.C.: U.S. Institute of Peace, 1996.

Macartney, C. A. *National States and National Minorities.* London: Oxford Univ. Press, 1934.

MacFarlane, S. Neil. "The Internationalization of Ethnic Strife." In *Democratic Consolidation in Eastern Europe,* edited by Jan Zielonka and Alex Pravda, 139–62. Oxford: Oxford Univ. Press, 2001.

Malcolm, Neil, Alex Pravda, Roy Allison, and Margot Light, eds. *Internal Factors in Russian Foreign Policy.* New York: Oxford Univ. Press, 1996.

Manas, Jean E. "The Council of Europe's Democracy Ideal and the Challenge of Ethno-National Strife." In *Preventing Conflict in the Post-Communist World,* edited by Abram Chayes and Antonia Handler Chayes, 99–146. Washington, D.C.: The Brookings Institution, 1995.

Mandelbaum, Michael. *The New European Diasporas: National Minorities and Conflict in Eastern Europe.* New York: Council on Foreign Relations Press, 2000.

Marshall, Monty G. "States at Risk: Ethnopolitics in the Multinational States of Eastern Europe." In *Minorities at Risk: A Global View of Ethnopolitical Conflicts,* edited by Ted Gurr, 173–216. Washington, D.C.: USIP Press, 1993.

———. "Systems at Risk." Chapter 6 in *Wars in the Midst of Peace: The International Politics of Ethnic Conflict,* edited by David Carment and Patrick James. Pittsburgh: Univ. of Pittsburgh Press, 1997.

Mathews, Jessica T. "Power Shift." *Foreign Affairs* 76, no. 1 (1997): 50–66.

McCalla, Robert B. "NATO's Persistence After the Cold War." *International Organization* 5, no. 3 (1996): 445–75.

McFaul, Michael. "A Precarious Peace: Domestic Determinants of Russian Foreign Policy." *International Security* 22, no. 3 (1997–98): 5–35.

McHugh, Heather S. "USAID and Ethnic Conflict: An Epiphany?" In *Carrot, Stick and Ethnic Conflict. Rethinking Development Assistance,* edited by Esman and Herring, 49–89. Ann Arbor: University of Michigan Press, 2001.

McMahon, Patrice C. "Rebuilding Bosnia: A Model to Emulate or Avoid?" *Political Science Quarterly* 119, no. 4 (2004–5): 569–93.

Mearsheimer, John J. "Back to the Future: Instability in Europe After the Cold War." *International Security* 15, no. 1 (1990): 5–56.

———. "Why We Will Soon Miss the Cold War." *The Atlantic Monthly* 266, no. 2 (1990): 35–50.

Medianu, Narcisa. 2002. "Analyzing Political Exchanges between Minority and Majority Leaders in Romania." *The Global Review of Ethnopolitics* 1, no. 4 (June 2002): 28–41.

Melescanu, Theodora. "The Accession to the European Union: The Fundamental Option of Romania's Foreign Policy." *Romanian Journal of International Affairs,* 2, no. 4 (1996): 1–10.

"Memorandum by the Democratic Alliance of Hungarians in Romania on Romania's Admission to the Council of Europe." Available online at the Hungarian Human Rights Foundation, http://www.hhrf.org/hhrf/index_en.php.

Mendelson, Sarah E., and John K. Glenn, eds. *The Power and Limits of NGOs.* New York: Columbia Univ. Press, 2002.

Miall, Hugh, ed. *Minority Rights in Europe: The Scope for a Transnational Regime.* New York: Council on Foreign Relations, 1994.

———, ed. *Redefining Europe: New Patterns of Conflict and Cooperation.* London: The Royal Institute of International Affairs, 1994.

Miko, Francis T. "American Perspectives on the Helsinki Review Conference and the Future Role of the CSCE." In *The CSCE in the 1990s: Construction European Security and Cooperation,* edited by Michael R. Lucas, 61–71. Baden-Baden: Nomos, 1993.

Miller, Linda B. *World Order and Local Disorder: The United Nations and Internal Conflicts.* Princeton: Princeton Univ. Press, 1967.

Miniotaite. Grazina. "Lithuania and NATO Enlargement." *Baltic Defence Review* 2, no. 6 (2001): 30–35.

"Minority Rights and European Union Enlargement to the East." *Report of the First Meeting of the Reflections Group on the Long-Term Implications of EU Enlargement: The Nature of the New Borders.* European Union Institute: RSC Policy Paper no. 98/5 (1998).

Montville, Joseph, ed. *Conflict and Peacemaking in Multiethnic Societies.* Lexington, Mass.: Lexington Books, 1991.

Motyl, Alex. *Sovietology, Rationality, Nationalism.* New York: Columbia Univ. Press, 1990.

———. *Will the Non-Russians Rebel?* Ithaca: Cornell Univ. Press, 1987.

Moynihan, Daniel P. *Pandemonium: Ethnicity in International Politics.* New York: Oxford Univ. Press, 1993.

Mueller, John. "The Banality of 'Ethnic War.'" *International Security* 25, no. 1 (2000): 42–70.

Muiznieks, Nils, and Ilze Brands Kehris. "The European Union: Democratization and Minorities in Latvia." In *The European Union and Democratization,* edited by Paul. J. Kubicek, 30–50. London: Routledge, 2003.

Mungiu-Pippidi, Alina. "Identity Crisis: Romania Self-Analyzes Its Way West." *Transitions* 5, no. 4 (April 1998).

Nastase, Lucian, and Levente Salat, eds. *Interethnic Relations in Post-Communist Romania: Proceedings of the Conference the Romanian Model of Ethnic Relations; The Last Ten Years, The Next Ten Years.* Cluj: Ethnocultural Diversity in Romania Series, 2000.

North, Douglass C. *Institutions, Institutional Change and Economic Performance.* Cambridge: Cambridge Univ. Press, 1990.

North Atlantic Treaty Organization. "Fact Sheet: NATO." U.S. Department of State, Bureau of Public Affairs, Nov. 22, 1995.

———. "London Declaration on a Transformed North Atlantic Alliance," July 6, 1990.

———. "NATO Applicant Status: A Status Report." Report for Congress, Congressional Research Service, RL30168. Updated Apr. 25, 2003.

———. "Partnership with the Countries of Central and Eastern Europe." Statement issued by the North Atlantic Council meeting in Ministerial Session, Copenhagen, June 7, 1991.

———. *Report to Congress on the Enlargement of the North Atlantic Treaty Organization: Rationale, Benefits, Costs and Implications,* Feb. 24, 1997. *http://www.fas.org/man/nato/off-docs/us_97/wh970224.htm.*

———. "Study on NATO Enlargement," 1995. http://www.nato.int/docu/basictxt/enl-9502.html.

Nuemann, Iver B. "Regionalization and Consolidation." In *Democratic Consolidation in Eastern Europe,* edited by Jan Zielonka and Alex Pravda, 58–75. Oxford: Oxford Univ. Press, 2001.

Nye, Joseph S. and John D. Donahue, eds. *Governance in a Globalizing World.* Washington, D.C.: The Brookings Institution, 2000.

Oberschall, Anthony. "The Manipulation of Ethnicity: From Cooperation to Violence and War in Yugoslavia." *Ethnic and Racial Studies* 23, no. 6 (2000): 982–1001.

Okey, Robin. *Eastern Europe 1740–1980.* Minneapolis: Univ. of Minnesota Press, 1982.

Oltay, Edith. "Minorities as a Stumbling Block in Relations with Neighbors." *RFE/RL,* May 8, 1992.

Organization for Security and Cooperation in Europe. *Annual Report on CSCE/OSCE Activities,* 1998.

———. *Annual Report on Interaction between Organizations and Institutions in the CSCE/OSCE Area.* Nov. 1, 1999-Oct. 31, 2000.

———. "Contribution by the North Atlantic Treaty Organization," REF.S/97/96 29. Lisbon Summit, Nov. 29, 1996.

———. *Cooperation of the Naturalization Board with Foreign Institutions and International Organizations, 1994–2004.* Riga: Naturalization Board Foreign Relations Department, 2004.

———. *Co-operation with International Organizations and Institutions: Selected Documents and Catalogue of Forms of Co-operation.* COOP_DRF.DOC/04.11.94. 1995.

———. "Letter dated 15 March 1996 to the Minister for Foreign Affairs of the Republic of Latvia." REF.HC/5/96. April 22, 1996.

———. "Letter dated 28 October 1996 to the Minister for Foreign Affairs of the Republic of Latvia." REF.HC/2/77. Dec. 10, 1996.

———. "Letter from the Prime Minister of Latvia, Mr. Guntars Krasts." HCNM.GAL/3/98, 1998.

———. "Letter of 21 November 1996 to the Minister for Foreign Affairs of the Republic of Latvia, Mr. V. Birkavs, as well as the letter of republic, dated 27 February 1997." REF.HC/3/97. 1997.

———. Mission to Latvia Activity Reports:

No. 7, Aug. 2, 1994, restricted.

No. 9, Oct 10, 1994.

Spot Report No. 12, Nov. 29, 1994.

No. 12, Jan. 30, 1995.

No. 13, Feb. 28, 1995.

No. 15, Apr. 24, 1995.

No. 21, Nov. 20, 1995, restricted.

No. 26, Apr. 26, 1996, restricted.

No. 27, 3 June 1996.

No. 34, Jan. 10, 1997, restricted.

No. 51, Oct. 13, 1998, restricted.

No. 52, Nov. 1, 1998, restricted.

No. 53, Dec. 18, 1998, restricted.

No. 37, July 16, 1999, restricted.

———. Mission to Latvia. "Background report: Background information for Ambassador Orns' Permanent Council Appearance." Mar. 15, 2000, restricted.

———. Press Release of the OSCE HCNM in Riga on the abolition of the so-called "window" system for naturalization. Apr. 17, 1998.

———. Press Statement of the OSCE HCNM, Mr. Max van der Stoel, Riga 17 April 1998. INF./1/98, April 20, 1998.

———. Secretary General Intervention at CSCE/OSCE Permanent Council, PC.DEL/668–00. Nov. 2, 2000.

———. Structures and Institutions SEC.GAL/94/02. June 6, 2002.

———. "The U.S. Delegation to the CSCE Office of the Public Affairs Adviser: Joint News Conference by the President of the U.S. with the Presidents of Latvia, Lithuania, and Estonia July 6, 1994." OSCE Doc. 469. July 7, 1994.

———. Survey of CSCE/OSCE Long-Term Missions and Other CSCE/OSCE Field Activities, SEC.INF/115/04. June 2, 2004.

Ottaway, Marina, and Thomas Carothers, eds. Funding Virtue: Civil Society Aid and Democracy Promotion. Washington, D.C.: The Carnegie Endowment for International Peace, 2000.

Ottaway, Marina, and Theresa Chung. "Toward a New Paradigm." Journal of Democracy 10, no. 4 (1999): 99–114.

Pabriks, Artis. "From Nationalism to Ethnic Policy: The Latvian Nation in the Present and Past." Berlin: Berliner Interuniversitare Abreitns gruppe Baltische Staaten, Nr. 17, 1999.

Packer, John. "Considerations on Procedures to Implement the Right to Self Determination." In *The Implementation of the Right to Self-Determination as a Contribution to Conflict Prevention,* edited by Michael van Walt van Praage. Report of the International Conference of Experts. UNESCEO Division of Human Rights, Nov. 1998, 21–27.

———. "Making International Law Matter in Preventing Ethnic Conflict: A Practitioner's Perspective." *International Law and Politics* 32 (2000): 715–24.

———. "On the Content of Minority Rights." In *Do We Need Minority Rights?* edited by J. Raikka, 121–78. Netherlands: Kluwer Law International, 1996.

———. "United Nations Protection of Minorities in Time of Public Emergency: The Hardcore of Minority Rights." In *Non-Derogable Rights and States of Emergency,* edited by D. Prémont, C. Stenersen, and I. Oseredczuk, 449–548. Brussels: Etablissements Emile Bruyland, 1996.

Payton, Philip. "Ethnicity in Western Europe today." In *Ethnicity and Democratisation in the New Europe,* edited by Karl Cordell, 24–37. London: Routledge, 1999.

Pearson, Frederic S., Jonathan Nagle, and Mark Suprun. 2000. "Overcoming Wilsonianism: American Conflict Resolution and Ethnic Nationalism in Eastern Europe and the Former Soviet Union." In *Reconcilable Differences. Turing Points in Ethnic Conflict,* edited by Sean Byren and Cynthia L. Irvin. Bloomfield: Kumarian Press, 2000.

Pei-neng, Chiang. *NGOs at the United Nations.* New York: Praeger Publishers, 1981.

Pentassuglia, Gaetano. "On the Models of Minority Rights Supervision in Europe and How They Affect a Changing Concept of Sovereignty." *European Yearbook of Minority Issues* 1 (2001–2): 29–64.

Petrescu, Dan. "Civil Society in Romania." In *Civil Society Aid and Democracy Promotion,* edited by Martina Ottaway and Thomas Carothers, 217–42. Washington, D.C.: The Carnegie Endowment for International Peace, 2000.

Phillips, Ann L. "Exporting Democracy: German Political Foundations in Central-East Europe." *Democratization* 6, no. 2 (1999): 70–98.

Plamentaz, Janusz. "Two Types of Nationalism." In *Nationalism, The Nature and Evolution of an Ideal,* edited by E. Kamenka. Canberra: Australian National Press, 1973.

Poleshchuk, Vadim. "Accession to the EU and National Integration in Estonia and Latvia." Baltic Seminar 2000, Dec. 7–10. ECMI Report no. 8, March 2001.

Pond, Elizabeth. *The Rebirth of Europe.* Washington: The Brookings Institution, 2002.

Popa, Oana C. "Ethnic Nationalism and Regional Security in Southeast Europe: A Multi-dimensional Perspective." *NATO Final Report,* March 1999.

Posen, Barry. "The Security Dilemma and Ethnic Conflict." In *Ethnic Conflict and Interna-*

tional Security, edited by Michael E. Brown, 103–25. Princeton: Princeton Univ. Press, 1993.

Powell, Walter W. "Neither Market Nor Hierarchy: Network Forms of Organization." *Research in Organizational Behavior* 12 (1990): 295–336.

Power, Samantha. *A Problem From Hell: American and the Age of Genocide.* New York: Basic Books, 2002.

Project on Ethnic Relations. "Political Will: Romania's Path to Ethnic Accommodation." Report by the Project on Ethnic Relations. Bucharest, Romania, Feb. 22–24, 2001.

Quigley, Kevin F. F. *For Democracy's Sake: Foundations and Democracy Assistance in Central Europe.* Washington: The Woodrow Wilson Center, 1997.

———. "Lofty Goals, Modest Results: Assisting Civil Society in Eastern Europe." In *Funding Virtue: Civil Society Aid and Democracy Promotion,* edited by Martina Ottaway and Thomas Carothers, 191–216. Washington, D.C.: The Carnegie Endowment for International Peace, 2000.

———. "Philanthropy's Role in East Europe." *Orbis* 37, 4 (1993): 581–99.

Ram, Melanie H. "Black Sea Cooperation toward European Integration." Unpublished paper presented at the Black Sea Regional Policy Symposium, Mar. 29-Apr. 11, 2001, Leesburg, Va.

———. "Sub-regional Cooperation and European Integration: Romania's Delicate Balance." Unpublished paper presented at the International Studies Association annual meeting, Feb. 20–24, 2001, Chicago, Ill.

Ramet, Sabrina P. *Balkan Babel: The Disintegration of Yugoslavia from the Death of Tito to the War for Kosovo.* Boulder: Westview Press, 1999.

———. *Whose Democracy? Nationalism, Religion and The Doctrine of Collective Rights in Post-1989 Eastern Europe.* Lanham, Md.: Rowman and Littlefield, 1997.

Ratner, Steven R. "Does International Law Matter in Preventing Ethnic Conflict?" *Journal of International Law and Politics* 32, no. 3 (2000): 591–642.

———. "Drawing a Better Line: *Uti Possidetis* and the Borders of New States." In *International Law and the Rise of Nations,* edited by Robert J. Beck and Thomas Abriosio, 250–83. London: Chatham House Publishers, 2001.

Reincke, Wolfgang H., and Francis Deng. *Critical Choices: The UN, Networks and the Future of Global Governance.* Ottawa: International Development Research Center, 2000.

Reiter, Dan. 2001. "Why NATO Enlargement Does Not Spread Democracy." *International Security* 25, no. 4 (2001): 41–67.

Rhodes, R. A. W. *European Policy-Making: Implementation and Subcentral Governments; A Survey.* Maastricht: European Institute of Public Administration, 1986.

———. "Policy Network Analysis." In *The Oxford Handbook of Public Policy,* edited by M. Moran, M. Rein, and R. E. Goodin. Oxford: Oxford Univ. Press, 2005.

Rieff, David. *Slaughterhouse: Bosnia and the Failure of the West.* New York: Simon and Schuster, 1995.

Risse-Kappen, Thomas. "Bringing Transnational Actors Back In: Introduction." In *Bringing Transnational Relations Back In: Non-state Actors, Domestic Structures and International Institutions,* edited by Thomas Risse-Kappen, 3–36. Cambridge: Cambridge Univ. Press, 1995.

Risse, Thomas, Stephen C. Ropp, and Kathryn Sikkink, eds. *The Power of Human Rights.* Cambridge: Cambridge Univ. Press, 1999.

Roe, Paul. "The Intrastate Security Dilemma Ethnic Conflict as Tragedy." *Journal of Peace Research* 36, no. 2 (1999):83–202.

Roter, Petra, ed. "Managing the Minority Problem in Post-Cold War Europe within the Framework of a Multilayered Regime for the Protection of National Minorities." *European Yearbook of Minority Issues* 1 (2001–2).

Rothman, Jay. *From Confrontation to Cooperation: Resolving Ethnic and Regional Conflict.* Newbury Park, Calif.: SAGE Publications, 1992.

Rothschild, Joseph. *Eastern Europe Between the Two World Wars.* Seattle: Univ. of Washington Press, 1979.

———. *Ethnopolitics: A Conceptual Framework.* New York: Columbia Univ. Press, 1981.

Rudenshield, Eric. "Ethnic Dimensions in Contemporary Latvian Politics: Focusing Forces for Change." *Soviet Studies* 44, no. 4 (1992): 609–38.

Rummel, R. J. *Death by Government.* New Brunswick: Transaction Publishers, 1997.

Rupnik, Jacques. "Eastern Europe: The International Context." In *Globalization, Power, and Democracy,* edited by Marc F. Plattner and Aleksander Smolar, 51–68. Baltimore: The Johns Hopkins Press, 2000.

Ryan, Stephen. *Ethnic Conflict and International Relations.* Aldershot, England: Dartmouth Publishing Company, 1990.

Saideman, Stephen M., and R. William Ayres. "Pie Crust Promises and Silence Procedures: Understanding the Limited Impact of NATO and EU Membership." Unpublished paper presented at the 2005 International Studies Association Conference, Honolulu, Hawaii, March 2–5, 2005.

Scheppele, Kim Lane. "The Soros Empire." In *American and German Cultural Policies in Eastern Europe: Assessing Developments in the 1990s,* edited by Frank Trommler, 18–26. Washington, D.C.: American Institute for Contemporary German Studies, 1998.

Schimmelfennig, Frank. "Introduction: The Impact of International Organizations on the Central and Eastern European States: Conceptual and Theoretical Issues." In *Norms and Nannies: The Impact of International Organizations on Central and East Europe,* edited by Ron H. Linden, 1–29. Lanham, Md.: Rowman and Littlefield, 2002.

———. "NATO Enlargement: A Constructivist Explanation." *Security Studies* 8, no. 2–3 (1998–99): 198–234.

Schimmelfennig, Frank, Stefan Engert, and Heiko Knobel. "Costs, Commitment and Compliance: The Importance of EU Democratic Conditionality on Latvia, Slovakia, and Turkey." *Journal of Ethnopolitics and Minority Issues in Europe* 3 (2003): 495–518.

Schopflin, George. *Nations, Identity and Power.* New York: New York Press, 2000.

Seton-Watson, Hugh. *The East European Revolution.* London, Methuen, 1950.

Shafir, Gershon. *Immigrants and Nationalists: Ethnic Conflict and Accommodation in the Basque, Country, Latvia and Estonia.* Albany: State University of New York Press, 1995.

Shafir, Michael. "Ethnic Tensions Run High in Romania." *RFE/RL* 3, no. 32 Aug. 19, 1994.

———. "The Hungarian Democratic Federation of Romania: Actions, Reactions, and Factions." In *Ethnicity Unbound: The Politics of Minority Participation in Post-Communist Europe,* edited by Robert W. Mickey, 110–25. London: St. Martin's Press, 1996.

———. "Minorities Council Raises Questions." *RFE/RL* 2, no. 24, June 11, 1993.

———. "The Political Party as National Holding Company: The Hungarian Democratic Federation of Romania." *The Politics of National Minority Participation in Post-Communist Europe: State-Building, Democracy, and Ethnic Moblization,* edited by Jonathan P. Stein. Armonk, N.Y.: M. E. Sharpe, 2000.

———. "Romania's Road to 'Normalization.' " *Journal of Democracy* 8, no. 2 (1997).

Singh, Anita Inder. *Democracy, Ethnic Diversity and Security in Post-Communist Europe.* Westport: Praeger, 2001.

Sisk, Timothy. *Power Sharing and International Mediation in Ethnic Conflict.* Washington, D.C.: United States Institute of Peace Press, 1996.

Slaughter, Anne-Marie. *A New World Order.* Princeton: Princeton Univ. Press, 2004.

———. "The Real New World Order." *Foreign Affairs* 76, no. 1 (1997):183–97.

Smith, Anthony D. *The Ethnic Origins of Nations.* Oxford: Basil Blackwell, 1986.

Smith, David. "Framing the National Question in Central and Eastern Europe: A Quadratic Nexus." *The Global Review of Ethnopolitics* 2, no. 1 (2002): 3–16.

Smith, Graham, ed. *The Nationalities Question in the Soviet Union.* London: Longman, 1990.

Smith, Karen E. "Western Actors and the Promotion of Democracy." In *Democratic Consolidation in Eastern Europe,* edited by Jan Zielonka and Alex Pravda, 31–57. Oxford: Oxford Univ. Press, 2001.

Snyder, Jack, and Edward Mansfield. "Democratization and War." *Foreign Affairs,* May-June 1995: 79–97.

Spendzharova, Aneta Borislavova. "Bringing Europe In? The Impact of EU Conditionality on Bulgarian and Romanian Politics." *Southeast European Politics* 4, no. 2 (2003): 141–56.

Stein, Jonathan P., ed. 2000. *The Politics of National Minorities in Central Europe.* Armonk, N.Y.: M. E. Sharpe.

Stroschein, Sherrill. "NGO Strategies for Hungarian and Roma Minorities in Central Europe." *Voluntas* 13, no. 1 (2002): 1–26.

Svekis, Elmars. "Latvia's Compliance with the OSCE Principles: Domestic Choices or International Commitments?" M.A. Thesis, The Central European Univ., Budapest, Oct. 30, 2001.

Szplorluk, Roman. "Belarus, Ukraine, and The Russian Question." *Post-Soviet Affairs* 9, no. 4 (1993): 366–74.

Taras, Raymond, and Rajat Ganguly. *Understanding Ethnic Conflict: The International Dimension.* New York: Longman, 2002.

Tarrow, Sidney. *Power in Movement.* Cambridge: Cambridge Univ. Press, 1998.

———. "Transnational Politics: Contention and Institutions in International Politics." *Annual Review of Political Science* 4 (2002): 1–20.

Taylor, Trevor. "Security for Europe." In *Redefining Europe: New Patterns of Conflict and Cooperation,* edited by Hugh Miall, 166–85. London: The Royal Institute of International Affairs, 1994.

Tesser, Lynn M. "The Geopolitics of Tolerance: Minority Rights under EU Expansion in East-Central Europe." *East European Politics and Societies* 17, no. 3 (Summer 2003): 483–532.

Thomas, Daniel C. "The Helsinki Accords and Political Change in Eastern Europe." In *The Power of Human Rights: International Norms and Domestic Change,* edited by Thomas Risse, Stephen Ropp, and Kathryn Sikkink, 205–33. Cambridge: Cambridge University Press, 1999.

Thompson, Cecilia. "United Nations: The Protection of Minorities within the United Nations." In *Minority Rights in Europe: European Minorities and Languages,* edited by Snezana Trifunovska, 115–37. 1st ed. The Hague: Springer, 2001.

Thornberry, Patrick. "An Unfinished Story of Minority Rights." In *Diversity in Action Local Public Management of Multi-Ethnic Communities in Central and Eastern Europe,* edited by Anna-Maria Biro and Petra Kovacs, 47–54. Budapest: OSI Publications, 2001.

Tindemans, Leo, Lloyd Cutler, Bronislaw Geremek, John Roper, Theo Sommer, Simone Veil, and David Anderson. *Unfinished Peace: Report of the International Commission on the Balkans.* Washington, D.C.: The Carnegie Endowment for International Peace, 1996.

Tolz, Vera. "Russia: Westernizers Continue to Challenge National Patriots." *RFE/RL* 1, no. 29, Dec. 11, 1992.

Trifunovska, Snezana, ed. *Minority Rights in Europe: European Minorities and Languages.* 1st ed. The Hague: Springer, 2001.

Tsilevich, Boris. "EU Enlargement and the Protection of National Minorities: Opportunities, Myths and Prospects." http://www.eumap.org/journal/features/2001/oct/euenlarge.

United Nations. *An Agenda for Peace: Preventive Diplomacy, Peacemaking and Peace-keeping.* Doc. A/47/277-S/2411, 1992.

———. *Supplement to an Agenda for Peace: Position Paper of the Secretary-General on the*

Occasion of the Fiftieth Anniversary of the University Nations. Doc. A/50/60-S/1995/1, Jan. 3, 1995.

——. *UN General Assembly Resolution 47/135,* www.unhcr.ch/html/menu3/b/d-minor.thm, 1992.

United States Agency for International Development. *A Decade of Change: Profiles of USAID Assistance to Europe and Eurasia.* Washington, D.C.: Agency for International Development, 2000.

——. *Lessons in Implementation: The NGO Story.* Washington: D.C.: Agency for International Development, 1999.

United States Department of State. "Central and Eastern Europe: A Year Later." U.S. Department of State Dispatch 2, no. 20, May 20, 1991.

——. "Focus on Central and Eastern Europe: Overview of U.S. Assistance," U.S. Department of State Dispatch 2, no. 11, Mar. 18, 1991.

——. *1996 Country Reports on Human Rights Practices.* Washington, D.C.: Bureau of Democracy, Human Rights, and Labor, U.S. Department of State, 1997.

——. *1999 Country Report on Human Rights Practices.* Washington, D.C.: Bureau of Democracy, Human Rights, and Labor, U.S. Department of State, 2000.

USIS. "Presidents of Estonia, Latvia, Lithuania Hold Briefing." USIS Washington File, 1998. Available online at http://www.fas.org/man/nato/national/98011503_wpo.html, accessed Feb. 2004.

Vachudova, Milada Anna. *Europe Undivided: Democracy, Leverage and Integration After Communism.* Oxford: Oxford Univ. Press, 2005.

——. "Strategies for European Integration and Democratization in the Balkans." *Slovak Foreign Policy Affairs* 1 (Spring 2003): 92–105.

Van der Stoel, Max. "International response to ethnic conflicts: Focusing on Prevention." Keynote Address by the CSCE HCNM to the Fourth International PIOOM Symposium: Ethnic Conflicts and Human Rights Violations in Europe, June 25, 1993, Leiden, The Netherlands.

——. "Principles and Pragmatism: Twenty Five Years with the Helsinki Process." In *OSCE Yearbook 2000,* 25–34. Baden-Baden: Univ. of Hamburg, 2001.

——. "The Role of the CSCE/OSCE High Commissioner in Conflict Prevention." Address by the CSCE/OSCE High Commissioner on National Minorities, Oct. 18, 1996, Skopje, Macedonia.

——. "The Role of the OSCE High Commissioner in Conflict Prevention." In *Herding Cats. Multiparty Mediation in a Complex World,* edited by Chester A. Crocker, Fen Osler-Hampson, and Pamela Aall, 65–84. Washington, D.C.: USIP Press, 1999.

Van Dyke, Vernon. "Self-Determination and Minority Rights." *International Studies Quarterly* 13, no. 3 (1969): 223–53.

Van Evera, Stephen. "Hypotheses on Nationalism." *International Security* 18, no. 4 (1994): 5–39.

———."Managing the Eastern Crisis: Managing War in the Former Soviet Empire." *Security Studies* 1, no. 3 (1992): 361–81.

Van Tongeren, Paul, Hans van de Veen, and Juliette Verhoeven. *Searching for Peace in Europe and Eurasia.* Boulder: Lynne Rienner, 2002.

Varshney, Ashutosh. *Ethnic Conflict and Civic Life.* New Haven: Yale Univ. Press, 2002.

Verdery, Katherine. "Nationalism and Nationalism in Post-Socialist Romania." *Slavic Review* 52, no. 2 (1993): 179–203.

Vermeersch, Peter. "Advocacy Networks and Romani Politics in Central and Eastern Europe." *Journal of Ethnopolitics and Minority Issues in Europe,* Autumn 2001:1–19.

Vetik, Raivo. "Ethnic Conflict and Accommodation in Post-Communist Estonia," *Journal of Peace Research* 30, no. 3 (1993): 271–80.

Walker, Jenonne. "European Regional Organizations and Ethnic Conflict." In *Central and Eastern Europe: The Challenge of Transition,* edited by Regina Cowen Karp, 37–59. Oxford: Oxford Univ. Press, 1993.

Wallander, Celeste A. "Institutional Assets and Adaptability: NATO After the Cold War." *International Organization* 54, no. 4 (2000): 705–35.

Wallensteen, Peter, and Margareta Sollenberge. 1998. "Armed Conflict and Regional Conflict Complexes, 1989–1997." *Journal of Peace Research* 35, no. 5 (1998): 621–34.

Wallerstein, Immanuel. *The Modern World System: Capitalist Agriculture and the Origins of the European World Economy in the Sixteenth Century.* New York: Academic Press, 1974.

Walter, Barbara F., and Jack Snyder, eds. *Civil Wars, Insecurity, and Intervention.* New York: Columbia Univ. Press, 1999.

Wandycz, Piotr Stefan. *The Lands of Partitioned Poland, 1795–1918.* Seattle: Univ. of Washington Press, 1993.

Wedel, Janine. *Collision and Collusion: The Strange Case of Western Aid to Eastern Europe, 1989–1998.* New York: St. Martin's Press, 1998.

Weir, Fred. "Latvia Gives Russia Cold Shoulder." *The Christian Science Monitor,* Nov. 26, 2002.

Weiss, Thomas G. "Nongovernmental Organizations and Internal Conflict." In *The International Dimensions of Ethnic Conflict,* edited by Michael Brown, 434–59. Cambridge, Mass.: MIT Press, 1996.

Weiss, Thomas G., and Leon Gordenker. 1996. *NGOs, the UN, and Global Governance.* Boulder: Lynne Rienner, 1996.

White, George W. *Nationalism and Territory.* New York: Rowman and Littlefield, 2000.

Whitehead, Laurence. *The International Dimensions of Democratization in Europe and the Americas.* Oxford: Oxford Univ. Press, 1996.

Witt, Andrea. "National Borders: Images, Functions, and Their Effects on Cross-Border Co-operation in North America and Europe." In *Caught in the Middle: Border Communities in an Era of Globalization,* edited by Demetrios G. Papademetriou and Deborah Waller Meyers, 166–99. Washington, D.C.: Carnegie Endowment for International Peace, 2001.

Woodward, Susan L. *Balkan Tragedy: Chaos and Dissolution after the Cold War.* Washington, D.C.: The Brookings Institution, 1995.

Worner, Manfred. *Change and Continuity in the North Atlantic Alliance: Speeches by the Secretary General of NATO Manfred Worner.* Brussels: NATO Office of Information and Press, 1990.

Zaagman, Robert. "Conflict Prevention in the Baltic States." *Journal of Ethnopolitics and Minority Issues* 1 (April 1999): 1–75.

Zellner, Wolfgang, Randolf Oberschmidt, and Claus Neukirch, eds. *Comparative Case Studies on the Effectiveness of the OSCE High Commissioner on National Minorities: The Possibilities for Preventive Diplomacy.* Baden-Baden: University of Hamburg, 2004.

———, eds. "The CSCE/OSCE: Uniquely Qualified for a Conflict-Prevention Role." In *Searching for Peace in Europe and Eurasia,* edited by Paul van Tongeren, Hans van de Veen, and Juliette Verhoeven, 15–26. Boulder: Lynne Rienner, 2002.

Zielonka, Jan, ed. *Europe Unbound: Enlarging and Restructuring the Borders of the EU.* New York: Routledge, 2002.

Zielonka, Jan, and Alex Pravda, eds. *Democratic Consolidation in Eastern Europe.* Oxford: Oxford Univ. Press, 2001.

Interviews

Aboltins, Reinis. Director of the Department of Social Integration, Secretariat of the Minister for Social Integration Affairs, Riga, Latvia, July 2004.

Adam, Gabor. Director, Ethnocultural Diversity Center, Cluj-Napoca, June 2004.

Aldermane, Eizenija. Head, Republic of Latvia Naturalization Board, Riga, Latvia, July 2004.

Alexander, Paige. Vice President for Programs, International Research and Exchange Program (IREX); United State Agency for International Development, 1993–2001, European Country Affairs, Washington, D.C., June 2003.

Andreescu, Gabriel. Director, Romanian Helsinki Committee, Bucharest, Romania, June 2004.

Ashman, Peter. Senior Adviser, EuropeAid, and former director, European Human Rights Foundation, Brussels, Belgium, March 2004.

Aukmanis, Andris. Director, Soros Foundation Latvia, Riga, Latvia, July 2004.

Batinic, Havoje. Civil Society and Roma Program, Open Society Fund BIH, Sarajevo, Bosnia, September 2000.

Birkavs, Valdis. Former Prime Minister and Minister of Foreign Affairs of Latvia, Riga, Latvia, July 2004.

Bluhm, Nathan. Formerly Officer in Charge, U.S. Information Office, Cluj, Romania, 1994–97; written correspondence, July 26–29, 2004.

Brands Kehris, Ilze. Director, Latvian Center for Human Rights and Ethnic Studies, Riga, Latvia, July 2004.

Cermak, Franz. Adviser, Coordination of Negotiations and Pre-accession, Enlargement, Directorate General, European Commission, Brussels, Belgium, March 2004.

Chifu, Iulian. Director, Center for Conflict Prevention and Early Warning, Bucharest, Romania, June 2004.

Cowles, David L. Former Deputy Director (1995–98), the Center for Economic Growth and Agricultural Development; Director for European Country Affairs, United States Agency for International Development, Washington, D.C., June 2003.

Dizdarevic, Ismet. Professor, Univ. of Sarajevo, Bosnia, September 2000.

Doyle, Michael. Political Analyst, International Crisis Group, Sarajevo, Bosnia, September 2000.

Dzino-Silajdzic, Velida. Program Manager, Catholic Relief Services, Sarajevo, Bosnia, September 2000.

Farnsworth, Sarah. USAID, International Cooperation Specialist, Eastern Europe, United States Agency for International Development, Washington, D.C., June 2003.

Fertig-Dykes, Susan. Senior Desk Officer, Bosnia and Herzegovina, Eastern Europe, United States Agency for International Development, Washington, D.C., June 2003.

Finci, Jakob. President, Truth and Reconciliation Association of Citziens, Sarajevo, Bosnia, July 2001.

Fraenkel, Eran. Southern and Eastern Europe, Regional Director, Search for Common Ground, Brussels, Belgium, March 2004.

Ganibegovic, Majda. Project Manager, International Rescue Committee, Sarajevo, Bosnia, July 2001.

Ganic, Emina. Political Adviser, Council of Europe, Sarajevo, Bosnia, September 2000.

Ginsburg, Marianna. Senior Program Officer, Environmental Partnerships, The German Marshall Fund, Washington, D.C., June 2003.

Golubeva, Maria. Professor Univ. of Riga, PROVIDUS, Public Policy Center, Board Member of the Baltic-American Partnership Foundation, Riga, Latvia, July 2004.

Graves, Peter D. Senior Media Adviser, Eastern Europe, United States Agency for International Development, Washington, D.C., June 2003.

Gutmanis, Armands. Under Secretary of State, Ministry of Foreign Affairs of the Republic of Latvia, former adviser in the State President's Office, Riga, Latvia, July 2004.

Havlicek, Sasha. Deputy Director. Regional and Transfrontier Cooperation Program, East-West Institute, Brussels, Belgium, March 2004.

Henderson, Phil. Director of Programs. The German Marshall Fund, Washington, D.C., June 23, 2003.

Holma, Daigma. Head of Program Unit, United Nations Development Program, Riga, Latvia, July 2004.

Horvath, Istvan. Sociologist, Babes-Bolyai Univ., Cluj-Napoca, Romania, June 2004.

Jones, Judith. Special Assistant to the Supervisor, Office of the High Representative, Brcko, Bosnia, June 2003.

Kemp, Walter. Senior Adviser, OSCE, Vienna, Austria, June 2004.

Klimkiewicz, Slawomir. Democratisation Team Manager, Head of Brcko Team, OSCE Bosnia and Hercegovina, Brko, Bosnia, June 2003.

Kondonis, Haralambos. Expert on Democratization and Human Rights, Stability Pact for South Eastern Europe, Brussels, Belgium, March 2, 2004.

Kuhne, Bjorn. Political Adviser, Stability Pact for South Eastern Europe, Brussels, Belgium, March 2004.

Kulenovic-Latal, Selia. Catholic Relief Services, Seila Project Officer II, Sarajevo, Bosnia, July 2001.

Lange, Falk. Senior Adviser to the High Commissioner on National Minorities, The Hague, the Netherlands, March 4, 2004.

Lempke, Roger. Major General, Nebraska National Guard, May 2003.

Levente, Salat. Associate Professor and Vice Rector, Babes-Bolyai Univ., Cluj-Napoca, formerly director, Open Society Foundation, June 2004.

Mates, Michael. Officer in Charge, U.S. Information Office, Cluj, Romania, June 2004.

Morica, Ieva. Director, The Baltic-American Partnership Program, Riga, Latvia, July 2004.

Munari, Liina. Administrator, Commission for External Relations, Committee of the Regions, European Union, Brussels, Belgium, March 2004.

Niculescu, Toni. Executive Vice President, Democratic Alliance of Hungarians in Romania, Department for European Integration, Bucharest, June 2004.

Oprescu, Dan. Senior Adviser, Government of Romania, Office on Romania Issues, June 2004.

Pimenov, Igor. Former Director of LASHOR: Latvian Association of Schools of Russian, Riga, Latvia, July 2004.

Rasavac, Zineta. Civil Society Program Manager, OSCE Bosnia and Herzegonia, Sarajevo, Bosnia, September 2000.

Reina, Inga. Representative of the Government of Latvia, Ministry of the Foreign Affairs, Riga, Latvia, July 2004.

Rolett, Jonas. Director for the Eastern Europe/Former Soviet Union Project, The Soros Foundation, Washington, D.C., June 2003.

Roux, Franck-Oliver. International Organizations, EuropeAid Co-operation Office, European Commission, March 2004.

Sahinpasic, Asim. Communications Manager, World Vision, Sarajevo, Bosnia, July 2001.

Sakss, Nils. Director of the Secretariat, Society Integration Foundation, Riga, Latvia, July 2004.

Schriefer, Paula G. Director of Programs, Freedom House, June 2003.

Stanisic, Vladimir. Human Rights/Rule of Law Department, Office of the High Representative, Sarajevo, Bosnia, September 2000.

Stawe, Malin. Coordinator Europe, EuropeAid, European Commission, Brussels, Belgium, March 2004.

Stuart, Lisa Jennifer. Adviser, Civil Society Development, Eastern Europe, United States Agency for International Development, Washington, D.C., June 2003.

Svekes, Elmars. Project Technical Adviser, Ministry of Foreign Affairs and UNDP Latvia project, Riga, Latvia, July 2004.

Swerer, Daniel. Director, The Balkans Program, U.S. Institute of Peace, Washington, D.C., June 2003.

Terauda, Vita. Director, PROVIDUS, Center for Public Policy, former director of Soros Foundation Latvia, Riga, Latvia, July, 2004.

Tokaca, Mirsad. Secretary, War Crimes Commission, Republic of Bosnia and Herzegovina, Sarajevo, Bosnia, September 2000.

Van der Stoel, Max. High Commissioner on National Minorities, OSCE, 1993–2002, The Hague, Netherlands, July 2004.

Weber, Renata. Director, Open Society Institute, Bucharest, Romania, June 2004.

Windsor, Jennifer. Executive Director, Freedom House, formerly at USAID from 1994–2000, Office of Democracy and Governance, Washington, D.C., June 2003.

Index